Follow the Moon and Stars
A Literary Journey through Nottinghamshire

*To my parents, Sheila and John.
For the mileage, the photos
and moving those bins*

Follow the Moon and Stars
A Literary Journey through Nottinghamshire

John Baird

Follow the Moon and Stars
A Literary Journey through Nottinghamshire
by John Baird

Published by Five Leaves Publications,
14a Long Row, Nottingham NG1 2DH
in association with
Nottingham UNESCO City of Literature

www.fiveleaves.co.uk
www.fiveleavesbookshop.co.uk
www.nottinghamcityofliterature.com

ISBN (paperback): 978-1-910170-89-2
ISBN (hardback): 978-1-910170-90-8

Copyright © John Baird, 2021

Photographs by John Baird
unless otherwise stated

Design and layout by
Four Sheets Design and Print

Printed in Great Britain by
TJ Books Ltd, Padstow, Cornwall

Contents

Book One: Nottingham City Centre

Foreword	11
Chapter 1 The Arboretum – A Walk in the Park	15
Chapter 2 Arkwright Building, Shakespeare Street – A Place of Learning	20
Chapter 3 Broadway Cinema, Broad Street – From Booth to Bouchercon	26
Chapter 4 Bromley House Library, Angel Row – A Living History	32
Chapter 5 The Council House – The Power and the Glory	35
Chapter 6 The Emett Clock, Victoria Centre – A Moving Sculpture	39
Chapter 7 Exchange Arcade – Years of Promise	41
Chapter 8 Express Building, Upper Parliament Street – Nottingham's Greeneland	45
Chapter 9 Five Leaves Bookshop, Swann's Yard – Radically Independent	53
Chapter 10 The Loggerheads (former), Cliff Road – City of Crime	58
Chapter 11 Mechanics' Hall (former) – What the Dickens!	63
Chapter 12 Mushroom Bookshop (former) – Nottingham's Lost Bookshops	68
Chapter 13 New Foresters, St Ann's Street – Pride and Prejudice	76
Chapter 14 Newstead House, St James Street – The Boy Byron	91
Chapter 15 Nottingham Arts Theatre, George Street – Nottingham Crusoe	94
Chapter 16 Nottingham Castle – Of Curious Rebels	99

Chapter 17
Nottingham Mechanics – Various Homes of the NWC   106

Chapter 18
Nottingham Playhouse – Made in Nottingham   111

Chapter 19
The Pitcher and Piano, High Pavement – Little St Mary's   118

Chapter 20
The Playwright, Shakespeare Street – Shakespeare in Nottingham   124

Chapter 21
Raleigh Street – A Design For Life   128

Chapter 22
Regent Street – Keeping Mum   131

Chapter 23
School of Art – Illustrious Illustrators   134

Chapter 24
St Mary's Church and the Lace Market – Historic Happenings   140

Chapter 25
Tanners, Pelham Street – Pan's People   147

Chapter 26
Theatre Royal – Putting on a Show   151

Chapter 27
Weavers, Castle Gate – Against the Barons   155

Chapter 28
The White Lion (former) – Filling A Gap   159

Chapter 29
Yates's (former) – Poet, Mother, Free Spirit   162

Chapter 30
The Zara Building – A Booklovers' Library   167

Book Two: Nottingham

Chapter 31
Basford House – Home of the Long Poem — 175

Chapter 32
Beaconsfield Street – Nottingham's Black Writers — 179

Chapter 33
Bertrand Russell House, Gamble Street – Building the Foundation — 184

Chapter 34
Broxtowe – Estate of Mind — 191

Chapter 35
Caledon Road, Sherwood – Nottingham's Booker Prize — 198

Chapter 36
Danethorpe Vale, Sherwood – Back to the Beginning — 202

Chapter 37
Ebers Road, Mapperley Park – The Twentieth Century's Austen — 205

Chapter 38
First Avenue, Sherwood Rise – The Social Psychologist — 208

Chapter 39
The Forest Recreation Ground – Ball Park Figures — 211

Chapter 40
Maggie's, City Hospital – The Big C, Creativity — 216

Chapter 41
Nottingham Girls' High School – On the Write Path — 219

Chapter 42
The Old General (former), Hyson Green – A Lovable Rogue — 221

Chapter 43
The Park Estate – Private Lives — 224

Chapter 44
Sneinton Market – Common People — 227

Chapter 45
St Ann's – Getting By — 234

Chapter 46
Victoria Crescent, Mapperley Park – When Bertie Met Frieda — 242

Chapter 47
The White Horse, Radford – Down the Local — 244

Book Three: Nottinghamshire

Chapter 48
All Hallows Church, Gedling – Gandalf of Gedling?   253

Chapter 49
Annesley Hall – The Forsaken   256

Chapter 50
Aslockton – The Book of Common Words   260

Chapter 51
Bingham – Shakespeare's Nottingham Knight   263

Chapter 52
Bridgford Road, West Bridgford – The Genre-hopping All-rounder   268

Chapter 53
Car Colston – The First History of Nottinghamshire   271

Chapter 54
Devonshire Avenue, Beeston – A Place of Poetry   274

Chapter 55
Eastwood – The Country of My Heart   277

Chapter 56
Elston – An Evolved Man   282

Chapter 57
Gonalston Mill – Twist in the Tale   287

Chapter 58
Haggs Farm – Sowing the Seeds   291

Chapter 59
Halam – Little Village of Words   296

Chapter 60
The Hemlock Stone, Bramcote – Inspiring Legend   299

Chapter 61
Keyworth – Read All About It   301

Chapter 62
Langar – The Butler Did It   304

Chapter 63
Lowdham – A Literary Lowdown   309

Chapter 64
Newark – Pieces of History   312

Chapter 65
Newstead Abbey – A Resplendent Home   320

Chapter 66
Eakring – Cresswell Country　　　　　　　　　　　　　　　330

Chapter 67
The Old Library, Edwinstowe – Festival in the Forest　　　334

Chapter 68
The Rancliffe Arms – The Wrestling Baronet　　　　　　　340

Chapter 69
Retford – Our Friends in the North　　　　　　　　　　　343

Chapter 70
The Robin Hood Theatre, Averham – Play by the River　　347

Chapter 71
Rufford Abbey – A Secret World　　　　　　　　　　　　350

Chapter 72
Sherwood Lodge, Arnold – Family Fortunes　　　　　　　353

Chapter 73
Southwell – A Literary Town　　　　　　　　　　　　　　358

Chapter 74
St Mary Magdalene Church, Hucknall – What Lies Beneath　368

Chapter 75
St Mary's Church, Edwinstowe – Of Phrase and Fable　　　376

Chapter 76
Stapleford – It's All About Mee　　　　　　　　　　　　　380

Chapter 77
Thrumpton Hall – An Obsession　　　　　　　　　　　　385

Chapter 78
University of Nottingham – A Special Collection　　　　　392

Chapter 79
Welbeck Abbey – Going Underground　　　　　　　　　　400

Chapter 80
Wilford and Clifton Grove – Down by the River　　　　　　405

The Journey Continues...　　　　　　　　　　　　　　414
Acknowledgements　　　　　　　　　　　　　　　　　415
Printed Primary Sources　　　　　　　　　　　　　　　416
References　　　　　　　　　　　　　　　　　　　　　419
Index　　　　　　　　　　　　　　　　　　　　　　　439

Foreword

Do people inhabit places or places inhabit people? The answer, surely, is both. The role of writers in "place-making" is a worthy subject: they form (and inform) cultural memories; and by force of imagination, tell of how places once were, and how they might yet be. But the city and county in these pages are present and real. That is why a book about the places where the literature of Nottingham and Nottinghamshire has been made — and continues to be made — is of itself a great treasure to hold. Think of it as a guide not only to where the precious metals are found, but also how and why they have been forged and fashioned.

The course of this book, indeed these books, is to take the reader on ever-increasing circles. It spirals, rather wonderfully, from the very centre, out to Nottingham in all its social layers and neighbourhoods, and then beyond to the county surrounds. As the Irish poet, Patrick Kavanagh wrote: *'To know fully even one field or one land is a lifetime's experience. In the world of poetic experience it is depth that counts, not width.'* John Baird has been loyal to meeting the demands of that truth. The attention he has given to place has made it special to him, even sacred. That is a gift and one he shares with us here through his dedication to writers and to writing. Indeed, his book reflects something of a journey, as its first steps began with blogging on "Notts Lit". That was born of his pride in the best of literary heritage with a Nottinghamshire connection, and it shines through the pages of his book.

That is a rightful pride, as recognised by Nottingham's designation as a UNESCO City of Literature in 2015. Such accreditation cherishes not only the City's literary pedigree but also the importance of its declared ambition to make a better world with words. This book plays its part in realising that aim.

In part out of sentiment — as the book belonged to my late father — I still have the *Oxford Literary Guide to the British Isles*, first published in 1977. The authors devote less than a column and a half to Nottingham. The last two sentences tell of how 'D.H. Lawrence was at the High School and University College (now Nottingham University). The riots in the town form the background of his story "Goose Fair".' As John Baird's book attests, so much more could have been told by way of story. Of riots, there are Luddite, reform and race, to note but three. Of that celebrated Fair, take your pick from losing 'all idea of time and place locked in the belly of its infernal noise' (Alan Sillitoe) or 'following the custom of centuries [as] the good people of the city whose Sheriff was so soundly abused by Robin Hood, take leave of their senses' (Cecil Roberts), to draw on just a couple of the various references offered.

A writer who did make a trip to Nottingham, back in 1705, was Edward Ward. In rhyming couplets, he wrote of how:

To my joy, I arrived at fair Nottingham Town
Whose streets, and whose buildings, I shall not describe.
I'll leave it to some historical tribe.
But this I must say, in its praise, if I had
it merited all that my Muse could have said.

Though John Baird does describe the streets and buildings, he is not just from "some historical tribe". The welcome irony of this book about place is that it is not easy to place — and it is all the more interesting for that. Yes, it's part historical, but it's also anecdotal, biographical, cultural, and littered with gems for those in the grip of "quote-o-mania".

Whilst Baird's book ranges assuredly over literary pedigrees of old, he casts an unfailingly knowledgeable eye over what has occurred here, for example, in the way of independent book-selling, a burgeoning poetry scene, and the contribution made by writers of colour. In doing so, he traverses not only the last several years (since becoming a City of Literature) but also how the roots for that grew many decades before. Readers may not actually reach the "Moon and Stars" — read on further for that reference — but in following this literary journey of the resonant names of the "Queen of the Midlands", wherever they be reading from, they will be enriched. May this book be alive in your keeping!

Patrick Limb,
Chair, Nottingham UNESCO City of Literature
November 2021

Book One:
Nottingham City Centre

Chapter 1
The Arboretum – A Walk in the Park

'Second star to the right and straight on till morning.'
JM Barrie, *Peter Pan, or The Boy Who Wouldn't Grow Up*

The Arboretum was Nottingham's first public park. Close to the two high schools and a university, it has been a source of recreation and inspiration for many a writer. The park's design of winding paths and sweeping lawns was set out in 1850 under the supervision of the botanical publisher and editor Samuel Curtis (1779–1860), who created it for the relaxation and education of Nottingham's city dwellers. Its twelve acres host a number of attractions. In addition to a small lake, an aviary, a cockatoo's grave (the bird did live to be 114) and a bandstand, there are several areas of interest to bibliophiles, and the park is even situated on Waverley Street, the only Nottingham street named after a novel.

Inside the grounds, near the Western Gates and Waverley Lodge, and facing the park's entrance, is a bronze bust of Samuel Morley (1809–86), created by the principal of Nottingham's School of Art, Joseph Else, he of the Council House's lions. The monument describes Morley as an "MP, merchant and philanthropist". In 1882 Morley founded the first separately-housed public lending library for children in Britain, in a turreted building – attached to Bard House, the former Adult Education Centre, once the home of many evening classes in literature and courses for trade unionists – towards the Mansfield Road end of Shakespeare Street. The well-furnished, pioneering library was created with Morley's £500 grant. Believing that the working classes were being 'poisoned with cheap, noxious fiction of the most objectionable kind,' Morley personally selected the donated three-and-a half thousand books.

The first children's library, on Shakespeare Street.

15

It was after hearing that Nottingham's Central Library only opened to users aged fifteen and over that Morley funded the new library. Books were made available to children over the age of seven who were allowed to borrow two free books a week. By limiting this number, and keeping the opening hours between 4pm and 8pm weekdays, it was assumed that the children's reading would not interfere with their home studies.

The writer John Potter Briscoe (1848–1926), Principal Librarian of the Nottingham Free Public Libraries, and an original member of the Library Association, also deserves a mention here. As a leading figure in the development of professional librarianship, and a driving force behind the extension of library services in Nottingham, he was keen to provide books for children and helped in the establishment of The Children's Free Public Lending Library and Reading Room, as the children's library was known. Potter Briscoe lived within easy walking distance of the new library, at 2 Forest Grove, Colville Street, and later at 38 Addison Street, where he died. One of Potter Briscoe's assistant librarians had been Paul Herring, who went from being the city's first certified librarian to becoming a popular novelist with his thrillers and humourous romance novels.

Samuel Morley's bust was part of a whole statue which used to stand outside the Theatre Royal but in 1929, when it had to be moved for traffic purposes, the statue fell off the back of a lorry.[1] Morley was the youngest son of a manufacturer with premises in Nottingham and London. He took managerial control of the business after his father and brothers retired and, after his uncle and cousin died, he became the sole managing partner. He became very wealthy, success that coincided with his introduction of pensions and allowances for his workforce.[2] A Liberal and political radical, Morley was an abolitionist and campaigner, supporting universal suffrage and donating to worthy causes. He also gave money to Nottingham Castle and the city's university. Morley was elected MP for Nottingham in 1865, and later in Bristol. He declined a

The Arboretum lake.

peerage from the Queen, not wanting to be seen as above the people.

Near the Arboretum's Addison Street side, bordering the bowling green, is another statue of a radical, Feargus O'Connor (1794–1855), the first and only Chartist Member of Parliament. Erected by his admirers, the statue of O'Connor holding a scroll was designed by JB Robinson in 1859. O'Connor was MP for Nottingham 1847–52, and his statue is the only one in the UK dedicated to a Chartist leader. It was paid for by the working people of Nottingham without any contribution from the borough, who only allowed it on condition that it contained no controversial inscriptions and was regarded as a work of art. The Chartists were the first national working-class political reform movement in Britain. In the 1830s, millions of excluded people clamoured for the right to the vote and Nottingham was a centre of this agitation. With the arrival of new workers for the growing textile trades, the population increased, and workers were subjected to dire conditions. Hailing from County Cork in Ireland, Feargus O'Connor became the movement's popular leader. An acclaimed public speaker and known drinker, he was declared insane in 1852. There's a 2008 book about him by Paul A Pickering.

It took until 1918 for women over the age of thirty to be given the right to vote. The daughter of a Lenton vicar, Helen Kirkpatrick Watts (1881–1972), was arrested three times and imprisoned twice whilst campaigning for votes for women. The activist wrote that 'Votes for women will not be won by drawing-room chatter. It has got to be fought for in the market-places, and if we don't fight for it, no one else will.'

Watts helped establish the Nottingham branch of the Women's Social and Political Union. A juniper tree was planted in the Arboretum in her honour, with a plaque later unveiled. Eight of her written speeches (1909) are held at Nottinghamshire Archives.

On one occasion in 1911, at a weekly meeting of Nottingham's Cosmopolitan Debating Society, or Cosmo, their Sunday lecture was delivered by Miss Adela Pankhurst, daughter of Emmeline Pankhurst. She gave a speech entitled, "Sweated Women Workers and how the Women's Votes can help them". The Cosmo was a place for Nottingham's working-class autodidacts, like those in Philip Callow's Nottingham novel *The Hosanna Man* (1956) and Alan Sillitoe's *The Open Door* (1989). It was like 'a working man's House of Commons,' according to Ray Gosling. In an edition of

Nottingham Quarterly (1978), he recalled, 'I once went to that most famous of Nottingham ancient working-class venerations – the Cosmopolitan Debating Society – as an incited, advertised speaker.' He added, 'they tore me to shreds before I began.'

Geoffrey Trease (1909–98), another rebel, was born in Chaucer Street, a road facing the Arboretum, which became an important part of his childhood. Trease was educated at Nottingham Boys' High School, where he was head boy. For some time, the writer had more books in print than any other British author. A pioneer of children's fiction, Trease also penned novels, autobiography, criticism and historical studies.

The Arboretum itself has provided much literary inspiration. It features in Rose Fyleman's (1877–1957) children's book *A Princess Comes to Our Town* (1927), and it is claimed that JM Barrie (1860–1937) used the park with its lake and aviary as a source for his, and Peter Pan's, Neverland. The cannons in the Chinese Bell Tower certainly wouldn't look out of place. The two Russian cannons were captured in the Crimean War and placed with two replicas within an octagonal tower. Barrie introduced Neverland as the Never Never Land in his 1904 play, which became the novel, *Peter and Wendy: Peter Pan; or, the Boy Who Wouldn't Grow Up*, in 1911. Like the Arboretum, Barrie's Neverland is compact enough that adventures are never far between, and he would take regular journeys through the park from his digs at 5 Birkland Avenue, just off Peel Street, to his job at the *Nottingham Journal*.

Chinese Bell Tower and the cannons, in the Arboretum.

Forty years later, Graham Greene (1904–91) would stroll through the Arboretum when lodging at Ivy House, just off Waverley Street. During his time as a trainee sub-editor on the *Nottingham Journal* Greene would take his dog to the park.

Michael Standen (1937–2011) used his schooldays in Nottingham as inspiration for his successful debut novel, set here in the early 1960s. Standen's *Start Somewhere* (1965) follows a group of unconventional teenagers as they enter adulthood, and it opens with humorous high jinks in the Arboretum as we get to know eighteen-year-old Frank Griffin, his mates, and his working-class family.

In *Harris' Requiem* (1960), Stanley Middleton has his eponymous hero, '...walk in the frowsty park, past the Victorian busts and the Chinese pagoda, and watch the ducks on the pond behind the low, lurching railing.'

And there's a meeting in the Arboretum between John Harvey's two great detectives, Charlie Resnick and Frank Elder, in *Flesh and Blood* (2004).

A twelve-year-old DH Lawrence (1885–1930) became the first boy from Eastwood to win a twelve pounds a year county council scholarship to Nottingham High School (situated just outside the Arboretum), a school 'considered the best day school in England,' he wrote, and he recalled the boys and girls from both the high schools mingling. In Lawrence's *The Rainbow* (1915), Ursula Brangwen mentions the school and park in this description:

> The school itself had been a gentleman's house. Dark, sombre lawns separated it from the dark, select avenue. But its rooms were very large and of good appearance, and from the back, one looked over lawns and shrubbery, over the trees and the grassy slope of the Arboretum, to the town which heaped the hollow with its roofs and cupolas and its shadows.

Various educational buildings are situated close to the Arboretum, adding to the wave of writers familiar with the park.

---

[1]Mee, 1938.
[2]Mellors, 1924

Chapter 2
The Arkwright Building, Shakespeare Street – A Place of Learning

> 'The big college built of stone, standing in the quiet street, with its rim of grass and lime-trees all so peaceful: she felt it remote, a magic-land.'
>
> DH Lawrence, *The Rainbow*

Once known as the finest pile of public buildings in Nottinghamshire, the Arkwright Building is one of England's most important places of learning, built with the aim of bringing education to all those who desired it, regardless of class, sex or financial means.

It was in the mid-1870s that Nottingham Corporation decided to bring together a further educational college, a public library and a museum to provide quality education in the centre of Nottingham. The desire was to open up university education to people unable to attend the traditional universities of Oxford or Cambridge. Work began in 1877 on this superb example of late nineteenth-century architecture, with its Gothic revival style of gables, arches and pinnacles, many of which survive to this day. The building was designed by Lockwood and Mawson after they beat off competition from other architects.

Arkwright Building, University College.

Nottingham Corporation received an anonymous £10,000 private donation on condition that suitable accommodation for lectures was provided and that the corporation would pay the rest. They found the extra £61,000 and used land they already owned, known as Horse Pool Close, which had had Shakespeare Street built across it since 1852.

In 1881 the grand development was complete, and courses began at University College in the autumn. The former public library – which had taken over the old Artisans' Library in 1867 – moved its books from Thurland Street to Nottingham's Central Library, where it remained until 1977. The new adult education centre, with its fine lecture rooms and inclusive daytime and evening classes, was the first municipally-funded college of further education, leading *The Times* to predict that it would eventually become Nottingham University.

Completing the Arkwright Building's trinity of educational establishments was the Natural History Museum, which moved to Wollaton Hall in 1927. Not only was the Arkwright Building Nottingham's most significant educational venue, it would play an important role in the history of both the city's universities.

There were one hundred and thirty students in the first term, attending day lectures on Shakespeare. The majority were aged fourteen and upwards, their "university extension classes" paving the way for the college to align itself with the University of London, an affiliation that allowed students to study to degree level. Only six first degrees were obtained before 1890, the first BA being awarded to Henry T Saville.

The Arkwright Building was a place of learning and inspiration for DH Lawrence. He was due to start his studies at University College in 1905 but, monetarily challenged, he decided to continue teaching for another year. By the time he started his teacher training, he had already spent three years as a pupil-teacher in Eastwood and Ilkeston. Lawrence was twenty-one when he began his teacher's certificate course. His professors thought he'd 'make an excellent teacher of upper classes,' but added, '...for a large class of boys in a rough district he would not have sufficient persistence and enthusiasm.'

Elementary teachers had been trained at the college from 1890, Nottingham being one of the first places in the country to establish day training for teachers. The students studied a combination of educational theory and academic subjects, in addition to undertaking teaching practice in local schools.

Largely unimpressed by his college education, Lawrence wrote that his professors:

> ...went on in such a miserable jogtrot, earn-your-money manner that I was startled... I came to feel that I might as well be taught by gramophones... I doubted them, I began to despise or distrust things.

Lawrence left the college two years later, having gained his certificate to teach at elementary schools but without staying on for a bachelor's degree. He did admit to gaining maturity from the experience and it was during his time here that he completed the second draft of *Laetitia,* later to become his first novel *The White Peacock* (1911).

It was also during this period, in 1907, that Lawrence wrote three stories for the *Nottingham Guardian*'s Christmas story competition, winning with "A Prelude".

In *The Rainbow* (1915), the Arkwright Building is described thus by Ursula Brangwen:

> The big college built of stone, standing in the quiet street, with its rim of grass and lime-trees all so peaceful: she felt it remote, a magic-land. Its architecture was foolish, she knew from her father. Still, it was different from that of all other buildings. Its rather pretty, plaything, Gothic form was almost a style, in the dirty industrial town. She liked the hall, with its big stone chimney-piece of cardboard-like carved stone, with its armorial decoration, looked silly just opposite the bicycle stand and the radiator, whilst the great notice-board with its fluttering papers seemed to slam away all senses of retreat and mystery from the far wall.

Just inside the building's main entrance, to the left, remains that big stone chimney-piece. To its right is a plaque with the familiar Lawrence phoenix. Opposite the stone chimney is a stone stairway up to the windows. From Lawrence's "From A College Window", from *New Poems* (1918):

> The glimmer of the limes, sun-heavy, sleeping,
> Goes trembling past me up the College wall.
> Below, the lawn, in soft blue shade is keeping,
> The daisy-froth quiescent, softly in thrall...

In 2021 a new plaque was erected outside the building, commemorating Lawrence's time here.

After qualifying as a teacher Lawrence took up a post at an elementary school in Croydon. The experiences informed *The Rainbow,* in which Ursula becomes a teacher.

In the 1920s University College moved most of its faculties to the new Highfields site where it achieved university status after the Second World War, becoming what is now the University of Nottingham. During the war, the Luftwaffe bombed the Arkwright Building, damaging both the textile and mining departments and destroying part of the façade and roof. Two casualties were the statues of James Watt and Georges Cuvier. The four other figures, William Shakespeare, John Milton, Francis Bacon and Isaac Newton, survived and can be seen on the Shakespeare Street side.

Following the war, the Arkwright Building continued its role in education, becoming home to the Nottingham & District Technical College and, in 1958, the Newton Building opened nearby. It was Nottingham's first high rise (nine floors). The name changes continued, and by the 1970s the Arkwright Building was part of the College of Technology which, together with Nottingham School of Art and other institutions, amalgamated to form Trent Polytechnic.

In the early 1970s Slavomir Rawicz (1915–2004) was a technician on an architectural ceramics course at Trent Poly's School of Art and Design, before a heart attack brought forward his retirement. After the war, Rawicz was one of the many Polish people to settle in Nottingham. In 1941 he had escaped from a Russian gulag and made his way from Siberia to British India, by way of China, the Gobi Desert, Tibet and the Himalayas. This journey was told in the 2010 film *The Way Back* and, earlier, in Rawicz's ghost-written book *The Long Walk* (1956). The memoir is an epic tale of physical and mental resilience. By the time Rawicz was rescued, he weighed just five stone. His wife Marjorie, a local librarian who had helped with the book, assisted "Slav" in answering the many

Lawrence's "big stone chimney".

letters he continued to receive from admirers. *The Long Walk*, never out of print, has sold half a million copies.

Trent Poly became Nottingham Polytechnic, and achieved its own university status in 1993, becoming Nottingham Trent University (NTU). In that same year Sue Thomas and others devised an MA writing course which has become one of the longest established postgraduate courses of its kind in the UK. The country's first course had been set up by the former West Bridgford schoolboy Malcolm Bradbury (1932–2000), author of *The History Man* (1975), who launched the MA in Creative Writing at the University of East Anglia in 1970. NTU admitted its first intake of students in 1994. The poet and author Gregory Woods was one of the colleagues assisting Thomas in setting up the Nottingham MA course, which has mostly been taught at NTU's Clifton site where it has proved to be both popular and productive.

To celebrate twenty-five years of the course, Shoestring Press published *25* in 2019, a book featuring twenty-five contributions, from writers with a connection to the MA course. Including work from members of staff (past and present), visiting professors and former students, it's a unique book of original writing from a host of award-winning writers.

Teachers on the early MA course were, or would later become, published writers. There was Sue Thomas herself (*Correspondence*), the biographers Katherine Frank (*Crusoe*) and Kathryn Hughes (*George Eliot*), the multi-genre author Graham Joyce (*The Facts of Life*), and poets Catherine Byron (*Settlements*) and Mahendra Solanki (*The Lies We Tell*), the latter becoming course leader in 1999.

Sue Thomas later founded trAce Online Writing Centre (1995–2006) at NTU, an early global online community. Other previous leaders of the MA course are the writers David Belbin (*The Great Deception*), who changed the course's title to MA Creative Writing, Vicki Bertram (*Kicking Daffodils*) and Sarah Jackson (*Pelt*). The poet Rory Waterman (*Sweet Nothings*) has been course leader since 2013.

Current staff members on the MA also have a wealth of publications to their name. Belbin runs a module on children's and young adult fiction, the poet Andrew Taylor (*Not Here — There*) teaches English and creative writing, Anthony Cropper (*Nature's Magician*) leads the script module and Eve Makis (*Spice Box Letters*) leads the fiction module. Cropper and Makis collaborated in

2018 on *The Accidental Memoir*, a book for anyone wanting to document their lives and explore their creativity. Sue Dymoke, who has had several collections of poetry published as well as academic works on writing poetry, works at NTU as an Associate Professor in the Nottingham Institute of Education.

Guest speakers on the MA have included some of the nation's best writers for the page, stage and screen, such as Jon McGregor (*Reservoir 13*), Alison Moore (*The Lighthouse*), Kate Mosse (*Labyrinth*), Amanda Whittington (*Be My Baby*), Miranda Seymour (*In Byron's Wake*) and Alan Sillitoe (*Saturday Night and Sunday Morning*). Visiting professors include Peter Porter (*Once Bitten Twice Bitten*), David Almond (*Skellig*), William Ivory (*Made in Dagenham*) and Michael Eaton (*Lockerbie*).

Each year the students write, produce and publish an anthology of original creative writing and the MA has a strong record of publication by its graduates, some of whom have themselves become publishers. Di Slaney now owns and runs Nottingham's Candlestick Press, an independent publisher of poetry pamphlets with offices in Arnold. Slaney is a poet herself with the collections *Reward for Winter* (2016) and *Herd Queen* (2020). She lives in a Grade II listed four-hundred-year-old farm house in Bilsthorpe where she provides a home for over 170 needy animals. And Colwick's Stephan Collishaw runs Noir Press, which brings Lithuanian fiction to an English-reading audience. Collishaw has authored four novels of his own including 2017's *The Song of the Stork*.

A further selection of alumni with selected titles to look out for are: Nicola Monaghan (*Dead Flowers*), Kim Slater (*Smart*), Clare Stevens (*Blue Tide Rising*), Clare Littleford (*Beholden*), Maria Allen (*Before the Earthquake*), Maxine Linnell (*Breaking the Rules*), Lynda Clark (*Beyond Kidding*), Kerry Young (*Pao*), Frances Thimann (*Cello and other stories*), Freda Love Smith (*Red Velvet Underground* – part memoir, part cookbook); and poetry from Rebecca Cullen (*Majid Sits in a Tree and Sings*), Mark Goodwin (*The Ground Aslant*), Rich Goodson (*Mr Universe*), Jo Dixon (*A Woman in the Queue*) and Zayneb Allak (*Keine Angst*).

It's no surprise that NTU now runs its own creative writing hub for writers at the University.

Chapter 3
Broadway Cinema, 14–18 Broad Street – From Booth to Bouchercon

> 'The rescued are appallingly few – a ghastly minority compared with the multitudes who struggle and sink in the open-mouthed abyss.'
> William Booth, *In Darkest England and the Way Out*

Where Broadway Cinema now stands was the Broad Street Wesleyan Chapel. Erected in 1837 with impressive Corinthian columns, the venue witnessed the conversion of a fifteen-year-old pawnbroker's apprentice called William Booth.[1] In 1890 Booth wrote *In Darkest England and the Way Out*, which highlighted the desperate straits in which many ordinary people found themselves. Profits from the book helped fund projects for the homeless. Booth then founded The Salvation Army and was their first General. On Notintone Place, Sneinton, is the William Booth Birthplace Museum, comprising three houses c1825. Booth was born in the middle one, no 12. The building was used as a hostel by the Army in the 1930s before it became a museum in 1959.

William Booth's Birthplace Museum, Notintone Place.

In 1905 William Booth (1829–1912) became a freeman of Nottingham, travelling to his ceremony in an open carriage, past the well-wishers in the Great Market Place and orator's corner where, as a boy, he'd stood on a box and preached the word.

Unable to afford the costly roof repairs, Broad Street's Wesleyan Chapel closed in 1954 and was sold to the Nottingham Co-operative Society for use as the country's first co-operative educational centre, complete with a five-hundred-seat theatre, known to hold poetry evenings. By the end of the decade, it had become an arts theatre and begun screening films. It was adopted by the British Film Institute as one of their regional film theatres, and in 1966 the Nottingham Film Theatre opened, later to be known as City Lights Cinema. Sunday night showings were popular with a regular, dedicated audience – so regular that Alan Simpson, later MP for Nottingham South, quipped, 'Most cinemas announce changes in the programme, here they announce changes in the audience.'

Broadway Cinema arrived in 1990 as a charity born out of a consortium of four local media organisations: Nottingham Film Theatre, New Cinema Workshop, Midland Group, and Nottingham Video Project, with support from the BFI, East Midlands Arts, and the local city and county councils. The cinema had re-opened before it had even been re-branded as Broadway. The first public event was a showing of *Fellow Traveller*, a film written by Nottingham's Michael Eaton and starring Ron Silver as a blacklisted Hollywood screenwriter.

Back then, Broadway had a large sprung dancefloor and the Rainbow Rooms, replaced in 1992 by Screen Two and a café bar. Screens Three and Four were added in 2006, Paul Smith assisting with the design. *Total Film* rated Broadway as one of the ten best cinemas in the world.

Broadway Cinema, Broad Street.

The current CEO of Film London, Adrian Wootton, was the founding Director of Broadway Media Centre and he 'wanted to put Nottingham onto the new media map.' That year, 1990, Wootton travelled with his close friend Michael Eaton to the Noir in Cinema Festival in Cattolica, Italy. They both realised 'We could do this in Nottingham.' Their aspiration was always to hold a literary event as well as a film festival, and that Italian celebration of film and literature provided the template to launch Nottingham's own International Crime & Mystery Festival, *Shots in the Dark*.

Broadway's small team put together a ten-day event which launched in 1991. The programme included film previews, retrospectives and writers' events, and included the British premiere of *Silence of the Lambs*. In the festival's first few years Broadway welcomed several notable guests, such as the American screenwriter, novelist and film director Sam Fuller (1912–97), the French film director, producer and screenwriter Claude Miller (1942–2012), and the Czech–English actor Herbert Lom (1917–2012), star of *The Ladykillers* and *The Pink Panther.*

By the June festival of 1992, *Shots* included a new three-day crime writing convention, *Shots on the Page.* This ran alongside the main festival and featured visiting novelists Colin Dexter, Julian Symons and Donald E Westlake, author of the hard-boiled Parker books (as Richard Stark) and the wonderful Dortmunder series of capers.

In November 2021 Broadway commemorated the thirtieth anniversary of Shots with an all-day event which included a Michael Eaton solo performance remembering the famous "Never Mind the Bollocks" court case, when the local Virgin record shop manager was arrested for displaying the Sex Pistols' album cover in his window in 1977.

Adrian Wootton said, 'From [June 1992] onwards, *Shots in the Dark* started confidently preparing for a bigger third year, helped in no small way by the establishment of Broadway as a major cultural and social centre.'

1993's *Shots on the Page* brought more authors to the city, including Val McDermid, Peter Lovesey and Sara Paretsky, creator of the tough female private eye VI Warshawski. It was during *Shots* that David Belbin met one of his heroes, Evan Hunter (better known as Ed McBain). Michael Eaton, who was interviewing Hunter for *Shots,* invited Belbin to dinner with the American author. McBain's 87th Precinct novels always open with the line 'The city in these pages is imaginary.' In a nice twist and nod to McBain, Belbin began his Nottingham-based Beat series with the line 'The city in these pages is real.'

The eleven-day extravaganza of *Shots '93* had its usual mix of film previews, panel discussions and educational events, as well as a photography exhibition and a theatrical show devised by Eaton. But the festival will be best remembered for a visit by Quentin Tarantino, the world's hottest young director, a visit that resulted in 'a large amount of press attention and terrific public support which established our event as a truly popular festival,' said Wootton.

Adrian Wootton had met Tarantino that spring and persuaded him to come to Nottingham for the British premiere screening of *Reservoir Dogs.* When Tarantino returned in 1994 it was as an honorary patron and he spent several days in and around the festival. Speaking to the *Nottingham Evening Post,* Tarantino said:

People ask me 'Why are you coming here?' I come here because I really like the festival. I like the city. I think that Nottingham is a really cool city. Coming here and seeing the different movies and hanging out with all the people here who I have got to know a little bit, it's fun and I get a big kick out of it.

On the festival's last Saturday, Broadway had its biggest coup, as Tarantino presented a secret "mystery" film, playing a reel he'd brought over with him from France, complete with French subtitles. David Belbin was there and told me:

> I'd had the nod and knew what was coming: the second ever showing of Tarantino's second movie, *Pulp Fiction*. The previous showing had been at Cannes, where it won the Palme D'Or. Quentin gave a brief introduction to the packed cinema. Afterwards, following tumultuous applause, he answered questions until we ran out of them, gone three in the morning.

Tarantino was heavily involved in the festival, programming a Blacksploitation season and speaking before each movie. He also found time to take in the local sights. 'He gobbled up Nottingham,' said Eaton, 'we even chauffeured him to see the Major Oak.'

In 1994, the scale of *Shots on the Page* was expanded, and plans were well underway to enter the international spotlight. Wootton was eager to crack the big one, *Bouchercon*, the world's largest and most prestigious annual crime mystery convention. Named after the American critic and editor Anthony Boucher, *Bouchercon* sees hundreds of writers, publishers, reviewers, booksellers and readers convene on a city; but in its fifty-year history the world mystery convention has only been held outside of North America twice. The first time was in London (1990). John Harvey told me:

> It was the first *Bouchercon* I attended and I can testify to the sad fact that it was, in organisational terms, less than successful. Which may have been one of the driving forces behind the ambitious bid to bring *Bouchercon* to Nottingham. 'Anything London can do, we can do better.'

Wootton's plan to land *Bouchercon* had been launched in 1990, inspired by that trip to Italy with Eaton. In 1991 the two men visited Pasadena for that year's event. Their campaign was afoot. 'Having experienced the excesses of the crime writers at play, we once again had the vain-glorious reckoning: "We could do this",' said Eaton. Joining Wootton and Eaton on the *Nottingham Bouchercon* programming committee was the British Film Institute's Paul Taylor, key figures from the city, and the crime fiction writer, editor, publisher and critic Maxim Jakubowski, who did much to run the writers' programme for both *Shots in the Page* and *Bouchercon*. Harvey chaired the committee. Eaton said, 'Thus it was that the following year a merry band came riding through the glen to Toronto to mount an Olympian bid to host *Bouchercon*.' Key members of the committee kept up the lobbying at the next festivals too, in Omaha 1993 and Seattle 1994, where the Nottingham bid to host *Bouchercon '95* was subject to a vote. 'It was all rather tense,' said Eaton, adding:

> Nottingham was definitely the rank outsider. Our city did not have the hotels, did not have the economic support (tell me about it), did not have the background or experience to mount such a significant international jubilee. But somehow we must have hit the spot. We had the enthusiasm. We had the desire. And we pulled it off. We won the vote.

Harvey said, 'I was in the room when the result was announced and remember vividly the excitement that followed. Job done. Or, more accurately, job just begun.'

Wootton recalled the 'arduous activity that it took to win the bid, then persuade the Americans to come, to get the funding and to stage it with all the sensitivities and, to be frank, egos of the personalities attending as guests.'

The twenty-sixth *Bouchercon* arrived in Nottingham on Friday 28 September 1995 as part of the year's *Shots in the Dark* festival. Delegates registered at the Royal Hotel and highlights from the first day included Sue Grafton and Walter Mosley at the Concert Hall and a crime cabaret evening. On the Saturday morning you could catch Minette Walters with Frances Fyfield, and that night, back at Broadway, Linda Barnes, Walter Mosley, John Harvey and Bill Moody performed in *Blues and All That Jazz*. The next morning, it was time for Lawrence Block and Donald E Westlake. Breathless stuff.

There were many, many events across several locations, with Sara Paretsky, Ian Rankin, Val McDermid, Tony Hillerman and Jonathan Coe all speaking on panels that addressed a wide variety of subjects. There was also a crime quiz and a tribute to Patricia Highsmith.

Among the venues employed was the Theatre Royal, where local crime writers Frank Palmer, Keith Wright, John Harvey and

Raymond Flynn discussed Nottingham in *The Most Violent Place in England? How far does Nottingham live up to its reputation, and how close are the fictions set there to the facts?* Joining them on the panel was Professor Stephen Jones and Harvey's advisor on the Resnick novels, Detective Superintendent Peter Coles.

Knowing in advance that Nottingham was to host Bouchercon, Harvey shrewdly set his seventh Resnick novel, *Living Proof*, at a crime writing festival in Nottingham and timed its release with *Bouchercon*'s opening. The festival also held a guided Resnick walk with its own map.

The year's international guest of honour was James Ellroy, who also compiled a programme of noir films for Broadway. Inspector Morse creator Colin Dexter was the British guest of honour, and there was a lifetime achievement award for Ruth Rendell. Harvey said:

> All in all, it was a great four days, during most of which I wandered around on a high. Everyone, but everyone – save for James Ellroy – seemed to be having a good time. For me, being part of the general atmosphere aside, one of the most memorable moments came in hearing the wonderfully dry wit of Reginald Hill in his role as toastmaster at the Anthony Awards Banquet.

Wootton told me, 'The *Shots/Bouchercon* festival was a really important part of my history and during the 1992–5 period it really dominated a large part of my life.'

Shots in the Dark left Nottingham with the last century but returned in 2018. Revived by Broadway's Caroline Hennigan and Steve Mapp, and once again under Wootton's patronage, it welcomed the French director, screenwriter, actor and producer Bertrand Tavernier as guest of honour. *Shots on the Page* also returned, giving me the chance to interview CJ Tudor, who had recently gone from walking other people's dogs on Woodthorpe Park to becoming a bestselling writer of chiller thrillers, starting with *The Chalk Man*.

The film producer Jeremy Thomas was guest of honour in 2019 while 2020's recipient was due to be the director Stephen Frears, a son of West Bridgford. In a virtual *Shots in the Dark* Wootton hosted the writer and director Marco Bellocchio and presented him with an award before a special screening of *The Traitor*, all in benefit to Broadway.

---

[1] Mellors, 1924.

Chapter 4
Bromley House Library – A Living History

'The oldest books are still only just out to those who have not read them.'

Samuel Butler

In the heart of Nottingham, tucked away between a charity shop and a newsagent, is the entrance to Bromley House Library. It was in 1816 that Nottingham's oldest subscription library was founded, moving to Bromley House in 1821. The house itself had been built as a town house in 1752 for the Nottingham banker George Smith, grandson of the founder of the oldest known provincial bank in the country. Smith named the house after his son changed his name to Bromley. In 1804, the diarist Abigail Gawthern (1757–1822) recorded attending a sandwich party at Thomas Smith's Bromley House, noting down, '...above fifty people: Captain Fothergill intoxicated and behaved rude to Mr Ray.'

The library became a hub of the city's intellectual life and encouraged the forming of educational societies such as the Literary and Science Society (est 1824) and the Literary and Debating Club (est 1837). The visitors' book at Bromley House Library is a record of Nottingham's intellectual and cultural heritage, with past members such as George Green, a father of quantum physics, included alongside notable guests like the scientist Michael Faraday. Formally capped at 265 subscribers, the library had required each member to purchase a share. The cap was removed in 1998 when charitable status was obtained, and there are now well over a thousand members with more being welcomed. Former regulars include notable members of the Nottinghamshire literati: William and Mary Howitt, Rose Fyleman, Philip James Bailey and Robert Mellors.

As a boy Cecil Roberts visited the library and '...went out, dazed, making a vow that one day, in the affluent future I planned, I would belong to it'.[1] The novelist never did join but he did have a room named after him in the nearby Central Library.

Bromley House Library adds a thousand new books annually and meets modern demands whilst retaining its grand history. Holding nearly 50,000 books and manuscripts, the beautiful Grade II listed building has recently undergone some needed structural repair, having received a grant of £385,000 from Historic England towards the cost of fixing its 267-year-old roof.

The library has a working meridian line. A small hole in the upper left of a window sends a beam of light along a brass strip on the floor precisely at true solar noon. It was used to set the clocks of Nottingham in days before standard time. There's also an 1830 longcase clock inscribed with the time differences that occurred across the country (Nottingham time was over four minutes behind Greenwich). More striking is the library's iconic spiral staircase, added in 1857. It was crafted by William Stevenson, Nottingham's master-carpenter, cabinetmaker, and the writer of *Bygone Nottinghamshire* (1893).

Bromley House Library's spiral staircase.

On the top floor of the library is a studio that operated as the first photographic studio in Nottingham, and one of the first commercial photographic studios in the country, a venue where many of Nottingham's wealthier families of the mid-nineteenth century had their images captured. Nottingham's first professional photographer, Alfred Barber, put in a skylight at his own expense, a circular and glass structure incorporating a cog wheel mechanism that could follow the passage of the sun. At the rear of the library is a hidden Victorian garden, a haven in the heart of the city. The garden features in Philip Jones' book *Great Nottinghamshire Gardens* (2001).

Bromley House Library gardens.

The poet Ruth Fainlight, widow of Alan Sillitoe (1928–2010), donated a number of items to the library after his death. The library's Alan Sillitoe Collection includes lots of books that had belonged to Sillitoe and Fainlight from their holiday cottage in Derbyshire. Many of the books contain messages and dedications from family, friends and fellow writers, and there are personal notes from Sillitoe, plus many maps, befitting of his lifelong passion for them ever since his grandfather had given him an old Ordnance Survey map. Sillitoe and Fainlight were joint presidents of the library in 2009 and 2010.

For more on Bromley House Library and its writers, read *The Literary Ghosts of Bromley House* by Rowena Edlin-White, and take one of the library's guided tours.

---

[1]Roberts, 1967.

Chapter 5
The Council House – The Power and the Glory

> 'Inside the Council House all is municipal opulence – sweeping staircase of Italian marble, phone kiosk in bronze, walnut and black marble, sprung parquet dancefloor...'
>
> Emrys Bryson, *Portrait of Nottingham*

When Ken Dodd first came to Nottingham, he took a taxi from Midland Station to the Empire Theatre for what was to be his first professional show. As the taxi passed our grand Council House with its big dome, Dodd asked the driver what it was.

'That's the Council House,' he replied.

Dodd said, 'Oh, I'll put my name down for one of those.'

Ken Dodd isn't the only celebrity to be impressed by our Council House, one of the finest municipal buildings outside London. It was officially opened on 22 May 1929 by the Prince of Wales, the same year the Old Market Square got its name, having previously been known as the Great Market Place. Slab Square, as many locals call it, was rammed in 1945 – the year the UN came into existence – when General Dwight D Eisenhower pledged friendship

Nottingham's Council House

between the United States and Great Britain and addressed the masses from the balcony of the Council House.

Designed by TC Howitt, the imposing building was built from Portland stone, from the same quarry used by Christopher Wren to build the similar-looking St. Paul's Cathedral in London. Its iconic sixty-one-metre-high dome rises above the city, and its deep-toned hourly bell, nicknamed Little John, can be heard seven miles away. The keystone of the central arch was salvaged from a London church after the Great Fire of 1666, and it is claimed that its two lifts were from a set of four, the other two being inside New York's Empire State Building.

The Council House has hosted some of Nottingham's most important literary events. It was here in 2008 that Alan Sillitoe became an honorary freeman of the city, and said, 'It really is an honour. It's something I never thought I'd get. I'm staggered.' Sillitoe wondered where he would be without Nottingham, 'without its scenery.' A few months after he died, in 2010, a celebration of his life and work was held at the Council House, with a series of talks and reflections. Among those involved was Alan's son David, plus local authors Gwen Grant, John Harvey and Nicola Monaghan. The event also had an Arthur Seaton inspired set from local band Blue Yonder, and there was the chance for people to have their photo taken at Sillitoe's writing desk. The main organisers were Five Leaves, the publisher of this volume, and Nottingham Writers' Studio.

The Council House appears in Alan Sillitoe's 1960 film adaptation of his most famous novel *Saturday Night and Sunday Morning* (1958). Arthur Seaton might not have ventured into the ballroom of the Council House but he took advantage of the famous meeting place outside, the stone lions (usually the left), where he meets with Doreen. In Sillitoe's *The Broken Chariot* (1998), Archie told Bert that 'if you stood between the lions in front of the Council House for an hour a week everybody who lived in the town would sooner or later pass by.'

The first writer to have been named a freeman of Nottingham was Cecil Roberts (1892–1976). In 1964, two aldermen travelled to Rome to inform Roberts of the city's desire to confer its freedom on him. He was received at the Council House the following year. The town clerk read out the citation, that Roberts was a 'distinguished son of the city' and he was given a parchment scroll from the Mayor in a large silver casket, engraved with an inkpot and quill pens (years later he discovered that a mouse had eaten the scroll).

Roberts gave a speech before a banquet of 180 guests. In volume five of his autobiography, *The Pleasant Years* (1974), Roberts recalled his speech:

> I am the only author on your list of Freemen. I can think of local authors more worthy, such as Lord Byron and DH Lawrence. Nearly sixty years ago I began my career as an employee of your Corporation. In the basement of this Council House I used the office typewriter and the office paper on which to write my poems, a preposterous office boy. Quite correctly the Press has called this occasion "a happy fairy-tale story". It is indeed, and thanks to you I am the Happy Prince in it.

Roberts was fifteen when he worked as a clerk in the market and fairs department, and he could smell the banquets upstairs. Young Roberts was based in a cubby-hole, bereft of daylight and fresh air, and he was more used to enduring the smells coming from the butchers, the stalls of poultry and the penny lavatories. The old Exchange Building had stood over a bloody basement known as "the shambles", mostly butchers' shops lit by gas flares that extended past the rear of the Exchange. The corporation did increase young Roberts' wages from eight to seventeen shillings a week after discovering that he had returned from the mortuary after identifying his father.

On receiving his Freedom of Nottingham title, Roberts presented some forty volumes of bound manuscripts to the City Library.

Half a century after Roberts became a freeman, Nottingham officially launched its bid to become a UNESCO City of Literature, at an event hosted by the Lord Mayor at the Council House, with David Belbin saying, 'We need to use literature to build literacy,' whilst acknowledging that achieving the UNESCO status would not be easy. One author that supported the bid was Catharine Arnold, a writer of popular history books. In 2018, Arnold became the Sheriff of Nottingham and was based at the Council House.

Belbin was back here in 2019 as the proud Chair of Nottingham UNESCO City of Literature, on what was the ninetieth anniversary of the building's opening. NUCoL and the University of Nottingham were there to host cultural leaders from twenty-six cities as part of Nottwich, the UNESCO Cities of

Literature summit. It was a memorable evening with many inspiring speakers including Sandeep Mahal, Director of NUCoL, Councillor David Mellen, Leader of Nottingham City Council, and Darren Henley OBE, Chief Executive of Arts Council England. There was also a chance for delegates from around the globe to share ideas and forge partnerships.

The highlight of the event was a lecture from the internationally acclaimed author Robert Macfarlane, movingly introduced with a video highlighting the impact of the Lost Words project that was inspired by his 2017 book of the same name. Macfarlane is renowned for his writing on landscape, memory, place and nature, and his talk was a vivid demonstration of the power of storytelling and how culture and creativity can help a world in deep trouble. With mutualism and interconnectedness as relevant now as ever before, Macfarlane proved the perfect speaker for a talk in front of the Creative Cities. The packed audience held on to his every word, many taking inspiration from them.

Chapter 6
The Emett Clock – A Moving Sculpture

> 'The first principle in science is to invent something nice to look at and then decide what it can do.'
>
> Rowland Emett

To some, he's an eccentric cartoonist, artist, designer and author. To many, he's the quirky inventor of Emettland, the Featherstone kite-flying machine and mechanical devices that capture the imagination. To most, he's the creator of the car and other inventions in the 1968 film *Chitty Chitty Bang Bang*. But for Nottinghamians, Rowland Emett (1906–90) is best known for his clock and fountain, a place to meet in the Viccy Centre. The legendary structure used to be near the Boots end of the Victoria Centre but has since moved ends, having had a well-deserved clean.

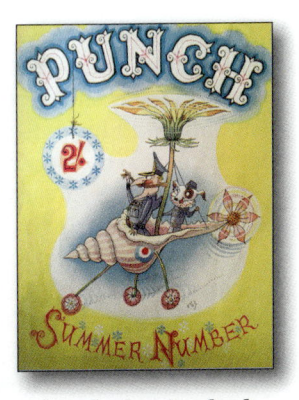

A regular cartoonist for *Punch*, Emett sold his images whilst working as an advertising illustrator, only to have his career postponed by the Second World War when he was drafted to the Air Ministry. Continuing to produce cartoons, he added book illustrations to his repertoire and produced a book with his wife Mary entitled *Anthony and Antimacassar* (1943). It included wonderfully whimsical drawings of trains, depicting the adventures and travels of Antimacassar in a work of comic art.

The Emett Clock in Victoria Centre.

Other illustrated books, *Engines, Aunties and Others* (1943), *Sidings and Suchlike* (1946), *Far Twittering* (1949), *Emett's Domain – Trains, Trams and Englishmen* (1953), and *The Early Morning Milk Train: The Cream of Emett Railway Drawings* (1977), are among those that followed. Early first editions in good condition are quite a find.

In 1954 Emett was commissioned to tour America, sketching his impressions as he went along and producing a colour spread in *Life* magazine. For this he was paid enough to buy a cottage in Ditching where he and his wife settled and he created his phantasmagorical inventions. When Ian Fleming's story *Chitty Chitty Bang Bang* was set to become a musical film, with a Roald Dahl screenplay, Emett set to work on bringing to life the inventions of Caractacus Potts.

Impressed by the film's brilliant props, Nottingham called, and Emett was asked to create an installation for the new Victoria Centre opening in 1973. The result was the Emett Clock, rhythmical time-fountain or aqua horological tintinnabulatory, the choice is yours. The kinetic sculpture looks down over shoppers, though now a little marooned in its new home on the first floor. The twenty-three-foot-tall clock boasts a combination of jets and metal rotating animals, and it keeps time with the playing of the tune "Gigue en Rondeau II".

In 1978, Emett was awarded an OBE for his services to art and science. His services to Nottingham haven't been bad either, although his imaginative books deserve more recognition.

Chapter 7
Exchange Arcade – Years of Promise

> 'Oh! what a noble heart was here undone, When Science' self destroyed her favourite son!'
> Lord Byron, *English Bards and Scotch Reviewers*

Facing the top of Peck Lane and off Smithy Row, behind the Council House, is a side entrance to the Exchange Arcade. Just inside and to the right you'll find a metal plaque depicting Henry Kirke White's birthplace. It states:

> Here on this site stood the birth
> place of Henry Kirke White
> Poet – Born March 31st 1785
> Died at Cambridge Oct 19th 1806

You'll have noticed from those dates that Kirke White died young, and yet Lord Byron acknowledged him, Robert Southey collected his poems, Wordsworth admired him, and his writing astonished Samuel Coleridge.

In the late eighteenth century, former butcher John White, 'a coarse and ignorant man,' and his wife Mary (née Neville), 'gentle in her manners, and possessing an educated intellect,'[1] lived above one of the six butchers' shops in what was known as Rotten Row, now Cheapside, between 1784 and 1798. It was here that their son Henry was born. Years after his death the inn to the right was named after him, The Kirke White Tavern.[2]

Henry Kirke White (he later added the e) was a bright lad and started school aged three, soon becoming a

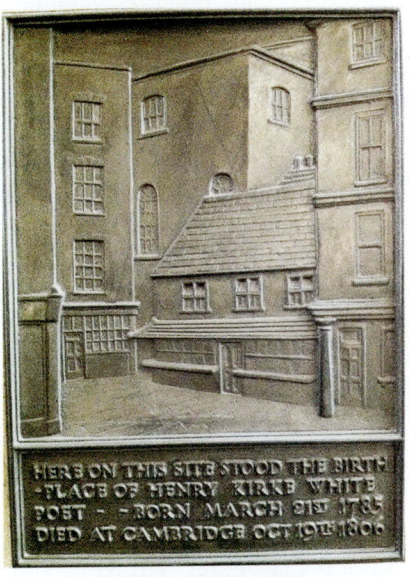

Henry Kirke White plaque, Exchange Arcade.

voracious reader. He later wrote a poem about his time at Mrs Grassington's school which includes the lines:

First at the form, my task for ever true
A little favourite rapidly I grew.

His work life was less fun as he hated the drudgery of spinning and folding stockings, and complained to his mother that he simply couldn't finish his apprenticeship. He even wrote to the editors of the *Nottingham Journal* describing his concern for the state of the town's women lace workers.

It was in Rose Yard, now called King John's Chambers, that he was permitted to join a law firm as an apprentice to an attorney. Kirke White applied himself to his legal studies with great industry, working twelve hours a day, but his poor hearing eventually ruled out a law career. In his free time he wrote poetry, including at lunchtimes and whilst walking, and he mastered several languages. He was beginning to burn himself out.

An ardent rhymer and a good essayist, aged fifteen Kirke White gave a talk to a Nottingham literary society on the poet Thomas Chatterton. He wanted to join the group but was rejected for being too young. They relented when his poems began to appear in periodicals like the *Monthly Preceptor*.

Kirke White's poetical productions had seen him acquainted with Thomas Hill (1760–1840), part proprietor of the *Monthly Mirror* and 'a lover of English literature, and who has probably the most copious collection of English poetry in existence,' according to Southey. Hill's encouragement led to Kirke White producing a small volume of poems for the press.

A string of prizes later, aged eighteen, he published his best-known poetry, including *The Fair Maid of Clifton* and *Clifton Grove*. This led to him becoming the protégé of the future Poet Laureate Robert Southey who, along with other patrons, encouraged him to go to St John's College, Cambridge, albeit with the intention of a career in the church. Kirke White's best friend in Nottingham, the Evangelical Henry Maddock, also gained admission to Cambridge as an undergraduate. Maddock was ordained and later became the vicar of Tadcaster in Yorkshire, living to the age of eighty-nine. As for Kirke White, his tuberculosis had other ideas. He did go to Saint John's and, despite his deafness and illness being a handicap, he did well, being named man of his year. But the illness, with its insomnia and palpitations, was shattering his nerves, and after a fit he was bled and blistered as treatment.

Henry Kirke White died at St John's, aged twenty-one. His letters and unpublished papers were put inside a box which was collected by Southey. Much of the writing had been done before he was thirteen. Amongst the papers – on law, divinity, electricity, languages and numerous poems – was a planned history of Nottingham. In 1807 Southey edited the collection and wrote an account of Kirke White's short life, *The Remains of Kirke White.*

The young poet was remembered at a centenary banquet in 1906 at which Professor F Granger of University College said that Kirke White and his contemporaries, Gilbert Wakefield, Richard Parkes Bonington and Marshall Hall, were the most eminent persons Nottingham had ever produced, making it a centre of genius and learning.

It was as part of the centenary of Kirke White's death that his plaque was put up. In addition, University College launched their annual Henry Kirke White prize for poetry.

On the corner opposite, the novelist Cecil Roberts worked as a snooper, a future inspector of weights and measures for Nottingham Corporation, and would slip out his office for half an hour to browse the shelves of the nearby Boots Library. It was at the office that Roberts learned to operate a typewriter, which he used to type out his poems and articles. Roberts couldn't help but notice the plaque dedicated to Henry Kirke White, and he became aware of the annual Henry Kirke White prize.

In 1908, aged fifteen, Roberts' father died suddenly. His father had been something of a scholar and had attended Southwell Grammar School. He had also been responsible for his son abandoning the 'awful' Nottingham accent. He'd tell him, 'In Nottingham you must mind not your Ps and Qs but your As and Us.' (Roberts, 1968). Cecil Roberts was lonely. In volume two of his autobiography, *The Years of Promise*, he wrote:

> I could find no companion of my own age in our working-class world, where the only interests were cricket, football and girls, where no house harboured a bookshelf; a world of the cloth cap over the dormant brain.

In 1912 Roberts entered his long poem *The Trent* into the Henry Kirke White prize competition. The poem, which lamented the loss of a friend, the banks of the Trent being their favourite haunt, won the prize, helping Roberts on his way to a career as a writer.

Having achieved success as a novelist, Cecil Roberts was on a ship sailing to New York for one of his lecture tours when he found himself lounging next to an English civil engineer called Hugh Lofting. Every night at six, Roberts' deck-chair companion would say 'I have to go,' and he'd pop off to tell his kids a bedtime story.

Enquiring about this, Roberts was told, 'Oh, I've invented a character called Dr Dolittle. It's a nickname I've given to my little boy Colin who has set himself up as a doctor for sick animals. They have all sorts of adventures.'

Roberts asked Lofting if he ever wrote the stories down. Lofting told him he did, and he showed them to Roberts, complete with his own illustrations.

'You should have these stories published,' said Roberts.

Lofting looked surprised. 'Do you think they're good enough?'

'Indeed I do,' said Roberts, and gave him a letter to present to his New York publisher, Frederick Stokes and Co.[3]

Within twelve months, Roberts received an inscribed copy of *The Story of Doctor Dolittle*, the first of a successful and lucrative series. When Lofting died, his third wife inherited the *Dolittle* copyrights, which later passed to her son Christopher, who became a millionaire. The original inspiration for Dr. Dolittle, Lofting's son Colin, never received a penny.

---

[1]Godfrey, Southey and Ward, 1908.
[2]Gill, 1904.
[3]Roberts, 1970.

Chapter 8
Express Building, Upper Parliament Street – Nottingham's Greeneland

'Over the way, fifty yards down towards the market, he could see the portico of the Royal Theatre.'

Graham Greene, *A Gun for Sale*

One of the twentieth century's greatest novelists, (Henry) Graham Greene, whose works include *Brighton Rock* (1938), *The Heart of the Matter* (1948), *The Third Man* (1949), *The End of the Affair* (1951), *The Quiet American* (1955), *Our Man in Havana* (1958) and *The Human Factor* (1978), spent four months in Nottingham in what was a crucially important period, influencing his life and writing.

There's a plaque inside the entrance of the Express Building on Upper Parliament Street that marks Graham Greene's time working there on the *Nottingham Journal*, and his 'happy memories of this bizarre old building...' As he recalled:

> One entered... through a narrow stone Gothic door, stained with soot... and the heads of Liberal statesmen stuck out above like gargoyles; on rainy days the nose of Gladstone dripped on my head when I came in.

That carved head of Gladstone is above the entrance, along with fellow Liberals Cobden and Bright. The Express Building had been built fifty years before Greene arrived in the city for the proprietors of the Liberal-leaning *Nottingham Express* newspaper. The building was one of Watson Fothergill's designs, his corner entrance tower inspired by the work of the architect Burges. In 1899 Fothergill added an upper level, providing the *Express* with room for linotype machines where the editor

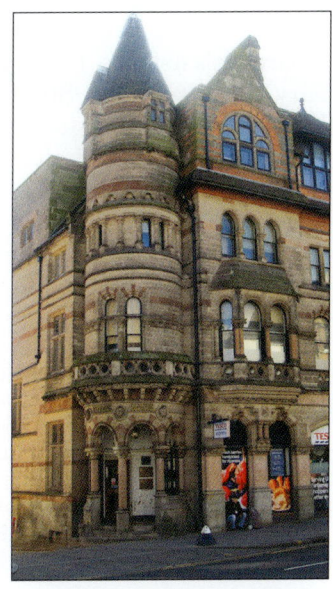

Express Building, Upper Parliament Street.

would compose the paper's layout and headings, all with a 2am deadline for the morning edition. Having earlier signed the building FW, the architect added the name Watson Fothergill, having swapped his names around in the interim.

It was in this building on 1 November 1925 that Graham Greene began working six hours a night as a trainee sub-editor at what was then the *Nottingham Journal,* described by Greene as 'a third-rate paper, run by third-rate people.'

In his first volume of autobiography, *A Sort of Life* (1971), Greene added:

> I arrived one wet night in Nottingham and woke next morning in the unknown city to an equally dark day. This was not like a London smog; the streets were free of vapour, the electric lights shone clearly: the fog lay somewhere out of sight beyond the lamps. When I read Dickens on Victorian London, I think of Nottingham in the twenties. There was an elderly 'boots' still employed at the Black Dog Inn, there were girls suffering from unemployment in the lace trade, who would, so it was said, sleep with you in return for a high tea with muffins, and a haggard blue-haired prostitute, ruined by amateur competition, haunted the corner by WH Smith's bookshop. Trams rattled downhill through the goose-market and on to the blackened castle.

In Greene's defence, the city wasn't looking its best. The Bloomsbury group's Lytton Strachey (1880–1932), author of *Eminent Victorians* (1918), visited Nottingham ten months after Greene and called it '...the oldest, grimmest place in the world, with a certain hideous grandeur.' His criticism was harsh, but during the winter months the city's air was often so thick that the city's bus conductors had to walk ahead of their ride in order to guide the driver.

Greene referred to the fog again in a letter to his fiancée Vivien:

> There's a most marvellous fog here today, my love. It makes walking a thrilling adventure. I've never been in such a fog before in my life. If I stretch out my walking stick in front of me, the ferrule is half lost in obscurity. Coming back, I twice lost my way, & ran into a cyclist, to our mutual surprise. Stepping off a pavement to cross to the other side becomes a wild and fantastic adventure... if you never hear from me again, you will know that I am moving round in little plaintive circles, looking for a pavement.

A recent Oxford graduate, Greene had worked for a short period as a private tutor before landing work here as an unpaid cub-reporter.

He had just turned twenty-one. His work began in the early evening and mostly involved typing up telegrams and interpreting handwriting. The late start meant he could attend matinées at the nearby Theatre Royal and several 'little dark cinemas' offering cheap matinées. Greene would often watch back-to-back films before work. The matinées eased his loneliness and satisfied his love of the pictures. He would have also visited The Elite supercinema that had opened in 1921 close to the *Journal*'s offices. The Elite was the height of luxury, boasting a grand concert organ and a full orchestra.

This was the era of classic comedies, starring Harold Lloyd (*The Freshman*), Buster Keaton (*Go West*), and Charlie Chaplin (*The Gold Rush*), of whom Greene was a great admirer. In 1952 he wrote an open letter to Chaplin defending him after Joseph McCarthy had labelled him a communist and denied his entry back into the United States. 'This is a letter of welcome,' wrote Greene, 'not only to the screen's finest artist (the only man who writes, directs and acts his own pictures and even composes their music), but to one of the greatest liberals of our day.' The letter ended thus: 'Intolerance in any country wounds freedom throughout the world.'

Upper Parliament Street would have appealed to any lover of the stage and screen, and yet Greene wrote to Vivien that, 'There's absolutely nothing worth doing in this place, no excitement, no interest, nothing worth a halfpenny curse.'

'[Nottingham] was the furthest north I had ever been,' he wrote in his autobiography, 'the first strange city in which I had made home, alone, without friends.' He wasn't quite alone as he had with him his dog Paddy, a sickly rough-haired terrier. Nor was he friendless, as he'd met Cecil Roberts who'd been at the *Journal* since 1920 and was already a successful author. On visiting Roberts' home, Greene gifted him a pamphlet of his poetry, *Babbling April*, published in the spring of 1925 at Oxford. The poetry had been poorly received and had failed to shift even half of the 300 published copies in the year of its release. Roberts offered some words of encouragement, but it would be Greene's first and last published verse. Cecil Roberts' first novel, *Scissors*, had been published by Heinemann two years prior to Greene's arrival at the *Journal*. In 1929, Greene would debut with the same publisher (as had DH Lawrence with *The White Peacock*).

While he was a student journalist at university Greene first received a letter from Vivien Dayrell-Browning, a Roman Catholic writing to chastise him for his article linking cinema, sex and religion. Greene responded with an apology and they began courting. By the time he was in Nottingham, they were engaged to be married. Greene would make trips back to London to see her, and tout for a job. One weekend she came up to Nottingham. Vivien was already a published author when she met Greene. Her first book, *The Little Wings*, a collection of poetry and prose, featured an introduction by GK Chesterton. A converted Catholic, she had rejected Greene's initial proposal of marriage on the grounds that he was an atheist.

To address their marital obstacle, and ease his boredom, Greene took Paddy for a walk to St Barnabas on Derby Road where he popped a note into the wooden inquiries box, asking for instruction. A week later he returned to St Barnabas and met Father Trollope, a 'very tall and very fat man with big smooth jowls which looked as though they had never needed a razor.' Trollope was a former West End actor who had 'mastered the art of repertory theatre, slipping in and out of various parts as the need arose,' wrote Shelden (1994). Trollope's bookshelves included plays alongside theological books, and the men met once or twice a week, for an hour at a time, sometimes in odd places like the upper deck of a tram. The purpose of Greene's initial visits was kept from his teacher. Greene then:

> began to fear that [Father Trollope] would distrust the genuineness of my conversion if it so happened that I chose to be received, for after a few weeks of serious argument the "if" was becoming less and less improbable.

St. Barnabas Church.

This deepening interest led to Greene adopting Catholicism, and he was received into the Roman Catholic faith at the cathedral church of St. Barnabas on 28 February 1926. It could be that he took some pleasure in being Catholic in a Protestant country. A couple of years ago St Barnabas celebrated their 175th anniversary with a day of talks entitled Faith, Nottingham and Graham Greene.

Following Greene's baptism was his first general confession, 'a humiliating ordeal,' which 'covers the whole of man's previous life,' he wrote, adding that:

> ...in the first Confession a convert really believes in his own promises. I carried mine down with me like heavy stones into an empty corner of the Cathedral, dark already in the early afternoon, and the only witness of my Baptism was a woman who had been dusting the chairs. I took the name of Thomas—after St. Thomas the doubter and not Thomas Aquinas—and then I went on to the *Nottingham Journal* office and football results and the evening of potato chips.

Greene married Vivien the following year, their children Lucy and Francis coming along in 1933 and 1936 respectively. The Greenes separated after twenty-one years of marriage but never divorced. Mrs Greene became the world's foremost expert on dolls' houses and lived to the age of ninety-eight.

Catholicism was to shape Graham Greene's writing career. He would say that he was a novelist who simply happened to be a Catholic, but it was from a Catholic perspective that he explored world issues. His works have been both hailed and criticised by Catholics for his treatment of the faith. It may even be that Greene's religious conviction kept him from killing himself – suicide being a mortal sin. He had made several attempts on his life prior to his conversion and continued to live with depression for many years.

Nottingham changed Greene. You might say that it was here that he got his first all-important look at how the other half lived. According to Norman Sherry, Greene's official biographer:

> He realised in Nottingham that he was a rather stuck-up, superior middle-class boy who had been brought up to look down on all those rather dirty, untidy people below him.

Those dirty, untidy people included one of the lodgers at Greene's digs on Hamilton Road, off Sherwood Rise, a man he described as 'the lowest cesspool of dirt I've ever come across.' Greene moved on after two weeks. The improved accommodation came with a less accommodating landlady, a busybody called Mrs Loney, who served up tinned salmon most evenings. She was a thin, complaining widow, a 'lazy woman who lived mostly in her basement from where she spied on her neighbours,' wrote Greene.

Mrs Loney inspired the character Mrs Coney in *It's a Battlefield* and *Brighton Rock*'s Mrs Prewitt, 'a bitter woman who likes tinned salmon'.[1]

Loney's basement was in Ivy House, All Saints Terrace, just off Waverley Street, close to a red-light area. Ivy House became Greene's model for disreputable houses in a number of his novels (*It's a Battlefield*, *Brighton Rock*, *A Gun for Sale*) and his play *The Potting Shed*.

Most mornings Greene would walk Paddy in the nearby soot-leafed Arboretum, 'I don't know why a certain wry love of Nottingham lodged in my imagination,' he wrote. Perhaps it was his fascination with the seedy side of provincial life, of which Nottingham had offered insight. The mean industrial wasteland certainly informed his 1936 noir novel, *A Gun for Sale*, set in a fictionalised version of Nottingham, a 'grim city a few hours from London.' In Nottwich, 'Fog lay over the city like a night sky with no stars.'

Greene wrote the book when he was writing film reviews for *The Spectator*, and the novel has a cinematic quality. The book's hired gunman is Raven, who spends a night in a Catholic cathedral, a fictional version of St Barnabas. Before Greene's Nottingham novel had been published, the film rights had already been sold, the first of five adaptations being *This Gun For Hire* (1942), starring Allan Ladd as Raven, and named after the superior US title of the book. Critics singled out Ladd for praise but, for my money, Veronica Lake as Ellen Graham, more than matches his performance.

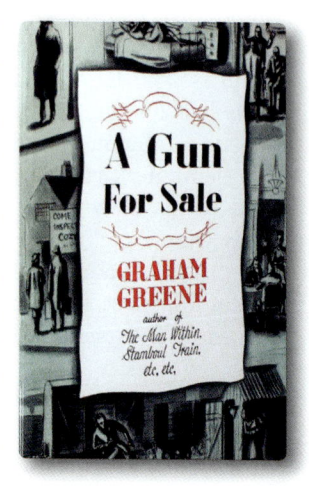

Nottwich is later referred to in one of Greene's classics, *Our Man in Havana* (1958).

Shortly after his time in Nottingham, Greene wrote to Vivien, 'Thank God Nottingham's over. It's like coming back into real life again...' Ten days later he landed a job on *The Times*, where he worked until 1929, a job he'd not have got without his four months in Nottingham.

According to Sherry (writing when Greene was in his eighties) the novelist 'now looks back nostalgically to the days he was [in

Nottingham].' Greene wrote, '[In Nottingham], I had fallen into a pocket out of life and out of time, but I was not unhappy.'

In volume three of his autobiography, *The Bright Twenties* (1970), Cecil Roberts remembered Greene as a 'tall, gangling, youth,' who 'looked undernourished.' Ten years before Greene arrived in Nottingham, Roberts had started at the *Nottingham Journal*. Like Greene, he began as a "gentleman pupil", in other words, a man willing to work for free. Roberts had chosen the *Journal* because of its literary tradition and its status as one of the oldest papers in the country, having been founded in 1712 as the *Weekly Courant*.

From this unpaid role, Roberts had gone on to work for the *Liverpool Post*. He'd been in and out of jobs – a literary editor, drama critic, schoolmaster, special correspondent – before he found himself sitting next to Sir Charles Starmer in London. Starmer knew Roberts' name as a war correspondent and, after an hour of conversation, he offered him the editorship of any of his fifteen provincial newspapers. Roberts picked the *Nottingham Journal*, and at twenty-seven he was the youngest editor in the UK, astounding the *Journal*'s staff who remembered him as an unpaid pupil there just four years earlier. Like Jesse Boot, who had financed the newspaper, Starmer was a committed liberal, and he asked Cecil Roberts to stand as the East Nottingham Liberal candidate.[2] Thinking he had four years to prepare, Roberts accepted, only to be thrust into a snap by-election in 1922 after the Conservative MP Sir John Rees opened a train door and fell to his death. Overworked, Roberts had a breakdown and withdrew on the orders of his doctor. Instead of a career in politics, he became a bestselling novelist.

In his time editing the *Nottingham Journal*, Cecil Roberts did assist another writer in his bid to win a Nottingham seat – Norman Angell, author of *The Great Illusion*, who had been selected as Labour's candidate for the Rushcliffe division. Angell was a tiny, frail, fifty-year-old with no local paper backing his party. Roberts gave him a weekly column in the *Journal* that he could use any way he wished. Angell's campaign had further support in the form of a document of approval, signed by Arnold Bennett, Jerome K Jerome and Bertrand Russell, among others. Despite this, Angell was defeated, having to wait until 1929 to enter Parliament after unseating a Tory in Bradford. Four years later he won a Nobel Peace Prize.

Other distinguished writers at the *Nottingham Journal* include the Parliamentary reporter Sir Dodds Shaw, the poet Philip James Bailey, the playwright JM Barrie, and John Foster Frazer, a Scottish travel writer who achieved fame by cycling round the world.

Years later, Cecil Roberts invited Graham Greene to his birthday party in Paris. Greene wrote back from Antibes, 'I would have broken my firm resolution to avoid cocktail parties for the pleasure of celebrating your seventy-ninth birthday but I'm afraid I can't get to Paris on the eighteenth.'

Three months later Greene greatly upset Roberts with a comment made in his autobiography, *A Start in Life,* when Greene referred to Roberts: 'He was said to be the son of a local tradesman, but other rumours, which he did not seem to resent, had it that he was the illegitimate child of one of the dukes of The Dukeries.'

Roberts objected immediately and Greene apologised, blaming reporters' room gossip. The offending passage was removed from future reprints.

---

[1]Greene, 1938.
[2]Roberts, 1970.

Chapter 9
Five Leaves Bookshop, Swann's Yard, 14A Long Row – Radically Independent

'A peasant that reads is a prince in waiting.'
Walter Mosley, *The Long Fall*

Just off Long Row, opposite the tourism centre, is an alley that dates back to medieval times. Known as Swann's Yard, the area has been occupied by a range of businesses from an inn to a bookshop.

It was in Swann's Yard that Thomas Miller (1807–74) once had a basket shop. The son of an unsuccessful wharf-keeper, Miller left school at the age of nine as a voracious reader. He came to Nottingham in 1831 and, after being a basketmaker's apprentice, set up his own business here. Miller wrote novels, children's books, penny dreadfuls and poetry.

In 1835 Miller sent some of his poetry in one of his ornate baskets to Lady Blessington (1789–1849), an Irish author – of *Conversations with Lord Byron* (1834) – known for her literary connections. Suitably impressed, Blessington invited Miller to her posh gatherings at Gore House, Kensington, (now the site of the Royal Albert Hall). From Hans Christian Andersen and Charles Dickens to Benjamin Disraeli and Edward Bulwer-Lytton, Gore House attracted many distinguished names, and Lady Blessington showed Miller off to them as a working-class poet.

After he'd hobnobbed with the elite, Miller's poetry was well received. In 1836 the *Courier* wrote that:

> There is so genuine a spirit, and such taste, harmony, and originality about [Miller's] poetry, as to stamp him a man whose conceptions emanate from the genuine sources of poetic inspiration. He is indeed nature's poet.

Henry Colburn commissioned three historical novels from Miller, who was prolific, producing more titles – over forty-five of them – than any other Victorian working-class author. He constantly struggled with poverty and, later, illness, and once (unsuccessfully) appealed to Dickens for financial assistance. Whilst on his death-bed, Miller did receive £100 from Disraeli, sent from the Treasury.[1]

Miller's entertaining working-class novel *Gideon Giles, The Roper* (1841), mostly set in Nottinghamshire, was written to raise attention of an unjust and cruel law which meant a poor salesman could be fined forty pounds or face three months in prison. It was a radical, political book, as Miller wrote in his introduction:

> To shew how great a check such a law is to honesty and industry, I have written this book, confident that every right-minded and honest-hearted man will agree with me, in wishing for the abolition of an Act, which has the power of imprisoning a poor man who, without a license, offers for sale the goods which his own hands have manufactured.

180 years after Miller worked at Swann's Yard, an independent radical bookshop moved in, the first independent bookshop to open in a city centre this century. Thomas Miller would have approved.

Since opening in 2013 Five Leaves Bookshop has been a hive of literary activity, hosting more authors than Lady Blessington. Before COVID-19 arrived, the bookshop was holding around a hundred events a year, reaching over 5,000 people. Quick to adapt when the pandemic arrived, Five Leaves has held live online events which later appear on their YouTube

lino cut: Gemma Curtis

channel. Funding from the National Lottery via Arts Council England has led to a series of themed high-profile online events and international collaboration with six other UNESCO Cities of Literature.

Ross Bradshaw set up Five Leaves Publications in 1995/6 after leaving Mushroom Bookshop where he had been for seventeen years. At the time he was secretary to John Heppell, Labour MP for Nottingham East, publishing in his spare time. He became Nottinghamshire County Council's Literature Development Officer, still publishing in his spare time until, after ten years, publishing squeezed out the day job. During his time there he edited a magazine called *County Lit*, later retitled *Nottinghamshire Book Reviews*. His job-share opposite numbers at the City Council, the poet Cathy Grindrod and Deirdre O'Byrne (later to work at Five Leaves, as well as teaching Irish and English literature, and the Irish language) edited a complementary listings paper, *On the Write Lines*. Ross organised events all over the county while Cathy and Deirdre did the same in the city, including the Poetry in the City series of festivals. There were also two Black writers' conferences and three literature- and history-based Changing Ireland conferences.

These posts vanished in rounds of local authority cutbacks.

Eventually, in 2013, Ross set up Five Leaves Bookshop, still publishing, but the organisation is largely focussed on bookselling and events now.

Five Leaves Bookshop stocks titles from major publishing houses but dedicates more space to independent presses, reprint houses, translation houses and poetry publishers, specialising in fiction and poetry, cityscape and landscape, politics, counterculture and more. They also stock seventy-plus magazines and journals covering a range of interests. Five Leaves was involved with Lowdham Book Festival for twenty years, they jointly organise States of Independence, an annual celebration of indie publishing, and they have their own mini-festival called Bread and Roses.

Five Leaves has been a firm supporter of Nottingham UNESCO City of Literature. They published a large print run of commissioned stories by local writers in an anthology called *These Seven* (2015), and long-time staff member Pippa Hennessy managed the process of writing Nottingham's successful bid for the UNESCO status. Another writer to have

photo: Pippa Hennessy

worked there is Beeston's Graham Caveney. A former journalist and lecturer at the University of Nottingham, Caveney has had four books published, including his emotional memoir, *The Boy with the Perpetual Nervousness* (2017). A second memoir, entitled *On Agoraphobia*, is set for 2022. Two other former members of staff, Emma Craddock and Marie Thompson, have published academic books, while Leah Wilkins has been one of the Costa Prize poetry judges. It was another Five Leaves member of staff, Jane Anger, that initiated Feminist Book Fortnight, an annual event running nationally (and in Ireland and Italy) since 2018.

The bookshop has been a regional finalist for the British Book Awards Independent Bookshop of the Year for six years in a row, 2016 to 2021, winning the national final in 2018, making the shop the year's best independent bookshop. The following year Five Leaves won the Midlands section (which it did again in 2021) and picked up a Nottingham Rainbow Heritage Award for their support for the city's LGBT+ communities.

The first radical bookshop in Nottingham appeared in 1826, on Hockley's Goose Gate. It was at the bottom end of the road that a fifty-four-year-old former Nottingham lace worker, Susannah Wright, opened her shop, which had to fight for its survival against violence and daily picketing from the Committee for the Suppression of Vice. During this time, Wright's shop was broken into, with attempts made to drag out the proprietor. Inciting the riots was Rev G Wilkins of the powerful St Mary's Church. Refusing to be intimidated, the free-thinking atheist held out and, on one occasion, confronted by threatening picketers, she withdrew her pistol from under the counter and calmly asked if they should like it fired at them. With many supporters, including the Nottingham Friends of Liberty group, Wright defeated the Committee and moved her successful bookshop to larger premises higher up Goose Gate, where she continued to promote free discussion and provide access to ideas.

Wright had arrived in Nottingham after being released from prison, serving time for unlawfully publishing and selling scandalous and blasphemous material. She had defended herself in court, using the opportunity to assert her right to free expression and calling for the people, not the church, to make the laws. After insisting that her opinion be heard, Wright was indicted for profanity, becoming the only woman to be imprisoned on this charge. Before opening her shop on Goose Gate, Wright had sold books at Trademen's Mart, roughly where Argos is now, on Lower Parliament Street. Wright's story is included in *A City of Light: Socialism, Chartism and Co-operation – Nottingham 1844* (2013) by Christopher Richardson (1947–2020) and *Unrespectable Radicals? Popular politics in the age of reform* (2008) edited by Michael T Davis and Paul A Pickering.

---

[1]Mellors, 1924.

Chapter 10
The Loggerheads, 59 Cliff Road – City of Crime

> 'Resnick took his warrant card from his pocket and opened it under the man's nose.'
>
> John Harvey, *Rough Treatment*

Narrow Marsh sits beneath St Mary's Cliff and the Lace Market. The old thoroughfare of Narrow Marsh covered the marshy land between the cliff and Leen Side (now Canal Street), an area once notorious for its slum dwellings, diseases – and crime. The area features in AR Dance's novel *Narrow Marsh* (2008), set in the early nineteenth century.

By the mid-eighteenth century, Alfred Coney, a disposer of stolen goods, lived at The Loggerheads on Cliff Road where he mixed with highwaymen such as Dick Turpin. Coney and his wife Martha also knew the dodgy duo Bouncing Bella and Lanky Dobbs, who lived just behind them. Dobbs worked as the local chimney sweep, a job that allowed him to discover where people kept their valuables. He fed this information back to Coney. Coney would then whistle out of a window in code, each different whistle signalling for a different type of burglar, whatever the job required. One toerag awaiting a whistle was Slimmy, purportedly the best robber in Nottingham.[1]

In Victorian times the master criminal Charlie Peace was in Narrow Marsh. Having murdered Constable Cock in London, Peace was in disguise and on the run. He met Sue Thompson, who became his mistress. She knew he was a wrong 'un but, as he never stole any of her goods, she put up with him for a while before giving his whereabouts to the police. Peace evaded capture by exiting through a skylight. Not

The Loggerheads, Cliff Road.

unlike Robin Hood, his exploits have been romanticised in popular culture, his legend living on in penny dreadfuls, music halls, ballads, theatre and early cinema. In 2017, Michael Eaton published a book about him: *Charlie Peace: his amazing life and astounding legend.*

At the turn of the twentieth century, Narrow Marsh remained a rabbit warren of alleys, courts and yards, and was still notorious for crime and poverty. In 1905 the area had a name change, becoming Red Lion Street after a local inn, in a forlorn hope that its fortunes would improve. Much of the area was demolished in the 1920s and 1930s, the slums cleared for some of the very first purpose-built council houses.

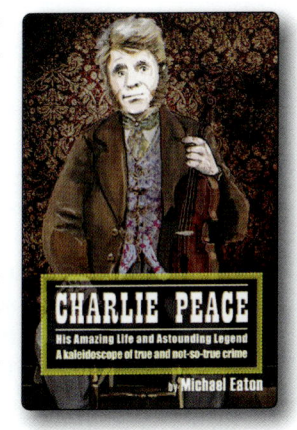

It's at the foot of the seventy-foot-high sandstone rock of St. Mary's Cliff, beneath landmarks like Nottingham Contemporary and the National Justice Museum, that you'll find the former Loggerheads. No longer a pub, the building still stands and is the setting for much of Nicola Monaghan's crime novel *Dead Flowers* (2019).

In Monaghan's book, The Loggerheads' ownership passes through key characters. *Dead Flowers* is a quintessential Nottingham novel, written by a Nottingham author and set entirely in the city. The book has a gripping dual narrative, featuring a busy Loggerheads of the late 1960s and early 1970s and its 2017 neglected version. Living in the former pub is ex-detective Sian Love, a forty-six-year-old forensic analyst who takes matters in hand after finding human remains in the basement. It's fitting that Love works in forensics, as it was in Nottingham that the first national police forensic science laboratory opened in 1934. Two years earlier, the UK's first message sent over a police car radio had occurred in the city.

Cliff Road had always fascinated Monaghan, with its 'strange position right at the bottom of a cliff,' and she brings to life her two fictionalised versions of the street. Cliff Road is the last surviving stretch of the old Narrow Marsh, and the retaining walls that run alongside it once belonged to the county jail. You can still see the dates 1829 and 1833 in the brickwork.

Nottingham's reputation as a City of Crime or "Shottingham" was unjust, but it accompanied a wave of crime fiction. The 1997 anthology *City of Crime* brought together some of Nottingham's crime writers, alongside writers known for other literature, each author writing a crime story.

David Davis MP once declared that Nottingham was 'reminiscent of 1930s Chicago,' a reputation that brought the director of the Scandi drama *The Killing* to the city. The Danish director and screenwriter Birger Larsen filmed his gritty crime drama, *Murder* (2016), in Nottingham, shooting the city through a blood-red filter. It was to be the last of Larsen's dramas as he died a few months later.

Nottingham's gift to televised crime drama has been notable. Beeston-born Barry Foster played the Dutch Detective Van der Valk on ITV in the 1970s, Retford-born Philip Jackson played Chief Inspector Japp in *Poirot* and DS Sharp in *A Touch of Frost*, Nottingham-born Tala Gouveia (DCI McDonald in ITV's *McDonald & Dodds*) spent much of her childhood running around backstage at the Playhouse, and Nottingham's Vicky McClure gives scene-stealing performances in hits like *Broadchurch* and *Line of Duty*. McClure is just one former member of Nottingham Television Workshop to have starred in crime dramas. The workshop is based at the edge of the old Narrow Marsh.

The dramas *Silent Witness* and *New Tricks* were created by the writer and former Nottingham murder squad detective Nigel McCrery, and John Harvey's *Resnick* made his way onto our screens in the early 1990s with Tom Wilkinson playing Nottingham's favourite sleuth. Harvey's twelve-book Charlie Resnick series follows Nottingham's changing inner city of the late twentieth century, and its struggles with poverty, unemployment, violence, weapons, drugs and gang culture. The series began with *Lonely Hearts* (1989), named as one of the top hundred crime novels of the century, and finished with *Darkness, Darkness* (2014) in which Resnick reflects on the turmoil of the 1980s miners' strike and how a fractured Nottinghamshire coped in its aftermath. Together with *Cold Light* (1994) and *Easy Meat* (1996) these are two of the best books in the series.

Before focusing on crime fiction, Harvey had been writing mostly westerns. One of his writing partners had been Angus Wells (1943–2006), who wrote with Harvey on several series of novels before writing epic fantasies and the Raven series. Wells died in a fire at his Nottingham home.

Fifty years before John Harvey's Nottingham novels were becoming popular at home and abroad, Ottwell Binns (1872–1935), was achieving considerable success with his crime novels. During the 1920s the prolific Binns, Minister of the Old Meeting House in Mansfield, was thrilling readers with his action-packed mysteries and adventures. His son, Max Dalman Binns, was another mystery writer, under the name Max Dalman. You will meet Nottingham's leading 'golden age' crime writer, Francis Vivian, in a future chapter.

Be it the University Hospital (KL Slater's *Blink*, 2017) or Nottingham Forest's City Ground (Frank Palmer's *Final Score*, 1998), Nottingham's crime fiction takes readers all over the city. Maybe it's time the "city of crime" label was buried and Nottingham became known as a city of crime writers.

Other selected crime novels set in Nottinghamshire are Ruth Rendell's *To Fear A Painted Devil* (1965), Keith Wright's procedural *Trace and Eliminate* (1992), Phil Whitaker's disturbing *The Face* (2002), Clare Littleford's suspenseful *Beholden* (2003), Rod Madocks' psychological debut *No Way To Say Goodbye* (2008), Rebecca S Buck's historical and modern *Truths* (2010), Stephen Booth's coalfield crime *Top Hard* (2012), Michael RD Smith's tale of corporate law *The Deed Room* (2013), Gary Bell QC's legal thriller *Beyond Reasonable Doubt* (2013), Chris Parker's mind-bending *Influence* (2014), David Belbin's political thriller *The Great Deception* (2015), Glenis Wilson's equestrian crime *Dead Certainty* (2015), Alan Williams' journey through time *The Daylight Thief* (2015), Jaq Hazell's student chiller *I Came To Find A Girl* (2015), retired judge Michael Stokes' *Blackmail* (2016), Rebecca Bradley's procedural *Shallow Waters* (2015), Trevor Negus's miners' strike story *The Coal Killer* (2016), Jacques Morrell's debut *The Showman* (2017) and CJ Tudor's horror-tinged psychological thriller *The Taking of Annie Thorne* (2019). Phew.

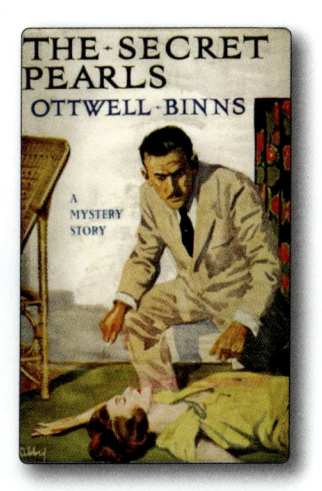

Ex-Nottinghamshire police officer Raymond Flynn, who worked in CID and headed up the fraud squad, applies his twenty-six years of expertise to his Eddathorpe novels, his fictional east coast town being known as Nottingham-by-the-sea, and, of course, Graham Greene fictionalised his 'grim' Nottingham in *A Gun for Sale* (1936).

Nottingham Noir is at large!

---

[1]Holland Walker, 1926.

Chapter 11
Mechanics' Hall, Milton Street (former) –
What the Dickens!

'A day wasted on others is not wasted on one's self.'
Charles Dickens, *A Tale of Two Cities*

The idea of the Mechanics' Institutes emerged in the late eighteenth century when two professors at the University of Glasgow started offering free lectures to the city's workers. Henry Brougham's *Observations Upon the Education of the People*, addressed to the working classes and their employers, helped to popularise the institutions. Founded in 1837, the Nottingham Mechanics' Institution (NMI) aimed to improve the knowledge of the city's workers with classes, lectures, performances and a library. By 1845 the NMI opened its own hall at the junction of Milton Street, Burton Street and Trinity Square, opposite the original entrance to Victoria Station. Its library contained 40,000 volumes.

Many famous literary men and women performed at the hall, including Oscar Wilde (twice), Anthony Trollope, Jerome K Jerome, GK Chesterton, Marie Corelli, Fanny Kemble, Sir Arthur Conan Doyle and Charles Dickens. Dickens' first visit was in 1852, by which time he was a celebrity and halfway through writing his ninth novel, *Bleak House*. It was at this point in the story that Inspector Bucket appears, arguably the first professional detective in English crime fiction. I mention this because joining Dickens on stage in Nottingham was his friend Wilkie Collins, who went on to write *The Moonstone* (1868), considered to be the first detective novel and first serialised in Dickens' magazine *All the Year Round*. Dickens and his friend Collins were performing at the Mechanics as part of a travelling

photo: nottingham-mechanics.org.uk

Mechanics Hall.

company called the Guild of Literature and Art, a charity group that Dickens had founded. The writers had met a year earlier during a production of *Not So Bad as We Seem*, a drama by another of Dickens' friends, Edward Bulwer-Lytton.

Charles Dickens referred to his group as the amateurs, and they toured halls or lecture rooms rather than provincial theatres. There was nothing amateurish about their staging and scenery. As usual, Dickens and his group arrived the day before the show, to set up their portable theatre. Their arrival wasn't well received by the Nottingham Wesleyan reformers who were hoping to hold their weekly Sunday morning meeting.

Showtime was Monday evening at 7pm. Among the audience were Charles Dickens' wife Catherine and her sister Miss Hogarth. The amateurs opened with the aforementioned *Not So Bad as We Seem*, with Wilkie Collins standing out in what proved for the audience a generally perplexing performance. The next act went down much better, a farce called *Mr Nightingale's Diary*, written by Dickens and Mark Lemon, founder and editor of *Punch*, who was also in the cast. Here's a snippet:

> Charles Dickens (as Gabblewig): 'Has anybody seen that puppy of mine with a gold-lace collar? (Dickens Enters) O' here you are! You scoundrel, where have you been?'
> Wilkie Collins (as Lithers): 'Good gracious me! Why if it ain't Mr. Gabblewig, Junior!'

Also in the cast was John Tenniel (*Punch* cartoonist and illustrator of *Alice in Wonderland*) but, as they ended at midnight with a one-act performance of *Past Two O'clock in the Morning*, it was Dickens who had taken on the most characters, male and female, old and young. The audience offered a cheer when their favourites appeared. Dickens' successful evening ended at Nottingham's oldest hotel The George, Hockley. Now known as the Mercure Hotel, there are suites named the Charles Suite and the Dickens suite. On display is the cheque with which Dickens paid his bill.

The following day Dickens and his troupe walked sixteen miles to Derby where their Mechanics' lecture hall awaited what was to be another triumph for the writer-come-theatrical impresario. His next visits to Nottingham would be quite different.

During this same month in 1852 Dickens visited Ada Lovelace. Lord Byron's daughter had previously attended dinners at Dickens' London home, but this time he travelled to her. Lovelace was

The Mercure Hotel, George Street.

seriously ill from uterine cancer, practically on her deathbed, when Dickens obliged her request that he read her favourite scene from his 1848 novel *Dombey and Son*. He read the moving passage in which the gentle six-year-old boy Paul Dombey dies, his cold, arrogant, business-obsessed father in attendance. 'Don't be so sorry for me, dear Papa! Indeed I am quite happy!'

Ada Lovelace died three months after Dickens' visit. The scene he had read to her was to be the next work he performed to a Nottingham audience.

In 1853 Dickens had given a solo reading of *A Christmas Carol* in Birmingham. This led to a second lucrative career, as Dickens realised there was money to be made from reading his own work. In October 1858 he was back in Nottingham reading scenes from *Dombey and Son* and *The Trial of Mr Pickwick*. As before, he arrived early to inspect and prepare, but this time the scenery was replaced by a simple platform with a maroon-curtained screen which curved behind him, hiding the orchestra. When reading, Dickens took to a raised block and stood alone behind a red stand, his elbow resting on a shelf designed for his glass of water.[1] He began with instructions for the audience: 'If you feel disposed as we go along to give expression to any emotion, whether grave or gay, you will do so with perfect freedom, and without the apprehension of disturbing me.'

In both readings Dickens read scenes that he had adapted from his original work, changes that were crafted to allow him to possess his characters in the most dramatic manner. Largely reserved, the Nottingham audience did laugh during *The Trial of Pickwick* but when Dickens returned to the Mechanics' Hall the following

October, the attendance was down. The smaller crowd may have been because the exact same readings were advertised, or maybe the audience was waiting for *A Christmas Carol* set for the following afternoon.

Dickens cancelled his planned reading of *A Christmas Carol*, perhaps sulking at the disappointing turnout for his reading of *Dombey* and *Pickwick* the previous night. A statement was made that he had been 'unavoidably impelled to return to London.'

In 1867 a fire damaged the Mechanics' Hall. Two years later a new hundred-and-ten-foot-long hall opened, with double the seating capacity. A month after the rebuilt hall had opened, Dickens returned to give his last Nottingham performance, part of his farewell tour. The advice was clear, 'On no consideration will Mr Dickens be induced to appoint an extra night in any place in which he shall have been announced to read for the last time.'

On this occasion the audience was full and appreciative, absorbed throughout *Dr Marigold* as Dickens played the cart-pushing hawker of sundries, roaring their approval and laughter during *The Trial of Pickwick,* and paying up to seven shillings for the honour. Dickens put his heart into his performances. His energetic, at times manic, stage-managed shows were so in demand on both sides of the Atlantic that they gave birth to ticket touts. In the States he would be reading to audiences of two thousand, each paying two dollars a ticket. Capitalising financially on this success, he undertook gruelling tours that affected his health, not helped by the committed way he inhabited his characters, a style which could be frightening to witness. Dickens died in 1870, a year after his final Nottingham reading.

The new Mechanics' building on North Sherwood Street (purpose-built in 2003) houses a superb bust of Dickens, randomly placed in the corner of a room, and, in 2007, there was a lecture at the new Mechanics by Lucinda Hawksley Dickens, great-great-great granddaughter of Charles and the author of a biography of his daughter Katey.

Nottingham has many other links to the great writer. The Nottingham branch of The Dickens Fellowship is one of only two branches that has operated continuously from its inception; John Lucas authored *The Major Novels* (1992), a critical study of five major Dickens' works; Michael Eaton adapted Dickens for BBC Radio (*The Pickwick Papers*, 2004) and he adapted *Great Expectations* for the stage; and a BBC television adaptation of *Great Expectations* was filmed (in part) at Nottinghamshire's Thoresby Hall.

---

[1]Payne, 2004.

Chapter 12
Mushroom Bookshop, 261 Arkwright Street – Nottingham's Lost Bookshops

> 'The shop was to be called "Mushroom", after Keith rejected my initial suggestion of "Dung" (I liked its resonance)'
> Chris Cook Cann, *Face Blind in Berlin, Suffolk and Gedling*

Alan Sillitoe owes a lot to Nottingham bookshops – his marriage for one, and arguably his career. He first encountered books at his maternal grandparents' cottage. Like Sillitoe's father, his grandfather was illiterate, but he had in his parlour a healthy collection of fiction, collected for his wife and children. Set on his own collection, it was in the basement of Frank Wore's second-hand bookshop that a ten-year-old Sillitoe bought his first books, Dumas' *The Count of Monte Cristo* among them.[1] At that time there were no books in Sillitoe's home and his father threatened to throw this one in the fire as reading, it seemed, unnerved him.

After returning to Nottingham in 1949 Sillitoe became a regular visitor to Paul Henderson's bookshop in central Nottingham, and the two men became friends. The shop hosted an open night on Saturdays where regulars could have a drink and a chat. In Sillitoe's novel *The Open Door* (1989), the real-life bookseller becomes Tom Boak. In chapter twenty-two, Brian Seaton is in the bookshop talking to Boak: 'My God, another customer,' Tom says. 'My heart can't stand two in one day. It must be the rain.'

In the novel, that other customer was Anne Jones, a tall woman buying a book by DH Lawrence. Brian takes an interest in her and 'Her remark that she loved Lawrence's work suggested that he'd have to read them, even if only to find out something about her.'

Anne Jones was based on the American poet Ruth Fainlight, who Alan Sillitoe met in Henderson's bookshop, and it was Paul Henderson that introduced Sillitoe to his future wife. Sillitoe was instantly attracted to

Mushroom Bookshop.

her and immediately fascinated. Fainlight was twenty years old and married.

After Sillitoe completed *By What Road*, his first attempt at a novel, it was Paul Henderson and Ruth Fainlight's opinion to which he turned, and they gave criticism that he accepted and heeded. Henderson supplied Sillitoe with the names of publishers to approach with other examples of his writing.

Ruth Fainlight told me:

> As far as I remember, Paul Henderson's bookshop was on Mansfield Road, more or less opposite the old Victoria Station. Nearby was another bookshop run by a man named Noel Dilke or Dilkes. It must have been 1950 when Alan and I met in Paul's bookshop.

Trent Bookshop opened in 1964 next to the City Ground on Pavilion Road, West Bridgford. The shop was founded by part-time teachers Stuart Mills and Martin Parnell, who wanted an avant-garde outlet for good modern literature in all its forms. The Tarasque Press operated from this bookshop. Co-edited by Mills and Simon Cutts, eleven issues of *Tarasque* were published between 1965 and 1971, the first edition featuring work by Ray Gosling (1939–2013). The magazine aimed to be the voice of Nottingham. Simon Cutts is now based in Ireland where he runs Ugly Duckling Press.

Trent Bookshop aspired to be a major poetry holding outside of London, and they soon introduced a series of monthly poetry readings held at the bookshop and elsewhere. A year later they helped stage a large poetry conference at Nottingham's Albert Hall, a gathering of about seventy poets including Alan Brownjohn, George MacBeth, Robert Garioch, Gael Turnbull, Spike Hawkins, Pete Brown, Michael Horovitz, Christopher Logue, Adrian Mitchell, Brian Patten, Roger

Albert Hall, North Circus Street.

McGough, Adrian Henri and Tom Pickard. This two-day festival, hosted by Jonathan Williams, was later acclaimed as a major event in the poetry world, even if all the writers were male!

In 1966 Trent Bookshop moved location, becoming BUX – labelled as "a branch of the Trent Bookshop" – at 16 Drury Hill, near the top of the ancient narrow street that ran up from Midland railway station to the Broadmarsh bus station. BUX, unlike Trent Bookshop with its modern art gallery interior, was a dusty little shop painted red, with an exposed wood frontage. Covering three floors, and with trestles out in the street, it was said to be a shoplifter's paradise (Neate, 2012), but with its piles of books and knowledgeable staff, BUX was doing nicely, selling the commercial and the controversial. Plans for the new Broadmarsh centre forced them to move to Lincoln Street, off Clumber Street. The larger store provided an outlet for Nottingham's underground culture.

Together with John Clark AKA Brick, Martin Parnell of BUX started an independent film club called Peachy Street Flick, run from the lecture theatre at the back of the Adult Education Centre on Shakespeare Street. Brick told me:

> On the back of us wrangling good deals from obscure distributors and our large, enthusiastic audience, the "Flick" was very successful, so much so that the centre refurbished the lecture hall with a projection sound booth for us. But it was becoming obvious that Martin's devotion to Peachy Street was having a detrimental impact on the bookshop and his relationship with Stuart. I harbour a small pang of guilt that the young whippersnapper that I then was brought down the town's first truly independent bookshop!

BUX closed in 1972, bankrupt, but having achieved what it set out to do: providing a home for many small presses. Stuart Mills went on to launch *Aggie Weston's*, an occasional magazine which ran to twenty-one issues between 1973 and 1984, but Nottingham was needing a new independent bookshop.

In 1972 Mushroom Bookshop opened at 261 Arkwright Street, a former jeweller's that had seen better days. Chris Cann and Keith Leonard rented the crumbling premises from the city council, living in the accommodation above. They sold books in the front room and joss sticks, clothes, crafts and other paraphernalia out back. Mushroom's focus was anti-war, anti-nukes, and anarchism. Advertised through word of mouth this political bookshop became a hub for Nottingham's radicals. There was a notice board for local campaigns and events, and a 'free corner' where books could be left or taken.[2]

When the council began demolishing shops on Arkwright Street it was clear that Mushroom needed a new home, so Chris and Keith rented a space at 15 Heathcoat Street in Hockley. Business picked up and Mushroom Bookshop moved over the road to number 10's larger premises, later expanding into the premises of the second-hand bookshop, Drury Hill Bookshop (no 12) next door when the owner retired. The former site of Mushroom Bookshop is now taken up by Jam Café and Paramount Picture Framing.

Mushroom stocked books that were 'useful personally and socially, literature that allows people to create their own alternatives,' according to their annual Christmas and New Year catalogue. A member of the Federation of Alternative Bookshops – which became FRB ("radical" replacing "alternative") – Mushroom Bookshop ran as a collective on non-commercial lines. In 1983 Mushroom won a court case against the police, who had seized forty-one books from their section on drugs, mainly concerning cannabis. By this time the shop had sections on feminism, gay writing, Black writing, vegetarianism, war and peace and self-help and they had become involved in literary events, bringing authors from far afield to a Nottingham audience for the first time.

In 1994 a large group trashed the shop, damaging equipment, wrecking bookshelves, and injuring two workers and a customer. The group responsible, known as Blood and Honour, was a fascist group allied to the BNP. One eyewitness said, 'We saw some people dressed like skinheads rushing out of the shop and throwing things back into the shop window.' Arrests were made. It wasn't the only attack made on Mushroom by fascists.

It was in the radical tradition of Mushroom Bookshop that Ross Bradshaw, who had worked at Mushroom between 1979 and 1995, opened Five Leaves Bookshop.

In her book *Winter at the Bookshop* (2019), Sylvia Riley tells of Pat Jordan's place on Dane Street, St Ann's, home to the International Group founded by Pat, Ken Coates and Peter Price in 1962. The bookshop, which also sold comics, was home to revolutionary groups and local movements. Not far from there, on Alfred Street Central, was a large bookshop that sold pricey pin-up books and doubled as a brothel. Around the corner from the brothel was

Orange for Books which catered for a different kind of tackle – fishing.

There were several other radical bookshops in the city, including the far-left Pathfinder Bookshop which closed in the mid-1970s; the People's Bookshop on Fletchergate, run by the Communist Party of Great Britain; the Socialist Bookshop, sometimes known as the Progressive Bookshop, on 24 North Sherwood Street, which, in the 1930s also used to show Russian films at the Co-operative Employees' Institute on Carrington Street; and Concord Books, a small shop owned and run by the late David Lane, a committed pacifist and vegan. The now-demolished Concord was at the Mansfield Road end of Woodborough Road. After the shop closed, David Lane became a national wholesaler for vegetarian/vegan books and green books. There was another political bookshop near the present NTU students' union building. And Bertrand Russell House in Gamble Street had a trade counter for Spokesman's books and pamphlets.

It was in the 1970s, back when he worked for an insurance brokers off Slab Square, that the comedy writer, poet, film producer and Nottingham Poetry Festival co-founder Henry Normal used his lunch hour to scour the city centre bookshops for any comedy books he'd not read. It was from these books that he learned how jokes were constructed and discovered their mathematics and musicality. He told me:

> The Marx Brothers scripts I loved, and biographies of great comics like Jack Benny or Abbot and Costello. I loved the fact that Abbot and Costello, who became the first millionaire comedians, were so poor when they first started that they had to sneak into a field and milk a cow for something to drink. I read many non-comedy books, too, including Alan Sillitoe's *Saturday Night and Sunday Morning* and *The Loneliness of the Long-Distance Runner*. I could relate to both of these, having been born in St Ann's and with my dad and my brother both working at Raleigh.

Henry Normal's favourite Nottingham bookshop was Sisson & Parker. 'It was like WH Smith but as though run by Grace Bros,' said Normal. 'A posh old-fashioned shop that also sold Parker pens and desk tidies.'

He once applied for a trainee position at Sisson & Parker. He'd spotted the job in the *Evening Post* and managed to get an interview. However:

It became apparent the interviewer took one look at me and decided I wasn't their type. He asked me the strangest question: 'Do you play football?' I told him I did and loved to watch Forest. This seemed to seal my fate. He asked no more questions and I was told he had more candidates to see. I never heard from them again. What was it that he thought he saw in me that meant I wasn't the type that would be right for a job working with books? I worried that I was pigeonholed and discarded. There was something at the time that felt unfair. Was it my working-class Nottingham accent? My Burton's suit? My schooling?

'It made me set my jaw to succeed,' said Normal. 'I was determined to make my way in the world and do it by being myself.' He joined a writers' group at the library on Angel Row, part of the Worker Writers' Federation. Jimmy McGovern was a member of the sister group in Liverpool. Normal recalled:

> The UK groups had an annual conference at Nottingham University where I read some poems that seemed to go down well. This encouraged me to keep writing and performing, which I did at any chance I could in the pubs around Nottingham. The Black Boy, The Thurland Arms, even the bar at the Nottingham Playhouse were host to poetry events in which I tried out material.

Normal went on to perform around the country, learning his trade on bills which included Seamus Heaney and John Cooper Clarke. In addition to his comedy writing and TV scripts Normal has written several books, mostly poetry and comedy stocking-fillers like those he loved to read in Nottingham. He sometimes thinks back to that interview at Sisson & Parker and wonders, 'If I'd have got that job where would I be now?'

In 1972 Alan Sillitoe was signing books in Sisson & Parker when an ex-girlfriend of his, Doreen Greatorex, showed up. Doreen had been Sillitoe's first girlfriend from back when they worked together on the factory floor at Raleigh, and she was the inspiration for *Saturday Night and Sunday Morning*'s Doreen Gretton, played by Shirley Anne Field in the film version. Sillitoe chatted with Doreen and learned that she was married with children and her husband was a disabled collier, information that allowed Sillitoe to base another character on her, in this case Jenny from *Birthday* (2001).

A Sainsbury's Local now occupies the former home of Wheeler Gate's Sisson & Parker. Sisson & Parker (est 1854) moved to this former hotel from number thirteen where it sold novels and dictionaries, later supplying textbooks for schools and colleges as well as religious books and stationery. They also housed a lending library in their grand premises, where they remained until the early 1980s. At one time there was a second-hand bookshop next door.

Another bookshop, Hudsons, replaced Sisson & Parker on Wheeler Gate and, before the decade was out, Dillons had moved in. Dillons was well-stocked and covered several floors. It folded in 1999 and, as with many of their stores, Waterstones took over the premises. Nottingham soon had two large Waterstones bookshops within close proximity and something had to give. The writing was on the wall, or literally on the floor, for the Wheeler Gate store never did change its Dillons-branded carpet. Nottingham had another branch of Sisson & Parker, a small paperback shop opposite the Victoria Centre Clocktower, on the corner where you'd now find a branch of PC World.

The former home of Sisson & Parker

Next to the current Waterstones, on the Bottle Lane/ Bridlesmith Gate corner, was where the Sutton family of printers and booksellers lived and had their premises. The property was purchased by Nottingham Corporation in 1861 as part of a street-widening scheme.

The most recent edition to our lost bookshops is Jermy & Westerman, whose shell remains at 293 Mansfield Road. Pete Jermy and Roger Westerman established the shop in 1978. Jermy ran it almost singlehandedly, Westerman was a sleeping partner who awoke for one weekend a month. In 1990 Jermy emigrated to Tasmania to be with his family, settling in a small town in which he quickly opened a second-hand bookshop.

Jermy & Westerman was bought by father and son team Geoff and Richard Blore. Geoff already owned a Mansfield Road bookshop, Geoff Blore's in Sherwood, and Richard had recently joined him as a business partner. Both their shops were chock full of books, covering every wall and crevice of each floor, but competition, notably from charity shops, ultimately defeated them.

Other bookshops from the past include the Christian bookshop on Heathcoat Street, a near neighbour to Mushroom, Penguin Books on Bridlesmith Gate, Bookscene on Alfreton Road and Hyson Green's Ujamaa, so far Nottingham's only Black bookshop. From Sven's Books (an adult bookshop on Talbot Street then Mansfield Rd) to the Christian Bookshop inside the Congregational Centre on Castle Gate, Nottingham has lost many city centre bookshops. How many can you remember?

---

[1]Bradford, 2008.
[2]Cook Cann, 2019.

Chapter 13
New Foresters, 18 St Ann's Street –
Pride and Prejudice

> 'I should like to know why nearly every man that approaches greatness tends to homosexuality, whether he admits it or not.'
>
> DH Lawrence, *Letters of DH Lawrence Vol 2*

Nottingham City Council's LGBT+ Employee Network ran a poll in 2021 to decide which building should feature a new plaque marking its place in the city's LGBT+ history. The winning venue was the New Foresters pub, beating Nottingham Women's Centre, The Flying Horse Inn and the National Justice Museum. These locations and others have played an important role in the LGBT+ literary history of Nottingham.

Without its LGBT+ writers and writing, Nottingham would not be a UNESCO City of Literature, and there might not even be a legend of Robin Hood. It's widely thought that the story of Robin Hood, as we know it, comes from the ballad *A Geste of Robyn Hode* which, according to local historian Tony Scupham-Bilton, was written by Sir John Clanvowe. Clanvowe, a knight and accomplished poet, was as good as married to Sir William Neville, the constable of Nottingham Castle from 1381, a connection that Scupham-Bilton has said, 'formed all the background to Robin Hood.'

Sir John and Sir William had their close relationship recognised in a church ceremony, and their tombstone displays their coats of arms as if they were married. In his republished 2019 book, *Robin Hood: Out of the Greenwood: His Gay Origins*, Scupham-Bilton suggests that Sir John wove new characters and plots into the existing Robin Hood stories, creating the legends from his partner's family connections such as the Sheriff of Nottingham, Little John and Guy of Gisborne, and bringing the folk hero closer to Nottingham.

New Foresters, St Ann's Street.

The writer Lady Mary Wortley Montagu (1689–1762) challenged attitudes towards women. She married the British ambassador to Turkey, having previously had a relationship with his sister Anne. In one collection of letters to an unnamed woman, Wortley Montagu describes sensual encounters with Turkish women. Born at Holme Pierrepont Hall, Wortley Montagu gained much of her early education from the library at Thoresby Hall, her family home. She often referred to herself as a poet and became a famed travel writer.

Lady Mary Wortley Montagu.

Wortley Montagu is also known for advocating the use of the smallpox inoculation, which she introduced to Britain. Having already inoculated her son in Turkey, she deliberately infected her three-year-old daughter with a tiny dose of smallpox, the first successful inoculation on English soil. 'There was such a severe outbreak in 1721, she thought she had to take action,' said Jo Willett, who has written the biography, *The Pioneering Life of Mary Wortley Montagu* (2021). Wortley Montagu's action can ultimately be seen as leading the way to the eradication of smallpox, and the development of the first safe vaccine.

In Lord Byron's (1788–1824) day homosexuality was a serious offence. In her 2002 biography *Byron: Life and Legend*, Fiona MacCarthy suggested that it was the poet's fear of prosecution for sodomy that drove him to flee England forever in 1816. Mythology and Victorian cover-ups have clouded the facts, not helped by the destruction and removal of passages from Byron's diaries and letters, but his bisexuality is now well-known, as it was in his time, both within his own close circle and "on the street".

Byron had had many gay friends in England, the most notable being Charles Skinner Matthews at Cambridge. They belonged to a circle of friends that spoke and wrote in the coded gay slang of the age, where sensitive words were replaced with euphemisms. In Byron's letter to Matthews, written about sailor boys he'd seen in Falmouth, he uses the word hyacinth, slang for a younger man one fancied. The use of encrypted messages was not new to Byron, who had exchanged such text with the young chorister John Edleston.

Byron's *Don Juan* (1819–24) is filled with references that hint at male love, such as his disclosure that he is writing for the initiated, a word used in Byron's time (including by Shelley) as code for gay. Byron's popular *Oriental* poems were coded gay love stories, according to Peter Cochran, who shows that the poems' female lovers are really male, again something only gay readers would have understood. Cochran's book *Byron and Orientalism* (2006) was based on a conference held in 2005 at NTU.

The necessary gay subterfuge was not required in Greece, where Byron had at least two male lovers: Eustathios Georgiou in 1810 and Lukas Chalandritsanos in 1824. Ralph Lloyd-Jones told me, 'In Greece, the problem was that you should do your duty and liberate the country before enjoying its pleasures!'

In *The Intersexes* (1909), Xavier Mayne stated that Byron was 'Greek in his intellectual and sexual nature' and he argued that in Byron's poem *Manfred*, the 'burden on the conscience' and the 'unspeakable sin' is not incest but a hidden male relationship.

Louis Crompton's *Byron and Greek Love: Homophobia in 19th-Century England* (1992) addressed the role and significance of homosexuality in Byron's life and work. The book showed Byron to be on the side of all rebels and, like DH Lawrence and Samuel Butler, with attitudes that were ahead of his time.

Langar's Samuel Butler (1835–1902) escaped the institutions of religion and family when he sailed off to New Zealand in 1859 and became a sheep farmer. Butler, who had relationships with men and women, returned to England with his lover Charles Pauli, an Oxford-educated accountant, whom Butler provided with a regular allowance for thirty-four years.

In 1885 the Labouchère Amendment made all homosexual acts of "gross indecency" illegal. Ten years later Oscar Wilde became the law's most prominent victim, spending two years in prison at hard labour. The amendment was used to perpetrate fear and hatred of male homosexuality for more than eighty years. Nottingham's National Justice Museum held a 2008 exhibition called "Prisoner C.3.3: Oscar Wilde", which commemorated his imprisonment. Wilde's grandson Merlin Holland, author of *The Real Trial of Oscar Wilde* (2003), recreated the trial in the museum's old court where twenty-three men had been prosecuted for homosexuality in 1961.

'I myself never considered Plato very wrong, or Oscar Wilde,' wrote DH Lawrence in *Letters of DH Lawrence, Vol. 2: 1913–16* (1981). Lawrence depicts same-sex desire and intimacy in his novels *The White Peacock* (1911), *The Rainbow* (1915) and *Women in Love* (1920). All these characters – Rupert and Gerald, who wrestle naked in *Women in Love*, George and Cyril, who give each other a rubdown in *The White Peacock*, and Ursula, who has a same-sex relationship with her teacher in *The Rainbow* – also desire members of the opposite sex. *The Rainbow* was banned by court order two months after it had been published, partly due to Lawrence's brief depiction of Ursula's affair.

"Gross indecency" between females almost became illegal in 1921 after an act modelled on the Labouchère amendment was introduced by the Conservative MP Frederick Macquisten. The section, which passed in the House of Commons, was defeated in the House of Lords.

By the end of *The Rainbow*, Rupert tells Ursula, 'I wanted eternal union with a man too: another kind of love.'

She says, 'You can't have it, because it's wrong, impossible.'

'I don't believe that,' he answers.

Many scholars and writers have suggested that Lawrence had homosexual desires and he was certainly interested in the full range of human sexual experience. He once said, 'the nearest thing I've come to perfect love was with a coal-miner when I was sixteen,' and he's known to have had an intimate relationship with a Cornish farmer by the name William Henry Hocking, a relationship that was not likely to have been sexual according to the biographer Mark Kinkead-Weekes (1996).

Lawrence was involved with homosexual men, including John Maynard Keynes, Maurice Magnus and EM Forster. Forster later defended *Lady Chatterley's Lover* at the Chatterley trial of 1960, and his own book *Maurice* (1971) was labelled a gay Lady Chatterley, because it contained an aristocratic desire being met by a gamekeeper.

During the Second World War homosexuality had been off the moral agenda, but the twenty years that followed were 'one of the worst times in recent history to be gay if you were British' wrote Paul Baker in *Fabulosa!* (2019). Even drag shows were banned in the 1950s, and anyone out in drag was likely to be arrested for soliciting. At that time in Nottingham one of the few places lesbians and gay men could congregate and dance together was the jazz nights run by the Communist Party.

In the 1960s the police were arresting gay and bisexual men in record numbers. They were an easy target, often cooperating rather than face publicity and its many consequences. By the mid-1960s Polari was being spoken in Nottingham as a way that one gay man could identify another without their sexuality being made public. Polari derives from various sources and slang. The use of unfamiliar words and switching pronouns (he/omee to she/palone) all helped to create this secret gay language. The key to Polari, according to Baker (2019), was to sound like you're having a good time and to use lots of exaggerations, drama and gossip. Polari lost its secret status after it entered the mainstream with BBC Radio's *Round the Horne* (1964–68), a show created by Barry Took and Marty Feldman, starring Kenneth Williams and Hugh Paddick.

Edwinstowe-born Geoffrey Palmer (1912–2005) was educated in Nottinghamshire where he became a teacher. He later formed his own theatre group and met his partner, the actor Noel Lloyd. Palmer's only adult novel, *To Church on Sunday*, was published in 1940, but he went on to have a prolific writing career with Lloyd. In the early 1960s they wrote three children's books set in the Sherwood Forest area (Edwinstowe becomes Edwinston).

In 1965, nineteen-year-old John Clarkson was investigated by the police for shoplifting. On discovering that he lived with a man, the police searched Clarkson's house before interviewing both him and his partner and bullying them into confessing that they had slept together. A court trial (at what's now the National Justice Museum) revealed how the police had humiliated the men, with their bed sheets held aloft and a jar of lubricant passed around the jury to the words 'notice the pubic hair.' Ray Gosling reported on the case, and later re-interviewed John Clarkson about the case for the TV documentary *Socially Unacceptable*. Clarkson had been sent to prison for two years, his partner Billy for three. Gosling was a writer and a campaigning man of the people who had written and presented several hundred television and radio programmes. His later documentaries focused on his personal life and emergence as a gay activist.

In the same year Clarkson was arrested, Nottingham-born Cecil Roberts was becoming the first author to be named a Freemen of the City. According to the novelist and literary critic Francis King, in his autobiography *Yesterday Came Suddenly* (1993), Roberts, who never came out publicly, boasted in private of having various famous lovers including Laurence Olivier, Ivor Novello, Baron Gottfried von Cramm (a tennis player), Somerset Maugham, and the Duke of Kent. 'For Cecil, snob that he was, the last of these represented the highest achievement,' wrote King.

On the fiftieth anniversary of the 1967 Sexual Offences Act, the National Justice Museum hosted an exhibition devoted to Joe Orton. The Act had made gay sex no longer unlawful, which meant part-decriminalisation. Police harassment towards lesbians and gay men continued for decades after, the remaining laws being actively enforced.

The late Ike Cowen started the Nottingham Campaign for Homosexual Equality (CHE) group in 1971 and people soon travelled from surrounding towns and cities to attend meetings in Nottingham at the Friends Meeting House or the Albert Hall. Ray Gosling was among those involved with CHE, which became a mass movement supporting gay men who had been discriminated against whilst also seeking reform and an assimilation into mainstream society.

The Gay Liberation Front (GLF) also emerged in the early 1970s. Christopher Pious Mary "Kris" Kirk was in Nottingham at the time studying American Literature at the University of Nottingham. He came out as openly gay and founded the university's first Gay Liberation Society. Kirk was also part of Nottingham's Gay Street Theatre, produced by GLF and CHE. He played Maid Marian in *Robina Hood and her Gay Folk*, performed on the steps of the Council House in 1975 before the police moved them on. Kirk went on to work in television and had a successful career as a journalist writing pioneering articles about homosexuality for *Gay News* and *Gay Times*, including an interview with Boy George. Kirk was also an acclaimed music journalist, writing for the magazine *Melody Maker*.

Kris Kirk co-wrote the book *Men In Frocks* (1984), an illustrated history of British crossdressing from the war to the 1980s. Kirk isn't the only Nottinghamshire writer to have written on this subject, there's also Edwinstowe-born Roger Baker's *Drag: A History of Female Impersonation in the Performing Arts* (1995). Sherwood-born Douglas Byng, AKA the Queen of Pantomime Dames, had been an openly gay and camp drag artist back in the 1940s. A star of the musical halls, his saying, 'tits like coconuts,' got him banned by the BBC.

Post-1967, Nottingham witnessed increasing opportunities for socialising, with more groups and 'legitimate' gay-friendly pubs springing up. In need of a listings magazine, Nottingham GLF and CHE produced their own newsletter, *Chimaera*, surreptitiously printed at The Manning Girls' School. It ran for ten years from 1972.

Addressing a need to provide support and information in the form of a helpline, Nottingham Gay and Lesbian Switchboard – now the Nottinghamshire LGBT+ Network – developed out of CHE in the mid-1970s. Founding member David Edgley, who has been a leading voice and active member of LGBT+ groups across Nottingham over the last fifty years, wrote *A History of a Lesbian and Gay Telephone Helpline* (2000) chronicling the charity's struggles and achievements.

Throughout the 1970s Nottingham's *Evening Post* refused advertising space to CHE, the *Post*'s boss writing, 'I do not approve of homosexuality.' It was an attitude shared by the leader of the Conservative group in 1977, who 'always regarded homosexuality as one form of perversion.'

The fortnightly publication *Gay News*, founded in 1972, had been an important mouthpiece for its former collaborators CHE and GLF. For years WH Smith refused to stock *Gay News* and wouldn't allow their distribution company to transport it to other outlets. The newspaper's editor, Dennis Lemon, attended a meeting of Nottingham CHE. When *Gay News* ceased publishing, Nottingham's writers responded with their own publications.

Colin Clews who, together with Bob Emerton, Nigel Leach, Dave Pitt, Michael (a.k.a. Mitzi) Scholes and cartoonist Cathy White, produced *GEM* (Gay East Midlands) in Nottingham, campaigned to get the Nottingham Labour Party to take up lesbian and gay rights, and was instrumental in setting up Nottingham's first AIDS Information Project. *GEM* was Britain's only gay and lesbian publication when the AIDS crisis struck. Clews examined the challenges faced by LGBT+ people in the 1980s in his book *Gay in the 80s: from fighting for our rights to fighting for our lives* (2017).

Back in the mid-1980s Clews had helped Hockley's Mushroom Bookshop establish what became a comprehensive section of lesbian and gay books, the first such collection in a Nottingham bookshop. Mushroom continued to stock Nottingham's many LGBT+ magazines and free sheets including *Diversion* (1986); *Gay*

Nottingham ('85–87), *Metrogay* ('87–89), *Outright* ('89–97) and *Lookout* ('96–), until the shop closed in 2000.

Gay Nottingham and its successor *Metrogay* were started by Richard McCance, an openly gay member of the Labour Party who was asked to stand as a candidate in the local council elections. Defying expectations, McCance won his seat, becoming a Nottingham city councillor in 1983. His gay and lesbian free sheet became a sixteen-page magazine with a circulation of 5,000 providing news and information for the LGBT+ community. McCance recounted his experience in "The Skaters Waltz" which appeared in *Late Outbursts: LGBTQ Memoirs* (2014). His partner, Christopher Richardson, wrote *A City of Light: Socialism, Chartism and Co-operation – Nottingham, 1844* (2013), which delves into the history of Nottingham's many operatives' libraries, halls and reading rooms.

Mushroom Bookshop prominently displayed the local gay free papers, and *Gay Times* became the shop's biggest selling magazine. Mushroom was the first venue in Nottingham to hold regular author visits, with many events hosting LGBT+ writers (and authors of LGBT+ writing): including Armistead Maupin at the height of his fame; Suniti Namjoshi, whose inventive writing challenged racism, sexism and homophobia; Maureen Duffy, one of the first modern writers of explicitly lesbian fiction; Jeanette Winterson, author of novels exploring gender polarities and sexual identity; and the gay rights activist Jane Rule, who came over on a rare visit from Canada to talk about her book *Desert of the Heart* (1964), which had been adapted for the popular lesbian film *Desert Hearts* (1985).

Nottinghamshire Rainbow Heritage recognised Mushroom Bookshop for their service and support for the local LGBT+ community, awarding them a posthumous certificate in 2012.

It was under the Mushroom Books imprint that Gregory Woods' *This Is No Book: A Gay Reader* (1994) was published. Woods had been a member of the local writing group Pink Ink, having joined shortly after moving to Nottingham in 1990 to teach at the Polytechnic (now NTU). The Lord Roberts pub in Hockley played an important role in Pink Ink's history. The gay-friendly pub with its art-deco style, on the corner of Broad Street and High Cross Street since 1936, was named on Nottingham Civic Society's list of local heritage assets of the city of Nottingham. The Pink Ink group was founded in the

1980s by Tony Challis, current Chair of Nottingham Poetry Society, and over the years the group met at a variety of locations including in The Lord Roberts' cellar and at the Forest Tavern. Challis went on to initiate Rainbow Writers, an LGBT+ Writers' Group at Nottingham Writers' Studio.

The Lord Roberts, Broad Street.

Gregory Woods is now Emeritus Professor of Gay and Lesbian Studies at NTU, where he carries out research in the areas of LGBT+ literary and cultural studies. Woods is the author of *Articulate Flesh: Male Homo-eroticism and Modern Poetry* (1987), *A History of Gay Literature* (1998), and *Homintern: How Gay Culture Liberated the Modern World* (2016), a work that crosses continents and languages, tracing the networks of writers, artists, intellectuals and film stars who transformed western twentieth-century culture. His poetry includes *We Have the Melon* (1992), described by *Time Out* as 'graphic, beautiful, gay love poems,' *An Ordinary Dog* (2011) and *Records of an Incitement to Silence* (2021). Woods is writing a long dramatic monologue in the voice of Samuel Butler.

In 1986 there was a lesbian library inside a new community centre on Mansfield Road. Around this time, the Closet Library opened (books by and about lesbians) which was based at the Lesbian Centre, part of the Women's Centre on Chaucer Street. Melanie Duffill-Jeffs was manager of the Women's Centre for six years before becoming Director of Bromley House Library in 2017. She was in charge of the centre during the re-development of its library, which still contains a sizable collection of lesbian-themed literature. Duffill-Jeffs has done much to support lesbians, bisexual and trans women in Nottingham.

In 1987 the front window of Nottingham Central Library featured a lesbian and gay exhibition which was vandalised several times. This was at a time of the AIDS outbreak, when the tabloid media further demonised gay and bisexual men, contributing to the fact that, in this year, three-quarters of the population agreed that homosexual activity was always or mostly wrong. This was election time, and during the campaign Conservative MP Jill Knight argued that Labour wanted to glorify homosexual intercourse, giving young children access to gay and lesbian books. Knight, who later campaigned against same-sex marriage, also linked discussion of homosexuality in schools to the spread of AIDS.

Knight's protests led to Prime Minister Margaret Thatcher introducing Section 28 of the Local Government Act 1988 and its enacted amendment which stated that a local authority 'shall not intentionally promote homosexuality or publish material with the intention of promoting homosexuality.' Thatcher had been complaining that Labour councils were damaging 'traditional values' in promoting same-sex 'pretend' parenting and the 'right to be gay'. Section 28 suited the PM's anti-gay agenda, and it was the first anti-lesbian law introduced in Britain. Boris Johnson, then a journalist on the *Daily Telegraph*, wrote, 'We don't want our children being taught some rubbish about homosexual marriage being the same as normal marriage, and that is why I am more than happy to support Section 28.'

Across the country gay-themed literature was removed from library shelves and many positive depictions of LGBT+ life were gone from schools. Section 28 was not repealed in England until 2003, and in its early years it helped spread discrimination.

This homophobic prohibition of books and other gay information was opposed and defied by many members of Nottingham's literary community. Mushroom Bookshop produced and distributed thousands of double-sided leaflets; on one side was a listing of lesbian and gay writers and gay writing, on the other was the case against Section 28. Working with Nottinghamshire Libraries, they also produced a booklist called *Unsilenced Voices*, part of a campaign that included readings by Francis King and Adam Mars-Jones and a performance of Philip Osment's play *This Island's Mine*. Local libraries produced their own defiant display of the unsilenced voices' books promoted by Alan Guest, an openly-gay man in the literary service at that time.

In the 1990s, under the nose of Section 28, David Belbin's YA series The Beat introduced PC Gary Monk, the first recurring gay character to feature in a British YA series. The decade was seeing gradual social reforms and the start of incremental law changes that would alter attitudes.

It was in the 1990s that Narvel Annable published the first of his autobiographic novels, described as gay thrillers. From 1978 to 1995 Annable was a history teacher at Valley

Comprehensive School in Worksop, too frightened to come out. This experience informed his book *Double Life* (2019), which covers the cruelty of the Thatcher era and the panic of AIDS, set against a blighted colliery landscape. *Lost Lad* (2003) was inspired by his early gay experiences during his adolescence at William Howitt Secondary Modern. And Annable, a campaigner for gay rights, wrote a biography of His Honour Judge Keith Matthewman QC of Nottingham Crown Court entitled *A Judge Too Far* (2001).

MP Ann Widdecombe, then Shadow Home Secretary, wasn't happy in 1998 when Gregory Woods was made Britain's first Professor of Lesbian and Gay Studies at NTU. Widdecombe called it 'a phenomenal waste of public money.' A spokesman for Stonewall – the UK gay rights charity set up in the wake of Section 28 – said, 'There is tremendous ignorance about lesbian and gay issues. This will help redress the balance.'

'Small but pioneering,' was how Woods described his appointment, adding, 'It's encouraging that the university has taken what is a slightly brave decision.'

In 2005, with Section 28 now history, Nottinghamshire Libraries bought over one hundred LGBT+ themed books, including novels, biographies, non-fiction, and self-help on issues such as LGBT+ parenting. The year also saw the resurrection of *QB* (Queer Bulletin) magazine which is still being produced.

Nottingham's Sapphist Writers group was set up in 2007. Founded by counsellor and trainer Sam Hope, Sapphist Writers was ostensibly for bisexual women and lesbians (including bi and lesbian trans women) but was open to all women (and non-binary) writers. Hope told me, 'We met once a month at Nottingham Women's Centre and were an informal group focused on creativity and support rather than critique, our ethos being inclusivity and encouragement rather than formality.'

Sapphist Writers ran for seven years providing lots of support and inspiration to writers, for which they won a Rainbow Heritage Award. Sam Hope, author of *Person-Centred Counselling for Trans and Gender Diverse People: a practical guide* (2019) is one of the many former members to have had their work published. Others include Nicki Hastie, a lesbian writer whose work has appeared in various anthologies and magazines, including reflections on her involvement in activism around lesbian and LGBT+ identities. There's Rebecca S Buck, author of *The Locket and the Flintlock*

(2012), Giselle Leeb, an award-winning writer of short stories, and Victoria Villasenor, writer of novels under the names Brey Willows and Victoria Oldham.

Now displaying its plaque in recognition of its place in Nottingham's LGBT+ history, the New Foresters has been gay-friendly since the 1950s. Debbie Law has run the pub for the last two decades and every year she hosts the Bold Strokes Festival's meet and greet. Usually held at Nottingham's Waterstones, Bold Strokes Festival is the longest running LGBTQ book festival in the UK.

The East Midlands largest bookshop, Waterstones, is situated on the historic Bridlesmith Gate, nos 1–3, where it occupies a grand Victorian building that covers four floors beneath a large events' room (the Sillitoe Room). The venue was built in 1873–75 and extended to the Bottle Lane corner in 1927. Since hosting Nottinghamshire's Rainbow Heritage Exhibition in 2009, Nottingham Waterstones has been a strong supporter of LGBT+ writers and writing.

Victoria Villasenor organises the annual Bold Strokes Festival. She is the consulting editor and UK rep for Bold Strokes Books, the largest LGBTQ publishing house. When asked about the festival she told me, 'It's so incredibly gratifying to have such a big turnout year after year that brings people back as well as welcomes new people in; all who want to be part of the LGBTQ book world.'

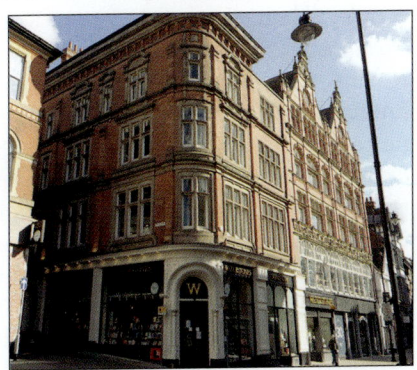

Waterstones, Bridlesmith Gate.

Sapphist Writers published an anthology in 2012 entitled *The Big Tree*, a collection of poetry, short stories and flash fiction from ten of their members, on the theme of relationships. Nottingham Sapphist and Rainbow Writers collaborated for Nottingham's 2013 Festival of Words, showcasing their poetry at NTU's Newton Building. The compere was Russell Christie, former travel writer for *Gay Times* and *The Pink Paper*. Christie has a long history in LGBT+ rights and political activism. His novel, *The Queer Diary of Mordred Vienna* (2015), is loosely based on his five years in San Francisco in the early 1990s.

Since opening in 2013, Five Leaves Bookshop has supported Nottingham's LGBT+ community. Five Leaves is a friendly, safe space that stocks a large selection of relevant literature including the magazines *DIVA, Curve* and *Gay & Lesbian Quarterly*. The bookshop has held regular LGBT+ events, hosting many poets, fiction and non-fiction writers, and it's the only place in Nottingham that regularly puts on public events with trans speakers/readers.

Five Leaves has also published a handful of LGBT+ books over the years, including *Unorthodox: LGBT+ Identity and Faith* (2019) edited by Séan Richardson, an academic, curator and writer then based in Nottingham whose research tackles the lasting resonances of queer history in contemporary society through literature and heritage. *Unorthodox* tells the stories of LGBT+ people of faith throughout the country.

Several LGBT+ support groups held meetings at The Health Shop on Broad Street. One of these is Outburst, a group for young people. Their powerful memoirs are collected in the anthology *Speaking OUT* (2014). Along with Victoria Villasenor, Nicci Robinson, who writes under the pen name Robyn Nyx, edited and published the group's anthology through Global Words. There are more true stories in *In Different Shoes: Stories from the Trans Community* (2016), written by young people from Nottingham's transgender community, many of the contributors from the Nottingham youth group Trans4me.

Villasenor and Robinson ran creative writing workshops as part of an LGBTQ memoir project run in conjunction with the British Museum. This collaboration resulted in *Desire, Love, Identity* (2019), an anthology of personal stories from members of Nottingham's LGBTQ community in response to artefacts and histories on display at the National Justice Museum. Its writers include the aforementioned Challis, Woods, Edgley, Hastie and Buck, and the poets Thom Seddon and Kevin Jackson.

Jackson's poetry includes the collection *Loves Burn* (2020), locally published by Big White Shed. Jackson, an activist, told me:

> Queer writers are a rich strand of Nottingham's spoken word scene, diverse truth-telling activists, then and now. My aim has shifted and I would say so has that of other queer writers: from giving voice to exceptionalism, making meaning (entertainment?) out of otherness, to a full-on project of social justice.

Nottingham has its own writers of LGBT+ literature. Anne Goodwin's *Sugar and Snails* (2015) is set in 2004, the year of the Gender Recognition Act. The novel flashes back to a woman's childhood in the 1960s and 1970s and her gender transition at the age of fifteen. Kristina Adams' novel *Behind the Spotlight* (2019), set in Nottingham, tells the story of Cameron, whose ex-boyfriend is now one-quarter of the world's biggest boy band. Dr Hongwei Bao's nonfiction book *Queer Comrades* (2018) is the first to look at gay identity and queer activism in China from a cultural studies perspective. Irish author Christopher Pressler's semi-autobiographical *Canning Circus: a Novel Under and Over Nottingham* (2003) is a collection of stories about local characters, including several young gay men. *These Seven* (2015), includes a story by Megan Taylor which features a lesbian character. And in 2021 Gareth Peter wrote *My Daddies,* about his experience of adopting two children with his partner. The result is the first Puffin picture book to feature same-sex parents.

Nottingham has a growing number of LGBT+ writers and poets.

Rich Goodson's poetry has appeared in the *Penguin Poetry of Sex* (2014) and *A Queer Anthology of Rage* (2018), and his own pamphlet *Mr Universe* (2017). After completing his doctorate in writing under the supervision of Gregory Woods, Goodson founded Word Jam (now World Jam), a collective of poets and musicians whose first language is not English.

Lise Gold is an author of lesbian romance. Her eleven novels include the award-winning *French Summer* (2018) and *Living* (2019). Gold moved to Nottingham with her wife in 2011 and finds it 'a very open-minded city where anyone would feel welcome.'

Joe Andrews' poetry has featured in various anthologies and literary magazines including Bad Betty's *Alter Egos* (2019), *Homology Lit* and *Anomaly,* the international journal of literature and the arts. A former events coordinator for the University of Nottingham's Poetry and Spoken Word Society, their poetry explores the relationship between gender and family.

Joshua Judson, the founder of Poetry Is Dead Good, has had his poetry published in *The North, Brittle Star* and *Magma,* among other journals. His first collection, *Gongoozler,* (def. *noun* a person who enjoys watching boats and activities on canals) was published in 2021.

Pippa Hennessy – a long-term Five Leaves worker – is one of three featured poets in *Take Three* (2019). Her poems "The

Observer Effect" and "The Uncertainty Principle" are about the experience of watching her daughter change from a little boy to a grown-up young lady, and coming to terms with her daughter's trans-ness, poems that are part of a collection inspired by quantum theory.

And the trans model Paris Lees' autobiographical novel, *What It Feels Like for a Girl* (2021), will feature in this book's Hucknall chapter.

650 years after Sir John Clanvowe was writing his poetry of Robin Hood, Nottingham's LGBT+ writers are still producing words that help define the city. One such writer is Troy Jenkinson, writer of LGBT+-focussed children's books, who has compiled *An LGBT Walking Tour of Nottingham*, available free from city centre venues.

Chapter 14
Newstead House, St James Street – The Boy Byron

'Adversity is the first path to truth.' Lord Byron, *Don Juan*

Newstead House is an elegant Grade II-listed townhouse that spans five levels and has its own caves. More impressively, it's the city centre's best brick-built link to the romantic poet Lord Byron.

The story of how Lord Byron came to live in Nottingham is as follows. Captain John Byron, also known as "Mad Jack" – son of John Byron, author of two books of voyages and shipwreck – eloped with Amelia Osborne, the wife of the future Fifth Duke of Leeds. Byron later married her and, as a gambler, he squandered away much of her money. They had three children, of which only one daughter survived beyond infancy. Amelia died in 1784, her inheritance dying with her, leaving Byron looking for a new wife and source of income.

Enter Catherine Gordon of Gight, Aberdeenshire. John Byron met the Scottish heiress in 1785 and within a few weeks they were wed. In the *Memoir of Robert Chambers* (1872), it is suggested that Catherine had been primed to fall in love with Byron a year earlier after attending *Isabella, or the Fatal Marriage* at Edinburgh's Theatre Royal. Catherine was so overcome by the onstage distress of the married Isabella, who had just found out her first and beloved husband Biron was still alive, that she became hysterical and had to be carried out of her box, screaming loudly the actress's words: 'Oh, my Biron! my Biron!'

To claim Catherine's Scottish estate, the real Byron took the surname Gordon. Her inheritance was used to pay off his debts and fund his extravagant, unscrupulous lifestyle. Whilst being a waster, he was also a known spendthrift and they moved to France for its cheaper cost of living.

Newstead House, St James Street.

Catherine Gordon returned to England, alone, for the birth of their son George in 1788. A year later, after her husband had deserted her, Catherine and her son moved to a flat in Aberdeen, living in comparative poverty. She became a heavy drinker. John Byron stayed in France and died three years later, never seeing his son.

In 1794, at the age of six, George became heir to the family estate and the title of Rochdale after the premature death of his cousin at the siege of Calvi. When George's great-uncle himself died, George inherited the largely ruinous Newstead Abbey, its estate and the attached title.

Now Lord Byron, George left Aberdeen Grammar School in 1798, where he'd been educated for four years, and arrived in Nottingham, aged ten, taking up residence with his mother, in the house on St James Street, at the invitation of the Parkyns family. Whilst here, Lord Byron received treatment for his lame foot, a problem since birth. A "trussmaker" at the nearby General Hospital, John Lavender applied a vice and braced shoe to Byron's foot in a botched repair job that was as useless as it was painful. The "surgeon", as he was listed in the *Nottingham Directory for 1814*, wasn't even qualified. He seems to have gained a reputation for treating misshapen limbs, but made his living making surgical appliances.

Young Byron's time in Nottingham was not easy. His difficult relationship with his mother was not helped by her mood swings, her kindness ruined by a strong temper and a drink problem. For much of the time, Byron was "looked after" by a drunken servant, Mrs Gray, who would often beat the boy and was known to bring dubious company back to the house, most likely exposing him to sexual acts. Catherine was spending time in London trying to secure a pension for her titled son.

During this period, Byron did enjoy the tutorage of Dummer Rogers, who quoted Virgil and Cicero to him. According to the journal *Notes and Queries* (1870), Rogers was an American loyalist pensioned by the English Government and was living in Hen Cross, Nottingham.

It's claimed that Byron wrote his first verses in Nottingham. The most famous of these early efforts was said to have been written about a woman in Swine Green, a short walk away (now part of Hockley). The woman had offended the young poet with reference to his lameness. A green plaque on the front of Faraday's states:

Faradays, Pelham Street.

This site was formerly known as Swine Green
Lord Byron wrote his first piece of poetry in 1798,
with the verse
'In Nottingham County there lives at
Swine Green as curst an old lady
as ever was seen...'

The verse continues:

And when she does die,
which I hope will be soon,
She firmly believes she will go the moon.

There's another plaque on the outside of Newstead House:

Lord Byron
1788. The Poet 1824.
Lived in this house
in the years 1798 and 1799

When Byron's plaque was put up, Newstead House was a Trade Union office. The four-bedroom end-of-terrace townhouse was sold in 2018 with an asking price of £850,000.

Chapter 15
Nottingham Arts Theatre, George Street – Nottingham Crusoe

> 'After a time, I was induced to yield to their allurements, to imitate their manners, and to join them in their sins.'
>
> George Vason

It was here on George Street that George Vason, dubbed Nottingham's Robinson Crusoe, attended the Baptist church. Vason was Governor of the town jail and the secret narrator of an extraordinary true story.

The story was written by a local Anglican clergyman – in Vason's first-person voice – who had taken down his words. Both men remained anonymous when the book was published in 1810 under the title *An Authentic Narrative of Four Years' Residence at Tongataboo: One of the Friendly Islands, in the South-Sea.* Vason was deeply ashamed of his story and only ever told it as a warning to prospective missionaries.

George Vason was a working-class man from North Muskam. After a childhood helping his father, a butcher, he decided he didn't want to lug meat around any longer and became an apprentice bricklayer. He moved to Nottingham to work as a builder and soon became a member of the Baptist church in Park Street, where he was baptised in 1794.

'I was addicted to swearing and cursing,' he said, grasping the chance for forgiveness. He soon learned of the "blessed truth of the gospel" and, after hearing of a planned missionary journey to the newly-discovered islands of the South Seas, Vason offered to help fit out the good ship Duff. In doing so, he found that they wanted a man of his skills to join them on their quest. And

Nottingham Arts Theatre, George Street.

so it was that in 1796, aged twenty-four, Vason set out with twenty-eight other missionaries to the Friendly Islands (modern-day Tonga). Knowing little of their destination, the men and women were prepared to suffer death to bring the word of God to heathens.

Vason disembarked at Tongataboo, the Duff's captain providing Vason and eight other men with gifts for the natives (axes and scissors) before leaving the missionaries ashore. The men were pleased with the prospect of the island's hills and vales, adorned as they were with fruit trees.

Nature provided an all-year round supply of food, and Vason took to the diet; the baked sweet potato, the abundance of fish and the coconut milk, 'as refreshing as lemonade.'

His book tells of a Pacific paradise of carnal enjoyment – and of a savage barbarity: 'a place where the natives were keen on inspiring terror into the minds of strangers,' wrote Orange (1840). The locals appreciated the provisions given to them and welcomed the missionaries. At first. Vason existed in a state of internal conflict; for he had arrived certain that his religion was the right path, only to feel himself slipping into a new way of life.

Two Europeans harassed Vason and attempted to seize his goods. They also influenced the natives, inciting murder. Vason's pistol was wrestled from him and spears were pointed at him, in what was to become one of many near-death experiences. On one occasion Vason was saved by the moon. This was after he has been dragged and restrained, with a club about to strike him dead. He was on his back when the moon suddenly emerged from under a cloud, shining full in his face. This was enough to spare him, as an islander recognised him as a friend of their chief.

Vason had been at the former chief's funeral, a sight that would never leave him. As his body had been placed in a tomb, two of his wives were strangled. Then:

> Hundreds ran about it, with ferocious emulation, to signalize their grief for the venerated chief, or their contempt of pain and death, by inflicting on themselves the most ghastly wounds, and exhibiting spectacles of the greatest horror.

In the hours before a new chief was elected, men continued running aimlessly, cutting themselves and fighting. After time had passed, the chance to escape and set sail to New South Wales presented itself, but Vason chose to remain on the island. 'The remembrance of this has caused me bitter remorse,' said Vason, 'and often fills me, still, with deep contrition, shame and self-abhorrence.'

Vason resided with Chief Mulikha'amea and experienced the natives' ways and customs. He enjoyed the dancing and singing, and he neglected his prayers and Bible reading.

Adopting their ways, he was tattooed, swapped his western clothing for a piece of cloth, and was persuaded to take a wife, a near relation of the chief's, 'a handsome girl of the age of eighteen.' He said:

> I lament to say, that I now entered, with the utmost eagerness, into every pleasure and entertainment of the natives; and endeavoured to forget that I was once called a Christian, and had left Christian land to evangelize the heathen.

Vason gained his own estate and took a further wife. He had gone native, but life was a perilous one. The islands were often at war and Vason joined the army of Tongataboo into battle. After one conflict he witnessed the roasting and eating of the enemy. The time had come for him to make his escape.

His luck was in. Noticing a passing English ship, he turned his canoe towards it. When other canoes gave chase, Vason dived into the water and headed for the ship, attempting to avoid darts as he swam. The captain ordered a boat to be lowered but Vason failed to communicate his need for help. Under great stress, he had forgotten how to speak English. A young midshipman from

An illustration from Vason's book.

Nottinghamshire commanded that Vason be pulled out of the shark-infested water.

Via China, New York and London, Vason worked his way back to Nottingham where he gained employment as keeper of St Mary's Workhouse before being dismissed. Vason's story had captured great sympathy and interest from Philip Bailey, father of the writer Thomas Bailey and grandfather of the poet Philip James Bailey. Philip Bailey resigned as governor of Nottingham Jail on Vason's behalf, allowing him to fill the vacant position.[1] Vason worked as the governor from 1820 until his death in 1838, aged sixty-six. He was interred in Mount Street's Baptist burial ground (now gone) alongside his Nottingham wife who had died eight months earlier.

Vason had met his wife, Miss Leavers, at the Baptist Church which moved to George Street in 1815, a newly-built building designed by Edward Staveley which could seat a thousand people. The Vasons worshipped there for the rest of their lives. During this time, Pritt, the Coddington man who had rescued Vason from the sea, met with him in Nottingham.

Vason's 1810 book was republished two years after his death as *Narrative of the Late George Vason of Nottingham* (1840) by Rev James Orange, a book that has been hailed as an important early and accurate account of Polynesian life and culture before it became forever changed by European contact. In the same year that Orange published Vason's story, he authored *The History of Nottingham*, a book which explored local institutions, manners, customs and arts. An early study in social history, Orange's book looked at working and workhouse conditions. With a particular concern for the framework knitters, the minister wrote *A Plea for the Poor* (1841), introducing the idea of allotment gardens for the working man.

In 1946 the Nottingham Co-operative Wholesale Society (CWS) bought the then disused Particular Baptist Church on George Street where, using voluntary labour, they founded the People's Theatre in 1948, later renamed the Co-operative Arts Theatre. The need for a theatre had arisen after the choral, operatic and drama groups had outgrown their previous venue at Co-op House. The Nottingham playwright Stephen Lowe's love of the theatre grew when he joined the youth group at the theatre, a place he enjoyed so much he was known to sleep there at weekends.

When the CWS intended to close the Arts Theatre in 1999, and sell its prime land for re-development, a theatre group started a campaign to buy the building. With help from Nottingham City Council and Broadway Media Centre, the asking price was met and it was able to remain a community venue. In 2007 the theatre survived another threat of closure and it now boasts a raised stage area with tiered seating for 300. In 2015, the theatre partnered up with the Nottingham based Confetti Institute of Creative Technologies.

The small pink theatre is home to an educational charity which aims to provide opportunities for all within the performing arts. Now simply known as Nottingham Arts Theatre it has played host to a large number of amateur and professional visiting companies. Next to the theatre is a 1946–48 remodelling of Vason's 1815 Baptist chapel by AH Betts.[2]

---

[1]Potter Briscoe, 1917.
[2]Pevsner, 2020.

Chapter 16
Nottingham Castle – Of Curious Rebels

'Nottingham Castle, foursquare, squat and respectable, not unlike the Queen herself in shape, frowned from its rock southwards over the slums, frowned northwards over the bright grass of its lawns set about with formal patterns of daffodils and hyacinths.'

Hilda Lewis, *Penny Lace*

A victim of our rebellious past, Nottingham Castle has been rebuilt several times and remains the city's best-known building. William Peveril constructed the first Nottingham Castle for William the Conqueror in 1086, Henry I added stone walls and new buildings, and Henry II provided defences, but the Castle was at its most impressive by the time Richard III and Henry VII rode from Nottingham to fight in battle, in Richard's case, to his death at the Battle of Bosworth in 1485.

In *Antiquities of Nottinghamshire* (1677) Robert Thoroton writes of the Castle that there is 'no other place so far distant from London which hath so often given entertainment and residence to the Kings and Queens of this realm since the Norman Conquest.'

On raising his standard here to start the Civil War in 1642, King Charles found little support in Nottingham as it became a stronghold for Parliament in a region dominated by those supporting the King. Parliamentary troops held the Castle under Colonel John Hutchinson, who became its governor in 1643. Hutchinson stood firm throughout the war despite Royalist raids from Newark.

His wife Lucy wrote an entertaining diary which has become an important source for historians.

Lucy Hutchinson had been twenty-three when the first of the Royalist's attacks was made. A poet who enjoyed translating Classical writers, she wrote a first-hand account of the war, its build-up and aftermath, in one of the earliest personal books written by an Englishwoman. It was written as a tribute to her husband, enhancing his reputation, and it reads like an historical adventure, with dramatic escapes and disguises, priests and aristocrats behaving badly, spies with coded information, a bitten-off nose, and death from a broken heart.[1] There are descriptions of the Castle's towers and passages as they were before its demolition in 1651 on the orders of her husband.

Memoirs of the Life of Colonel Hutchinson came to the public's attention as late as 1806, at which point it became a best-seller. Nottingham Castle holds a handwritten manuscript of the memoirs which is on display in the new Rebellion Gallery.

After the Civil War, Lucy Hutchinson returned to the family's seat in Owthorpe, Nottinghamshire, and it was here that she completed the memoirs. Her other works include the first epic poem published by a woman in English, *Order and Disorder* (1679). Lucy Hutchinson is buried in the crypt at Owthorpe beside her husband.

Owthorpe and the Hutchinsons feature in the children's historical novel *Uncivil War: Twin Tales of Nottinghamshire* (2016) by Noel Harrower. The author spent most of his working life as a careers officer in Nottinghamshire where he has won several awards for his one-act plays. The book also features Pierrepont Hall.

In 1663 William Cavendish, the Duke of Newcastle, set to work clearing the site for the building of a renaissance-style palace which was completed in 1679 after the duke's death. The fourth Duke of Newcastle, Henry Pelham Clinton, was its absent owner in 1831 at the time of the Reform Riots. The duke was not only an opponent of electoral reform, he also led the defeat of a bill that would have extended the vote to more people and halted corrupt voting practices. When news reached Nottingham that the bill had been voted down, the town rioted, and the Castle was stormed.

In *Mary Howitt, an autobiography* (1889), edited by her daughter Margaret, William Howitt (1792–1879) describes the scene he witnessed from their home in the Market Square:

> First in the dusk of the evening, the vast market-place of six acres filled with one dense throng of people, their black heads looking like a sea of ink, for the whole living mass was swaying and heaving in the commotion of fury seeking a vent. Suddenly there was a cry of 'To the castle! To the castle' to which a fierce roar of applause with the ominous echo, and at once this heaving, raging ocean of agitated life became an impetuous, headlong torrent, struggling away towards Friar Lane, leading directly to the castle.

William Howitt recalled the deafening yells as the mob scaled the walls and surrounded the vast building, and how, 'The flames rapidly spread, filled the whole place with a deep fiery glow, mingled with clouds of smoke that burst from the windows and streamed up roofwards, tipped with tongues of flame, hungry for the destruction of the whole fabric.' It was raining steadily but, 'Soon the riotous, voracious flames burst through the roof, sending down torrents of melted lead, and to heaven legions of glittering sparks and smoke as from a volcano.'

In Alan Sillitoe's novel, *A Man of His Time* (2004), Ernest Burton references the Reform Riots when mentioning the castle:

> Fifty or so years ago it was set on fire, an old codger told him who'd seen it as a youth, one of a thousand cheering the rioters, the sky all flame when not blotted out by smoke. 'I watched the fire till it started to rain, then walked home. Some of those who stayed were caught, and hanged.' The Duke of Newcastle got twenty-one thousand pounds to have it built up again, so the poor paid for the bonfire out of their own pockets. All the same, it must have been a treat to see it go up.

The whole castle was consumed by the fire, its remaining furnishings stripped, and statues destroyed. After the duke deliberately neglected its ruined shell, TC Hine was given the job of renovating the castle and turning it into a museum of fine art, and in 1878 the castle became the first municipal museum of art in the country. To mark its opening, Philip James Bailey wrote his *Historical Ode on the Opening of the Castle as a Permanent Art Museum*, eighteen verses that celebrated 900 years of turbulent history, from 'freeborn outlaws' to the castle becoming an 'intellectual beacon burning bright.'

By this time Nottingham had established itself as a world leader in the design and manufacture of lace, and lace machines are on display in the castle's museum. In Hilda Lewis's *Penny Lace* (1946), it's here in the Long Gallery that the ambitious Nicholas Penny and equally rebellious Heriot Ware first sit down and talk. The castle and its gardens are perhaps a natural setting where a working-class man and an upper-class lady might have met and this is the case for Penny and Ware in several of the book's scenes.

In the first chapter of his first novel, *The White Peacock* (1911), DH Lawrence's George and Meg visit the castle. 'We stood on the high rock in the cool of the day, and watched the sun sloping over the great river-flats...,' wrote Lawrence. They then explored the picture galleries and listened to the military band playing in the grounds outside.

There are several more visits here in Lawrence's most autobiographical novel, *Sons and Lovers* (1913). When Paul Morel visited with Clara, 'The Castle grounds were very green and fresh.' By the time they'd climbed the 'precipitous ascent,' Lawrence wrote:

> There was scarcely time to go inside the squat, square building that crowns the bluff of rock. They leaned upon the wall where the cliff runs sheer down to the Park. Below them, in their holes in the sandstone, pigeons preened themselves and cooed softly. Away down upon the boulevard at the foot of the rock, tiny trees stood in their own pools of shadow, and tiny people went scurrying about in almost ludicrous importance.

Nottingham Castle's museum held a superb DH Lawrence exhibition in 1972, organised by Arnold Rattenbury. Costing over six thousand pounds, it featured a collection of documents, photographs, paintings, sketches, objects and other material from Lawrence's early years in Eastwood, Nottingham, Croydon and elsewhere, spanning his earliest recorded childhood to the First World War, his paintings taking centre stage.

In *Sons and Lovers*, Paul sends paintings to the Castle's exhibitions. To the delight of Paul's mother, two of his paintings are displayed in the autumn exhibition of students' work, both of them are awarded prizes.

Alan Sillitoe's Arthur Seaton (1958) hated the Castle:

> ...more than I've hated owt in my life before, and I'd like to plant a thousand tons of bone-dry T.N.T. in the tunnel called Mortimer's Hole, and send it to Kingdom Cum, so's nob'dy 'ud ever see it again.

Mortimer's Hole refers to the cave tunnel that the king's raiders used to enter the Castle in 1330. Edward's supporters' successful coup d'état against Isabella of France and her lover Roger Mortimer led to Mortimer being seized and later executed for treason.

Seaton's Castle was 'a crowned brownstone shaggy lion-head slouching its big snout out of the city, poised as if to gobble up uncouth suburbs hemmed in by an elbow of the turgid Trent,' and in Sillitoe's *A Man of His Time* (2004) it becomes 'squat and bleak on its high rock, thunderclouds piling above...'

Sillitoe's poem *Nottingham Castle*, from the first edition of *Nottingham Quarterly* (1978), featured in a 2021 exhibition at the Castle called *Revolutions in Print: Reform, Rebellion and the Press*. NTU produced the event which focused on the city's radical print heritage from the nineteenth century through to the present day, expanding on the Castle's permanent theme of rebellion.

Nottingham Castle makes a cameo appearance in Ian Fleming's eighth full-length James Bond novel. The Castle was chosen by John Player as his first trademark in 1877 and the image is described in *Thunderball* (1961). In the chapter "Cardboard Hero", Bond girl Domino Vitali, an Italian chain-smoker described as being 'beautiful, sexy, provocative, independent, self-willed, quick-tempered, and cruel,' tells Bond she'd like a packet of Players. She then goes into a dreamlike state, creating a lengthy backstory for the iconic sailor on the front of her packet; portraying him as her one true love, the man of her dreams and the first man she ever sinned with. The packet of Players conjures up a romantic, heroic image on which, according to Domino, 'the whole of England is there.' Over several pages she moves on to explain how John Player came to have the sailor on his packets before talking about the sons in Player and Sons.

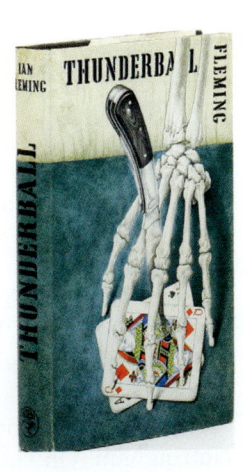

Just when you think Domino has finished with Nottingham, she flips the packet over and describes the other side saying, '...and that extraordinary trade mark of a doll's house swimming in chocolate fudge with Nottingham Castle written underneath.' (The doll's house is the Castle.) Sherwood Forest also gets a mention in *Thunderball*, which was the first novelisation of a yet-to-be-filmed James Bond screenplay, a collaborative work by five writers. At least one of them had been stirred by Nottingham.

On 16 May 1966, a black Daimler limousine pulled up outside the gates to Nottingham Castle and three men emerged. One was holding a photographic camera, another had a cine camera and a microphone. They were focused on the third man who was sporting a curly mop of hair, dark sunglasses and pinstriped trousers – Bob Dylan.

Fifty years before he won the Nobel Prize for Literature, Dylan arrived in Nottingham in the middle of a controversial tour that changed music history. He had his photo taken coming back through the gates by the photographer Barry Feinstein, who also snapped the singer outside L.S.D (sic) Partners, a bookies at 18 Castle Boulevard (Egan, 2017). That evening Dylan played Sheffield's Gaumont Theatre where he sang "Desolation Row", a song that mentions Robin Hood, perhaps with the outlaw's statue in mind.

It was a day later that Dylan played Manchester's Free Trade Hall, a legendary night mistakenly known as the Royal Albert Hall concert, the most bootlegged concert in rock history, that captured the moment 'Judas' was shouted from the balcony as Dylan and the Band went electric. Like Alan Sillitoe, Dylan objected to being labelled. He didn't like being called a folk singer, a protest singer or a poet. The phrase "Whatever people say I am, that's what I'm not" could have been said by Dylan if Arthur Seaton hadn't beaten him to it.[1]

It would be another thirty-nine years before Dylan performed in Nottingham. On the setlist was "Masters of War", a song with a Nottingham connection as it's written to the tune of "Fair Nottamun Town", a folk song the Ritchie family believed to be about Nottingham in old England. Jean Ritchie gained the copyright to "Fair Nottamun Town" in 1964. The Ritchie family of Kentucky hailed from all over the UK, first arriving in America in 1768, and bringing their songs with them. Nottamun Town was an old "magic song", said to be cursed and that whoever uncovers its meaning will lose all of their luck. It comes from Nottingham mummers' plays. These folk plays were performed by amateur actors, traditionally all male, and featured several different stock characters including Tom Fool and Dame Jane. The plays were taken door to door and performed in exchange for money or gifts, with threats of destruction if the audience didn't pay up. They were like an adult version of trick or treat, the actors hiding their true identities.

Dylan would have come across the tune to "Nottamum Town"

from Jackie Washington, who had sung a version of the song (in 1962) that Dylan loved. Dylan would go to Gerde's Folk City every night Washington performed and repeatedly ask him to sing it, later demanding a copy of the record. The next time Washington heard the tune it had become "Masters of War". When Dylan played "Masters of War" in Nottingham (in 2005) it was the only time he played the song during that UK/Ireland eleven-show leg of the tour.

---

[1]Lock, 2017.
[2]Sillitoe, 1958.

Chapter 17
Nottingham Mechanics, North Sherwood Street – Various Homes of the NWC

'Keep on writing.' Godfrey Winn

It was at the Black Boy Hotel on Long Row that the Nottingham Writers' Club (NWC) was established in 1927 after a group of writers known as the Nottingham Writers' Circle placed adverts in the local *Evening Post* and *Nottingham Guardian*. Still going strong, the club can count Helen Cresswell, Alan Sillitoe and a largely forgotten golden-age bestseller among its former members.

The painter and decorator Arthur "Ernest" Ashley (1906–79), played an important role in the literary history of Nottingham. A founder member of NWC, Ashley swapped brush for pen in 1932, writing short stories for newspapers and magazines. His first detective novel, *Death at the Salutation*, arrived five years later, written under the name Francis Vivian. A series followed, featuring Scotland Yard's Detective Knollis. Here's a taste from the series opener, *The Death of Mr. Lomas* (1941):

> Lomas was poisoned, shaved after death, and placed in the river. He is full of whisky and the post-mortem examination will undoubtedly prove that cocaine was in the alcohol. The murderer worked on him with a lavish hand, one so lavish that it may eventually prove to be his undoing.

In 2018 Dean Street Press republished ten of Francis Vivian's crime novels with new cover art, giving readers a chance to discover this lost Nottingham writer.

Ashley worked on the *Nottinghamshire Free Press* newspaper whilst writing nine more books in his Knollis series. Francis Vivian's books were hugely popular when it came to hardbacks and library loans.

Black Boy Hotel.

According to the *Guardian*'s John Hall, 'Francis Vivian was neck and neck with Ngaio Marsh in second place after Agatha Christie.'

In 1950, during the peak of his success, the co-creator of NWC was invited back to select the winning entry in their short story competition. Ashley picked a story called *The General's Dilemma* by a twenty-two-year-old aspiring writer by the name of Alan Sillitoe. In his autobiography, *Life Without Armour* (1995), Sillitoe recalled, '...a crime novelist who earned his living by writing... gave [my story] first prize, telling me it was so well written and original that nothing further need to be done, and that I should try and get it published.'

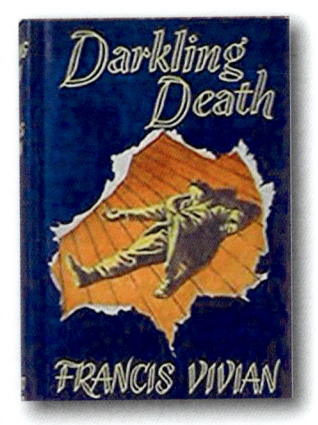

This story later developed into Sillitoe's second novel, *The General* (1960), and its plot was used by the 1968 American film *Counterpoint* starring Charlton Heston and Leslie Nielsen. However, in the opinion of John Hall, Sillitoe never reached the heights of Francis Vivian, who Hall described as 'the best local author after Byron and DH Lawrence.' Adding, 'People who wouldn't know Alan Sillitoe from George Eliot will stop [Ashley/Vivian] in the street and tell him they solved his latest detective story.'

"Ernest" Ashley had similar interests to Arthur Conan Doyle – psychology, beekeeping, the spirit world – and he featured these subjects in his books and lectures. His writing achievements were noted in NWC's magazine *Scribe*, first published in 1933.

When Ashley first attended club meetings it was in the Haddon Room of the Black Boy Hotel on Long Row (to the right of Five Leaves Bookshop). The famous hotel had been extended and reconstructed by the architect Fothergill Watson, who had become Watson Fothergill by the time he last worked on the hotel in 1878. The Black Boy boasted Gracie Fields, George Formby, Gregory Peck and Laurence Olivier among its customers, and NWC also attracted some fine guest speakers, including Leslie Charteris, known for his *The Saint* books featuring the adventures of Simon Templar, and the journalist and actor Godfrey Winn, whose advice to the members was to, 'Go out on every possible occasion and meet people.'

NWC had left the building long before then, moving their meetings to The Elite in 1937, where Francis Vivian had returned as their first guest speaker. The Elite was another grand building, a super-cinema that had showed Nottingham's first "talkie" in 1929. The Elite's shell remains in place on the Upper Parliament/King Street corner. NWC moved on after a year to the nearby Albert Hotel on Derby Road where they regularly met until the outbreak of the Second World War.

The club reconvened at the adult schoolroom on Friar Lane. Back in 1798, a literacy school for adults had been set up there by William Singleton of the Methodist New Connection Church. The Quaker Samuel Fox later took it over and it became the Quaker School. The purpose-built premises also witnessed the country's first Women's Adult School, started by Caroline Howitt and Alice Scanlon. From there the adult school movement spread nationwide.

NWC remained in the Quaker building until 1960, so it was here that Alan Sillitoe would have attended his meetings in the early 1950s. Sillitoe joined the club at the prompting of his friend, Flight Lieutenant Hales, and his wife Madge, a poet.[1] Sillitoe had been impressed by her poetry collection, *Pine Silence* (1950). An article in *Bygones* claimed that Sillitoe won a NWC short story competition with "Mountain Jungle", of which the adjudicator said, 'I have no criticism of it, as it came perfectly into my vision as I read, and I felt that it was something that had been imprinted on the author's mind. The atmosphere has been caught perfectly.' The story appears in the April 1951 edition of *Scribe*, for which Sillitoe also wrote the article "Disaster at Menton" about a French flood.

After briefly meeting in the guild room of the Nottingham Co-operative Society Education Centre in Broad Street, they moved to the Bell Inn on Angel Row in 1960. It was then back to Friar Lane and a new venue, St Luke's House, where the club regularly met between 1966 and 1987. During this spell, in 1970, two of the club's former homes, the Black Boy Hotel and the Albert Hotel, were demolished.

One NWC president was the novelist Eric Malpass (1910–96), who was a household name in Germany. The man from Long Eaton won the *Observer* short story competition in 1955 and the first of his nineteen novels followed two years later. That debut book, *Beefy Jones*, won the Palma d'Oro in Italy for the best humourous novel of the year. In the mid-1960s Malpass ditched his four-decade-long banking career and became a full-time writer. His novel *Morning's at Seven* (1966) was a smash hit across Europe, spanning sixty editions. The story introduced the character Gaylord Pentecost, an innocent seven-year-old hero who observes the lives of his chaotic family with amusement and incredulity. German readers enjoyed Malpass' witty descriptions of rural English family life, and they loved Gaylord, who featured in five more bestsellers, some of which were adapted for German TV. James Last's theme tune for *Morning's at Seven* (*Morgens Um Sieben*) was used by the BBC as their ice-dancing theme. The book's sequel, *The Height of the Moon* (1967), was made into a movie. Malpass' other books include a trilogy of Shakespeare's life and a novel based on the life of Nottinghamshire's Thomas Cranmer entitled *Of Human Frailty* (1987).

A highlight of this time at St Luke's was that NWC had their own radio show, recorded at York House for BBC Radio Nottingham. After leaving St Luke's House it was off to Birkbeck House in Trinity Square, a rather ugly building that wasn't a patch on the old Mechanics Building that it replaced. NWC met in the card room on the first floor, where the Nottingham Mechanics were then based.

By this time another successful writer had succeeded Eric Malpass as club president, Peter Walker (1936–2017). In 1967 Walker wrote *Carnaby and the Highjackers*, the first of eleven books about a flamboyant detective. In 1979 his new series began, *Constable on the Hill*, set in the fictional village of Aidensfield, Yorkshire, and written under the pen name Nicholas Rhea. At this time Walker was a serving policeman. He retired from the force in 1982. Rhea's Constable series with its fictional village bobby inspired the 1960s-set TV show *Heartbeat* which ran for eighteen series, averaging audiences of fourteen million in 2001. An author of over 130 books, Walker founded the Crime Writers' Association's northern chapter. His advice to his fellow NWC members was, 'Ideas are all around. Everything I do, everywhere I go, everything I see is potential material.'

In 2003 NWC relocated to the new home of the Nottingham Mechanics on North Sherwood Street where they still gather. The then Mansfield-based writer Roy

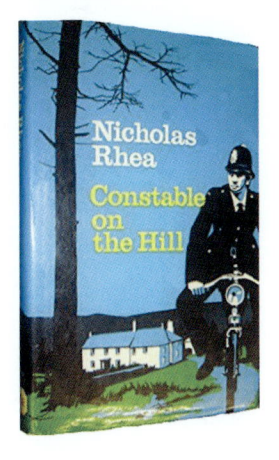

Bainton took over as President in 2007. Bainton has written TV scripts, radio dramas, music tour brochures, biography, novels and poetry, and regularly wrote for NWC's quarterly magazine *Scribe*.

NWC still holds regular poetry and prose competitions, with former members Ena Young, Rosemary Robb, Dolly Sewell and Gladys Bungay all lending their names to trophies. A four-time recipient of the Gladys Bungay Novel Award is long-time member Glenis Wilson, whose reluctant sleuth, Harry Radcliffe, is keeping up the club's great tradition for crime fiction. I'm sure that Francis Vivian, the club's once-famous co-founder, would approve, and of the fact that NWC have entertained the crime writers Stephen Booth, Simon Brett and John Harvey as guest speakers.

Nottingham Writers' Club aims to, 'Provide friendly co-operation among writers and to promote activities for their mutual interest and benefit,' and it welcomes writers at any stage in their writing life.

---

[1] Bradford, 2008.

Chapter 18
Nottingham Playhouse – Made in Nottingham

'Audiences know what to expect, and that is all that they are prepared to believe in.'
Tom Stoppard, *Rosencrantz and Guildenstern Are Dead*

Nottingham Playhouse, North Circus Street.

Nottingham Playhouse has been around for over seventy years, producing world-class theatre, but its origins go back much further, to Hyson Green. At 2 Radford Road, on the corner with Gregory Boulevard, was the Grand Theatre (established 1886), with a fine painted panel on its ceiling and busts of Macready, Bacon, Shakespeare and Byron. Joan Wallace described the Grand in her historical novel *Ragtime Joe* (1998):

> The Grand Theatre did not look too grand from the outside, Joe observed, but as he stepped inside the foyer he changed his mind. A carpet of red and gold spread out before him flanked by ornate gilt framed mirrors that reached up to the ceiling. The carpet flowed up a staircase which had an archway built in the Grecian fashion: either side of the archway, statues of Greek goddesses held torches which displayed flickering gas lights underneath shades of red patterned glass. Miniature palm trees sat in large brass urns and beautiful oil paintings competed with the magnificence of their ornate frames.

By 1920, Hyson Green had a growing working-class population but a falling reputation, and audiences for the Grand's succession of melodramas had suffered. As the once glorious theatre decayed, so the people began avoiding the evening tram ride home. When the

Grand closed, in stepped Virginia Bateman Compton (1853–1940), taking over the lease.

Virginia was the widow of Edward Compton. Together they had headed the Compton Comedy Company, and she thought that she could set up a resident repertory company in Nottingham, and so she revived the ailing theatre. Nottingham had wanted a repertory theatre for some time but, with no public money forthcoming, all attempts had failed. Using money left by her late husband, Mrs Compton splashed out on renovating the venue with new carpets, curtains, oil paintings, antiques and furniture, and it was renamed the Nottingham Repertory Theatre (NRT). One regular visitor to be inspired was the schoolboy Geoffrey Trease.

The theatre opened with *School for Scandal* (as the Theatre Royal had done in 1865). Two of Compton's daughters, Ellen and Viola, helped manage the theatre as well as acting in the plays with their husbands. The third, most famous daughter, Fay, was a celebrated West End actor, playing Ophelia to the Hamlets of Barrymore and Gielgud[1], while Virginia Compton's son, the author Compton Mackenzie – now known for his comic novels *The Monarch of the Glen* (1941) and *Whisky Galore* (1947) – visited Nottingham to put on his specially written play *Columbine*, adapted from his novel *Carnival* (1912). Mackenzie addressed his Nottingham audience at the end of the show. DH Lawrence later contacted Compton Mackenzie after his sisters had attended the play, writing, 'Heard from my elder sister that Nottingham thought [the play] a great success.'

Despite this encouragement, the theatre was soon running out of money. Jesse Boot coughed up some cash, and the recently-formed Nottingham Playgoers' club hosted George Bernard Shaw for a fundraising event, but the Comptons' efforts to establish a repertory theatre was ultimately in vain, and it closed in 1924. In its short time the NRT had staged works by a range of dramatists from JM Barrie to Shakespeare, the last play being Du

Nottingham Repertory Theatre.

Maurier's *Trilby*. The building was sold to Gaumont British and it became a cinema before being demolished in 1964.

After the Second World War the desire for a new repertory theatre resurfaced. As a boy Hugh Willatt had loved his visits to Hyson Green's repertory theatre, of which he later said, 'I had a tremendous diet, chiefly of Shakespeare and the classics, at this theatre early in the 1920s which had a great effect on me.' It also motivated his father and others who, after the NRT closed, yearned for a replacement. 'Because of that failure,' said Willatt, 'they were determined to get another repertory theatre of high quality, a professional theatre, established in Nottingham'.[1]

Despite little civic backing, plans were afoot for the Pringle's Picture Palace on Goldsmith Street, which had been a cinema since 1910. Not knowing if moving pictures had a future, the venue had been originally built as a cine-variety theatre, with a small stage known as the Little Theatre. After much wrangling, in 1948 the small cinema, with its domed corner, became the first Playhouse Theatre in Nottingham. This was under the directorship of André van Gyseghem (1906–1979) with his distinguished company of young actors. The Playhouse opened with George Bernard Shaw's *Man and Superman* and was soon doing well and also providing thirty to forty children's matinées a year. There were limited backstage facilities, no foyer and no bar. The writer and critic Emrys Bryson (1928–2021), in *Portrait of Nottingham* (1974), wrote of people 'battling with a vest-pocket stage, dressing-rooms foetid with boiler fumes, wings so puny that scenery had to be put out in the street, and the sort of acoustics which meant that whenever a fire engine left the station nearby it drowned out the actors' lines.'

In 1958 a twenty-two-year-old Brian Blessed, a coal miner's son straight out of drama school, came to Nottingham to work on the set of Agatha Christie's *Spider's Web*. 'The stage door opened onto the street,' recalled Blessed, who remembered being alone in the theatre when the door opened and a tall elderly lady in a long overcoat appeared. She descended the small staircase and said, 'Hello. My name is Agatha Christie. You can call me Clarissa, my favourite name' (Clarissa was her middle name). Blessed spent a fortnight with the author, who helped him with the set, travelling with him all over Nottingham to secure props for the production. They got on amazingly well, according to Blessed, and had tea in the Arboretum. Christie revealed to Blessed that she was never mad on Poirot, who could overbalance a play. A year later Blessed performed at

Nottingham Playhouse in *Two for the Seesaw*. By now, Val May had joined the Playhouse as Artistic Director, a time of great discussion regarding the building of a new, more suitable venue on Wellington Circus.

A main player in the campaign for a new Playhouse was Hugh Willatt who, as a boy, had been so inspired by Nottingham's first repertory theatre in Hyson Green, and would later become Secretary-General of the Arts Council of Great Britain. In 1961, thanks to a casting vote from the Labour Lord Mayor, the authority finally committed some funding and the new Nottingham Playhouse was to open. The theatre on Goldsmith Street became a furniture shop. It's now a bar called Spankies.

Frank Dunlop, Artistic Director during 1961–1964, oversaw the new Playhouse's inaugural season along with John Neville (a hugely influential, popular and charismatic figure in Nottingham – a studio at the Playhouse bears his name). Nottingham Playhouse was officially opened in 1963 by Lord Snowdon – Princess Margaret was unwell – with a gala performance featuring excerpts from *Coriolanus*, which opened the following evening. The cast included Neville, "Leo" McKern, a young Ian McKellen and an even younger Michael Crawford. In the audience was the theatre's author-in-residence Peter Ustinov.

The Playhouse has always backed local talent and productions with a Nottinghamshire link. In 1965, as part of the Arts Festival, Emrys Bryson's *'Owd Yer Tight* entertained Nottingham and later became a book of the same name. Young Pat McGrath's novel, *Green Leaves of Nottingham* (1972), was adapted and performed by teenage members of the Saturday morning theatre workshop. And by the late 1970s Stephen Lowe was breaking through.

In his mid-teens Lowe had discovered that DH Lawrence had written plays, so he borrowed them from Central Library. Fascinated, especially by *The Daughter-in-law*, a kitchen-sink drama, Lowe hung around the newly-opened Playhouse discussing plays. A decade later Richard Eyre was running Nottingham Playhouse. As a champion of new writers, Eyre commissioned Lowe to write a play. The result was *Touched*. Set around the terraces of Sneinton in 1945 during the days between VE Day and VJ Day, *Touched* focuses on working-class women living with loss and hope as they experience this extraordinary and changing time. The award-winning play celebrated its fortieth anniversary in 2019 with a Playhouse production starring Vicky McClure.

In 1985 the Playhouse marked DH Lawrence's centenary with a performance of *Phoenix Rising*, written by Nottingham's Campbell Kay. Set in France in 1928, the play depicts Lawrence in ill health, reminiscing about his early life.

A more recent Playhouse adaptation has been *Darkness, Darkness* (2016), based on John Harvey's 2014 book of the same name. The then new Nottingham Playhouse and John Neville had been a big factor in Harvey's decision to first come to live in Nottingham, back when he was a newly-qualified teacher. It's fitting that it was here that Harvey's final Resnick novel was brought to the stage, a play that was produced by Giles Croft. Croft became Artistic Director at the Nottingham Playhouse in 1999, a position he would hold for eighteen years, doubling the theatre's in-house productions and producing more than fifty new plays. His directing credits include *Polygraph* (2001), *Any Means Necessary* (2016) and the European premiere of *The Kite Runner* (2013). He also oversaw the implementation of the Nottingham European Arts & Theatre Festivals (neat). Croft has a passion for Tom Stoppard's Olivier Award-winning *Arcadia* – he was one of the first people to read the play when he was literary manager at the National Theatre – and in his fifteenth year at the Playhouse Croft produced the play.

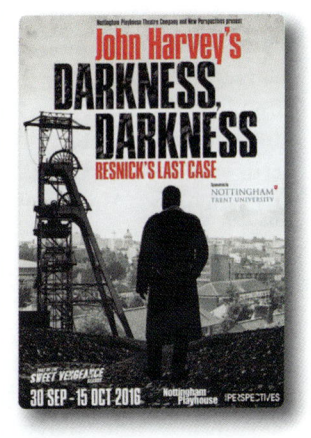

Arguably Britain's greatest living playwright, Sir Tom Stoppard has a strong connection with Nottinghamshire, having been to school here between 1946 and 1951. Stoppard was born Tom Straussler in 1937, in Czechoslovakia. Two years later his Jewish family fled to Singapore to escape the Nazis. Due to the Japanese invasion, which later saw his father killed, Tom moved to Darjeeling, India, with his mother and brother. In 1946, the family emigrated to England after Kenneth Stoppard, a major in the British army, married the boys' widowed mother. Some of this story comes out in Stoppard's latest play *Leopoldstadt*.

When Tom arrived in Nottinghamshire he was eight years old. Within three weeks, he and his brother were adopted by Major Stoppard, and they took his surname. Tom Stoppard was enrolled at the Dolphin Preparatory School. Langford Hall, a Grade II listed country house in Langford, situated in eighty-three acres of parkland, had been bought by Charles Roach who had established a Dolphin school. Stoppard's education in Nottinghamshire, and later Yorkshire, is associated with him feeling 'depressed, longing for the holidays, and a bit homesick, usually to do with the severity of one or two of the teachers'.[3]

His education may have left him feeling 'totally bored by everyone from Shakespeare to Dickens aside,' but he left school wanting to be a great writer, albeit a journalist. After moving to Bristol, a trip to the theatre had a 'tremendous' effect on him and he began writing plays. He has also co-written screenplays and been secretly, and lucratively, hired to improve film scripts, such as for the blockbusters *Robin Hood* and *Indiana Jones and the Last Crusade*.[4]

Of all the playwrights associated with the theatre, the most famous of all is arguably Tennessee Williams. The American writer was in Nottingham in 1978 to see the British premiere of his play *Vieux Carré* at the Playhouse.

Another fine playwright-come-screenwriter is Nottingham's Michael Eaton, who has written four plays for Nottingham Playhouse, including *The Families of Lockerbie* (2010), about how the families of victims of the Lockerbie bombing came to terms with their loss, and *Charlie Peace – His Amazing Life and Astounding Legend* (2013), which starred Peter Duncan as the master criminal and Norman Pace as a Goose Fair showman.

Nick Wood has seen several of his plays performed at Nottingham Playhouse. The former actor, freelance journalist and teacher has been a full-time playwright for the past two decades. Wood is passionate about the Playhouse and the help it has given to writers.

A Playhouse favourite, the former *Evening Post* columnist Amanda Whittington, entered the mainstream with a string of popular and accessible plays featuring the experiences of women. The Playhouse has staged productions of Whittington's *Judy Garland's Life*, *Satin 'n' Steel* and *Amateur Girl*, the story of a woman who lives in a Viccy Centre flat. Whittington has also adapted Alan Sillitoe's *Saturday Night and Sunday Morning* for the stage.

Back in 1964 Frank Dunlop directed David Brett's adaptation of *Saturday Night and Sunday Morning* (April–July 1964) which starred Ursula Smith and Joan Heal, with Ian McKellen as the antihero. McKellen was just one of a number of Seatons to struggle with the Nottingham accent. 'It's not all that difficult, actually, to say "note" instead of "knout",' wrote Sillitoe to his brother in 1992. Twenty years later a musical version of *SN&SM* came to the Playhouse.

The current Artistic Director is the former Arnold Hill School pupil Adam Penford, who opened his tenure with Beth Steel's *Wonderland*, a superb play about the miners' strike. Other Penfold picks include the five-star-rated production of Alan Bennett's *The Madness of George III* (2018), starring Olivier Award-winner Mark Gatiss, and the world premiere of James Graham's new play about the pandemic, *Bubble* (2020), part of a series of live and live-streamed shows. A former Ashfield Comprehensive School student, James Graham fell in love with theatre when working on the door at Nottingham's Theatre Royal. His work for the stage and screen includes *Brexit: The Uncivil War* (2019), *Quiz* (2017) and *Labour of Love* (2017), the latter set in a Mansfield MP's constituency office.

It's impossible to do justice to the vast number of Nottinghamshire writers, poets and performers that have appeared at the Playhouse, which continues to create up to ten new shows each year and employs a full in-house production department.

Take a bow.

---

[1]Bailey, 1994.
[2]McCarthy, 1971.
[3]Gussow, 1995.
[4]Lee, 2020.

Chapter 19
Pitcher & Piano (The Unitarian Church), High Pavement – Little St Mary's

'The church was like a great lantern suspended.'
DH Lawrence, *Sons and Lovers*

Before its various rebuilds, the Unitarian Church on High Pavement was affectionately referred to as Little St Mary's. Now the Pitcher & Piano, the building has links with a number of our writers, including Byron, Lawrence, and the reformer Rev George Walker (1734–1807), Minister of High Pavement Chapel for twenty-four years.

George Walker arrived in Nottingham as a respected mathematician who had recently become a Fellow of the Royal Society. Ordained in Durham, he became a minister on High Pavement, in the Lace Market, in 1774. The congregation had become Unitarian in the early to mid-eighteenth century. Together with the scholar Gilbert Wakefield, with whom he shared an interest in literary matters, Walker ran a discussion group and a weekly literary club. Wakefield said of Walker that he possessed 'the greatest variety of knowledge, with the most masculine understanding of any man I ever knew' (Wakefield, 1804).

Wanting to bring education to as many children as possible, Walker helped to form the Presbyterian High Pavement Charity School (Gordon, 1900). Perhaps inspired by the first Sunday school in England – which had opened nearby in St Mary's Church in 1751 – the High Pavement school began in 1788 as a 'charity school for the children of poor persons,' and it was one of the first non-sectarian charity schools in the country. Manned by volunteers, the school offered a basic level of literacy as part of a full day's education. The plain, brick premises used by the original High Pavement school were built

Pitcher and Piano, High Pavement.

in 1758 (rebuilt in 1846) and it was situated behind the chapel, on the cliff edge.

An annual charity sermon took place for the purpose of fundraising[1] and, in 1796, the 'celebrity' speaker was the then little-known poet Samuel Taylor Coleridge (1772–1834). Before arriving in Nottingham, Coleridge had stopped off at Derby where he met with the better-known poet Erasmus Darwin (1731–1802). Coleridge was doing the rounds as part of his Watchman tour, seeking subscribers for his poetry.

The radical Nottingham bookseller, John Sutton, is likely to have compiled Coleridge's list of subscribers, about 1,200 of them, with the chapel member and silk merchant John Fellows (or Fellowes) (1757–1823) collecting the subscriptions. Coleridge later wrote to Fellows, 'The Ladies, who have honoured me by so delicate an act of liberality, will accept my sincerest acknowledgments. The Poems will be sent forthwith, directed to you & to be left at Mr. Sutton's'.[2]

It was probably at the High Pavement chapel itself that Coleridge delivered his charity sermon to an audience he said was made up of 'all sorts'. The names on his subscription list included members of the leading Whig families who controlled much of the town's wealth. Many of the subscribers were politically active, including Walker's daughter Lady Cayley.

Coleridge's time in Nottingham coincided with a turbulent general election. Nottingham had a reputation as a centre for radicalism, and Walker's congregation was politically the most powerful and opinionated in Nottingham, with twelve of the town's fifteen mayors worshipping there between 1775 and 1800. Walker was to wield much influence, leading special sermons and drafting petitions. He was an early advocate for the abolition of the slave trade, an opponent of the war with America, a campaigner against religious tests in England, and an advocate for Parliamentary reform. His Appeal to the People of England, in opposition to the Test and Corporation Act, was praised by the prominent statesman and champion of liberty, Charles James Fox.

As a highly distinguished pulpit orator, Walker's sermons helped his chapel to attract many of Nottingham's intellectuals and his dissenting voice travelled the county. His reform speech at a meeting in Mansfield in 1782, led William Henry Cavendish-Bentinck, Third Duke of Portland, to compare him with Cicero. The substance of Walker's Mansfield speech is now available in a twenty-page booklet (2010).

Walker was a partner in Major John Cartwright's cotton mill at Retford, known as Revolution Mill, and he looked after Cartwright's business dealings in Nottingham. Cartwright (1740–1824), known as the father of reform, wrote one of the earliest works on reform in Parliament, entitled *Take your Choice*, and he founded the Society for Constitutional Information, advocating universal male suffrage. Like Cartwright, Walker became a leading figure, and he chaired the Associated Dissenters of Nottinghamshire, with an objective to repeal the Test Acts which meant that only people taking communion in the established Church of England were eligible for public employment. In his *Essays* (1809), Walker wrote that, 'it came to be in a considerable degree unsafe to express a difference of opinion from those who were attached to the measures of ministers.'

By 1790, opinion on the French Revolution was dividing the people of Nottingham into two hostile parties, the so-called "democrats", who considered delegated authority, and not titles of nobility, as the only legal power, and the "aristocrats", who submitted to the will of the king, nobility and clergy. Walker's sympathies were with the democrats, whose persuasive means and political pamphlets prompted much vengeful anger from their rivals.

In simply drafting a petition calling for the end to the war with France, Walker had been accused of treason by the aristocrats. One man, for expressing the opinion that England should have its own revolution, had been imprisoned for three months.

With its population of around 25,000, Nottingham was a battleground, the year's general election leading to violent disturbances with windows smashed[3] and stones thrown. After the police had been driven out of the Market Place, troops were sent in and an innocent bystander was shot dead.

In 1792, a letter was sent to the landlady of the democrat-friendly Sun Inn on Pelham Street, threatening to burn down her house.[4] Political rioting, and rioting in general, was commonplace in Nottingham. Many poor people were inspired by the revolutionaries in France, and the town established the Nottingham Constitutional Society, dedicated to advancing the principles of liberty and equality. The reformer Thomas Hardy led a similar society in London and he visited Nottingham to offer his support. The Market Place saw an act of counter-revolutionary nationalism as a rival mob of conservatives burnt a straw effigy of the radical hero Thomas Paine (1737–1809), author of *The Rights of Man* (1791).

In response to the popularity of Paine's book, and the growth of radicalism in Britain, the Royal proclamation against seditious writings and publications was issued by George III, limiting radical literature. It was in this dangerous era that Walker composed a petition for Parliamentary reform, arguing that 'the constitution of these Kingdoms has passed into the grossest abuses, so as to insult the common sense of the nation,' and insisting on universal male suffrage. His petition was signed by 2,000 people in Nottingham and was presented to the House of Commons, only for it to be rejected as seditious.[5]

1794 brought the duckings, when ducking and pumping 'became now the order of the day,' wrote Walker:

> ...and those who live at a distance from Nottingham, will scarcely credit the relation, that such outrages were continued, under the nose of the Chief Magistrate, for upwards of four days; the unfortunate victims having no protection offered them, than being sent to gaol for their further personal security.

A seven-storey mill belonging to Robert Denison, a member of the High Pavement chapel, became a refuge for the democrats before it came under siege from a mob. Walker wrote[6] that:

> the windows of the mill were much demolished before young Denison remonstrated with the mob, and told them the consequence of further outrage. Those within the mill were at last, however, compelled to fire, to prevent the completion of the most horrid threats, not only against the mill, but against the lives of its protectors.

Walker was critical of the local press, whose continued attacks upon those who dared to maintain an independent opinion were making them targets. He wrote, 'It is here seen that even Mr. Denison's respectability (so well known to the inhabitants of Nottingham) could not protect him from popular outrage; because his conduct ran counter to the stream of popular prejudice.'

In his account of the duckings, Walker added:

> This conduct was continued with unabating perseverance, and two countrymen, coming to complain of some outrage they had suffered from their neighbours, on account of their differing from them in political sentiment, were violently taken from the place where the county magistrates were sitting, and conducted to a pump, just at hand, where they were completely drenched, and suffered every

other species of insult and indignity, which the wanton imagination of a mob could suggest.

Of one altercation, Walker wrote that the 'Mayor, apprised of the tumult, repaired to the spot, where he remained a tame and patient spectator of breaking windows, dragging the peaceable inhabitants from their houses, kicking, beating, rolling them in the mud, pumping upon them and ducking them...'

The following year the Seditious Meetings Act 1795 was approved by Parliament. It was another gagging act, with a purpose to restrict the size of public meetings to fifty people. Walker rallied against these measures for the suppression of public opinion, which stated that any place where political meetings took place, with the purpose of discussing the injustice of any law, constitution, government and policy of the kingdoms, must be declared a house of disorder and punished.

Another violently-contested election occurred in 1796 and, by the end of the century, Walker had left Nottingham, resigning in the May of 1798. It was in this month that the poet Lord Byron inherited his title and, by August, the boy Byron was in Nottingham where he became a regular visitor to the church (1798–99), just missing Walker's time here.

George Walker ended his days in Manchester where, from 1804 until his death, he was the President of the Manchester Literary and Philosophical Society.[7] His own writing includes many works published during his time in Nottingham, such as the treatises *Conic Sections* and *On the Doctrine of the Sphere*, *A collection of Psalms and Hymns*, *Life*, *Essays* and *Sermons*, with collections of his speeches and political addresses.

Ruth Bryan (1805–1860) lived on High Pavement at Bethel Cottage, close to the Unitarian church. In *Exploring Nottinghamshire Writers* (2017), Rowena Edlin-White describes Bryan as, 'a mystic and spiritual writer, forgotten in Nottingham but still celebrated in America.'

One unforgettable Nottingham writer is DH Lawrence, and it was at the High Pavement Unitarian Church that Paul comes across Miriam singing hymns towards the end of Lawrence's *Sons and Lovers* (1913). Paul approaches her after the service:

> The large coloured windows glowed up in the night. The church was like a great lantern suspended. They went down Hollow Stone, and

he took the car for the Bridges.

"You will just have supper with me," he said; "then I'll bring you back."

"Very well," she replied, low and husky.

High Pavement Chapel ceased to be a place of worship for Unitarians in 1982 when it was converted into the Nottingham Lace Hall, a museum. Lawrence's great lantern suspended, designed by S Coleman (1874–76) is a fine rebuild, the ornate Gothic style rightly warranting its Grade II listing. The building was converted into the Pitcher & Piano bar in 1998.

---

[1]Thomis, 1968.
[2]Magnuson, 2003.
[3]Gurnham, 2010.
[4]Blackner, 1815.
[5]Thomis, 1969.
[6]Sutton, 1852.
[7]Magnuson, 2003.

Chapter 20
The Playwright, 38 Shakespeare Street – Shakespeare in Notts

'When I read Shakespeare I am struck with wonder that such trivial people should muse and thunder in such lovely language.'

DH Lawrence, *Pansies*

The carving of William Shakespeare on the front of the Arkwright Building now looks across to The Playwright pub (formerly The Orange Tree). In honour of the Bard's *Hamlet* there are lounges called Gertrude's Gaff and Hamlet's Hideout. Back in 1865, when it was the Clinton Arms, Nottingham Forest FC was formed here and there's now a plaque outside stating as much.

Ray Gosling 'escaped' to Nottingham in the early 1960s, first living here in Shakespeare Street at 7 Stratford Square. His tiny, barely furnished room is now part of NTU. Gosling wrote that he 'slipped in and stayed for fifteen years,' hitting the ground running with his first memoir, *Sum Total* (1962). Written when the 1960s were about to take off, it captured England at that moment. Gosling pushed for a life beyond conformity, at a time when the working-class youth were challenging the norms and redefining culture.

If William Shakespeare ever visited Nottingham it was probably in 1615, the year before his death.[1] Nottingham's old Guild Hall, on the south side of Weekday Cross, hosted The King's Players, Shakespeare's company, and the playwright may have joined the group, perhaps even playing a role on stage. The troupe were paid thirteen shillings and four pence by civic leaders. The medieval building has long since been demolished.

The Playwright, Shakespeare Street.

The first Black actor to perform Shakespeare did so in Nottingham.[2] There's an advertisement for a performance of *Julius Caesar*, which played here in 1827, in which an extraordinary novelty is referred to. This "novelty" was the appearance of Ira Aldridge, who became known as the African Roscius.

One of the twentieth century's greatest Shakespearian actors was Sir Donald Wolfit (1902–68). Born in Balderton, near Newark, Wolfit attended the Magnus Grammar School before making his first appearance at the Old Vic Theatre in 1929 as Claudius. By 1937 he had formed the Donald Wolfit Shakespeare Company for which he played most of the major roles. Wolfit was renowned for his portrayal of King Lear.

'How boring, how small Shakespeare's people are! Yet the language so lovely! like the dyes from gas-tar,' wrote DH Lawrence who critiqued the Bard in "When I Read Shakespeare" from his 1929 collection *Pansies*.

Founded in Lawrence's time, in 1904, the Nottingham Shakespeare society meet fortnightly (Sept to May) at Nottingham Mechanics to study the works of Shakespeare and his contemporaries. With readings and lectures, the society enjoys much discussion and learning, with regular visiting speakers. There's now a new fringe/amateur company dedicated to producing quality Shakespeare in Nottingham through readings, workshops and full productions. They go by the name of the Nottingham Shakespeare Company.

In his lifetime, the Chartist-come-Radical Liberal, Henry Thomas Hall (1823–94), amassed a large collection of editions of Shakespeare's works plus related historical and critical works about the dramatist. Since 1960 this collection of over 1,700 volumes has been held at the University of Nottingham. *The works of Mr. William Shakespear*, from the early 1700s, is the earliest book in the collection. The first edition to be illustrated, it was destined for private reading as much as for stage performances.

In the mid-nineteenth century, a local circus clown and music hall star called William Wallett often included Shakespeare's work in his performances. Having memorised vast sections of verse, Wallett would recite them with great gusto, earning himself the title The Shakespearian Jester. Typically wearing a court jester's costume, he combined his humour with a talent for self-promotion, his "Wallett is Here!" posters helping him to sustain his popularity for over half a century.

In 1844 Queen Victoria sent for Wallett, and she was quite amused after seeing his performance at Windsor Castle in front of a large and distinguished party of guests. He may have had no official royal approval but it didn't prevent Wallett from rebranding himself as The Queen's Jester. The title stuck, making Wallett a household name. In the 1871 census, Wallett's mother even listed herself as "Queen Victoria's Jester's mother".

Wallett is said to be the only man to have pawned himself. As Emrys Bryson wrote in his book *'Owd Yer Tight* (1967), Wallett was due to perform in Nottingham when a brace of burly bailiffs accosted him, demanding payment of a debt. Wallett walked the men to a pawnbroker's where he pawned himself for ten pounds. Knowing he was required at the big top, the pawnbroker allowed the jester to remain with him until the ringmaster turned up to buy him out. When Wallett finally appeared in the circus ring, he addressed the crowd:

> Good evening, folks in the pit and the stalls.
> I've just had a rest 'neath the three golden balls.
> I popped myself in for a tenner or more
> To satisfy Shylock's own dogs of the law.

Beeston had become Wallett's home shortly after his second wedding in 1862. In marrying Sarah Farmer his career received a further boost, as her family was connected with many of Nottingham's entertainment venues. In 1879 they moved to 220 Station Road, and on this attractive white house is a blue plaque:

William Frederick Wallett
(The Queen's Jester)
1813–1892
International circus
and stage entertainer
Moved to Beeston in 1862
lived here from 1879

220 Station Road, Beeston.

Having settled in Beeston, Wallett worked as a lecturer and professor of elocution. He died at his home in 1892. A memorial survives in Nottingham's General Cemetery where the jester is buried. Wallett wrote an autobiography, *The Public Life of WF Wallett, The Queen's Jester* (1870).

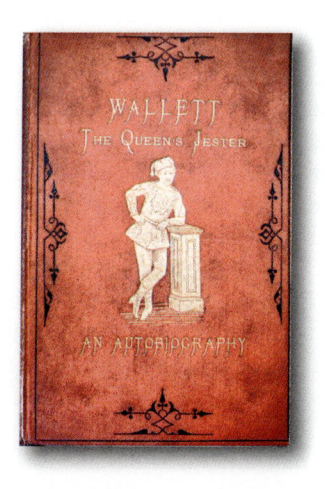

[1] Keenan, 2016.
[2] Wilcox, 2016.

Chapter 21
73 Raleigh Street – A Design for Life

'...the first effects of newly acquired wealth are always seen in the buildings of a town.'

Ken Brand, *Thomas Chambers Hine*

When thoughts turn to architects associated with Nottingham, two names spring to mind, Thomas Chambers Hine and Watson Fothergill. Whilst the latter may be the more flamboyant in his designs, the former leaves the better legacy – and part of this legacy is a literary one, through his granddaughter.

TC Hine designed the majestic Adams Building on Stoney Street, the Great Northern Railway Station (now a gym), the layout and development of The Park estate (including the Park tunnel and many of the estate's houses), Broadway's Birkin Building, the General Hospital (the clock and the chapel) and many other important Nottingham buildings.

Hine was born in Covent Garden, London, in 1813. He was the eldest son of hosiery manufacturer Jonathan Hine. He moved to Nottingham in 1837, forming a partnership with the builder William Patterson and winning a national competition. This led to several important commissions, the first being Nottingham Corn Exchange (1849–50), a building referenced by DH Lawrence in *The Rainbow* (1915). Adjoining the Corn Exchange was the former Artisans' Library. Hine's reputation further grew in the 1850s when he worked for Henry Pelham-Clinton, the Fifth Duke of Newcastle.

A keen autograph collector – Hine's scrapbook of letters and autographs from famous people (including royals, scientists and authors) is in the University of Nottingham's Manuscripts and Special Collections – TC Hine was also a member of Bromley House Library for fifty-five years. The last of his business partners, from 1867, another Bromley House subscriber, was his son George Thomas Hine (1841–1916).

After TC Hine retired in 1890, his son George started his own practice in Westminster on Parliament Street. Moving to London with him was his wife Florence and their two children, Thomas, a future physician, and Muriel Florence Hine (1874–1949), a future novelist.

Born and raised in Nottingham, Muriel Hine was educated at London's Queen's College and in Paris. Her popular light fiction had *The Times* describing her as having a 'gift of infusing life into the characters and an equally striking gift for description.' Several of Hine's novels are set in the 1880s Nottingham – or, as she calls it, Lacingham – of her youth and they provide insight into life here at that time. The semi-autobiographical *A Great Adventure* (1939) covers this period up to her family's move to the capital.

In the book, George Henty, an architect who works in his father's firm, is nearly ruined by his involvement in the collapse of a building society due to fraud and must give up his large house in the village of Whittington. Henty returns to public life and financial stability through the award of the contract to build a large asylum in Lacingham.

Similarly, in real life, George Hine was implicated in a case of malpractice in the early 1880s and the family gave up their large house in Wollaton for lodgings on Standard Hill. Hine's reputation survived the bad press and he won a design competition with his plans for the large new asylum in Mapperley.

In Muriel Hine's version of Nottingham, the Duke of Newcastle becomes the Duke of Tyne and The Park is named the Chase; and as her characters navigate their way around Lacingham their paths exactly match those of Nottingham at that time. Two of her former Nottingham homes feature in her work, 73 Raleigh Street and 25 Regent Street. In 1887, after their struggle, the Hines moved to the house on Raleigh Street known as Simla Villa, a home built by the author's grandfather for her father in 1870, according to Hartwell/Pevsner (2020).

The Regent Street house, on the corner of Oxford Street near the Playhouse, is described accurately in *A Great Adventure*. There is a plaque on the wall of this fine Gothic revival-style home denoting its relevance to TC Hine, who had designed it for his family. The architect lived there until his death in 1899. He was laid to rest in Rock Cemetery in an unmarked grave as he had requested.

Simla Villa, Raleigh Street.

Hine House, Oxford Street.

His fine house also features in Muriel Hine's *Wild Rye* (1931), in which a young woman breaks with expectations, and its sequel *Jenny Rorke* (1932).

In many of her thirty-five novels, Muriel Hine explored the challenges faced by women, including the fight for the vote. One of her books, *The Best in Life* (1918), was made into the silent film *Fifth Avenue Models*, produced by Universal Pictures in 1924. She also wrote plays and song lyrics. After marrying the New Zealand test cricketer Sidney William Coxon she lived in Chelsea, London, where she died.

From *The Man With the Double Heart* (1914):

> You see – to cut it short – you're by way of being a freak! You've got – by want of a better name – what I call a Double Heart. One heart's on your right side and one's in the proper place. It's the most amazing thing I've ever come across. You're perfectly healthy – sound as a bell. I shouldn't wonder, upon my soul, if you hadn't two lives!

Muriel Hine's father and grandfather worked together on many projects in Nottingham, such as the renovations of the burnt-out Nottingham Castle, which they turned into the first municipal museum of art outside of London. For more on TC Hine and his Nottingham buildings, I recommend Ken Brand's *Thomas Chambers Hine: Architect of Victorian Nottingham* (2003).

Chapter 22
15 Regent Street – Keeping Mum

'...the origin, development, and significance of the beautiful customs which have entwined themselves around the fourth Sunday in Lent, the true and ancient day in praise of mothers.'
Constance Penswick Smith,
The Revival of Mothering Sunday

It was on Regent Street that Constance Penswick Smith (1878–1938) and her friend tried to resist Mother's Day and re-establish the true Christian celebration of Mothering Sunday, a campaign that was to last for thirty years.

Mothering Sunday originated in the UK, evolving from a time when Christians would visit their "mother" church. This later became a day when domestic workers were given time off. Many would pick flowers for the church and for their mothers. Other traditions included making a simnel cake for Mother. As the poet Robert Herrick wrote,

'I'll to thee a Simnel bring,/Gainst thou go'st a Mothering.'

Over the pond, Philadelphia's Anna Jarvis was leading a movement that wanted a designated day to celebrate mothers. Jarvis's Mother's Day would be separated from religion and take place on the second Sunday in May, when her own mother had died. Backed by the Mums' Groups established during the American Civil War, President Woodrow Wilson formalised the date in 1914, and it was Jarvis' intention that the American Mother's Day festival should head to the UK. Constance Penswick Smith was outraged and objected immediately to plans for a May Mother's Day in Britain, in addition to the Lent time Mothering

15 Regent Street.

Sunday. She had previously read of Jarvis' campaign in America, and written a play, *In Praise of Mother: A story of Mothering Sunday* (1913). She was primed to respond. Penswick Smith founded The Society for the Observance of Mothering Sunday and warned that the American version would lead to the commercialisation of a meaningful Christian event.

Together with her friend Ellen Porter, Superintendent of the Girls' Friendly Society Hostel in Nottingham, Penswick Smith set up the campaign's headquarters at 15 Regent Street,[1] the end townhouse in a row of five designed by TC Hine. Smith and Porter designed Mothering Sunday cards for children to give to their mothers, while Penswick Smith collected appropriate hymns, and wrote plays and articles. After writing *A Short History of Mothering Sunday* (1915), she published her influential *The Revival of Mothering Sunday* (1921), aiming to reconnect simnel cakes with other surviving local customs.

Religious groups were not entirely accepting of her plans but, in time, *A Short History of Mothering Sunday* made a mark. After Rev Mr Killer of Sneinton's St Cyprians chose to give life to Penswick Smith's collected hymns, she went to live in his parish.

Penswick Smith first arrived in Nottinghamshire at the age of twelve, when her father was appointed the vicar of All Saints, Coddington. She was schooled in Newark and there's a plaque in the centre of the town, at Church House, 3 Church Walk – an attractive building in the grounds of the Church of St Mary Magdalene – which says:

Constance Penswick Smith
1878-1938
Who revived Mothering Sunday, attended school in this building.

Church House, Newark.

After two years as a governess in Germany, Penswick Smith returned to Nottingham and worked for Dr Thomas Mallett in Park

Row before dedicating her time to the defence and revival of Mothering Sunday. Constance Penswick Smith died in 1938, aged sixty. She had continued to write Mothering Sunday poems and cards until her death. She is buried in the grounds of All Saints Church, Coddington, where there are three stone cross headstones in a row belonging to the family. The largest of these is inscribed:

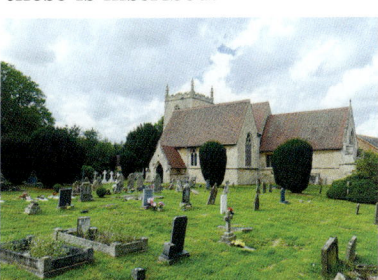

The gravestones of the Penswick Smiths.

In loving memory of Constance Penswick Smith, founder of the movement for the revival of the observance of Mothering Sunday and dearly loved daughter of Charles Penswick and Mary C. Smith, Born 28th April 1878, Entered paradise 10th June 1938. "Always abounding in the work of the Lord".

All Saints Church, Coddington.

The stone next to hers marks where her father is buried: 'Vicar of this parish for 32 years'.

Ellen Porter carried on the movement's work from her home on Marston Road in Bakersfield until her own death in 1942. Even today you'll find many people objecting to the use of "Mother's Day", insisting that it should be "Mothering Sunday", and the commercial nature of Mother's Day remains a bugbear. Even Anna Jarvis bemoaned the commercialisation, disapproving of Mother's Day cards with printed messages on them, saying, 'A printed card means nothing except that you are too lazy to write to the woman who has done more for you than anyone in the world.'

Constance Smith never became a mother, neither did Anna Jarvis. Both women agreed that their original sentiments had been sacrificed for profit.

---

[1]Wilcox, 2016.

Chapter 23
School of Art – Illustrious Illustrators

'It was a well-lighted building, with a tower, adjacent to the Arboretum Park, overlooking the General Cemetery.'

Cecil Roberts, *A Terrace in the Sun.*

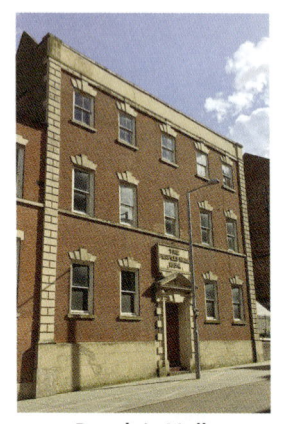

The Nottingham School of Art has had a hand in producing some of our nation's best-loved comic book characters. The Nottingham School of Design opened in 1843 at the People's Hall, on what's now Heathcoat Street, and moved to Plumptre House, Stoney Street, in 1852 and, six years later, to Commerce Square, off High Pavement. All three venues were chosen for their proximity to the Lace factories they served, for the school was established to provide instruction in design for Nottingham's manufacturers.

People's Hall, Heathcoat Street.

In 1863, a site was purchased on Nottingham's Waverley Street for the building of a new home for the school, and work shortly began. By 1865 architect F Bakewell's plans for the then College of Art and Design were realised.

Some of the school's former students have gone on to make great strides in illustrated storytelling. You may be unfamiliar with their names but you'll know some of their creations.

Thomas Henry Fisher was born in Eastwood in 1879, his family moving to Nottingham soon after, and it was here that he attended the Nottingham Government School of Design as it was then known. As a fifteen-year-old student, Thomas Henry (the name he was published under), began to work for the *Nottingham Guardian*, and it was for

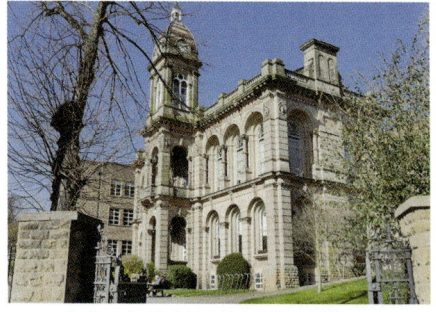

School of Art, Waverley Street.

134

the *Football Post* that his cartoons were first published. Representing the local teams, he created the characters Forester, Magpie and Stag, for regular cartoons until the late 1960s. By the time he lived in Cotgrave and then Plumtree, Henry's sketches were being featured in *Punch* after he'd impressed the satirical magazine with a drawing he'd made of his brother. Another break came when he took over as the artist on the Ally Sloper comic strips. The paper *Ally Sloper's Half Holiday* called itself 'the largest selling paper in the world.' It shifted copies to the working-class and gained a cult middle-class following. Sloper, an archetypal lazy schemer, was often depicted dodging his creditors.

Critical acclaim accompanied Henry's work with The Royal Academy, and the gallery at Nottingham Castle displayed his art. He also worked on the famous Player's Cigarettes' Sailor, used on the Navy Cut packets for Nottingham-based firm John Player's, an image described in Fleming's *Thunderball* (1961).

By 1920 Thomas Henry had established himself as an illustrator for many leading publications including *Strand Magazine* and *London Mail*, saucy postcards and children's books. But Henry is best known for illustrating the thirty-three book *Just William* series, chronicling the adventures of the unruly schoolboy William Brown.[1] First published in 1922, Richmal Crompton's popular stories followed an impish eleven-year-old, a grubby-kneed, unruly-haired, grinning character, brought to life by Henry for nearly fifty years. Throughout this time, Henry also crafted other characters in the stories, including Violet Elizabeth Bott, William's flame-haired nemesis and the spoiled daughter of the local millionaire. The characters changed little but the stories adapted to meet the time and settings right up to 1970. Henry's writer-illustrator relationship with Crompton lasted for forty-three years, but they met only once, at a book festival in Nottingham in 1958.

Born into poverty in 1870, Nottingham's Tom Browne became one of the most famous illustrators of the Edwardian era, and one of the most influential of all time. By the age of eleven, Browne had run away from school and was working as an errand boy in the Lace Market, before taking an apprenticeship at a firm of lithographic printers. Here he began moonlighting, sketching cartoons, one of which he sold to the comic paper *Scraps*. The Nottingham School of Art honed his skills before he moved to London and produced full-page strips and magazine illustrations for *Punch* and *The Tatler*. In an 1896 edition of *Chips*, his characters Weary Willie and Tired Tim first appeared. Browne's loveable tramps became a regular feature, adorning the front cover of *Chips* for fifty-seven years.

The famous striding upper-class character used as the logo for Johnnie Walker whisky was another of Browne's creations, but it's his comedic wandering tramps that have had the most enduring influence. From *The Beano* and *The Dandy* to Charlie Chaplin's famous little tramp with his ill-fitting jacket, many creations have followed suit. Chaplin said, 'I started the tramp to make people laugh because those other old tramps, Weary Willie and Tired Tim, had always made me laugh.'

Also famous for his postcards, Browne was a gifted watercolour artist, his postcard of Nottingham Castle is, typically, signed 'Tom B'. Browne and the writer Robert Machray depicted the inequality and poverty of London in their book *The Night Side of London*, for which Browne produced ninety-five illustrations that captured the era. Browne returned to Nottingham and, in 1897, he used the profits from his sketches to set up a lithographic colour printing firm that ran as Tom Browne & Co until 1954. Browne's art inspired many cartoonists and illustrators by the way in which his characters communicated nonverbally through their postures, mannerisms, gestures and facial expressions. Gifford (1990) said, '...his true living legacy may be seen in any copy of almost any British comic.'

Browne's style influenced the work of Dudley D Watkins, another graduate of Nottingham's School of Art, and a fellow founder of the Sketch Club of Chelsea. Watkins moved to Nottingham in 1910 when he was three years old. Before attending the School of Art, aged fifteen, he'd already had illustrations published in *The Beacon*, the in-house magazine of Boots the Chemist, when, in 1936, DC Thomson launched a comic supplement to the *Sunday Post* for whom Watkins created illustrations. He worked on RD Low's *The Broons*, about a working-class Scottish family who live in a tenement flat, and *Oor Wullie*, about a mischievous spiky-haired, dungaree-wearing, nine-year-old lad. Both of the *Sunday Post's* strips were hugely popular and still exist in bi-annual album form.

A couple of years later, Thomson's Publishing released their first childrens' comics *The Dandy*, for which Watkins drew Desperate Dan, and *The Beano*, for which he created Lord Snooty and Biffo the Bear. Watkins' later characters included Mickey the Monkey for *The Topper* and Ginger, for *The Beezer*. So important was Watkins' work that during the Second World War he was allowed to work his National Service in a way that allowed him to continue with his drawings, and from 1946 onwards, Watkins was given the unusual privilege of signing his work.[2]

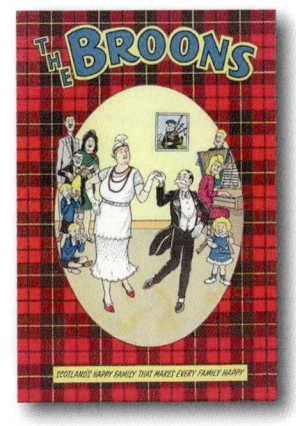

Watkins also produced serial comic adaptations of classic novels, with *Oliver Twist* and *Treasure Island* among his efforts. His intention to produce the Bible in comic form died with him in 1969. In Thomas Henry, Tom Browne and Dudley D Watkins, Nottingham and its School of Art has shaped the world of comic strips as we know them.

Daybrook's John Stuart Clark (AKA Brick) has been living and drawing in Nottingham for over half a century. A cartoonist on political, environmental and social issues, with regular slots in newspapers and magazines, Brick's first graphic novel *Depresso: or How I Learned to Stop Worrying and Embrace Being Bonkers* (2010) was shortlisted for the UK MIND Book of the Year Award. His latest as editor is the World War One anthology, *To End All Wars*, nominated for two Eisner Awards, and in 2021 he published *Mad Day at Gotham Village*, a humorous prose based on *The Merrie Tales of the Mad Men of Gotham*. He is the UK's only honorary visiting professor in comics.

Nottingham has grown a reputation as a centre for comic books. The first Nottingham cartoon festival, Big Grin, took place on Broad Street in 2002, a decade before Nottingham Comic Con was founded to celebrate comics and support charity. The annual family event with a comics theme was set up by Kev and Kel Brett, a husband-and-wife team. There's Nottingham Does Comics, a bi-monthly forum, by and for anybody interested in reading, creating, publishing, selling or studying new work and ideas in the medium. And there's Page 45, a bookshop that's been selling a wide range of comics and graphic novels since being created in 1994 by Mark

Simpson (1968–2005) and Stephen L Holland, the UK's Comic Laureate for 2021. Holland said, 'I want to empower young minds with the knowledge that they can create for themselves.' Page 45 won the Diamond Comics Award for Best Retailer in the UK, and the shop, at 9 Market Street, works with school libraries to promote literacy in and outside the classroom.

Also using the medium of comics to promote literacy is the book and project *Dawn of the Unread* by James Walker (producer/editor) and Paul Fillingham (art/digital producer), which imagines a scenario whereby dead writers from Nottingham's past return from the grave, incensed at the closing of libraries and low literacy levels.

Besides comics, the School of Art boasts other skilled illustrators and artists to have entered the literary world. The social historian and prominent author Dorothy Hartley (1893–1985) attended the school and returned as a teacher. Hartley's books cover six centuries of English history, but she's best-known for *Food in England* (1954). A huge seller, *Food in England* is both a cookery book and a history of British cuisine and culture. The book has had a big influence on many contemporary cooks and food writers. Still in print, it was described by Delia Smith as, 'A classic book without a worthy successor – a must for any keen English cook.'

In 1970 the School of Art merged with Trent Polytechnic and in 1992 it became part of NTU. The most famous artist to have attended the School of Art is Laura Knight (1877–1970). Born Laura Johnson, in Long Eaton, her father abandoned his wife and daughters, leaving Laura to grow up in Nottingham – there's a plaque on her Noel Street home – with her sister, mother, grandmother and great-grandmother.[3] Their financial difficulty was due to her family's repeated failures in the declining lace industry. Educated at Brincliffe School on Forest Road, and briefly in France, Laura returned to Nottingham and, aged thirteen, enrolled as an artisan student at the School of Art, paying no fees. Her mother taught art part-time at the school and at home. After she died, Laura took over her classes whilst studying herself. She was barely in her teens. Sitting on her right was the school's star student, palette in hand, a pale, dark-haired seventeen-year-old called Harold Knight. Three years later they were married, moving to Yorkshire when Laura was aged twenty. They were together nearly sixty years, both finding fame as artists.

Laura Knight often painted marginalised communities, including Travellers and circus performers – who she'd first spotted at Goose

Fair – and workers in the American South. In 1929 she was the only woman painter to have been made a dame. Knight confessed to being 'crackers about the theatre'[4] and her art studio often welcomed actors, writers and poets. Her own books include two autobiographies: *Oil Paint and Grease Paint* (1936) and *The Magic of a Line* (1965). The latter tells the story of an adventurous love of life and documents her work in the Second World War as a war artist and her work for the Royal Academy. *Oil Paint and Grease Paint* is arguably the better read. It tells of her perseverance as she became part of the male-dominated British art establishment. Knight's words paint a fascinating picture, just as her pictures tell a thousand words.

[1]Cadogan, 1990.
[2]Clark, 1989.
[3]Wilcox, 2008.
[4]McCarthy, 1971.

Chapter 24
St Mary's Church and the Lace Market –
Historic Happenings

'St Mary's, the beautiful mother church of Nottingham...'
Geoffrey Trease, *Nottingham: A Biography*

The Church of St Mary the Virgin (St Mary's) in Nottingham's Lace Market is the city's oldest medieval building. The present church is well over five hundred years old. This is at least the third church to have been on the site, as it has been repeatedly burnt down and rebuilt.

The church has thirty-seven stained or painted glass windows. One of these, in the Lady Chapel, depicts Nottingham-born Katherine Monica Wade-Dalton in her Nottingham lace wedding dress and veil, next to a depiction of her patron saint. A week after her wedding at St Mary's, Katherine was back there for her funeral, a victim of the 1918 Spanish flu. She was the daughter of Gustav Albert Flersheim who ran a nearby lace factory. The window was provided by her heartbroken husband and family who had it designed by the highly-regarded Burlison and Grylls company, best known for the South Rose window in Poets' Corner at Westminster Abbey.

The window at St Mary's is a rare surviving memorial to the more than one hundred million people that lost their lives to the virus, including 6,000 people in Nottingham in just one month. At that time, it was 'impossible to walk in the streets without meeting several funeral processions,' reported the *Nottingham Daily Express*, and there wasn't enough space in Nottingham to store the bodies. As a nine-year-old boy, the writer Geoffrey Trease had been aware of the deaths, later writing, 'I lay in bed with the influenza that was raging across Europe and listened to the horse-drawn funerals rumbling and clattering down our cobbled road on their way to the cemetery.'

St Mary's Church, The Lace Market

DH Lawrence may have left Nottingham by the time of the flu but he wasn't to escape the disease, which put him in bed for a month.

In 2018 Catharine Arnold wrote *Pandemic 1918: The Story of the Deadliest Influenza in History*. She told me that it was, 'a tough book to write, very upsetting. I wanted to tell the story of the pandemic – such a horrific tragedy – through hundreds of personal testimonies. Only that way can the true horror be brought to life.'

Both of Arnold's father's parents, Mr and Mrs Gladwin, died in the epidemic, a bereavement that left him with a lifelong depression. Catharine Arnold grew up in Nottingham, attending Hollygirt School and Clarendon College, and she's been back living here since 1988. For four years she worked on the *Nottingham Evening Post* as a trainee, then as a feature writer and sub, and has written novels and popular non-fiction around the subjects of death, sex, madness, crime and punishment.

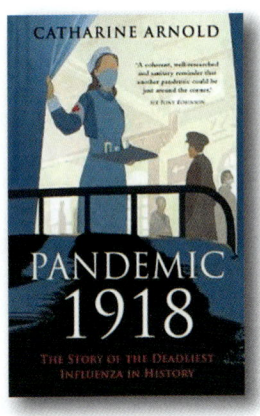

The pioneering journalist Gilbert Mabbot (1622–70) was baptised at St Mary's. The son of a Nottingham cobbler, or cordwainer, Mabbot was the official licenser of the press from 1647 to 1649. Mabbot, mentioned in *The Diary of Samuel Pepys*, became a prolific writer of newsletters and he assisted John Rushworth in compiling the *Historical Collections*, a history of the Civil War period.

Also baptised at St Mary's was the poet and writer Lucy Joynes (1782–1851), whose poems are published in several books. Often religious in nature and child-friendly, her 'original poetry for infant and juvenile minds,' has also recorded many notable Nottingham events. Joynes' 1844 book, *Original Rhymes Accompanying an Historical Chart of the Borough of Nottingham*, in particular, is of local interest.

Predominantly a writer for children, Jane Jerram (1815–72) wrote under two names, her birth name Jane Elizabeth Holmes and Mrs Jerram. She was married at St Mary's in 1836. Under the wing of Nottingham writer Mary Howitt (1799–1888), Jerram wrote in the easiest language she could command 'so that a child of three years old can understand it,' as she wrote in her introduction to her 1850 book *The Child's Own Story Book; Or, Tales and Dialogues for the Nursery.*

Dame Agnes Mellers, widow of the Mayor and bell founder Richard Mellers, established a Free School here in the parish of St Mary's in 1513,[1] partly as an act of atonement for her husband's wrongdoings against the people of Nottingham. King Henry VIII sealed the foundation, and an annual founders' day service still takes place in the church. The school later became the Nottingham High School which, after more than 500 years of teaching boys, is now co-educational.

As early as 1751, St Mary's had opened a Sunday school, pioneering Sunday education for children unable to attend day school. In addition to gaining religious understanding, pupils were taught to read and write.

George Fox (1624–91), dissenter and founder of the Quaker Society, was first imprisoned after attending a service at St Mary's in 1649, at which he had interrupted the sermon after disagreeing with the preacher.

Robin Hood was arrested in St Mary's in *Robin Hood and the Monk,* one of the oldest existing ballads, written about 1450. Robin was unhappy because he couldn't go to Mass. Devoted to the Virgin Mary, he decided to attend a service in Nottingham, accessing St Mary's through a tunnel from the law courts. Having ignored Much the Miller's son's advice to take at least twelve men, Robin had set off with just Little John, who left him after a disagreement following a bet. At St Mary's, a treacherous monk tipped off the Sheriff of Nottingham, whose men arrested Robin in the church porch as he tried to escape. Before his arrest Robin managed to strike the sheriff's helmet with enough force to break his own sword in half.

Among those buried in the grounds of St Mary's is Abigail Gawthern. The celebrated diarist left a fascinating record of Nottingham's cultural and social life in Georgian times. A gift for historians, the diary was discovered in the 1960s in a Norfolk bookshop and copied into one important volume.

The first history book of Nottingham was written by an immigrant, a German doctor by the name of Charles Deering (c1690–1749) who has an association with 1 Kayes Walk, the walkway adjacent to St Mary's Church, which is located on the site of the former Plumptre House. Born Georg Karl Dering (or perhaps Döring) in Saxony, he was educated in Hamburg, Leyden and Paris, receiving his degree in Rheims in 1718.[2] In 1735, when he was in his mid-forties, Deering came to live in Nottingham. Well-travelled and supremely knowledgeable, the skilled physician and speaker of eight languages arrived here with fine references, only to fail to establish a medical practice. Instead, he had to work at the practice of Dr Cox, a man who treated most of the paying patients, leaving Deering to pick up the rest.[3] Deering struggled to ingratiate himself with local society and was said to be short-tempered and always looking to be fed dinner.

He stayed in Nottingham for the rest of his life and authored work in 1737 and 1738 on *An Account of an impartial method of treating the Small-pox* and *A catalogue of Plants growing about Nottingham* respectively. The work on Nottingham's medicinal plants cost subscribers half a crown. He then focused on writing a history of the town of Nottingham.

Local MP John Plumptre, who lived in Plumptre House, supported Deering's endeavour, supplying documents and information. Unlike other local historians of his era, Deering was not tied to religion or political influence, and he pressed on with what he wanted to be the authoritative story of Nottingham. Nottinghamshire's first historian, Robert Thoroton, had been a committed Royalist and, in his role as a magistrate, had a record of persecuting the Quakers. Deering had no such leanings. Thoroton had obsessed over the county's churches and landowners, whilst Deering wanted to capture contemporary Nottingham and the lives of its working people. Deering's work was written to give 'an historical account of the ancient and present state of the town of Nottingham.'

Still practising as a doctor and living in poverty, Deering refused Plumptre's offer of financial assistance and finished his manuscript, which was ready to be printed in 1743. He addressed it to 'the candid reader' with a dedication to the Duke of Newcastle, then Lord Lieutenant. Only ninety-one people showed any interest in subscribing. Deering was forced to wait, using the time to expand and edit his work from his room on the south side of St Peter's Church. After five more years of asthma, gout and poverty, and still waiting for its publication, Deering died. He was surrounded by books and manuscripts.

There was no money to bury him. The only item of any real monetary value he'd left behind was his unpublished manuscript, entitled *Nottinghamia Vetus et Nova, or an Historical Account of the Ancient and Present State of the Town of Nottingham*. Two of the men to whom he was indebted, George Ayscough and Thomas

Willington, paid for Deering to be buried in St Peter's churchyard.[4] Two years later it was Ayscough, a printer, who published Deering's great work, complete with thirty-two attractive copperplates, including a plan of Nottingham produced by John Badder and Thomas Peat (in 1744), which was superior to earlier maps of Nottingham. With information on Nottingham's demography, food supply, climate, and local industries, the book provides a valuable record of the town as Deering knew it in 1749. At this time, framework-knitting was Nottingham's fastest growing industry, and the book includes detailed drawings and descriptions of the hand-operated stocking-knitting frame used at that time.

John Plumptre MP's (1712–91) support of Deering was crucial. His home, Plumptre House, was built in 1730 and designed by Colen Campbell, who intended its architectural standard to rival the Castle. The Georgian house, on Stoney Street near St Mary's Church, was befitting of the Plumptres, who had been a prominent land-owning family in Nottingham since the days of Edward I (1239–1307). John Plumptre was the last of them to live in Plumptre House, which was purchased in 1853 by Richard Birkin and demolished to make way for his new warehouses on Broadway, a new street, built by TC Hine in 1855–56, the orange-tinted warehouses positioned on an attractive serpentine route.

Broadway, The Lace Market.

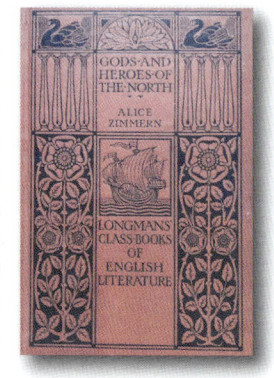

Lace merchant Hermann Theodore Zimmern, a German Jewish immigrant, and his wife Antonia Marie Therese Regina Zimmern's youngest daughter, Alice Zimmern (1855–1939), was born at Postern Street, Nottingham.[5] She became a writer, translator and pioneering advocate for women's education and suffrage. Zimmern's books made a big contribution to the debate on women's rights, and she mixed with fellow suffragist authors Edith Bland, Eleanor Marx and Beatrix Potter. A writer of popular children's books, Zimmern collaborated with her sister Helen in opening up much European culture and thought to the British public.

Based on diligent research into the declining Nottingham lace industry of the late nineteenth century, Hilda Lewis's novel *Penny Lace* (1946) captures the difficulties faced by the Lace Market's factories. In the book, Nicholas Penny sets out to take advantage of the changing industry, at a cost to his former boss and father-in-law's factory. Hilda Lewis (1896–1974) corresponded with several lace manufacturers before writing her novel. In the book we discover that as trade in the Lace Market suffered, Nottingham lace was being made in Paris – on Nottingham machines.

After serving his apprenticeship to a Newark draper, Worksop-born Thomas Adams (1807–73) was tricked into going to Paris where he was robbed and abandoned. In a story befitting that of a Hilda Lewis hero, Adams grew his lace business from a small house on Stoney Street, to 14/15 St Mary's Gate, where he remained for twenty years. He made his reputation building many of the Lace Market's warehouses. The largest and finest of these, and perhaps the grandest Victorian building in Nottingham, was designed by Hine for Thomas Adams. The Adams Building housed a library and hosted a book club for its many lace workers. It later held the Nottinghamshire Readers and Writers Festival, opened by Alan Sillitoe. In 1997–99 the building was converted to New College.

Thomas Adams' fortunes had first taken a turn for the better when he married Lucy Cullen, daughter of a Nottingham businessman, in St Mary's Church in 1830. Readers of *Penny Lace* will note the similarity.

The Adams Building, Lace Market.

Another of the big employers was I and R Morley Limited, hosiers of Nottingham. One of their workers was Rusticus (1827–1909) AKA George Hickling of Cotgrave, who received the accolade of being 'the truest poet in our locality' and who declared, 'O Nottingham! Nottingham! Glorious old town, So famous, so favoured, so high in renown!'

The writer Derrick Buttress (1932–2017) had been a Lace Market factory worker after leaving the Player school, a period he covers in his second memoir, *Music While You Work* (2007). Today you're much more likely to bump into a writer than a lace worker and the area is now part of Nottingham's Creative Quarter. The literature development agency Writing East Midlands (WEM) has its office on Stoney Street. For over ten years WEM have been supporting writers with mentoring programmes, workshops and events like its Lyric Lounge spoken word evenings, which have inspired many people from all walks of life to write or perform publicly, and Write Here Sanctuary, enabling asylum seekers and refugees in Nottingham to counter hostile attitudes via a poetry anthology *Riding on Solomon's Carpet* (2017).

For more on the Lace Market, seek out the Nottingham Civic Society book, *The Lace Market, Nottingham* (1991) by Geoffrey Oldfield, since updated (2002), and the booklet *Walkabout the Lace Market* (1990) by Doug Ritchie, which the author concludes with his poem, "The Lace Market".

---

[1]Carlisle, 1818.
[2]Becket and Smith, 1999.
[3]Evelyn, 1738.
[4]Mellors, 1924.
[5]Creffield, 2004.

Chapter 25
Tanners Estate Agents, Pelham Street – Pan's People

'He was a poet; and they are never exactly grown-up.'
JM Barrie, *Peter Pan in Kensington Gardens*

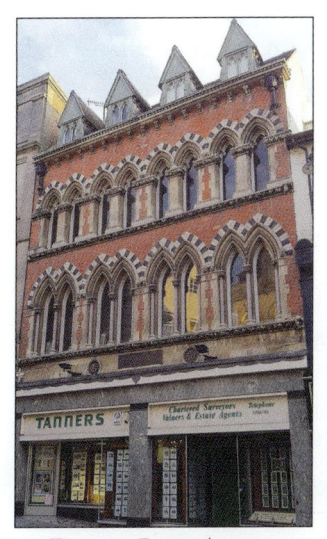

In 1883 a young James Matthew Barrie cut his literary teeth in Nottingham on Pelham Street. His sister Jane had passed him an advert she'd spotted in *The Scotsman* for a lead-writer on the *Nottingham Journal*. Barrie applied, having previously been turned down by *The Liverpool Post*. He sent the *Journal* one of his old university essays as an example of his style of writing. It worked and he was offered the job.

The *Journal* wanted him to start work the following Monday. Barrie failed to disclose that he'd no idea what leaders were or how they were written. Springing into action, he gathered together all the pieces of newspaper he could, emptying his mother's boxes for the lining of old papers and putting them on a pile. Then, he wrote, 'Surrounded by these, I sat down and studied how to become a journalist.'

It was on the cold February train to Nottingham that Barrie penned his first piece for the newspaper. On arrival at their Pelham Street office, he handed in the article, then found somewhere to stay. That place was 5 Birkland Avenue, off Annesley Grove, North Sherwood Street, where a green plaque now states:

Tanners Estate Agents, Pelham Street.

5 Birkland Avenue

JM Barrie,
author of "Peter Pan,"
lived here 1883–84

Each Monday Barrie was asked to contribute a special article for the daily paper. He would 'enter the mind of another for the space of a column, adopt the standpoint least expected by the reader, then proceed to inject into the affair as much cynicism and laconic humour as his spirits could muster'.[1]

Barrie's articles were written under the name Hippomeres and, writing the leaders and whatever else he wished, Barrie was quite happy in Nottingham, despite spells of loneliness and having no friends. In his spare time Barrie began planning a novel, his Nottingham novel,[2] which became *When a Man's Single* (1888), first published at Barrie's expense, before it was serialised in the Hodder & Stoughton-owned *British Weekly*. In the book, the *Nottingham Journal* becomes the *Daily Mirror*, and Nottingham is Silchester.

There's an attractive plaque on the side of Tanners, Chartered Surveyors, marking Barrie's time at the *Journal*. It reads:

> In Honour of James Matthew Barrie BART OM 1860–1937 who in 1883 & 1884 worked in this building on the staff of The Journal.

Barrie was let go in 1884 as the paper couldn't afford his wages of three pounds a week. Barrie's work in Nottingham as an editor-leader-writer was his first and last work as a journalist. His next job was in London, writing freelance, but Nottingham might have helped provide the playwright with inspiration for his most famous story, that of Peter Pan.

Pan didn't appear until 1902 in *The Little White Bird*, a novel Barrie had written for adults, but he is likely to have been living in Barrie's mind since childhood. Barrie was known to have constantly updated the story, and it is suggested that an early development came after the writer witnessed a street urchin wandering through Clifton Grove. One of Barrie's typically cynical articles for the *Nottingham Journal* in January 1884, entitled "Pretty Boys", offers a hint at what was to come, and there is much of the Arboretum about Neverland. However, the main inspiration for a boy for whom death would be 'an awfully big adventure' is likely to be traced back to his older brother, who died in a skating accident aged just thirteen. Barrie later said that his mother had taken some comfort from his story of the boy who would never grow up.

Perhaps Robin Hood also had an influence. In Barrie's original stage productions Peter would wear auburns, tans, browns and cobwebs, a Hood-like appearance. Disney's versions of *Peter Pan* and *Robin Hood* also share a similar look.

John Drinkwater (1882–1937) is another playwright who began his working life in this Pelham Street building. He worked as a junior clerk in the office of the Northern Assurance Company underneath the paper's offices. Drinkwater arrived here as a fifteen-year-old, straight from finishing his education. The office boy had charge of the stamp book and spent much of his time copying letters. He was so poor and hungry that he had to buy rotten fruit from the Market Place to augment his threepenny lunch. He hated the office but had no regrets regarding his three years in Nottingham. 'Well, I was quite happy there, quite happy,' he said.[3]

It was in Nottingham that Drinkwater made his first stage appearance, in an adaptation of *Tom Jones* at the Mechanics. He continued to experience Nottingham's amateur theatrical scene and may even have written his first poem here before moving to his employer's Birmingham branch, joining the local repertory theatre. Drinkwater has been credited with changing public perceptions of the poet Lord Byron for the better, thanks to his *The Pilgrim of Eternity* (1932).

The building where Drinkwater worked extended to Victoria Street, where Nottingham's literary society, the Nottingham Sette of Odde Volumes used to meet. The Sette of Odde Volumes, founded in 1878 by the German-born British bookseller and collector Bernard Quaritch, was a dining club for bibliophiles. The London club could count among its members many of the late nineteenth century and early twentieth century's literati, including Oscar Wilde, George Bernard Shaw and Bram Stoker. Their gatherings would include readings from the members and their guests. The Nottingham branch met fortnightly to discuss and read literature. JM Barrie became a member and, later in life, he was said to have been moved when he was made an honorary member of the group.

Barrie would have met John Potter Briscoe, who had co-founded the Nottingham Sette of Odde Volumes. A former sub-librarian in Bolton, Potter Briscoe was appointed as the Chief Librarian of the Nottingham municipal libraries in 1869, a role he undertook for forty-five years. An original member of the Library Association,

Briscoe was a leading figure in the development of professional librarianship and he extended Nottingham's services to provide children's books.

The year before he took the role around 70,000 volumes had been issued. The year he left, that number had risen to nearer half a million. On leaving his chief librarian role, Potter Briscoe was made Consulting City Librarian, his son getting his old job.[4] John Potter Briscoe authored many books, mostly of local interest, such as *Stories about the Midlands* (1883), a collection of anecdotes relating to Nottinghamshire and elsewhere, and the illustrated *Bypaths of Nottinghamshire History* (1905).

---

[1]Birkin, 2003.
[2]Roberts, 1970.
[3]Roberts, 1970.
[4]Mellors, 1924.

Chapter 26
Theatre Royal – Putting on a Show

'We must prove to the world that we are all nincompoops.'
Baroness Orczy, *The Scarlet Pimpernel*

In April 1865 the Lace Market's theatre-turned-music-hall in St Mary's Gate closed, having been there for over a hundred years. It reopened as Middleton's Alhambra Palace of Varieties but had gone for good by the end of the century.[1] Fortunately for Nottingham, in the September of 1865, the new Theatre Royal opened its stage doors.

Nottingham's only surviving Victorian theatre has been a recognisable local landmark ever since, in part due to Charles J Phipps' classic façade and Corinthian columns, Phipps being the first great theatre specialist. The brothers, lace dressers and councillors, William and John Lambert, provided the £15,000 for the six months of work needed to build the original theatre. They selected its location at the top of the steep gradient of Market Street as they wanted their 'temple of drama' to crown the vista. Intended as a place of 'innocent recreation and of moral and intellectual culture,' the theatre doors opened at 6.30pm on Monday 25 September. The national anthem was followed by Richard Sheridan's comedy of manners, gossip and amorous goings on, *The School for Scandal*, directed by Walter Montgomery, with GF Sinclair, GW Harris and Miss Reinhardt among the cast (as Joseph Surface, Charles Surface and Lady Teazle respectively). The evening concluded with the farce *The Rendezous!*

The first pantomime at the theatre occurred on the Boxing Day of 1865 with the production *The House that Jack Built*, the *Nottingham Journal* reporting the next day that 'The house was filled in all parts to overflowing, more than two-thousand being present.' William and John Lambert were praised from the stage, receiving 'a perfect furore of applause, which both men graciously responded to by bowing their acknowledgements from the box.'

Theatre Royal, Nottingham.

One of the world's first global stars was the pioneering nineteenth century French actress Sarah Bernhardt, and it was at the Theatre Royal that she captured the hearts and minds of the Nottingham audience. DH Lawrence brought her back here in his novel *Sons and Lovers* (1913), writing: 'One evening of that week Sarah Bernhardt was at the Theatre Royal in Nottingham, giving "La Dame aux Camélias". Paul wanted to see this old and famous actress, and he asked Clara to accompany him.'

In Lawrence's story, Paul Morel and Clara do indeed see Bernhardt at the Royal, but Paul is a little preoccupied with his date to fully appreciate the performance.

Theatre-goer Heriot Ware also finds her thoughts drift in Hilda Lewis' *Penny Lace* (1942). Despite this, she was still 'entranced by the sorrows of Iolanthe, and had laughed more than a young lady should, over the vagaries of the Lord Chancellor...'

In 1897–98 the theatre was remodelled by F Matcham as the Empire Theatre was added next door. Before the Empire building was demolished, in 1969, many famous names played there including Charlie Chaplin, Houdini, Arthur Askey, Tommy Trinder, Vera Lynn, Laurel & Hardy, Buddy Holly, Billy Cotton and Morecambe & Wise.

The writer Baroness Orczy (1865–1947) was born two days before the theatre opened. After struggling to find a publisher for her novel *The Scarlet Pimpernel* (1905), she rewrote it as a play, which was first performed at Nottingham's Theatre Royal in 1903, leading to the novel's publication. It was a book of great influence on the mystery genre, arguably creating the masked hero prototype; that person of wealth with an alter ego who operates in the shadows. Without the Pimpernel there may have been no Batman, a hero with other links to Nottinghamshire, such as Wollaton Hall, which has portrayed Wayne Manor.

The author Cecil Roberts attended his first play, *The Sign of the Cross*, at the Theatre Royal. In his first volume of autobiography, *Growing Boy* (1967), he wrote of being, 'Up in the gallery, sixpence entrance, we sat on wooden backless benches and looked down on the stage far below and into the well of the auditorium where sat the plutocrats.' Roberts recalled the columned portico and being overwhelmed by the plush and gilt luxury of the interior, the chandeliers, the gilt boxes and the great velvet curtain.

In 1952 Agatha Christie attended the opening of what would become the longest-running theatrical production, *The Mousetrap*. The play was first performed at Nottingham's Theatre Royal as part of a pre-West End tour. Its first Detective Sergeant Trotter was played by Richard Attenborough, starring alongside his future wife Sheila Sim. Its first review was given by the *Evening Post*'s theatre critic Emrys Bryson. The production opened here because Nottingham was regarded as a lucky city to launch new plays. Since its Nottingham opening, *The Mousetrap* has become the most watched play in theatre history.

Michael Caine once starred at the theatre, in former Nottingham resident Willis Hall's play *The Long And The Short And The Tall*. Not a lot of people know that Michael Caine had been the understudy to Peter O'Toole, but took his lead after O'Toole flew off to play Lawrence of Arabia.

In his time working as a lead-writer for the *Nottingham Journal* JM Barrie covered a wide range of topics in his twice-weekly articles, including several on the theatre. Barrie's *Peter Pan* has provided the Theatre Royal with many productions, from 1910 to 2018, including 2015's comedy of errors *Peter Pan Goes Wrong*. It may now be a familiar pantomime but it wasn't always that way. As recently as the summer of 1979 Anne Aston insisted, 'It's a play, a fantasy not a pantomime' when she was interviewed during her two-week run in Nottingham playing the swashbuckling hero.

Many pantomimes have borrowed from *Peter Pan* but the original version is perhaps the best child-play ever written. The early Peters were played by women, and it was Pauline Chase that first performed the role in Nottingham in 1910's *The Boy Who Would Not Grow Up*. JM Barrie often praised Nina Boucicault, the first actress to play the role, but he had a preference for Chase. In 1935 it was Jean Forbes-Robertson that took off as Pan in Nottingham, thanks to flying effects from Joseph Kirby and his Flying Ballet. Pat Kirkwood (1954) and Sylvia Syms (1966) remained faithful to Barrie's original vision but, as with the theatre itself, things were about to change.

The Theatre Royal has been owned by Nottingham City Council since 1969, and by the mid-1970s it was in need of a major redevelopment. At that time the balcony was still being served by gas lights, meaning that a fireman needed to be employed and a member of staff was required to stay in the theatre overnight. Restored by N Thompson and C Ferraby, who had previously worked on the Crucible in Sheffield and the National Theatre, London, the improved Theatre Royal was officially reopened by Princess Anne in 1978, signalling a new era.

Peter Pan returned in an all-singing all-dancing 1987 production, starring Bonnie Langford, and since then Barrie's play has become a pantomime. Chloe Newsome (1996), Sara Hillier (2002), Debra Stephenson (2007) and Barney Harwood (2013) wore the famous green, with Jack McNeill (2018) the most recent boy who wouldn't grow up, appearing alongside Joe Pasquale's Smee, of whom the critics spoke highly.

---

[1]Oldfield, 2002.

Chapter 27
Weavers, 1 Castle Gate – Against the Barons

> '*Cue for Treason* by Geoffrey Trease radicalized my young girl brain and made me want to be a gender-bending, sonnet-writing anarchist.'
>
> Miriam Toews

At the bottom of Castle Gate is the independent wine and spirit merchants Weavers, established in 1844. Above a door is the inscription:

> Site of the family business of Geoffrey Trease (1909–1998). An innovative children's author who made history come alive.

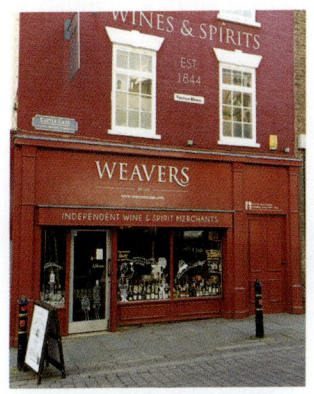

It was the grandfather of (Robert) Geoffrey Trease who came from Loughborough to take over the wine merchants in 1897. Born at 13 Chaucer Street, in the Arboretum area, Geoffrey Trease was the third and youngest son of the wine merchant George Trease and his wife Florence Dale, a doctor's daughter. He was mostly brought up on 142 Portland Road also near the Arboretum.

Weavers Wine Merchants, Castle Gate.

The family business provided access to paper on which Trease wrote his first stories. Doing well at school, he won an honorary foundation scholarship to Nottingham High School where he continued to write stories, poems, and a three-act play, inspired by his frequent visits to the theatre. He even published a school paper for private circulation, typed out on a Remington typewriter he'd persuaded his father to buy him. Aged thirteen, Trease sold an article to a popular boys' weekly on "Amateur Journalism". He left the school with a scholarship to Oxford University to study classics at Queen's College. He was there a year before leaving to focus on his writing.

The best known of his hundred-plus books are the classic historical children's books *Cue For Treason* (1940) and his first publication *Bows Against the Barons* (1934), which tells the story of a boy who joins a band of outlaws and takes part in a rebellion against the feudal elite. *Bows Against the Barons* sees the rich and poor clash in medieval England, a time of harsh winters and starvation, not a place for the merry. In this backdrop we get Trease's "Robin Hood for Boys and Girls!" in which a young Nottinghamshire lad must fight injustice after being made an outlaw for killing one of the king's deer. Thankfully he's helped by the commoners' great leader and his band of elite-battling rebels. This Leftist book was produced by the Communist Party of Great Britain's publishing arm, with illustrations by their official illustrator.

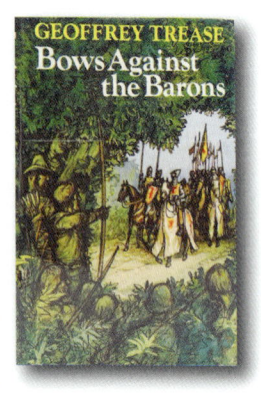

Trease never lectured to or patronised his readers, but the idea of Robin Hood as a role model put many parents off buying the book. A republished version took a less radical stance. In one rousing speech Hood claims:

> It won't be easy, comrades – if it was, we'd have done it long ago. It takes years to persuade men, to show them the one truth – that there are only two classes, masters and men, haves and have-nots. Everything else – Normans and Saxons, Christian and Saracen, peasant and craftsman – is a means of keeping us apart, of keeping the masters on top.

Like other rebel writers, Trease had work cancelled and censored (his books were even bombed by the Nazis) but his stories influenced many young minds for the better. George Orwell, in a *Tribune* book review, wrote of Trease that he was, 'that creature we have long been needing, a "light" Left-wing writer, rebellious but human, a sort of PG Wodehouse after a course of Marx.'[1]

Bows Against the Barons was a typical Trease story, written to help nurture the children of Britain. *The Red Towers of Granada* (1966) saw a sixteen-year-old outcast by the name of Robin, and featured Sherwood Forest and Nottingham's Jewish Quarter (between Hounds Gate and Castle Gate), before a quest for the elixir of life had him in the Moorish Spain of Cordoba and Granada. Another of his works, *A Flight of Angels* (1988), was inspired by the deep sandstone cellar-caves dug out under Nottingham by the old wine merchants.

Malcolm Gladwell, author of several international bestsellers, selected a random sample of Trease's stories when he was on *Desert Island Discs*. Gladwell described Trease's storytelling as 'a master at work,' and called him a 'wonderful English children's book writer' who reminded him of his early reading.

In addition to children's books, Trease's many titles include novels, biographies – including *Portrait of a Cavalier* (1979), the life of the duke who built Nottingham Castle, and works on Byron and Lawrence – criticism and historical studies. His *Nottingham: A Biography* (1970) is one of the most readable books on the history of the city.

To this day, the Trease family's wine merchants' business is still trading at 1 Castle Gate. It's now run by brother and sister Philip and Mary Trease, the fifth generation to work there. A few doors up Castle Gate, at no 17, is a former home of the Treases. Still in the family, the Treases' library has been preserved and contains all of the prolific author's titles, many in several different editions and translations.

Between this building and the wine shop is a green plaque, not for Geoffrey Trease but for DH Lawrence (1885–1930), for it was here that he worked when it was JA Haywood's surgical goods warehouse. The plaque reads:

Site of
Haywood's Factory
where DH Lawrence
worked in 1901

Lawrence's stint as a clerk came when he was a sixteen-year-old after leaving Nottingham High School. Lawrence only lasted three months, leaving his job following a serious pneumonia illness that would affect the rest of his life, and the unexpected death of his older brother Ernest from erysipelas. Shattered by the death of her son, Lawrence's mother turned her attention to her younger boy, nursing him tirelessly and transferring to him the hopes and ambitions that she had had for Ernest, creating a dynamic that formed the heart of *Sons and Lovers* (1913) – in which Ernest becomes William – a book written after the author lost his mother to cancer.

Lawrence's factory life provided much ground for the novel, from his older brother writing his job application, to the ribbing he received from the factory girls. A desk from Haywood's – where

Lawrence 'suffered tortures of shyness when, at half past eight, the Factory girls from upstairs trooped past him' – is on display at the DH Lawrence Birthplace Museum in Eastwood.

In the book, Paul Morel attended his interview at Thomas Jordan's, Manufactures of Surgical Appliances (at 21 Spaniel Row, close to Castle Gate), and he did so with concern, not wanting to become a prisoner of industrialisation. He dreaded the regulated, impersonal world of business and wished he were stupid. Morel also commented that he would sooner feel extreme physical pain than be exposed to strangers. He did, however, enjoy his day in Nottingham when his mother accompanied him. They had an adventure, visiting a bookshop and "big" shops.

Lawrence has Paul Morel walking up Castle Gate in *Sons and Lovers,* and he describes the street where the residents colour their doorsteps with yellow ochre. He's also heading up Castle Gate with Miriam, en route to the castle, when he meets Clara for first time.

The writer and poet Ann Gilbert (1782–1866) lived at 33 Castle Gate. Gilbert was known to collaborate with her sister Jane – the author of *Twinkle, Twinkle, Little Star* – on their children's writing.

---

[1]Walker, 2015.

Chapter 28
The White Lion (former) – Filling a Gap

'Teeth are always in style.' Dr Seuss

A Nottingham writer changed the face of dentistry. In the library of the British Dental Association is a copy of *A Treatise on the Disorders and Deformities of the Teeth and Gums*, arguably the first scientific written work on the subject, and the first to attempt to cover the whole field of dentistry. This early paper on the treatment of teeth appeared in 1770 and was written by a twenty-eight-year-old Nottinghamian, Thomas Berdmore, King George III's personal Operator for the Teeth.

In this valuable treatise, Berdmore described the most rational methods of treating diseases of the mouth, using example cases and experimental work to illustrate his techniques. Not an easy read for dentophobics, Berdmore wrote about visiting a young woman in a 'terrible state' after a botched extraction. The offending tooth had easily been removed but her practitioner had accidentally pulled out 'a piece of jawbone as big as a walnut and three neighbouring molars.' He offered advice too, writing 'Sugar is bad for you!' and 'I am inclined to think that smoking is hurtful to the teeth.'

The Lion Hotel, Clumber Street.

He also wrote that 'the boyish custom of carrying a table or chair in their mouth is as dangerous as it is absurd.'

The textbook became influential and was adopted by his fledgling profession with editions published in London, Ireland and America. Several translations followed as the work grew in reach and reputation. This was at a time when the care of teeth had only recently become a specialism. In the mid-eighteenth century, dentistry was usually the responsibility of barber-surgeons, called upon for tasks as varied as cutting hair to amputating limbs. In 2020, a copy of Berdmore's book was auctioned off in Derby where it fetched £2,000, six times its guide price.

Thomas Berdmore was born in Nottingham in 1740. He came from a family of Nottingham clergymen, his father being Thomas Berdmore, former vicar of St Mary's Church in the Lace Market, but young Thomas' calling was a medical one. Aged fifteen, he became apprentice to the surgeon Mark Skelton of Sheffield. By the age of twenty he was in London, working in the firm of Samuel Rutter and William Green, Operators for Teeth. Rutter and Green had been looking after King George II's teeth, and they introduced Berdmore to court life. In 1760, following the King's death, they took on their new royal client, King George III. As Green's young apprentice, Berdmore assisted the firm, but it wouldn't be long before he was the king's personal dentist. This was because within four years both Rutter and Green had died, leaving Berdmore to head the firm. Now in his mid-twenties, and having passed his examinations at Surgeons Hall, Berdmore acquired the lucrative practice and retained his royal client. He was ready to cash in.

The Surgeons' Company, the first professional body for dentistry, had been established, and Berdmore was a member. The writer continued to be the official surgeon general and teeth drawer to both His Majesty and his son, the Prince of Wales, whilst continuing his dental business. His wealth allowed him to travel and, in 1784, when in Paris, the celebrated dentist crossed paths with Benjamin Franklin.

By the time he died of stomach gout, aged forty-five, Berdmore had become a rich man. His death occurred in London's Fleet Street, but not before he'd written a detailed will. The childless bachelor left money to his housekeeper and friends, but the majority of his £50,000 went to a baby, his namesake and nephew Thomas Berdmore. He also stipulated that his body should be buried in Nottingham beneath the chancel in St Mary's Church, as this was where his father, uncle and grandfather had been laid to rest. He even wrote the inscription for his memorial stone: 'Near this place lies the remains of Thomas Berdmore, who acquired an ample and liberal fortune by toothdrawing.' This was later edited. Perhaps his family didn't like the word toothdrawing and its associations. The slab of marble can still be found on the church's north wall near the west window.

The body of Thomas Berdmore was brought from London in an elegantly decorated hearse to The White Lion Inn on Cow Lane (now Clumber Street), one of Nottingham's most important venues. A sign for The White Lion used to swing from a great beam which crossed Cow Lane.[1] Established in 1684, the coaching inn was a popular social venue with enough space for travellers to park up. On the occasion of Berdmore's arrival, two coaches of mourners and a large train of carriages and horsemen pulled into The White Lion. The building is long gone but a nineteenth-century rebuild remains in the shape of The White Lion Hotel. It retains its fine etched glass windows despite being an amusement arcade.

Berdmore's funeral procession gathered outside The White Lion and made their slow journey up to St Mary's. The streets were lined with mourners, the numbers boosted by the Berdmore family's strong connection to Nottingham. Six clergymen supported the coffin in recognition of the former ministers' links to St Mary's Church. It wasn't just Berdmore's father that had been a key figure at St Mary's, his uncle Scrope Berdmore – who he is buried next to, and whose portrait hangs in the church – and his grandfather, Samuel Berdmore, had also been reverends there.

Thomas Berdmore was a surgeon fit for a king, and another writer from Nottingham who shaped the world – of dentistry.

---

[1] Holland Walker, 1935.

Chapter 29
Yates's (former), 49 Long Row West –
Poet, Mother, Free Spirit

> 'Bring me a pen if you like because one can't have too many...'
> Sophie Curly

Yates's Wine Lodge (originally The Talbot and now a Slug & Lettuce) once had a theatre attached to its rear. Grade II listed for its architectural importance, Yates's combined grandeur with spit and sawdust. It's no surprise that Nottingham's Alan Sillitoe wrote of the inn, but it also has an association with an outsider, BS Johnson, who spent time here when visiting his friend Tony Tillinghast, as recalled in *The Unfortunates* (1969):

> ... surely I must have gone to a pub round here with Tony, yes, there, of course! Yates's Wine Lodge, marvellous, a drink, there, Tony introduced me to it, of course, the great bar downstairs, the gallery round, the sugary music, the soirées, the poem I wrote afterwards, after my first visit there. But first the Gents.

Johnson also wrote a poem called "In Yates's" (1964), and the inn has been part of Nottingham's history since 1876. With old wine barrels, copper pipes, a marble bar and its famous balcony bar, Yates's became an iconic venue. Through the double doors atop the stairs, you'd often find the Talbot Trio playing their old time music. When Johnson returned to Yates's in the late 1960s to make a short promotional film about *The Unfortunates*, the Talbot Trio were captured on film. When Yates's had been the Talbot it was a gigantic gin palace, the best of its kind in the Midlands, and it was full of mirrors, cut glass, statues, oil paintings, spirit fountains and the latest gas lights.

Yates's was one of the city centre venues that hosted But I Know This City, a large 2014 event involving a hundred readers, reprised in 2019 to

Slug and Lettuce, Angel Row.

mark the fiftieth anniversary of Johnson's *The Unfortunates*. As with the chapters in the book, which can be read in any order (apart from the first and last), the audience could plan their own route as the event spread out across the city centre's bookshops, pubs, churches, homes and a host of atmospheric nooks, all chosen to connect to each of the book's chapters, if not geographically then thematically. As the event's chief organiser, writer Andy Barrett explained, 'One chapter's read in a car, another in a darkened porch of St Mary's Church, and the tenderest chapter was heard in a living room next to a roaring fire.'

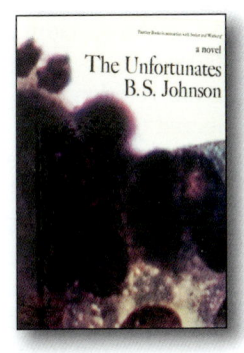

Johnson's book in a box is more a memoir than a novel, an exploration of memory, an enquiring melancholy. As the memories have no structure, they are randomly sieved through for meaning. Johnson took his own life at the age of forty.

Sophie Curly, another literary patron of Yates's, had her own mental health problems. For nearly thirty years the rebellious outcast could be found in Nottingham's city centre, walking the streets, sitting on a bench or supping at a boozer. You might remember her, a bag lady with a smiley face furnished with bright pink lipstick and a milky eye, ranting about Thatcher and preaching free love.

Fond of unjudgmental drunks, and not liking rich people, Curly preferred Nottingham's rougher establishments but frequented a range of inns including Yates's, The Bell, The Cricketers, The Sawyer's Arms and The Poachers (where her wake was held). She was quite a sight; her margarine-washed hair dyed in turmeric rice and curled with a pipe cleaner, her attire made up of a mixture of lace, cardboard and fishnet stockings, all topped off by a large Rasta hat.

This was before the Cloughie Statue (Speaker's Corner), so Curly's soapbox was a barstool or a bench, from which she was primed to offer her thoughts, attacking capitalism, attacking consumerism, attacking the Tories. In Thatcher's government she saw corruption and a refusal to look after the old and poor. She insisted that a Labour Party poster was put up at her care home during one election campaign. After the manager denied her the wall-space she transferred herself to another home. This wasn't a novel experience for Curly, who ended up in more homes than Kirsty Allsop. One time she was sent packing for propositioning male residents in the lift, another time a petition had been collected to have her evicted, and then there were those occasions in which she would evict herself after finding out the home wasn't run by the council.

Before the council caught up with her, Curly had been homeless, sleeping where she could, in an abandoned car, on a park bench. Between the streets and care homes she slept in a series of council flats, all her belongings in the one room, the windows covered in a web of string to catch burglars, with talcum powder on the sills to snag their prints. Paranoia was her shadow. She'd tell anyone who'd listen about child killers, evil scientists and others out to get her. Some refuge was found in the Catholic Church but she was not accepted there, her views on adultery being a God-given right didn't wash with the local priest.

Curly's poor physical health (including bowel cancer) and continual mental health problems (including the hearing of voices) resulted in spells in hospital. For the rest of her time in Nottingham it was the pubs in which she'd spend her days and pension, socialising using different accents, from posh Londoner to Nottingham local, as the situation required.

Throughout her time in the city Curly remained a reader, ordering books from the library. And she wrote. In one letter she put that she was saving up to live in the USSR and that, in the event of her death, her 'remains should be sent to the Kremlin.'[1] Some of her letters were written with her right/wrong hand to keep both sides of her brain exercised.

Sophie Curly had always been a writer. She had been born Joan Easdale and had grown up in Kent. Like her brother, Brian, she was a precocious talent. They would often put on shows and concerts for the family. Whilst Brian went on to win an Oscar for writing the score to *The Red Shoes*, Joan focused on her poetry and at the age of fifteen sent poems to Virginia Woolf (1882–1941), who declared her 'my discovery' and later published her works in two volumes. Easdale's *A Collection of Poems* (1931) was described by Hugh Walpole as 'astonishingly adroit, acute, accomplished.'

Joan Easdale regularly visited Woolf and also became close friends with the likeminded writer, socialist and free-love proponent Naomi Mitchison. In no time Easdale was accepted into The Bloomsbury Group, the London literary and intellectual elite of the

1930s. The attractive, glossy-haired Easdale fell in love with Jim Rendel, a man of science. They married and had three children.

Combining writing with home life, Joan Easdale wrote plays and talks for the BBC, but work and family demands were proving difficult to juggle. No longer did she have time for her poetry. Then came the war. Under the constant fear of being blown up during the Blitz, her life became unmanageable. Psychiatric advice was sought to help save her struggling marriage. Her analyst told her to give up writing and focus on being a good wife and mother. She took the advice and burned everything she had ever written on a big bonfire. In a last attempt to save her marriage she agreed to move the family to Australia after her husband had taken a job there.

It was in Sydney that she had a full-blown breakdown, becoming convinced that there were spies in the roof. It was decided that she should return to England to recover, and head back to Australia upon feeling better. She left but never returned. Saying goodbye to her children Jane (then aged thirteen) Polly (ten) and Sandy (six) hardly helped her mental state, and she entered Holloway Sanitorium where she was subjected to ECT and experimental drugs. Diagnosed as schizophrenic, she later felt well enough to discharge herself and caught a train up north. She got off at a random city, Nottingham, and reinvented herself, choosing the name Sophie Curly.

Curly enjoyed the company of most Nottingham people, finding them friendly. Nottingham allowed her to become her own person and she even reconnected with family members, some of whom would come up to see her. One such visitor was her granddaughter Celia Robertson, who has written a book about her, *Who Was Sophie? The lives of my grandmother, poet and stranger* (2018). Robertson's book includes "Amber Innocent", Easdale's 1939 poem, first published by The Hogarth Press, and a collection of great family photographs, some from Curly's time in Nottingham.

Sophie Curly's gravestone, in Wilford Hill Cemetery.

Sophie Curly's gravestone is in Wilford Hill Cemetery. It states:

> Joan Adeney Easdale,
> Joan Rendel, Sophia Curly,
> Sophie 1913–1998 Poet,
> Mother and Free Spirit.

---

[1]Robertson, 2018.

Chapter 30
The Zara Building – A Booklovers' Library

> 'Think of what our Nation stands for, Books from Boots' and country lanes, Free speech, free passes, class distinction, Democracy and proper drains.'
>
> John Betjeman, *In Westminster Abbey*

In David Lean's 1945 film *Brief Encounter*, the character Laura is seen in what looks like a public library, with a holiday reads section, a friendly librarian and a desk surrounded by shelves of books. 'I changed my book at Boots,' says Laura before walking through what viewers would have recognised as a branch of Boots. This scene reflects the opening of Noel Coward's *Still Life*, the play on which the film is based, in which a woman 'is reading a Boots library book at which she occasionally smiles.'

Between 1899 and 1966 Boots and books were known bedfellows, thanks to their popular circulating library which lent thirty-eight million books in one year. Yes, Boots the chemists once provided a great service to our country's readers. Their library system was the largest of its type in the world and its roots lie in Nottingham.

On Woolpack Lane in the Lace Market lived Sarah Boot, a keen user of natural remedies or medical botany. Her Methodist son John was drawn to these treatments as a means of providing affordable healthcare to the poor. To this end he opened the first purpose-built Boots' shop on nearby Goose Gate in Hockley (est 1884) and called it The British and American Botanic Establishment. As early as the mid-nineteenth century the shop was providing homemade remedies and private consultations. To promote sales Boot marketed his products with posters, window displays, newspaper adverts and even a brass band.[1]

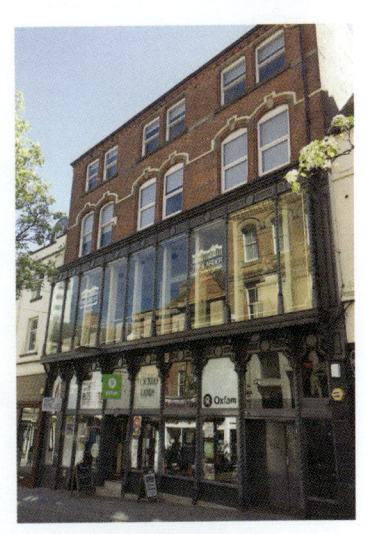

Boots former store, Goose Gate.

Whilst his business was successfully treating others, John Boot's own health suffered and he died in 1860 leaving behind a young family. His only son Jesse, aged ten at the time, revived the business (with the help of his mother and friends) and Boots grew. Now a man, work-related stress was taking its toll on Jesse's health, so much so that he considered selling up. His sister insisted that he take a holiday and, reluctantly, Jesse headed to Jersey where he met the daughter of a bookseller. Her name was Florence Rowe. Twelve years his junior, the vibrant Florence and the more restrained Jesse fell in love. A year later, despite opposition from Florence's mother, they married and returned to work in Nottingham.

Florence Boot quickly became a key member of the business and, after the Boots had children, she placed a cot in the corner of the office so that they could join her at work. Noticing poor literacy levels amongst the working class, she wanted to help, and installed a revolving bookcase in the small store on Goose Gate. Florence then came up with the idea of the Boots stores having a book department. A library followed in the store on Pelham Street, now Zara. This shop was an early, if not the first, Wonderstore, like a department store, with a café, hairdressers and gift shop.

Harrods, WH Smith and *The Times* all adopted similar libraries, but Boots was the biggest. London had six stores with libraries.

Zara, Pelham Street.

Nottingham had eight. In the bigger stores the libraries were upstairs at the rear, forcing readers to walk past the merchandise, whereas rivals often had their libraries in basements. Boots also had a much more organised distribution system, uniquely offering an inter-store exchange of books.

Unlike other subscription libraries that were around at the time, Boots Booklovers' Libraries were well-stocked with fiction, even titles they'd rather not stock. In 1905 Jesse Boot acknowledged:

> Whilst we do not intend to dictate to our readers as to either the quality or the range of their reading... we afford for the perusal of all literature, including some books that, personally, we regret to see published...

Once inside a Boots library there was no sense that you were inside a chemist's. The architect Percy Richard Morley Horder, who specialised in English country houses – and was responsible for the Trent Building at the University of Nottingham – was hired to design the library departments to look like posh country house libraries. They were adorned with rugs, sofas, rich curtains, thick carpets, plants and flowers.

Mercer Stretch was appointed Boots' first Head Librarian, a prestigious position that commanded the same salary as the Head Pharmacist and General Manager. He expanded the system, overseeing hundreds of libraries, with nearly half of all Boots' stores having one. Stretch was followed by FR Richardson, Head Librarian from 1911 to 1941, who had previously selected books for Queen Victoria.

Any work within the libraries was desirable. The First Literary Course provided librarians with an understanding of the publishing trade and a knowledge of bestsellers on which they were tested. Whilst all the chief librarians were men, all the shop floor librarians were women. Florence Boot called her female employees her "dear girls" and offered them free breakfast, outings and accommodation in the company's holiday homes.

Juniors would be required to dust the books every morning, a task that taught them where each title was placed, and by the age of twenty-one the workers were often moved to other stores, sent on relief. It was said that working at a Boots library helped a woman's social standing and marriage prospects. As women often had to leave work when they got married, some were reluctant to wed and there were reports of long engagements. Seventy percent of the libraries' members were women, the libraries providing an important social hub. Talking, unlike in many public libraries, was acceptable.

By 1920 there were over half a million "booklovers" and 3,500 requests each day. They had three types of membership. Their most expensive subscription was On-Demand, entitling readers to borrow any volume in circulation which, by the 1930s, meant any book from any branch, delivered within three days of ordering using the country's railway network. Their window posters proudly announced: 'Join Boots Booklovers Library, the finest Library Service in the Kingdom. You can change your books at any Boots Libraries.'[2] Snob-appeal existed with this more expensive membership. The Class A books were at eye level, with the Class B ones requiring bending or tip-toeing for perusal. There were special rates for book groups and educational societies, with schools taking advantage of the offers (yes, they also stocked children's books) and there were no fines for late returns. Worn books were sold to the public.

All members received a token and date of renewal. This could be attached to the borrowed book through a hole in the spine, the token then acting as a bookmark. Red labels were displayed on potentially offensive books which, once returned, were placed below the counter. All the other books wore green labels. A catalogue was produced featuring enticing blurbs and cannily advertising other Boots products. Amazon later adopted a similar strategy, knowing that an association with items as enriching and respected as books would help their brand and future sales.

The libraries ran as loss-leaders but managed to break even most years. With overseas subscribers and foreign travellers taking books with them, the famous green label was found all over the world.

During the Second World War the number of subscribers increased to a million, with detective novels proving most popular. One poster stated: 'One Blackout Benefit! More time for

READING!' Books were being bought for the libraries at the rate of 1,250,000 a year. Boots had real buying power and some publishers pandered to them. If a new title was not chosen by Boots it would suffer for it.

One publisher that turned the tables on Boots was Penguin who became, in part, responsible for the demise of the library departments. People liked to own books, and Penguin's affordable paperbacks made this possible. Penguin's paperbacks also proved difficult for libraries to stock as they were hard to protect against wear and tear. TV was another nail in the coffin, as were improvements in public libraries, with fiction becoming much more accessible.

WH Smith's libraries closed in 1961, *The Times*'s a year later. Boots took on many of their subscribers, managing to hold on a little longer, selling off 800,000 second-hand books in one year, but by 1965 the end was nigh. Book departments began taking over the library sections, and in 1966 the Booklovers' Libraries closed.

For sixty-seven years, Boots Libraries had brought books to the people, and it all began in Nottingham. Today, a branch of Boots sits on the site of the Rowe family's bookshop in St Helier, Jersey. In Nottingham, the City Council is building a new central library that aims to become the best children's library in England. It's an ambition befitting of Florence Boot.

There's a book about the story of Boots Booklovers' Library by Jackie Winter, entitled *Lipsticks and Library Books* (2016).

---

[1]Gurnham, 2020.
[2]Sears, 2008.

Book Two:
Nottingham

Chapter 31
Basford House, Church Street, Basford – Home of the Long Poem

> 'True fiction hath in it a higher end than fact.'
> Philip James Bailey, *Festus*

Basford House is where Thomas Bailey (1758–1856) compiled his *Annals of Nottinghamshire* and his son Philip wrote what would become the longest poem ever written in English. A favourite of Queen Victoria, it was said to be a sign of intelligence to have read it.

Aged twenty, Philip James Bailey (1816–1902) had read Goethe's *Faust*. The German play compelled Bailey to write *Festus*, his own version of the legend, in which he incorporated a more impressive spiritual content, his eponymous hero taking a pilgrimage that demonstrated the ultimate triumph of love and good over evil. Between 1836 and 1839 Bailey dedicated himself to the writing of his poem, working in isolation at Basford House. It was published by William Pickering in London without Bailey's name, although its dedication stated, 'Old Basford, near Nottingham, 1839'. It was seen as remarkable that a young man could produce a work of such insight and imagination and *Festus* attracted great interest from what was called the intelligent classes. The poem's first concentrated edition had great poetic power and was warmly received by the writers Edward Bulwer-Lytton, William Makepeace Thackeray and Alfred Tennyson, the latter writing to a friend, 'order it and read: you will most likely find it a great bore, but there are really very grand things in *Festus*.'

Tennyson's view is not uncommon, as *Festus* is wordy in the extreme and at times borders on the unreadable, yet it also contains passages of great force and beauty such as:

> We live in deeds, not years; in thoughts, not breaths;
> In feelings, not in figures on a dial.
> We should count time by heart throbs.
> He most lives who thinks most, feels the noblest, acts the best.

Philip James Bailey was a well-respected member of Nottingham's literary scene. Friends with fellow members of Bromley House Library, William and Mary Howitt, he read *Festus* to them in

Richard Howitt's pharmacy on Parliament Street and later visited the couple in Rome when holidaying with his second wife Anne, daughter of Alderman George Carey of Nottingham.

The 1845 second edition of *Festus* was the first of many new expanded versions up to an eleventh, jubilee edition, of 1889, by which time the poem contained over 40,000 lines in three volumes. Cecil Roberts wrote that '[Bailey] did very well out of it, for he got a civil list pension when quite young and spent the rest of his long life burying his poem with additions.' It was in theological and metaphysical treatises that Bailey buried the poetry, and *Festus'* popularity fluctuated. The poem remained well read in the United States with in excess of thirty editions throughout the second half of the nineteenth century.

Philip James Bailey dedicated *Festus* to his father with a poem that begins:

> MY FATHER! unto thee to whom I owe
> All that I am, all that I have and can

Philip's father, Thomas Bailey, was a distinguished Nottingham writer in his own right. In 1824 he wrote *A Sermon on the Death of Byron,* having taken young Philip to see Lord Byron's body lying-in-state. Philip inherited his father's love of poetry and committed to memory the whole of Byron's long narrative poem *Childe Harold's Pilgrimage.*

Thomas Bailey was largely self-educated. He became a successful businessman, initially living on Coalpit Lane, and he worked as a silk-stocking trader and Wheeler Gate wine merchant with premises on Low Pavement. A great believer in self-improvement, he developed into a fine public speaker (Brown, 1882) and, in 1830, had a failed attempt to represent Nottingham as a Liberal candidate. He did, however, contribute to a campaign that led to the 1832 Reform Act creating a more democratic House of Commons. He erected a memorial and column in the grounds of Basford House to commemorate the act's passing. The

Thomas Bailey's plaque, Basford Cemetery.

memorial plaque is now in the old cemetery opposite Basford House. A few years later he was elected to the town council on which he served for six years.

It was in 1832 that Thomas Bailey bought the red-bricked Basford House. Formerly named Manor House, the large building near Basford Church was built around 1700. Altered in the late nineteenth and twentieth centuries, it is now flats and offices. Thomas Bailey lived in Basford House for the remainder of his life. In 1845 he became owner and editor of the weekly *Nottingham Mercury* and, a great believer in the power of education and literature, he used his paper to help promote his views. His opinions proved too temperate for his readers and a declining circulation resulted in the newspaper folding in 1852, leaving Bailey to focus more on his own writing, producing prose and poetry full-time. He became a noted historian after compiling the four-volume *The Annals of Nottinghamshire* (1852–56). He also wrote *Village Reform: the Great Social Necessity of Britain* (1854) as well as handbooks on Nottingham Castle and Newstead Abbey, and many treatises such as *What is Life?* He wrote thirteen books in total as well as poetry.

A great collector of other people's books, Thomas Bailey continued to champion the importance of literature, and he set up a village library.[1] He died in Basford House in 1856, aged seventy-one, and was buried in the cemetery opposite. It was a source of great pride for Thomas Bailey that his son Philip became a celebrated poet.

Philip James Bailey was born in Nottingham in 1816 in a since-demolished house. There's a plaque on the corner of Fletcher Gate/Middle Pavement which states:

On this site
stood the house in which
Philip James Bailey
author of "Festus"
was born, April 22nd, 1816

The 'on this site' statement is incorrect but close enough.

Young Philip was afforded the best education Nottingham had to offer. He became a trained barrister but never practised. *Festus* was his obsession, and he continued to work on his magnum opus for fifty years. He is associated with the Spasmodic school of poetry, although his other poems *The Angel World* (1850), *The Mystic* (1855), *The Age* (1858) and *The Universal Hymn* (1867), were largely unsuccessful.

It was in 1856 that Philip James Bailey was awarded his civil list pension of a hundred pounds a year for services to literature. He lived in Jersey, Lee (North Devon) and Blackheath (London) before retiring to Nottingham. He is buried in Church/Rock Cemetery on Mansfield Road and shares a headstone with Annie Sophia, his wife of thirty-three years. The stone includes a quote from *Festus*:

> Death is another life. We bow our heads
> At going out, we think, and enter straight
> Another golden chamber of the king's
> Larger than this we leave, and lovelier.

In Newstead Abbey's writers' garden is a bust of Philip James Bailey by Albert Toft. For the best part of a century, it had stood at the entrance to Nottingham Castle. Toft received £300.84 for his creation (about £36,000 in today's money).

Thomas Bailey's grandson, John Henry Brown (1836–1911), was also a writer. The Nottingham wine merchant authored several books such as *The Rambler's Calendar* (1882), recounting his thoughts on observations of nature and the seasons, and the play *Love's Labyrinth* (1876). Brown's mother was Jane Brown (née Bailey).

Philip James Bailey's bust, Newstead Abbey.

---

[1]Mellors, 1914.

Chapter 32
Beaconsfield Street, Hyson Green – Nottingham's Black Writers

'Where are our heroes, martyrs and monuments?'

Len Garrison

The writer and poet, educationalist, community activist and historian, Lenford Alphonso "Len" Garrison, moved to London from Jamaica as a schoolboy in the 1950s. After gaining a degree in African and Caribbean History, he achieved his MA in Local History, his dissertation on Rastafari and identity forming the basis of his book *Black Youth, Rastafarianism and Identity Crisis in Britain* (1979).

Garrison was involved in a growing network of community-based initiatives and radical Black publishing. He realised that the British education system was failing Black children, denying the reality or existence of Black history or culture. To develop the Black British identity and record its history, Garrison believed that this information needed to be made available to schoolchildren. Having co-founded the Black Cultural Archives in Brixton in 1980, he formed Afro-Caribbean Education Resource (ACER) and began pioneering education packs.

ACER, an archive of Black history, created educational material for children of all ages and abilities, providing a proud sense of identity and belonging, and improving opportunities. Garrison also promoted the works of young Black writers, organising the Young Penmanship awards which helped to launch many careers. By 1988, ACER's educational packs had spanned the nation, giving inner-city African and Caribbean pupils materials and textbooks that concerned their heritage and history. After ACER ended due to a lack of funding, Len Garrison came to Nottingham.

By this time Garrison was an acclaimed poet and the author of *Beyond Babylon: Collection of Poems, 1972–82* (1985). He saw culture as another key community initiative and, once in Nottingham, he helped to develop the Afro-Caribbean Family and Friends (ACFF) Education and Culture Centre (which later became the Association of Caribbean Family & Friends), based at 28 Beaconsfield Street, Hyson Green. The venue hosted a series of Black bookfairs and, as the Director of ACFF, Garrison advanced the education of the public. Expanding his ACER concept, he also created a successful mentoring project known as BUILD.[1]

Having written the paper *Post-war Immigration and Settlement of West Indians in Nottingham 1948–1968*, Garrison helped produce the 1993 exhibition "The Black Presence in Nottingham", at Nottingham Castle's museum. It was thanks to Garrison and his development of local history research that the life of George Africanus, Nottingham's first Black entrepreneur, was featured at the castle. Ten years later, local historians were able to uncover the grave of Africanus in the churchyard of St Mary's in the Lace Market and plaques were put up in his memory at St Mary's and in Victoria Street, near where he ran a business.

Four years before that, Garrison was involved in the Anne Frank Exhibition that segued into Black History Month, with an overlapping committee. The combined events' speakers included Bernie Grant MP, Peter Tatchell (talking about the oppression of lesbian and gay men under the Nazis) and Denis Goldberg, who had been tried and imprisoned in South Africa for fighting apartheid. This was too much for Conservative councillors at the time who opposed funding the project and hit the front page of the *Nottingham Evening Post* after complaining about some of the speakers. In contrast, the then Conservative MP for Nottingham South, Martin Brandon-Bravo, sent a donation and happily came to the launch.

Marie Garrison, Len's wife, was a noted storyteller, working in many Nottinghamshire schools before the Garrisons returned to Brixton where Len died in 2003. There is a bust of him at the National Black Cultural Archives, which hosts an annual Len Garrison memorial lecture.

Due to Garrison's work, Black history is now part of the mainstream British educational curriculum. His legacy has inspired the likes of Sharmaine Lovegrow, publisher of the inclusive imprint Dialogue Books, and the Nottingham poet and archivist Panya Banjoko, who has described Garrison to me as 'a great cultural historian.' Banjoko shares his mission to ensure that Black history is properly recorded, celebrated and available to all, which she does with Nottingham Black Archive (NBA).

Forty years ago, the organisation Chronicle of Minority Arts (CHROMA) hosted workshops and poetry evenings, helping to produce a wave of Nottingham writers including Pitman Browne, Nezzle Saunders, Beverley Dennis, Christine Bell and Granville Levi, leading to the publication of the anthology *The Writers Club Book One* (1983), edited by Frederick Williams.

Building on this and the work of Garrison, Panya Banjoko and NBA has boosted the visibility of Black writing. She is currently researching the history of Black writing in Nottingham for her PhD on 'The Politics in Poetry and the role of African Caribbean Writers and Networks During the 1970s and 1980s in Nottingham'.

Panya Banjoko edited a book of thirty narratives from people moving to Nottingham, about why they came here and their lives in the city. She also edited the 2018 anthology *When We Speak: An Anthology of Black Writing in Nottingham*, a Real Creative Futures project in partnership with David Mathers, a collection that raised awareness of the city's African-Caribbean community's continuing literary tradition. In addition to her work in the recording of Black history, Banjoko is a writer, storyteller and performance poet. Her books include *Some Things* (2018), a poetry collection that reflects her position as one of the first generation of Caribbean people born in Britain. A further collection is due in 2022.

Every year, NBA organises a "read a Black author in public" event to promote diverse reading and authors of African descent, and there are plenty of Nottingham authors to choose from, many of whom have written about the experiences of African-Caribbean people in the city. Norma Gregory, author of *Jamaicans in Nottingham* (2015), has been researching this subject for three decades and has published many articles and academic papers including work on Black British literary and social history.

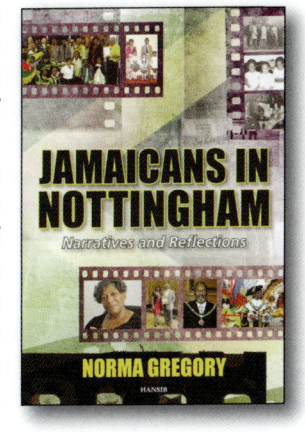

Lee Arbouin's *The Nottingham Connection* (2012) tells the story of four Jamaican women, from their childhoods to their experiences settling in England. Her daughter, Amanda, has written *British Black Graduates: untold stories*. Faith Gakanje's *A Life Robbed* (2019) chronicles her experience in Britain's complex and unwelcoming asylum system.

There are many examples of work portraying real experiences, with the aim of increasing awareness and helping the reader, such as Carrol Rowe's *Survivor: The Escape* (2016), about the courage to overcome violence, bullying and abuse, and Sherwood's Dr Courtney Alexander Smith's innovative self-help book, *The Wonderful You* (2016).

Many local Black writers have called on their pre-Nottingham experiences for inspiration. Director of the Africa Research Group at the University of Nottingham, Ken Kamoche's novels, *True Warriors* (2011) and *Black Ghosts* (2015), are based on his decade living in Hong Kong, and Freddy Fynn's collection of short stories, *Of Life and Love: Eight Moral Tales* (2010), are inspired by the traditional history of storytelling that he had enjoyed in his childhood in Ghana.

In recent years, Nottingham has seen publications from MA in Creative Writing graduate Sharon RM Stevens, with the children's book, *Oscar the Curious Cat* (2015), a debut novel from Betty-Maxine Onwuteaka, whose romance *Hired Fiancée* (2018) is the first in her 'Betty and Ryder' series, and Caroline Bell Foster has written eleven contemporary, multicultural and interracial novels, the locally set *The Cat Café* (2015) among them.

Retired nurse Lilleth Clarke's *Shared Thoughts: Poems for Everyday Living* (2017) is one of a number of recent poetry collections from Nottingham's Black writers and, aside from the written word, the city has an abundance of Black poets and spoken word artists. The large number of poetry nights, groups and publishers in Nottingham has helped provide a voice for poets, and two such groups, Mouthy Poets and Blackdrop, have given many people the opportunity to perform, be it spoken word, social commentary or poetic expression. Blackdrop was founded by the Irish-Jamaican poets Michelle "Mother" Hubbard, Lisa Jackson and David "Stickman" Higgins.

SlamOVision, the global spoken word community's Eurovision, hosted by the UNESCO Cities of Literature, was won in 2021 by Nottingham's Cara Thompson, whose poetry explores and embraces her Jamaican-British heritage. Nottingham will now host the 2022 event.

Nottingham's published Black poets include the aforementioned Banjoko, Ioney Smallhorne and Sarah "Rain" Kolawole, Associate Artist at Nottingham Playhouse, whose first play was *Notts Sweet Home*. We will meet the playwright and novelist Jenny McLeod in a later chapter, and the writer and labour activist George Powe, who was the subject of a 2021 exhibition at Nottingham Castle curated by Banjoko.

The writers and poets featured above are just some of Nottingham's Black writers, and it doesn't begin to include the wider population of BAME writers and poets in the city.

---

[1]Phillips, 2003.

Chapter 33
Bertrand Russell House, Gamble Street – Building the Foundation

'Man is a credulous animal, and must believe something; in the absence of good grounds for belief, he will be satisfied with bad ones.'

Bertrand Russell, *Unpopular Essays*

Bertrand Russell House, Basford.

There is a building in Basford with the name of Bertrand Russell emblazoned on its façade, a man whose links with Nottingham span three centuries. It's a story with an impressive cast that includes Viscount Amberley, Lady Ottoline Morrell and DH Lawrence, with Ray Gosling and even Alan Sillitoe making cameos. The links spawn hundreds of political publications and has resulted in Nottingham helping to highlight and counter the causes of violence, and to strive for peace, human rights and social justice.

Bertrand Russell's grandfather was a former British Prime Minister, and it is with him that the story begins. Lord John Russell, later Earl Russell, was the principal architect of the Great Reform Act in 1832 which gave more men the right to vote, an Act that included the redistribution of seats to the growing cities. A year earlier, after the House of Lords had rejected the Act, a crowd of Nottinghamians surged towards the castle and, taking their anger out on its proprietor who had opposed the Act, they broke through the gatehouse before setting the castle ablaze.

In 1865, when more people were clamouring for the right to vote, Lord Russell became Prime Minister for a second spell, having earlier had the role between 1846 and 1852. In preparing a second Reform Bill, John Russell became a leading instigator for voting reform. Charles Dickens dedicated *A Tale of Two Cities* (1859) to him, writing, 'In remembrance of many public services and private kindnesses.' In a later speech, Dickens said of him that 'there is no man in England whom I respect more in his public capacity, whom I love more in his private capacity.'

By the end of John Russell's premiership his son John, Viscount Amberley, had reluctantly entered politics and Nottingham was to be his destination. This was after the Nottingham Liberal committee had lobbied him to stand following the 1865 result being declared void, evidence of bribery and disruption forcing a by-election. Standing as their candidate, Amberley, together with his wife Katharine, arrived in Nottingham by train and stayed at the Flying Horse. As Kate recalled in her journal: 'We got into an open carriage with a postilion in blue and drove to our inn The Flying Horse, the old liberal headquarters – an old fashioned rambling inn...'.[1]

Kate had been warned about Nottingham's reputation for rebellion and rough politics, a concern shared by her father-in-law, the Prime Minister, who worried about the 'mob of ruffians' that backed the Conservatives. On their first night in Nottingham, Amberley and his wife were introduced to the hundred-and-fifty-strong committee at the Flying Horse before going the short distance to the Exchange building. 'As we went through the street, there were groans and hisses and cheers,' wrote Kate.

The Flying Horse, Old Market Square.

Later in the campaign, they were confronted:

> As we returned across the Market Place which was crowded, the mob rushed towards us and surrounded the carriage. When we got in I went to the window to show myself and had a stick thrown at me, also some dirt that hit me on the eye. There was a great mob in the street and they fisticuffed a good deal amongst one another and attacked one woman because she had yellow ribbons in her hair...

A progressive Liberal, Amberley won his seat. Weeks later, his father's second reform bill was defeated, leading to his resignation as PM. Amberley served as Nottingham's MP for two years, becoming known for his unorthodox views on religion, as well as his advocacy of birth control and women's suffrage, subjects that his wife Kate also campaigned on. A vivacious suffragist, Lady Amberley may even have done more for these causes than her shy and serious husband.

In 1872 John and Kate Amberley's youngest child, Bertrand Russell, was born in Wales. Before he was five, John and Kate had died, both in their early thirties. Russell was looked after by his paternal grandparents and he was home-schooled by a series of tutors. After a difficult adolescence characterised by loneliness and depression, Russell won a scholarship to study Maths at Trinity College Cambridge where he distinguished himself as an outstanding mathematician, a reputation secured after the publication of his book with AN Whitehead, *The Principles of Mathematics*. Russell would become equally well-known as a philosopher and political activist but his passport would come to show his profession as "author".

Russell, who wrote some seventy books and thousands of articles, received the Nobel Prize for Literature in 1950. Until the age of twenty-one he would spend hours trying to find the shortest way of saying something without ambiguity, and to this aim, he wrote, 'I was willing to sacrifice all attempts at aesthetic excellence.' Russell was able to express complex arguments and ideas in a direct, lucid style that benefited from his lack of a formal education and from his love of Percy B Shelley's poetry.

In 1926 Russell came to Nottingham to promote his most ambitious work on modern society, *The Prospects of Industrial Civilization*, in which he argued that industrialism is a threat to human freedom. He was invited back in 1937 by the psychologist and fellow Cambridge apostle, WJH Sprott. This time Russell would give a Byron Lecture at University College on Shakespeare Street. He had developed an interest in establishing the connection between the legacy of Byronic romanticism and the most disturbing ideology of the time, linked to the rise of Fascism. Russell was keen on Byron as an exemplar aristocratic rebel but not so much as a poet.

In the lecture, Russell referred to another Nottinghamshire writer, DH Lawrence, who had become something of an acquaintance. A one-time lover of Russell's, Ottoline Morrell (née Cavendish-Bentinck), had introduced him to Lawrence. Ottoline had her own links with Nottinghamshire as she grew up at Welbeck Abbey and, after her mother died, she returned to the estate. She had first met Lawrence and his wife Frieda in 1915 and, in that year, she took Russell to visit them in Suffolk. Like Ottoline, Russell had read Lawrence's books. The first meeting between Russell and Lawrence appeared a 'great success' to Ottoline. 'He is infallible,' said the forty-three-year-old Russell of the thirty-year-old Lawrence. 'He is like Ezekiel or some other Old Testament prophet, prophesying. Of course, the blood of his nonconformist preaching ancestors is strong in him, but he sees everything and is always right,' from *Ottoline at Garsington, Memoirs of Lady Ottoline Morrell 1915–1918* (1974). Russell also wrote:

> I have had a long long letter from Lawrence – saying it is no good to do anything till we get Socialism – and thinking (as the young do) that because he sees the desirability of Socialism it can be got by a few years' strenuous work. I feel his optimism difficult to cope with – I can't share it and don't want to discourage it. He is extraordinarily young.

Russell had been stimulated by Lawrence's ideas and their friendship lasted a year. 'Pacifism had produced in me a mood of bitter rebellion and I found Lawrence equally full of rebellion,' Russell later wrote in *Portraits from Memory* (1958).

> This made us think, at first, that there was a considerable measure of agreement between us, and it was only gradually that we discovered that we differed from each other more than either differed from the Kaiser ... I felt him to be a man of a certain imaginative genius and, at first, when I felt inclined to disagree with him, I thought that perhaps his insight into human nature was deeper than mine. It was only gradually that I came to feel him a positive force for evil and that he came to have the same feeling about me.

Russell's rebellion was rational and reasoned, Lawrence's wild and prophesising.

Russell's next connection with Nottingham takes us to the 1960s. In London he had established the Bertrand Russell Peace Foundation (BRPF) in 1963 after the Cuban Missile Crisis, to further the cause of peace and to assist in the pursuit of freedom and justice. In 1968, the BRPF opened an office and print shop, which became The Russell Press, in Nottingham. Why Nottingham? Because in 1965 Russell had invited Ken Coates to join the foundation, and by 1968 Coates was living in Greenfield Street, Dunkirk. He had recently been expelled from the Labour Party after criticising the Wilson government's support of US policy in Vietnam. Before his expulsion Coates had been President of Nottingham Labour Party and had a history of campaigning for left-wing causes. As a student he had been active in the National Association of Labour Student Organisations and became its National Secretary.

Vietnam was the big issue of the day, and the Foundation received support from Alan Sillitoe, who contributed the proceedings from the London stage premiere of *Saturday Night and Sunday Morning* in support of the people of Vietnam.

Ken Coates was a prolific Nottingham writer whose books, pamphlets and articles carried a strong voice for the Left. A former pit worker, he had gone on to win a state scholarship to Nottingham University, where he gained a first-class degree in Sociology before working as a teacher. His focus on poverty, industrial relations and working-class history influenced the outlook of many of his students.

Coates worked with Russell in his final years (Russell died in 1970, aged ninety-seven). By this time the printing arm of the foundation, Russell Press, had been established in Nottingham. Originally the Partisan Press, it shared premises with the BRPF on Goldsmith Street, in the Arboretum area, close to the General Cemetery. They moved into an old mill on Gamble Street just behind Alfreton Road. The road had a group of lace factories running along it and those buildings survive. Most of the premises are now used for student accommodation, but Bertrand Russell House retains its name and boasts original features from its days as a textile mill and printers, such as the lantern finishing rooms on top.

Opposite Bertrand Russell House on Gamble Street was Woolston Book Co, the book suppliers to libraries, later known as Woolston and Blunt then John Menzies Library Services, another impressive building to have escaped demolition.

In addition to printing for the BRPF's campaigns, Russell Press acted as printer for a raft of voluntary organisations and private clients. Russell Press and the BRPF moved to Bulwell Lane in Old Basford in the late nineties, and are now in Colwick near the country park. Some of Russell's materials can be found in the current office. Most of them had been collected and donated by his American wife Edith, a historian.

Ken Coates continued as director of the BRPF and was behind an extensive publishing programme under the foundation's Spokesman Books imprint, and in support of the campaign for European Nuclear Disarmament (END).

In the 1980s Ken Coates was elected MEP for Nottingham, and he continued to argue for a close alignment with Europe until his death in 2010. His many campaigns include opposing the abolition of the Labour Party's Clause IV – his book *Clause IV: Common Ownership and the Labour Party* (1995) making a powerful argument in favour of public ownership – as well as campaigning against military intervention in Afghanistan and Iraq as he continued to uphold his and Bertrand Russell's ideals. For four decades Coates edited the BRPF's journal *The Spokesman*.

Former Library Services building, Basford.

Since 1970, *The Spokesman* has been published in Nottingham. It still features independent journalism on peace and nuclear disarmament, human rights and civil liberties, as well as contemporary politics. Contributors have included Robert Fisk, Noam Chomsky, Naomi Klein, John Le Carré and Kurt Vonnegut and, increasingly, a number of local writers.

Forty years ago, Coates invited Tony Simpson to work at the BRPF as the European Nuclear Disarmament campaign was burgeoning. Simpson has worked for the Foundation ever since and has edited *The Spokesman* for the past twelve years, producing three journals a year. His work continues to promote the writing and ideals of Bertrand Russell worldwide, and helps to retain his many connections to Nottingham UNESCO City of Literature. In 1957 Russell won the UNESCO Kalinga Prize for his writing on science and society.

The people of Nottinghamshire have a history of standing up for social justice and it has often been the writers that have led the way.

Nottingham's reputation for promoting peace and justice was further strengthened in 1974 with the arrival of the radical magazine *Peace News,* which has been published as a grassroots paper since 1936. The editorial collective had proposed that *Peace News* move out of London to the provinces and organise itself as a printing and publishing co-operative, and free premises had been offered in Nottingham. The first of their new fortnightlies appeared that same year, with the masthead 'for nonviolent revolution'. For many years the paper was based at 8 Elm Avenue. Though the magazine's glory days and more literary days were in the past, it remained influential in national politics. During the mid-1970s *Peace News* itself became the subject of front-page news due to their coverage of David Stirling's plan to build a private army (BG75) and their involvement with the Old Bailey trial associated with the British Withdrawal from Northern Ireland Campaign. *Peace News* later used a venue by the canal before returning its main office to London in 1990.

---

[1]Simpson, 2016.

Chapter 34
Broxtowe Hall – Estate of Mind

'Broxtowe Estate was far from the scene of recent happiness, but it might be more interesting if my first day was anything to go by.'

Derrick Buttress, *Broxtowe Boy*

Broxtowe Hall.

Broxtowe's literary legacy spans the globe, boasting the first person to write a defence of universal religious freedom in English.

Broxtowe's Edmund Helwys and his wife Margaret both died in 1590, leaving behind five children. It was their teenage son, Askham-born Thomas Helwys, who then took over their lease of Broxtowe Hall. After he entered Gray's Inn in London – a professional association for barristers – Helwys returned to the Hall where he settled, marrying Joan Ashmore in 1595.[1] Their marriage caused some scandal, perhaps because Joan may have been his young housekeeper. Helwys came into contact with Puritans in the north of the county, such as Richard Bernard, the vicar of Worksop, and John Smyth, from Sturton, and this seems to have changed his direction. And all was not well. Objecting to being told how to pray, the group were demanding further reform of the Church of England.

By the century's end, the laws tightened once again, and those wanting to attend the church of their own choosing were left with little option – conform or leave. Many bided their time, but the new king turned out to be more conservative than they had hoped. In 1603, when King James made his stately rounds from Edinburgh to

London, knighting people en route at Worksop and Newark, Helwys did not claim his right. Under King James it was still illegal to play games (or even to run) on a Sunday; it was illegal for a priest not to wear a surplice; and illegal not to have your children christened. It was, however, legal to abuse others for their religious practices.

A conference was held in 1606 at which it was claimed that the best option was to move to the Netherlands, a place where all Protestants had been free to worship on their own premises, with no magistrate holding authority in matters of faith. Returning from the conference, Smyth fell ill and sought refuge, probably at Basford, where Helwys had now moved. He also preached, illegally, at the church in Basford where his friend Rev John Herring was minister. By this time, Smyth had renounced his ordination and organised a new congregation at Gainsborough, which attracted supporters from as far as Basford and Broxtowe, including Helwys.

In 1607, The High Court of Ecclesiastical Commission for the Province of York took active proceedings against members of the Gainsborough and Scrooby congregations. Local clergy were removed from office and Joan Helwys was arrested for refusing to take an oath according to law. After she declined to answer their questions, she was sent to York Castle.

Helwys had seen enough. The only lay leader in a group of rebels, he developed a Nottinghamshire network of some of the most religious radicals in England, and, facing further arrests, they prepared for action. He realised that life in England was becoming impossible and preparation to leave for the Netherlands was made. After a failed attempt to escape via Boston, Helwys provided the funds for another escape via Gainsborough and Stallingborough, although he and his wife were briefly arrested after being caught on the shore.

After helping to fund Smyth's move, Helwys joined the radical theologian and others at their Amsterdam premises. English authorities only allowed emigration by licence and so Broxtowe Hall was seized.

Influenced by the Mennonites in Amsterdam, Helwys and Smyth became the first two Baptists. Smyth baptised himself before baptising his friend. Helwys split from Smyth around 1610 when Smyth decided to join the fellowship of Waterlander Mennonites.

It was in Amsterdam that Helwys wrote one of the earliest English Baptist documents, *A Short Declaration of the Mystery of Iniquity*. Split into four books, it was a plea for religious liberty, in which Helwys argued that the State should have no control over religious faith, developing the view expressed by Smyth that magistrates should not be involved in matters of conscience. Helwys's writing called for complete liberty of conscience in matters of religion for all people. He argued for the same rights for all faiths, and that any relationship with God should be both personal and voluntary.

Identifying two beasts, the Roman Catholic Church and the Church of England, Helwys wrote of the cruel spiritual bondage of uniformity of interpretation, and stated that by forcing a single interpretation upon the people, the Church of England was guilty of spiritual tyranny.

His next act was one of huge bravery. For Helwys had not only decided to publish his radical work, he was returning to England with his new denomination of General Baptists, and taking his radical ideas to the king. Helwys believed in the power of the written word and also that the king could bring about the necessary reform.

It was risky. Another former Gray's Inn entrant, Henry Barrow, had previously been condemned to death for publishing and dispersing seditious books. Since then the Conventicle Bill had been amended, but an offender still faced prison and, if later refusing to attend public worship, banishment.

Helwys and twelve Baptists returned to England in 1612 where Helwys started the first Baptist Church on English soil, in Spitalfields, east London. Daring to challenge the king and state, a copy of Helwys' book was delivered to his Royal Highness with a handwritten inscription.

The appeal to accord full liberty of conscience was dismissed and Helwys and other Baptists were thrown into Newgate Prison.

It was in prison that *Persecution for Religion Judg'd and Condemn'd* (1616) was written, either by Helwys or his follower, fellow General Baptist John Murton (1585–1626) who had been greatly influenced by Helwys. Around 1615/16, Helwys died in prison, but his words would remain very much alive.

Aware of Helwys's death and in fear of persecution, many of the group from Scrooby, who had settled in Leiden, joined the Mayflower Pilgrims and crossed the Atlantic in 1620 where they established new colonies. It was Roger Williams (1603–1683), the father of Providence, Rhode Island, who continued to promote Helwys's arguments for tolerance. Williams married the daughter of Richard Bernard, the former Worksop vicar,[2] himself an author of many books and a likely influence on Bunyan's *The Pilgrim's Progress* (1678).

Three decades after Helwys's death, Williams used much of Murton's *An Humble Supplication to the King's Majesty* (1620) to develop his own defence of religious freedom, *The Bloody Tenant of Persecution* (1644), which was a defence of Murton's views (and a development of Helwys's).

Helwys's proposal for the separation of state and religion eventually made its way into the first line of the American Constitution's First Amendment, which reads: 'Congress shall make no law respecting an establishment of religion, or prohibiting the free exercise thereof...' and his call for tolerance and free will can be seen in Article 18 of the United Nations' Universal Declaration of Human Rights:

1. Everyone shall have the right to freedom of thought, conscience and religion. This right shall include freedom to have or to adopt a religion or belief of his choice, and freedom, either individually or in community with others and in public or private, to manifest his religion or belief in worship, observance, practice and teaching.
2. No one shall be subject to coercion which would impair his freedom to have or to adopt a religion or belief of his choice.

The argument that there should be a separation of State and the Church may not have been new but Helwys was the first to include all religions, or no religion, and to write the argument in such terms, including the point that anyone should be allowed to change religion. His courage and radical writing made the world a better place.

There are places in Nottingham that Thomas Helwys is better remembered. The Baptist church in Church Street, Lenton (rebuilt

Thomas Helwys Church, Lenton.

1967–68), is named after him and the church he visited in Bilborough, and married Joan Ashmore in, St Martin's Church, has a memorial to the Helwys family.

St Martin's also houses two murals painted in 1946 by the famous artist Evelyn Gibbs (1905–91). Thought to have been destroyed, these were uncovered behind a false ceiling by an electrician during repairs in 2009. The paintings depict a biblical scene set in Nottingham. Pauline Lucas, who wrote a biography of Evelyn Gibbs, was surprised and excited by news of their discovery. Gibbs had created the murals after coming to Nottingham during the Second World War. Staying here until 1960, she organised exhibitions and founded the Midland Group of Artists. She also taught at a school for children with special needs while writing an influential book on art, entitled *The Teaching of Art in Schools* (1948), a book illustrated by her pupils. Gibbs herself was a book illustrator and provided the art for several of Hilda Lewis's novels. Her husband was Hugh Willatt, one of the driving forces behind the creation of Nottingham Playhouse.

Lucy Hutchinson (1620–81), best known for *Memoirs of the Life of Colonel Hutchinson*, in praise of her husband, the roundhead governor of Nottingham during the English Civil War, wrote of Broxtowe Hall, which, during the war, was occupied as a garrison for Parliamentarians. Despite its position on the brow of a hill, the hall saw fighting and received considerable damage. Hutchinson tells of its setting for a story of romance and tragedy involving a gallant young Puritan commander, Captain Thornhaugh.

Broxtowe Hall was one of a number of country houses held by troops, another being the nearby mansion Aspley Wood Hall, which was held for the king by a member of the Willoughby family. A young Royalist and Papist, Agnes Willoughby, was returning home from Bilborough when she was jumped upon by three ruffians. On hearing her cries, Captain Thornhaugh came to her aid, shooting one of her attackers and sending the others running for cover. Agnes and the captain fell in love despite their religious and political differences. When Thornhaugh was fatally wounded, Agnes was heartbroken and vowed never to marry, devoting herself to prayer, fasting, and alms-giving. Their tragic love story is also told of in Robert Mellors' book, *In and About Nottinghamshire* (1908).

The grounds of Broxtowe Hall offered walkers a labyrinth of lanes and beautiful woods. This all changed after the hall was demolished in 1937, its land becoming part of the new Broxtowe Estate. There's just one bit of wall remaining from the old hall. Named after Broxtowe Hall, the new estate was built to accommodate families uprooted by slum clearances in the older areas of Nottingham such as Sneinton and Radford. As a seven-year-old, Derrick Buttress moved into a new red brick house on Frinton Road, one of the many new streets that radiated out from Denton Green.

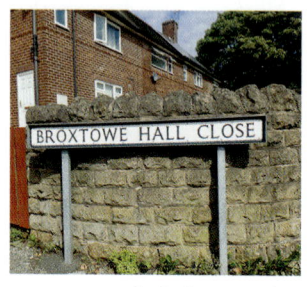

Buttress wrote about growing up in Broxtowe in his first volume of autobiography, *Broxtowe Boy* (2004), in which he described his childhood during the Second World War, hearing bombs land in the distance and feeling the vibrations beneath his feet. By the time he moved to Broxtowe his parents had only just reunited having separated for a year, and their marriage was to be the other 'war' in the young lad's life. His Mam, who lost her father and brother in the First World War, responds to her husband being called up by asking, 'How am I supposed to live on a soldier's pay?'

With conflict all around him, young Buttress found some comfort in friends, films and Aspley Public Library's junior library which, on first sight of, he 'felt like yelling in joy.'

Like Buttress's memoir, Nicola Monaghan's award-winning novel, *The Killing Jar* (2006), is a moving and at times amusing account of an impoverished life on the Broxtowe Estate where she lived. It's an unflattering, occasionally shocking, portrayal of a council estate ruled by drugs and violence. This powerful debut novel follows Kerrie-Ann, born into a life of struggle, who, by the age of ten, is selling drugs at school. Fiercely independent, she is an unforgettable character who narrates her story in an authentic Nottingham tongue. Monaghan dedicated *The Killing*

Jar to her cousin who was murdered after a drug-fuelled attack by one of his supposed friends, an incident that partly inspired the novel's setting.

From Helwys's plea for tolerance, to a tragic love story amid the Civil War, childhood memories of the Second World War and the horror of life as a young dealer, Broxtowe has a chequered but deserved place on Nottingham's literary map.

---

[1]Whitley, 1935.
[2]Gray, 2016.

Chapter 35
Caledon Road, Sherwood –
Nottingham's Booker Prize

'It's a little theory of mine that people who get on in the world do so because they are in some way personally vulnerable and make it up to themselves by chasing success.'
Stanley Middleton, *Married Past Redemption*

For nearly half a century the large Edwardian house at 42 Caledon Road was home to the quintessential Nottingham novelist, Stanley Middleton (1919–2009), who moved here with his wife Margaret and their two young daughters in 1961, by which time he was Head of English at High Pavement and an emerging novelist. From this home in Sherwood, Middleton wrote forty-five novels, averaging nearly one a year, a feat he combined with teaching until 1981.

42 Caledon Road, Sherwood.
photo: Dave Whittle

The centre-piece hallway looks up to a stunning skylight which illuminates an octagonal landing, off which was Middleton's study. He would write in here most mornings, his desk facing a mature rear garden that was lovingly tended by Margaret. Each manuscript was handwritten before being passed to somebody else to type up. By his desk were shelves of ex-library books. Middleton visited Sherwood Library on Saturdays and, when his daughters were young, they'd walk with him, listening to their father tell stories on the hoof.

Stanley Middleton may have been a prolific writer but never at the expense of his teaching or his daughters, who he always had time for. He was also a renaissance man, painting watercolours between writing novels and playing the piano. Middle-class creatives often appeared in his books. In one of his best, *Harris's*

Requiem (1960), the protagonist is a composer.

It was under Hutchinson's New Author scheme that Middleton was first published with *A Short Answer* (1958). This was the first of his many novels with Hutchinson. At no time did he have an agent or receive an advance. The novels are not driven by plot, they are about people, their relationships, careers, frustrations. Observations of provincial middle-aged lives. The realism is such that you can't help thinking that the author is writing about the everyday concerns and motivations of his own neighbours and colleagues, conversations he's had or overheard in a staffroom or over a garden fence. Middleton writes with compassion and a rare insight that amounts to wisdom. It's writing that's 'characterised by a deep sincerity, a single eye, an attachment to reality, a love of humanity and the townscapes of his Midland home...' said Davis (2009).

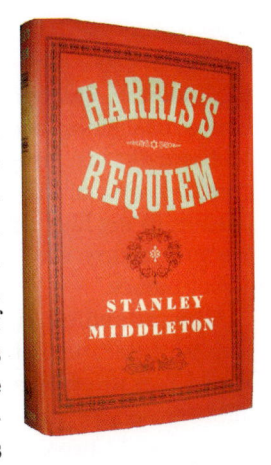

Most of the books are set in Nottingham, or Beechnall as he calls it. 'Beechnall is Nottingham, the whole thing,' admitted Middleton, who 'crossed Bulwell with Hucknall' when devising the name. 'I am invariably going to write about Nottingham,' he said, 'there are so many interesting things taking place hereabouts.' The local vernacular and humour in his dialogue is a welcome accompaniment to what are often moving reads.

Told through thoughts and flashbacks, his novel *Holiday* (1974) did venture away from his city. The story features a recently-separated lecturer who visits a seaside resort where he ponders the themes of life, death and broken relationships. It was for this novel that Middleton won the 1974 Booker Prize, an award he shared with Nadine Gordimer.

From his early novels the ingredients are there. Books two, three and four, *Harris's Requiem*, *A Serious Woman* (1961) and *The Just Exchange* (1962) being classic offerings, but if you've never read Middleton before, then *Holiday* is a good place to start. The 1970s were probably his best period for output, *Cold Gradations* (1972) being another of several highlights from this decade. For the 1980s, try *Entry into Jerusalem* (1983) or *Valley of Decision* (1985), the 1990s, *A Place to Stand* (1992) and *Married Past Redemption*

(1993), and for this century, *Brief Garlands* (2004) and *Her Three Wise Men* (2008) are all recommended.

Middleton was born in Bulwell on Menerva Street in 1919 (the house has since been pulled down) to working-class Wesleyan Methodists, his father a railway guard. At school in Bulwell, 'I received some of the best instruction I've ever had, or gave for that matter, in my life,' wrote Middleton (1996). 'And yet these teachers are not in any way commemorated in, for example, buildings or street names.'

After attending High Pavement Grammar School, he studied English Literature at University College Nottingham. The Second World War intervened and before his final year he was undertaking military service in the Royal Artillery and, mostly, in the Army Educational Corps, until 1946. By now Middleton was already writing (unpublished) novels and storing experiences for much later works. *Her Three Wise Men* takes its inspiration from his time teaching cadets in India.

After the war Middleton qualified as a teacher and was back in Nottingham for good. In 1951 he married Margaret Welch, later saying, 'I chose the right woman.' He was also settled at work, teaching at his former school, High Pavement. The school moved from, coincidentally, Stanley Road, Forest Fields, in 1955, to a large site in Bestwood. The English master may never have considered himself a great teacher, but many of his former pupils would disagree. Most days he walked to school, taking a right at the end of Caledon Road and walking up Hucknall Road. Each night, after completing his marking, Middleton would pick up his own exercise book and work on his latest novel.

In 1979 he declined an MBE, feeling that he was, like most people, simply doing his job. Never one for the spotlight, he was elected a Fellow of the Royal Society of Literature and held honorary degrees from the Open University and the University of Nottingham. For his eightieth birthday, Five Leaves published *Stanley Middleton at Eighty* (1999), a collection of his work, together with essays and poems from AS Byatt, Philip Callow, John Lucas and others. The book sported a front cover that featured one of Middleton's paintings. In a celebration of his career and birthday, the book was launched in the garden of Bromley House Library.

Stanley Middleton died in 2009 at the age of eighty-nine. His friend, the writer and first chair of Nottingham UNESCO City of Literature, David Belbin, arranged for a memorial plaque to be erected at his former home to coincide with Middleton's centenary. The plaque was crowdfunded by fans, friends and former pupils, and enough money was also raised for copies of a collection of Middleton's poems, *Poetry and Old Age* (2019), to be put in every library in the county. The black plaque proudly announces:

> Stanley Middleton
> Novelist
> Lived here
> 1961–2009

Poetry and Old Age – named after and including extracts from a late, unpublished novel – was published by Beeston's Shoestring Press and includes an introduction from Middleton's literary executor, Professor Philip Davis, a former pupil of his at High Pavement. Middleton had written poetry all of his adult life and thought it a higher calling than the novel, but this was his first published collection. Every bit as moving as his novels, the verse covers familiar Middleton ground. There's a poem about DH Lawrence (an early influence on Middleton) and plenty of other local interest.

It was a pleasure to be invited inside the former home of a true Nottingham novelist by its new owners, Felicity and Dave, who are adding to the home's literary legacy. Felicity Whittle leads the Gold Star Nottingham Booklovers Walk. The guided trail takes in many of the city centre's literary locations, and there's also a Nottingham's Women Writers walk. Middleton would have been delighted to see his former home in their hands.

Chapter 36
Danethorpe Vale, Sherwood –
Back to the Beginning

'If you insist that memory pays you a visit, keep it short.'
Peter Mortimer, *Forget Memory*

For his 2012 book *Made in Nottingham*, Peter Mortimer returned to Danethorpe Vale in Sherwood, a road he had left behind when he went to university some half a century earlier. Hoping to stay at the home he grew up in, Mortimer wrote a letter to 'The Occupants, 97 Danethorpe Vale, Sherwood Estate, Nottingham', only to hear back from Valerie and Derrick, the couple at no 85. It was their son (also Derrick) who lived at no 97, they explained, but he never has anyone in his house. Following their suggestion that Mortimer lived with them instead, the author travelled the hundred-and-sixty miles south from Tyneside to lodge with Valerie and Derrick, six doors along from his childhood home.

97 Danethorpe Vale, Sherwood Estate.

Danethorpe Vale is a long steep road that bisects the old Sherwood council estate, running from the busy Mansfield Road at the top to the busier Valley Road at the bottom. The estate was built a century ago to house veterans of the First World War.

Peter Mortimer is now known as an author, poet, playwright, journalist, artistic director (Cloud Nine Theatre Company) and publisher (IRON Press) but the Mortimer that lived in Nottingham never considered writing to be an option. He wasn't thinking beyond women, drink or football. He'd dreamed of playing professionally and got half-way there, wearing the colours of semi-pro Arnold St Mary's FC. As a fan he wore the black and white of Notts County – still his team.

As Mortimer takes up residence at no 85, the reader wonders what he'll make of the changes to his old patch. Will he ever get to see inside his old home at no 97? And what will Valerie do when she discovers he's been inadvertently using her toothbrush?

The book is part journal, part memoir, and has Mortimer revisiting old haunts such as the half-timbered Grade II listed pub, The Five Ways, named after the number of exits offered by the nearby Valley Road/Edwards Lane roundabout. The pub had been an important part of Mortimer's teenage years and its punters still sounded like he did, something he'd missed living up North. Even his own father shook off the vernacular after upgrading to Redhill two miles away. Now Mortimer was once again hearing words like 'bogger' and 'tuffy', and yet his reception was one of suspicion. 'Yo from the Child Support Agency or summat?' asked The Five Ways' landlord, paranoid at the sight of a stranger making notes (Mortimer, 2012).

Five Ways, Sherwood.

The Five Ways pub features in Alan Sillitoe's novel *Birthday* (2001) and at least one of his short stories. Sillitoe knew the pub well, and in the 1990s he campaigned to protect its interior from being altered when the building was up for sale.

In *Made in Nottingham* Mortimer proceeds to take in the Sherwood area with its strong artistic and independent vibe. He samples Nottingham's theatre life, its footy and pubs, mixing memories of Shippo's bitter with new experiences and rediscoveries. A former pupil at High Pavement, Mortimer had been taught English by Stanley Middleton, and he pays a visit to his former schoolmaster's widow, who was still living at their Caledon Road home. Middleton died in a Sherwood residential home called The Firs, sixty-five years after Mortimer had been born there (when it had been a maternity home). The Firs has

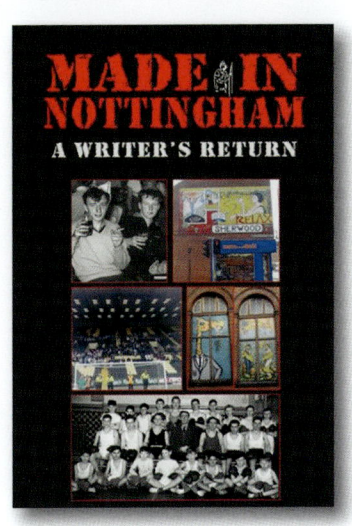

203

another literary connection as, in 1962, it was where the crime writer Andy Maslen was born.

Made in Nottingham contains loads of references to Nottingham writers, not least in many of the characters the author meets and the places he cycles to. The end result is one man's documentation of a life and place, then and now, an evocative journey that takes a series of unexpected routes.

This isn't the first time the author has taken himself out of his comfort zone and written about it. *Broke Through Britain* (1999), told in a similar style and structure to *Made in Nottingham*, follows Mortimer's five-hundred-mile trek from Plymouth to Edinburgh, on which he relied on the generosity of others, good fortune, and a little theft, to survive. *Camp Shatila* (2009) is about the time Mortimer lived in a Palestinian refugee camp in outer Beirut and set up a children's theatre group. The author also contributed to the collection of Nottingham crime stories *City of Crime* (1997).

Chapter 37
Ebers Road, Mapperley Park –
The Twentieth Century's Austen

'She had a good memory, too good, perhaps, since it held her imprisoned in the past.'

Dorothy Whipple, *Because of the Lockwoods*

35 Ebers Road, Mapperley Park.

Alfred 'Henry' Whipple was appointed Nottingham's first Director of Education in 1924, having held a similar post in Blackburn. It was Whipple who organised Nottingham's education system, dividing schools into three: Infant (up to seven/eight years), Junior (from seven/eight to eleven years) and Senior (eleven years and up), and the city into sixteen districts. He was also a strong advocate for the education of women, and that the new secondary schools should serve the wider community, providing evening access to culture for adults. The appointment had a hidden benefit for Nottingham in the form of the director's wife, for Henry had married Dorothy Stirrup in 1917, a woman half his age, who, between the World Wars, was the best-known novelist living in Nottingham.

Dorothy Whipple (1893–1966) had 'a kind of North-Country Jane Austen quality,' according to JB Priestley. She lived at 35 Ebers Road in Mapperley Park, and it was from here that she wrote her hugely popular novels. Whipple's *Greenbanks* (1932) was chosen as the year's Book Society's Choice, helping it to become the author's breakthrough novel. Following an ordinary family's joys and sorrows before and after the First World War, *Greenbanks* is a tale of infidelity, divorce, autocratic parents and rebellious offspring. Two characters, the emotional and irresponsible grandmother Louisa, and the unsentimental, charming granddaughter Rachel, were particularly well received.

From *Greenbanks*:

> It was queer, it was frightening, she thought, how in life you got what you wanted. Men, for instance, who admired above everything else, beauty in women, married beauty and, more often than not, found themselves with nothing but beauty.

Greenbanks brought with it a great success that continued with Whipple's subsequent tales of everyday life, most of which are set in Nottinghamshire, or as it appears, Trentham.

They Were Sisters (1943) tells the story of three siblings, the different marital choices they make, and how those choices impact on them; all set in an era when women stuck in a bad marriage had little or no option of reprieve. It's an authentic account of domestic middle-class life, with a menacing undertone that holds attention. From the novel:

> Moral failure or spiritual failure or whatever you call it, makes such a vicious circle... It seems as if when we love people and they fall short, we retaliate by falling shorter ourselves.

Tastes changed after the Second World War and Whipple's books fell out of favour. This was just as two of her novels had been made into films. 1945's *They Were Sisters* was voted one of the four best films of the year. The sisters are played by Phyllis Calvert (Lucy), Dulcie Gray (Charlotte) and Anne Crawford (Vera), whilst James Mason plays Geoffrey, one of their pursuers. He is an ambitious and cruel businessman, wanting a stay-at-home trophy wife, and the film is noted for its harrowing depiction of marital abuse.

A year later, the noirish *They Knew Mr Knight*, starring Mervyn

Johns, was released, featuring scenes of Ebers Road, Victoria Station and the Old Market Square.

The last of Whipple's sixteen novels, *Someone at a Distance* (1953), a tale about the destruction of a happy marriage, is another of her best.

One of a number of significant Nottingham writers to be have been published by John Murray, she wrote two memoirs: *The Other Day* (1950) and *Random Commentary* (1966), the latter offering reflection on Whipple's time in Nottingham. It contains the revealing line, 'I don't like having to concoct plots, I do people.' The author returned to Blackburn after her husband's death in 1958.

Persephone Books republished eight of Whipple's novels and a collection of her short stories. The writing has aged well, her characters are well-drawn and recognisable. There is a blue plaque on her former home, provided by Bromley House Library and Nottingham UNESCO City of Literature. It reads:

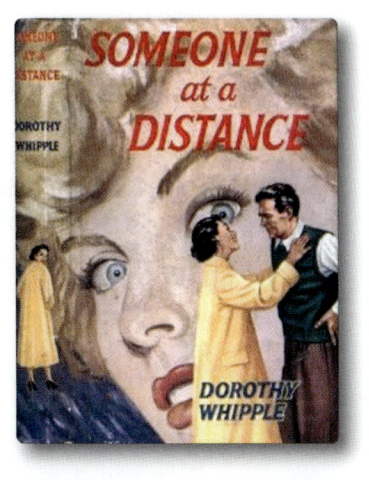

Dorothy Whipple
Novelist
lived here from 1926 to 1939
'the fullest years of my life'

Chapter 38
First Avenue, Sherwood Rise –
The Social Psychologist

'Good moods depend on physiological processes, some of which we understand.'

Michael Argyle, *The Psychology of Happiness*

One of the twentieth century's most respected social psychologists, (John) Michael Argyle was born on 11th August 1925 at 2 First Avenue, Sherwood Rise. A pioneer of experimental study, his work helped to establish the concepts of body language and social skills, and his forty-four books, both popular and scholarly, helped to define the scope of social psychology and promote its acceptance in academic circles.

Both of Michael Argyle's parents – his father George, a schoolmaster, and mother Phyllis (née Hawkins-Ambler) – died when he was eleven years old.[1] Argyle was educated at Nottingham High School for Boys and it was here that his interest in psychology began. Argyle had been concerned about a fellow pupil, a friend who suffered from shyness and a poor ability to interact with others, and he believed that the boy could be helped if only he could learn and develop "social skills".

After leaving the High School Argyle went to the University of Cambridge, initially reading Mathematics, but the Second World War intervened. Argyle served in the RAF, training as a navigator then working as a fireman during the Blitz, after which he completed an RAF science course and obtained a first-class degree in Experimental Psychology. It was as an undergraduate that he married Sonia, daughter of Marshall Dennis Kemp of Nottingham, and they had four children.

In 1952 Argyle became the first lecturer in Social Psychology at the University of Oxford and stayed there until his retirement. According to Lamb & Sissons Joshi (2002), he 'did more than any other individual in the UK to define the scope of social psychology, and to gain the nascent discipline's acceptance in academic departments and among the general public.' His great ability was to present complicated research in easily-read prose, and his work into nonverbal communication opened up a whole new line of inquiry, transforming human understanding of interpersonal communication.

It was *The Psychology of Interpersonal Behaviour* (1967), reputed to be the biggest-selling psychology paperback (Robinson, 2002) which, together with *Bodily Communication* (1975), established Argyle as a leading authority on the subject of nonverbal behaviour. He successfully put forward the hypothesis that spoken language is normally used for communicating information whereas nonverbal codes are typically used to express attitudes. He also established that there are many nonverbal aspects of behaviour (such as gaze, posture, proximity, facial expressions) that are more important than the words used when communicating with others. Of the two channels (verbal and nonverbal), Argyle suggested that nonverbal communication was twelve-and-a-half times more powerful than the actual words spoken, in terms of conveying attitudes.

Believing the psychology of happiness to be under-researched – psychologists were spending more time studying depression – Argyle decided to focus on the most positive aspects of human existence, asking what makes us happy. This was the subject of his 1987 book *The Psychology of Happiness*. His findings revealed that happiness is promoted by interpersonal relationships, and by sex, eating, exercise, music, and success, but not so much by wealth. He also wrote that happiness did not increase by removing causes of unhappiness, rather it required engaging in shared activities. Argyle himself allotted time in his daily schedule for writing and reading, research and teaching, as well as time for family, friends and fun. He later concluded that a happy marriage was the biggest single source of happiness, with dance and religion – for its mingling with the like-minded as much as anything else – also high on the happy list. Contentment, however, was best achieved through a fulfilling job pitched at a realistic level, together with the pursuance of an all-absorbing hobby, "serious leisure", such as reading, music, travel or art (or even housework), as long as you can become absorbed in it, as he described in *The Social Psychology of Leisure*

(1996). Watching television didn't promote happiness, but Argyle found that people who watched soap operas were, on average, happier than the rest of the population (most of this research was conducted before *EastEnders* hit our screens).

Argyle's work has been of scientific and practical importance, and he created training programmes for the workplace and everyday life. One of his programmes provided social skills training for psychiatric patients unable to cope with interpersonal relationships. And all this started with an idea from his Nottingham schooldays, when he thought that social skills were not only important but that they can be learned.

Michael Argyle was awarded honorary doctorates from several universities, including Oxford (1979), Adelaide (1982) and Brussels (1982), as well as many other awards. In 2002 Professor Argyle died in Nottingham, aged seventy-seven, following a swimming accident from which he never recovered. He left behind many theories on the human condition that have made a positive impact on people's lives.

---

[1]Colman, 2004.

Chapter 39
The Forest, Gregory Boulevard –
Ball Park Figures

'The Goose Fair was the cornerstone of the city's year... You never wanted to eat all your baby pink candyfloss but seeing it made with a stick around the barrel was like magic.'

Alice Levine

The Forest Recreation Ground.

The Forest Recreation Ground, about a mile north of the city centre, was once the southernmost part of Sherwood Forest. Best known for being Goose Fair's annual home and a site for park-and-riders, for over 300 years the Forest has hosted amateur sport. It began as the site of Nottingham Racecourse, whose grandstand was built in 1777, a hundred years before the ground was taken over by Nottingham Corporation when the racing moved to Colwick. In the eighteenth century Daniel Defoe was impressed by the people attending the races: the 'eleven or twelve noblemen and an infinite throng of gentlemen from all the counties around' and 'the train of coaches filled with the beauties of the north'.[1]

The son of a butcher, Herbert Kilpin – who grew up at 129 Mansfield Road (now no. 191) – played football on the Forest before moving to Italy in 1891. Picked to play for Internazionale Torino, Kilpin became the first Englishman to play in a foreign team. He later settled in Milan and founded the Milan Cricket and Football Club (now AC Milan). As a promoter, coach and player, Kilpin helped win the first three of Milan's many league titles. Robert Nieri's book *The Lord of Milan* (2019) tells the story of the man from Mansfield Road. The versatile novelist JC Snaith also played on the Forest, but his sport was cricket. A fellow Nottinghamshire cricketer invented shin pads after deciding to cut down his cricket pads and use them when playing football on the Forest. His name was "Sam Weller" Widdowson, a name his father had given him after his favourite fictional character, Charles Dickens' Sam Weller from *The Pickwick Papers*.

Situated at the south-east corner of the Forest is Church (or Rock) Cemetery, founded in 1848, and the resting place of many writers, including Philip James Bailey. Its location on the top of the Forest ridge had previously been the site of Gallows Hill, for centuries a place of executions. One person hanged there was Mary Voce, and her story inspired a leading author of the Victorian era.

Mary Voce from Fisher Gate (born Mary Hallam in Sneinton) was found in a state of shock and fear after her six-week-old baby had been poisoned with arsenic. The heart-broken mother was charged with her child's poisoning and, despite proclaiming her innocence, she was imprisoned to await execution.

In 1802 Voce appeared before a judge, who asked her if she'd anything to say. She handed him a piece of paper refuting the charge, blaming the poisoning on her neighbours' children, whilst admitting to have purchased the arsenic with the intention of poisoning herself after suffering much abuse from her husband. After ten minutes of deliberation, the jury declared her guilty. The Methodist preacher, Elizabeth Tomlinson, visited Mary Voce to pray with her and to persuade her to accept her crime. Tomlinson stayed with Voce through the night until, finally, the accused woman broke down and confessed. The preacher then travelled with her in the cart to Gallows Hill. Voce greeted her executioner with a smile and gave him her hand. 'Bless you,' she said to him. 'I have nothing against you. Somebody must do it.' Her body was left to hang for an hour, her dissected remains later placed on public display.

Two years later, Tomlinson got married. Her niece, Mary Ann Evans, became fond of her and would listen carefully to her recollections. Aged twenty, Evans heard all about Mary Voce and her aunt's time talking with her in the prison cell. Two decades on, Mary Ann Evans, better known for her pen name George Eliot, published *Adam Bede* (1859). The author recalled, 'The germ of *Adam Bede* was an anecdote told me by my Methodist Aunt [Elizabeth Tomlinson].' Eliot added, 'We were sitting together one afternoon ... probably in 1839 or 40, when it occurred to her to tell me how she had visited a condemned criminal, a very ignorant girl who had murdered her child and refused to confess...' (Eliot, 1858).

Predating Gallows Hill, Goose Fair has been a part of the Nottingham calendar for over 700 years, but it only moved to the Forest in 1928, the year Alan Sillitoe was born. In *Alan Sillitoe's Nottinghamshire* (1987), the author wrote, 'Goose Fair seems to have a magic all of its own, and an attraction for young people and children which I'm sure would be difficult to equal anywhere else.'

Sillitoe's short story, "Noah's Ark", from *The Loneliness of the Long-Distance Runner* (1959), tells of young Radford cousins, Colin and Bert, as they visit Goose Fair on its final Saturday with just fourpence between them for cakewalk and candyfloss, plus a few resourceful tricks at their disposal. They go looking for a free ride on the eponymous Noah's Ark, a carousel of painted animals. Before they head to the fair, there's the sight of:

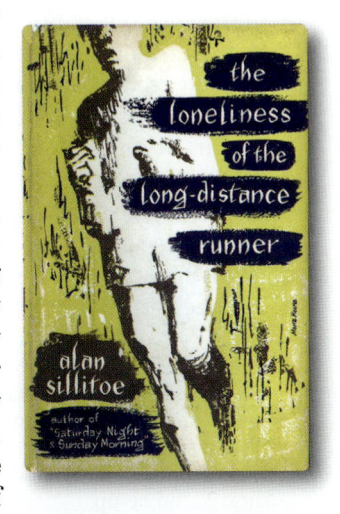

> a trundle of wagons and caravans rolling towards the open spaces of the Forest. [Colin's] brain was a bottleneck, like the wide boulevard along which each vehicle passed, and he saw, remembering last year, fresh-packed ranks of colourful Dodgem Cars, traction engines and mobile zoos, Ghost Trains, and Noah's Ark figures securely crated on to drays and lorries.

Goose Fair famously appears in Sillitoe's novel *Saturday Night and Sunday Morning* (1958), where Arthur Seaton loses 'all idea of time and place locked in the belly of its infernal noise.' Karel Reisz's 1960 screen version is filmed on location at the fair, Albert Finney (Seaton) and Shirley Anne Field (Doreen) riding the Waltzers and Dodgems, before Seaton tries to dodge trouble as he meets with Brenda (played by Rachel Roberts).

In 2001 a poetry festival, which claimed to be Nottingham's first, coincided with opening of Goose Fair. The event witnessed Brian Patten and Rosie Garner taking to a stage beneath the big wheel.

Local poet Garner read her poem *Fairground Music,* which was all about Goose Fair.

The fair has an edge, as anywhere might with such a 'crushing mass of gaping and sweating humanity,' as JB Priestley describes the crowds in *English Journey* (1934).

John Harvey might have avoided temptation to lean on Goose Fair for a story – though he certainly features the Forest, not least in *A Darker Shade of Blue* (2010) when Resnick attends a dead body on the site – but other crime fiction has taken advantage of the bustle and chaos of Goosey. In Keith Wright's fourth Inspector Stark crime thriller, *Fair Means or Foul* (1995), the death of a young girl at Goose Fair leads to a murder investigation. Wright himself was an inner-city CID Detective Sergeant.

Another retired detective, Alan Dawson, features Goose Fair in his debut suspense novel *The Showman* (2017), written under the pseudonym Jacques Morrell. In this scene, set in 1978, the character Michael is seeking answers:

> They got into a car on the Big Wheel, an open bench that behaved like a rocking chair ... Michael felt like he was on the second hand of a giant clock, time ticking away with each stop. He felt as though he had sixty hypothetical 'seconds' to get whatever information Bob Collins had for him. Once the wheel had turned its full circle, his time would be up.

The poet Kathy Pimlott was born in Radford between Players and the Forest. She later lived on Western Boulevard, where she would observe the fair arrive and leave. Having resided in London for four decades Pimlott still missed 'the specific, dangerous excitement that only happened once a year for two and half days.' In 2016 she wrote the poetry collection *Goose Fair Night*, reflecting on the fair and other places in and around Nottingham.

Goose Fair gets its name from when 20,000 geese were walked down from Lincolnshire to be sold, their feet dipped in tar to protect them on the long journey. DH Lawrence references this at the start of his short story, "Goose Fair", from *The Prussian Officer and Other Stories* (1914):

> Through the gloom of evening, and the flare of torches of the night before the fair, through the still fogs of the succeeding dawn came paddling the weary geese, lifting their poor feet that had been

dipped in tar for shoes, and trailing them along the cobble-stones into the town.

When Lawrence was a regular visitor, Goose Fair was still being held in the Market Square.

In the first volume of his autobiography, Cecil Roberts (1967) captured what it would have been like in Lawrence's day. 'Early in October every year there converged upon Nottingham from all over England all the travelling shows and hucksters,' wrote Roberts, who recalled seeing the fattest woman in the world and being peed on by a lion.

In his poem "The Fair", George 'Rusticus' Hickling captured all the fun when he wrote:

> There's Wombwell's menagerie and Holloway's stage
> And all the most wonderful things of the age:
> Fat pigs and fat children in plenty are there
> Descriptions of giants and dwarfs rend the air...

The Market Place hosted 'benign elephants and gloomy camels,' wrote Roberts, as well as lions, tigers, zebras, hyenas, monkeys and wolves, and 'helter-skelters like windmills,' and 'booths with prize-fighters who challenged all comers.' Roberts' depiction of the fair's rowdiness in the great crowds that grew before the midnight closing suggest good reason for its moving to the Forest, 'On the last night it was almost a matter of fighting one's way into the packed mass that swayed and circulated ... crushes that became near panic in which a rougher element delighted,' and 'an ugly temper began to raise its head.'

Perhaps letting off steam or escaping the routine of everyday life is what Goose Fair is all about. In his novel *Goose Fair* (1928) – published in England as *David and Diana* – Roberts sums it up nicely: 'Every first Thursday in October, following the custom of centuries, the good people of the city whose Sheriff was so soundly abused by Robin Hood, take leave of their senses.'

---

[1]Gurnham, 2010.

Chapter 40
Maggie's, City Hospital – This Big C, Creativity

'You can't use up creativity. The more you use, the more you have.'

Maya Angelou, *Conversations with Maya Angelou*

Maggie's, City Hospital.

Up in the trees at the City Hospital's Hucknall Road end is Nottingham's Maggie's cancer centre, a haven that provides practical, social and emotional support for people that have been affected by cancer. Architect Piers Gough's distinctive green building with its Paul Smith-designed interior provides a safe place to heal mentally and physically, with cancer support specialists on hand.

Maggie's user Ivory Longley told me, 'Maggie's is an emotional embrace that creates that wonderful feeling of not being alone in our cancer journey. The whisper of love, the strength of that gentle emotional hug: it's a place where I can be the real me.'

Open nine to five, Monday to Friday, there's a busy programme of free activities (most of which are drop-in) including a creative writing group that began soon after Maggie's opened in 2011. Former Reading and Literature Development lead for Nottinghamshire, Sheelagh Gallagher, ran the first group. Sheelagh had previously run a writing group at Nottinghamshire Hospice.

Maggie's inaugural writer-in-residence was Jo Weston, who said, 'Although everyone in the group has been affected by cancer, the focus is on an interest in reading and writing.' Weston is a writer of poetry, short fiction, travel writing and memoir. The NTU MA creative writing graduate's first poetry pamphlet is *How Not To Multitask* (2021).

The current writers in residence, Bridget Swinden and Sue Byrne, explained how the group has helped them: 'Maggie's is my safety net, where I can go for continuing support from staff and other centre users in the same situation, to deal with the physical and mental effects of having cancer, which have lasted long after the treatment ended,' said Swinden. Byrne added: 'Overcoming the death of my husband has been the biggest challenge of my life. The creative writing group has helped to process that grief and opened up an interest in poetry which I may not have developed without Maggie's.'

Members of the writing group find it beneficial to share their work and receive supportive feedback. It's not only a safe place to read work aloud, it's the ideal environment to express emotions around cancer.

The writing group has also welcomed along many local authors and poets. When I led a creative writing session there, I was joining a long list of writers to have done so, a list that includes Mark Barry, Paula Rawsthorne, Beth Moran, Jane Armstrong, Cathy Lesurf, Anne Goodwin, Helen Cross and Shreya Sen-Handley. The group also embarked on a literary tour of Nottingham.

On arriving at Maggie's you might notice poems displayed on the walls, or a basket of scrolls on the kitchen table, each with a piece of prose or poetry written on them. There is a library with a selection of books picked for their relevance to the centre's users, which includes two collections of writing produced by the group, *Between the Lines* (2015), a book of poems, short stories, memoirs and letters that was launched at Bromley House Library, and *Missing Pieces* (2017), launched at Waterstones. As you might expect, these collections include experiences of cancer and its effect on how the world is subsequently seen. The books are both entertaining and thought-provoking.

Clare Stevens was the creative writing group's tutor between 2015 and 2021. Stevens is a former journalist (*Nottingham Post* group) and government spin-doctor. After passing her MA in creative writing at NTU, she has seen the publication of her debut novel *Blue Tide Rising* (2019), which explores mental health issues using an otherworldly narrative thread. With both an urban and rural setting, including some Nottingham scenes, Stevens skilfully handles dark themes. Taking over from Stevens was Sarah Dale, an occupational psychologist, coach and author of *Bolder and Wiser* (2013) plus several published short stories.

Maggie's creative writing group meet fortnightly. If you've been affected by cancer then think about going along. It can be useful to put feelings and experiences onto paper in an environment in which hopes, fears and joys are cheered and comforted.

> With friends around to hold me,
> With a softness made of need,
> You wipe away the tear drops,
> And grow a loving seed.
> On my path you hold me steady,
> Holding hands so very tight,
> You guide me through the darkness,
> To a warm and shining light.
> I see the love you offer,
> As I stumble on my way,
> Your words so soft with kindness,
> That brightens up my day.
> I see you as a fountain,
> Spreading love and care,
> We feel the warmth around us,
> Just knowing you are there.

Maggie's Magic Moments, a poem by Maggie's user Ivory Longley (1945–2021).

Chapter 41
Nottingham Girls' High School, 9 Arboretum Street – On the Write Path

> 'You think you know someone – you could swear you knew what they were capable of – and then they go and surprise you.'
>
> Julie Myerson, *Something Might Happen*

Nottingham Girls' High School has had quite an impact on the city's contribution to literature. The school was originally on Oxford Street before relocating to a former lace manufacturer's home on Arboretum Street where it expanded into a neighbouring house. During the Second World War the school moved to Bestwood and Daybrook, only to move back to their current home as the war ended.

In DH Lawrence's *The Rainbow* (1915), the character Ursula Brangwen attends Nottingham Grammar School, which is the High School. '...its rooms were very large and of good appearance,' wrote Lawrence.

Among the school's alumnae are many published writers. The reviewer, journalist, columnist and author of fiction and non-fiction, Julie Myerson, attended in the 1970s. Born in Sherwood in 1960, Myerson grew up in several locations within the city and county. Sherwood features in her short story "Maureen", from *City of Crime* (1997), and in her book *Home* (2004), Myerson recalls almost every Nottingham house she's ever lived in. Her novel *Something Might Happen* (2003) was long-listed for the Booker Prize.

In the 1940s Janice Elliott, Helen Cresswell and Stella Rimington were all pupils of Nottingham Girls' High School. The novelist, journalist, reviewer and children's writer, Janice Elliott, was brought up in wartime Nottingham, a period of her life that provides the setting for her award-winning bestseller *Secret Places* (1981), which featured a girls' boarding school during the war. *Secret*

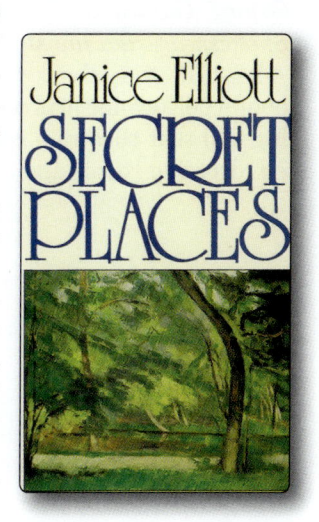

Places also became a prize-winning film in 1984. Elliott left a career in journalism (*Sunday Times*) for full-time writing in 1962. She has written more than twenty novels, five children's books and a collection of stories.

Helen Cresswell loved creating stories for children, and in a forty-five-year career the BAFTA award-winner penned well over a hundred of them. Cresswell missed a whole school year due to spinal problems when she was twelve (Brown, 2005). Much of her time in hospital was spent writing and reading, which she did voraciously, including the books of Enid Blyton, an author she'd later adapt for TV.

In 1969 Stella Rimington joined Britain's Security Service and, in 1992, she was appointed Director General of MI5, becoming the first woman to hold the post and the first to have her name publicly announced on appointment. Following her retirement in 1996, Rimington released her autobiography, *Open Secret*, and has since published ten bestselling thrillers featuring MI5 officer Liz Carlyle.

The literary scholar Helen Cooper was at the High School in the late 1950s/early 1960s. In 1978 she moved to University College Oxford, becoming the first woman fellow in its history, and taught medieval and early modern literature. Later, she became a Professor of Medieval and Renaissance English at the University of Cambridge and a fellow of Magdalene College. Cooper's research interests include Anglo-Norman and Middle English romance, Chaucer and Shakespeare. Her many published books include *Oxford Guides to Chaucer: The Canterbury Tales* (1996) and *Shakespeare and the Medieval World* (2010).

In 2017 the school raised the curtain on a new nine-million-pound performing arts centre known as The Space, a fully-functioning 260 seat theatre – complete with stage, auditorium, orchestra pit, dressing rooms and even a green room.

Chapter 42
The Old General, Radford Road – A Loveable Rogue

'He managed to rub shoulders with the most powerful men in Nottingham who indulged him in his harmless eccentricities.'
Ztan Zmith, *The "Green"– A journey through time*

The Old General pub/hotel used to stand on the corner of Radford Road and Bobbers Mill Road. It once proclaimed in neon lighting, "Welcome to Hyson Green", but it is its statue of a Nottingham pauper that caught the public's imagination.

The pub was built in 1883 by John Holmes. The sculpture that made the pub's name was crafted by his brother Joseph. Joseph Holmes, best known for his work with marble, was more used to commissions for funeral vases or stone angels when he was asked to carve a statue of local man Benjamin Mayo, AKA the Old General. Holmes carved the statue in an open field near the pub from a solid block of stone that came from Caen in France. After appearing in Nottingham Castle's museum, the statue was moved to a showroom before arriving in its recognisable location in the window above the main entrance of the Old General pub on the Bobbers Mill Road side. The statue was painted white, and every Christmas for over a century the Old General was dressed as Santa Claus, his red cloak and white beard becoming a yuletide landmark.

Benjamin Mayo, the real Old General, was born around 1779. Thought of as a "half-wit", the popular local eccentric was a fixture in and around Nottingham's Market Place where he sold ballads, broadsheets and chapbooks. Mayo's hunched stoop and deformed legs gave him a recognisable gait as he shuffled round with newspapers folded over his arm. The leading librarian John Potter Briscoe (1877) described him as 'very round shouldered and his stature was no more than four feet high. His eyes were dark grey...' and 'he wore his shirt unbuttoned revealing his copper coloured chest.'

Ben Mayo lived most of his life with his mother in the St Peter's workhouse where he was born (where the Broadmarsh Centre used to be). For years the pauper turned a profit selling the latest news, especially when it involved a disaster or scandal. Dying confessions were also in demand, as were any convicted criminal's final words before the public gallows. Often these were copies of a burglar's last letter to a loved one.

On dry news days, Mayo was known to sell speeches for a penny, advertising that he had copies of the latest words from the Duke of York or Prince of Wales, only to dupe his customers. When they protested that they'd received a blank sheet of paper, Mayo responded: "Is Royal 'ighness never said ought.'

After Mayo's mother had died and his workhouse was shut down, its master, Mr Hudson, took Mayo into his own home and provided for him, not wanting to see him go to the new workhouse. Thanks to his benefactor, Mayo got to ditch his grey clothing for a red coat with military epaulettes. Hudson took Mayo with him to St Peter's Church every Sunday. He wasn't the only local bigwig that the Old General mixed with, Mayo was well-known to most of Nottingham's authority figures, who put up with the lovable rogue.

The Old General came into his own on Mickleton Monday, a day when he led schoolchildren through the streets like a good-intentioned Pied Piper. In the days before maps were commonplace, the Mickleton Jury – consisting of the Mayor, two sheriffs and the corporation's important townsmen – would "beat the bounds" on the first Thursday in September, establishing the town's boundaries. The following Monday, the jury returned to note down any obstruction, irregularities or petty offences. Backing them up were Mayo and his band of youths demanding action. If anyone had kindling too close to their house or a loose pig in their yard, the General and his troop of minors would sort it. Their role, following behind the jury, was to enforce the immediate removal of obstructions or to remove them themselves.

The children loved Mickleton Monday. Those that weren't given permission to have the day off school either bunked off or were liberated by Mayo's battalion of kids shouting, 'Out, Out, Out,' and throwing mud at the school until those still inside were released. This one-day holiday ended at the entrance to Nottingham Castle with another tradition, in which the army of children demanded admission to the yard only to be denied access, then compensated by sweetmeats. These were thrown over the gateway of the Castle Lodge to the expectant crowd.

It wasn't just on Mickleton Monday that Mayo had his young followers. The Old General would regularly be seen in the Market Place drilling his army of truants like they were soldiers. Mayo saw himself as second only to the mayor in importance within Nottingham[1] and by the age of sixty he was wearing a military cap which, along with his red coat, gave him the look of the ringleader that, in many ways, he was.

After Mr Hudson left Nottingham, the Old General went to St Mary's Workhouse, also known as Nottingham Union Workhouse, between Mansfield Road and York Street (where BBC's York House used to be). He lived here with over a thousand other paupers.

Mayo died in 1843 after failing to recover from a fall. He was buried in the old St Peter's Churchyard, the Broad Marsh burial ground. He was so fondly remembered that subscribers paid for a tablet to be erected in his memory. This is in a quiet corner of the General Cemetery, mounted on a wall on the Clarendon Street side. It reads:

> Benjamin Mayo commonly known by the name of "the Old General" died in the Nottingham Union work-house 12th January 1831, aged 64 years. A few inhabitants of this town, associating his peculiarities and eccentricities with reminiscences of their early boyhood, have erected this tablet to his memory.

Benjamin Mayo's plaque, General Cemetery.

There's another nod to the Old General in Carrington, as Mayo Road is named after him. As for the Old General's statue, he's said to be hiding somewhere in Hyson Green. It's still missing a hand, a casualty of wartime damage.

Before we leave Hyson Green there's a forgotten writer worthy of your attention: William Hatfield (1892–1969), who was born here as Ernest Chapman. The son of a policeman, he briefly attended Nottingham University and was articled to a solicitor before migrating to Australia in 1912. A student of Aboriginal languages and customs, he worked as a bushman but dreamed of being a writer. Under the pen name William Hatfield, a name he later took by deed poll, he had a dozen books published, including *Sheepmates* (1931) and *Desert Saga* (1933), about an Aboriginal boy. In 1937 Oxford University Press published his autobiographical *I Find Australia*. Hatfield later focused on conservationist issues and lectured as a Communist.

---

[1]Holland Walker, 1926.

Chapter 43
The Park Estate – Private Lives

'There are fairies at the bottom of our garden!'

Rose Fyleman, *Fairies*

Famed for her fairies, the writer of more than sixty volumes of fiction, poetry and plays, Rose Fyleman, lived in the private Park Estate, at 29 Newcastle Drive, in a house designed by TC Hine in the mid-1850s. Fyleman left University College Nottingham to become a singer in Europe. After travelling she landed in London where the results of her training achieved a diploma from the Royal College of Music. Her work as an opera singer ceased on her return to Nottingham, where she conducted singing lessons and occasionally taught music. This led to regular classroom teaching at her sister's private school at 10 Pelham Terrace.[1] On finding a lack of suitable poetry for her students, Rose developed her own, tailored for use in the classroom.

Rose Fyleman was born in Nottingham in 1877, her father a German Jewish immigrant who worked in the lace trade. The family moved to the Park in 1912. Two years later, as war broke out, the Feilmanns anglicised their name to Fyleman. Rose Fyleman was nearly forty at this time and it coincided with the start of her successful career as a published writer. *Punch* magazine was the first to print her work, a fairy poem, and her association with fairies would endure. Fyleman's first collection, *Fairies and Chimneys*, followed in 1918 and it was reprinted twenty times over the next decade.

Fyleman's stories and poems avoided the darkness and evil that featured in many fairy tales of that time. Whilst continuing to write fairy stories, Fyleman edited the children's magazine *Merry-Go-Round* and wrote many other works for children, including plays such as *The Magic Pencil*. Popular with younger children, her short stories like *The Rainbow Cat* (1922) would lead readers into trying her more conventional books, *The Adventure Club* (1926) being one of them.

Her story, *A Princess Comes to Our Town* (1927), is set in Nottingham. In this fairy tale, the Fairy King and Queen have chosen the man they want their daughter to marry, but Princess Finestra doesn't want the prince, not yet anyway. Life would be far too boring, she wants to have real adventures first. To that end, the princess' godmother has her transported to Nottingham's Market Place where adventure ensues.

Robert Millhouse's (1788–1839) first published work included his poem "Nottingham Park" (1821). The long poem, published in Nottingham, is about The Park back when it was an open green space. Formerly the King's Park, then the Duke of Newcastle's, it became a private housing estate in Victorian times. 'England has no lovelier residential quarter,' wrote Cecil Roberts, in *The Growing Boy* (1974), 'secluded, sylvan, yet built into the heart of the city.'

'An address in The Park extracted immediate deference from the town tradespeople, and from the railway porters, who knew that residents therein always travelled first-class and tipped well,' wrote Roberts in his 1951 novel, *A Terrace in the Sun*.

The Park has been home to several literary folk. It was at 54 The Ropewalk that the poet Philip James Bailey lived his last days, dying from influenza. There's a photo of Bailey at his desk, pen in hand, gazing out the window from inside his Ropewalk home.

Rev John Elliotson Symes lived on The Park's Tattershall Drive. Born in London in 1847, he was the author of several non-fiction books from *The Prelude to Modern History* (1890) to *The Evolution*

Philip James Bailey at his desk looking out to the Ropewalk.

of the New Testament (1921). Symes was appointed Professor of Language and Literature at University College after it opened in 1881. He had responsibility for the whole arts department; his three lecturers teaching Shakespeare, history, political economy, Greek, Latin, French and German. Appointed Principal of University College in 1890, Symes established the teacher training that was later undertaken by DH Lawrence. He also supported the establishment of the first students' association.

William Bradshaw was involved in the management of University College. He was born in 1836 and lived at Carisbrooke House at 1 Cavendish Crescent North. A proprietor of the *Nottingham Journal*, he also founded and ran the *Leicester Daily Post*. Bradshaw was an important member of the Nottinghamshire Liberal Unionists and the Nottingham Naturalists' Society (Pike, 1901).

David Belbin's fictional Nottingham MP, Sarah Bone, lives in The Park. In the first of the Bone & Cane crime books (2011), it's revealed that she and Nick Cane had always aspired to live there. Cane rents a ground-floor flat on the Canning Circus side where he finds access to a cave in the sandstone. Illegal plans soon come to mind.

In the words of Geoffrey Trease, in his updated *Biography of Nottingham* (1984), 'The Park, as any snob will tell you, is not what it was.'

Carisbrooke House, 1 Cavendish Crescent North, The Park.

The jury is out as to whether the crime writer John Harvey raised or lowered the tone by living there!

---

[1]Edlin-White, 2017.

Chapter 44
Sneinton Market, Sneinton Square – Common People

'General Booth found the masses. He was the prophet of the poor.' Thomas FG Coates, *The Life Story of General Booth*

Sneinton's Market Square, which is not officially in Sneinton, was the site of a clay pipe workshop. Its nearest homes, back-to-back housing known as the Bottoms, were more like slums. In 1890, the Salvation Army's William Booth described the Sneinton of his youth, recalling 'the degradation and helpless misery of the poor stockingers, wandering gaunt and hunger-stricken through the streets.' Booth was born in 1829 in Sneinton's Notintone Place. The village of Notintone was formed in 900AD, becoming known as Sneinton in 1194.

Towards the middle of the nineteenth century the market area was hosting "blood tubs". These were plays that were performed by the poor, for the poor. A level below penny gaffs, the lewd and violent dramas were unlicensed shows that ranged from the recounting of Shakespeare to the recreating of local crimes. Often improvising, the performers would react to the crowd, doing whatever it took to part them from their loose change. The cobbled market space also hosted public and religious meetings. At one such event, the boxer Bendigo is said to have given a sermon atop a wagon. There have been many books written about Bendigo, but it's a little-known poem by Arthur Conan Doyle, entitled *Bendy's Sermon*, that best captures the spirit of the man. It was first published with illustrations in a 1909 edition of *The Strand Magazine*.

It's possible that some of Robert Millhouse's children were amongst those gathering to watch the Sneinton blood tubs. Working in a factory with a stocking loom from the age of six, and at a stocking frame from the age of ten, Millhouse spent most of his life in poverty, and writing poetry. The weaver-poet learned to write at Sunday school. On being selected to sing in the choir of St Peter's Church, Millhouse was no longer able to receive his weekly education. Undeterred, he began reading the poetry of Shakespeare, Milton and Pope, inspiring him to write his own verse.[1] Millhouse was named "The Artisan Poet" and "The Burns of Sherwood Forest". His works include *Blossoms* (1823), *The Song* of the Patriot (1826) and *Sherwood Forest* (1827). His best work is thought to be *The Destinies of Man* (1832 and 1834).

In 1828 Millhouse took part in a strike by the framework-knitters. According to Sir Richard Phillips, he suffered 'for his fidelity to his brethren, every kind of privation. He justified this strike, and displayed, with great energy and eloquence, the wretched situation of himself and others.'

Millhouse had lived in West Street, a stone's throw from Sneinton Market, before moving around the corner to 32 Walker Street where he died in 1839, aged fifty. Just three years earlier, Millhouse had married his second wife Marian at St Stephen's Church in Sneinton. Seven children survived him. A lover of nature, he wrote:

St Stephen's Church, Sneinton.

From my early boyhood until now
Thy forest, Sherwood, held alone the spring
Whence gushed my inspiration.

Thomas Ragg (1808–81) contributed a poetic appeal on behalf of Millhouse. Ragg become assistant to the Sneinton bookseller William Dearden, of 3 Carlton Street, in 1834. By this time Ragg was living on Haywood Street and had already contributed verses to the *Nottingham Review* and written his popular poem "The Incarnation", part of a twelve-book work called *The Deity* (1834), described by *The Times* as 'a very remarkable production; an elaborate philosophical poem by a working mechanic of Nottingham.'[2] Ragg was self-educated and wrote his popular books and poetry on the side. Robert Southey was an admirer of Ragg, who wrote ten books and later edited and owned the *Birmingham Advertiser*. His autobiography came out in 1858, and by 1873 his *Creation's testimony to its God, or the accordance of Science, Philosophy, and Revelation* had reached twelve editions.

An ancestor of Ragg's was the prominent radical George Ragg who, after being prosecuted in 1819 for selling the *Republican* newspaper, was sent to Warwick Jail.

William Dearden, the Carlton Street printer and bookseller – whose premises were later occupied by the printer Messrs J & H Bell Ltd – published *Dearden's Miscellany* from the 1830s. The monthly magazine combined local writing talent with general interest pieces, acting as a convenient book of reference for contemporary inventions and the advancement of science, on which Dearden was particularly focused. In addition to publishing books, Dearden also edited the magazine, whose contributors included not just Thomas Ragg but other local poets such as Richard Howitt and Sidney Giles.

Sneinton officially became part of Nottingham in 1877. This was two years after Arthur John Lawrence had married Lydia Beardsall at Sneinton's parish church, St Stephen's. Their fourth child, David Herbert Richards Lawrence, born in 1885, mentions the church in his early historical short story, "Goose Fair".

By 1920, Sneinton Market had made its way into literature, with this description in DH Lawrence's *Women in Love* (1920):

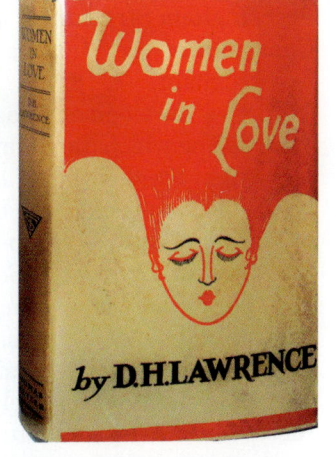

> The old market-square was not very large, a mere bare patch of granite setts, usually with a few fruit-stalls under a wall. It was in a poor quarter of the town. Meagre houses stood down one side, there was a hosiery factory, a great blank with myriad oblong windows, at the end, a street of little shops with flagstone pavement down the other side, and, for a crowning monument, the public baths, of new red brick, with a clock-tower. The people who moved about seemed stumpy and sordid, the air seemed to smell rather

dirty, there was a sense of many mean streets ramifying off into warrens of meanness. Now and again a great chocolate-and-yellow tramcar ground round a difficult bend under the hosiery factory.

Arthur Brown's tall clock tower remains a crowning monument. In chapter twenty-six of *Women in Love*, Ursula Brangwen is more concerned with the time she spends with the local people:

> Ursula was superficially thrilled when she found herself out among the common people, in the jumbled place piled with old bedding, heaps of old iron, shabby crockery in pale lots, muffled lots of unthinkable clothing. She and Birkin went unwillingly down the narrow aisle between the rusty wares. He was looking at the goods, she at the people.

At the time Lawrence last walked through Sneinton, the Reading Rooms and Libraries in Carlton Road and Hermit Street were catering for a thousand readers a day. By the 1930s, the wholesale market had been modernised and houses were demolished, replaced by strong, open-fronted, glazed-roofed units. Streets became Avenues A, B and C. The final one was named Freckingham Street after the man behind the developments, the Chairman of the Markets and Fairs Committee, Alderman HJ Freckingham.

Further development was put on hold due to the Second World War, during which Sneinton was heavily bombed. The Nottingham playwright Stephen Lowe, born in Sneinton in 1947, grew up in a typical back-to-back house before his family moved to the high-rise of Manvers Court. With no books at home, his library card became his salvation, Lawrence's *Sons and Lovers* having the most impact. A working-class lad wanting to be an actor, Lowe saw much of his own life and hopes in the character of Paul Morel, and the book convinced him that it was possible to be a writer.

Stephen Lowe was largely raised by his mother. His father had served in the army and returned home with meningitis and TB, the treatment for which rendered him deaf. Lowe used his tense home life as the source for his autobiographical *Moving Pictures*. His award-winning, breakthrough play, *Touched,* is set in Sneinton during the days between VE Day and VJ Day. The play focuses on working-class women living with loss and hope. It was written as a reaction to there being little recognition for women like his mother who had stayed at home, fighting their different battles.

A year after *Touched* first opened, Richard Eyre produced another of Lowe's Sneinton-set plays. This time it was an early screenplay for the BBC. Set and filmed in Sneinton Market, *Cries from the Watchtower*, his first Play for Today, tells of a small-time watchmaker who finds his livelihood threatened by cheaply imported digital watches in an era of new silicon chip technology. It was inspired by a friend's father, a Mormon, who had a stall at which he'd repair watches amid the bustling crowd. This was the kind of Nottingham scene Lowe had observed as a boy when visiting the Monday and Saturday morning markets. He loved the stallholders' comedic banter, free entertainment he harnessed in developing his ear for dialogue.

As a lad, Lowe would spend lots of time at the second-hand bookstall, looking for anything Penguin, or by Graham Greene or Raymond Chandler. He'd often read the first chapter before buying. With no other books in his house, his collection of paperbacks became an important addition, his choices more exciting than the hardbacks available from the library.

The filming of *Cries from a Watchtower* took over Sneinton Market for a day, with the extras made up of Lowe's family, notably his loud Aunt Hilda, while the legendary comedic actor Stan Stennett played one of the stall-holders.

By the late seventies, as Stephen Lowe's name was on the rise, Sneinton Market was falling into a state of disrepair. It didn't stop the writer returning in the 1980s when he would visit Victoria Leisure Centre's Turkish baths on Gedling Street. Victoria Baths had been Nottingham's first municipal baths and washhouses when they opened in 1851. Lowe also revisited the market, listening again to the patter to help hone his dialogue. In 1985 Lowe was writing for *Albion Market*, a new soap opera. He wrote half their episodes before moving on to write prolifically for another soap, *Coronation Street*.

The first part of *The Philosopher's Stone* (1969), a science fiction novel by Colin Wilson (1931–2013), is partly set in Sneinton. An earlier Wilson novel, *Adrift in Soho* (1961), formed the basis of a 2019 film of the same name, much of which was shot in Nottingham. Wilson's official bibliographer is the West Bridgford author and publisher (Paupers' Press) Colin Stanley.

Sneinton Market is the subject of a poem by Michelle "Mother" Hubbard, entitled "Market Day", based on her weekly visits there in the 1980s and '90s, and Gail Webb's poem "Sneinton Market" won a Nottingham City Arts competition.

During the 1980s, Dave Ablitt interviewed seven Sneinton residents for *Sneinton Magazine,* of which he was a founder. Ablitt has been involved in community groups and local politics for decades. Some of his diverse interviews are reproduced in his 2019 book *Sneinton People.* One of his recorded conversations was with John Tyson, the left-wing vicar of St Stephen's Church, who had an affection for Soviet Socialism and nuclear disarmament.

Stories of Sneinton Market (2016) by Colin Haynes is also based on interviews with local people. Haynes and Ray Gosling had worked together on the St Ann's paper *Chase Chat* and he was one of the first people to sort through his late friend's archive at NTU, an immense accumulation of Gosling's notes, papers, books, paintings (originals by local artists) and research that was salvaged by John Goodridge from his old house in Mapperley Park. It was due to bankruptcy that Gosling lost the three-storey Victorian house that he'd loved. His archive reveals that one of his many protests had been against council plans to build a flyover over Sneinton.

Haynes' *Stories of Sneinton Market* is full of contributions from the sellers and patrons of Sneinton Market, which, for many, was 'an outdoor community centre.' In 2014 the market received some much-needed investment and with it came a new era as part of Nottingham's Creative Quarter. Sneinton Market's Avenues are now home to over twenty creative businesses; a hub of artists, musicians, crafters, designers and more, embracing the original, the quirky and the independent. The "plaza" has hosted live music events and various performances.

In 2017 *LeftLion* moved its headquarters from Hockley to the end of Freckingham Street. It was also in 2017 that Nottingham's culture magazine went monthly and local poet Bridie Squires became the editor. Squires became NTU's first writer-in-residence in 2019 and she's since gone on to develop and perform her own full-length, one-woman show, *Casino Zero.*

LeftLion has been promoting Nottinghamshire writers, books and poets since 2003, from which time scores of local writers have contributed articles to their pages and website. The magazine enjoyed a literary takeover in January 2018, the whole edition being dedicated to Nottingham UNESCO City of Literature (NUCoL).

Before *LeftLion* moved to Sneinton, James Walker had been its literary editor. Over the past decade, Walker has done much to help to promote Nottingham's literary scene and celebrate its history. Developing a specialism for digital storytelling, with an emphasis on different platforms and multi-collaboration, Walker continues to explore the relationship between digital and literature. His projects include the graphic novel *Dawn of the Unread,* which has some great additional digital content; its follow-up, *Whatever People Say I Am,* created to dispel myths around identity and challenge stereotypes; and *DH Lawrence: A Digital Pilgrimage,* a memory theatre retracing Lawrence's self-imposed exile. Earlier projects of Walker's include *The Sillitoe Trail* (2013) and *Being Arthur* (2014), a live twenty-four-hour Twitter presentation of *Saturday Night and Sunday Morning.*

On the upper floor of *LeftLion*'s HQ was the office of Nottingham UNESCO City of Literature. The first Director of NUCoL Sandeep Mahal, formerly of the Reading Agency, operates on the national stage as a Trustee of the Women's Prize and is often to be found on prize-judging panels. She wrote, "I grew up in a home with no books, in a Derby community with no reading culture. But the fact that I ended up working with readers and writers is down to the fact that I had a library close to where I lived. Libraries showed me the power of great writing – and the power it gave me."

NUCoL's Executive Assistant is the poet Leanne Moden, whose collection *Get Over Yourself* (2020) contains social commentary, humour and wisdom, as Moden gives us her take on modern life. As a performance poet Moden has appeared at events across the UK and Europe. Her first solo poetry show, *Skip Skip Skip,* was full of stories of belonging, exclusion and teenage rebellion – much like Sneinton Market.

In 2021 NUCoL moved to Lakeside at the University of Nottingham, a regular literature venue, but plan to move into the new City Library near the train station once it's open.

---

[1] Wylie, 1852.
[2] Mellors, 1914.

Chapter 45
St Ann's – Getting By

'St Ann's is such a beautiful site and the life so varied.'
Ray Gosling, *St Ann's*

St Ann's is 'situated in a broad valley, bounded to the south by dour Sneinton; to the north by still elegant, affluent Mapperley Park; to the east a no man's land, suburbs of a suburb, the giant Gedling colliery and a scampi belt of villages – and to the west the city heart,' wrote Ray Gosling in the booklet *St Ann's* (1967).

The literary heritage of St Ann's is linked to its own social history. Take, for example, the race riots. For it was at the bottom of Robin Hood's Chase, in the late August and early September of 1958, that modern Britain's first race riot occurred, and 'The whole place was like a slaughterhouse,' according to the *Evening Post*. Sonia Davies, a Nottingham-born sessional lecturer in Black studies, said, 'I can remember my dad talking about the 1958 riots. He said that it wasn't a riot in the immediate sense of the word, it was more like gangs of white men beating on black men.'

At this time, in the midst of the racial tension, and in response to the "Keep Britain White" campaign, a local man, Oswald "George" Powe, wrote *Don't Blame the Blacks*, words to fight racism and industrial inequality. Written for British workers, Powe's pamphlet aspired to unite them – all races together. With sections on "Why we came?" and "Do we cause unemployment?", the Jamaican-born writer explained how political decisions by the ruling class were the real cause of unemployment. His words carried the message that 'the working class has been divided, for if it were to become united it might fight back.' Scapegoats were being made of Black immigrants because they stood out, argued Powe, whose pamphlet received orders from as far as America and Africa.

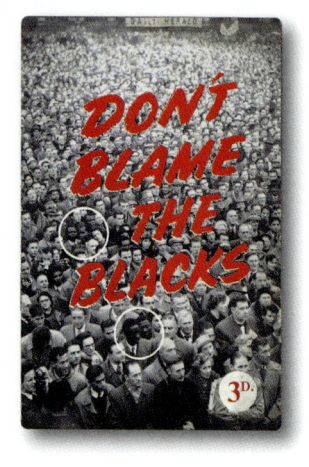

Powe's links with St Ann's began in 1952 after he followed his politically-minded friends to Nottingham. The Black population at this time was small and living four to a room in multi-occupied slum housing that was being rented by racketeers. It was at Pat Jordan's Dane Street bookshop – the second house of a long, terraced row of three-storey houses, off Alfred Street Central – that Powe's *Don't Blame the Blacks* was printed. Powe knew the radical bookshop to be a place where Black people could meet and chat.

'It was in a street in the heart of the worst of the district that little Pat Jordan kept his shop,' wrote Gosling in his memoir *Personal Copy* (1980), adding, '[His] front room was the shop, with tables piled shoulder-high with Zane Gray and Barbara Cartland... Schoolboys would always be in, passing through the dog-eared comic strips, looking for a juicy Nazi tale – not realizing what went on behind the curtained door, in the back room, but knowing something did.'

Sylvia Riley's memoir of the 1960s, *Winter at the Bookshop* (2019), tells of 4 Dane Street and what went on in its back room, when the bookshop was a meeting place for politically active revolutionary groups and local movements. Riley, writing as Carol Lake, won the 1989 Guardian Fiction Prize for her short story collection *Rosehill: portraits of a Midlands city*. In *Winter at the Bookshop* she wrote, 'From the front of the shop [Pat Jordan] sold second-hand books and comics, and in the back room he kept his duplicator ever turning, churning out documents and political statements and a weekly news-sheet.'

Winter at the Bookshop
Politics and Poverty
St Ann's in the 1960s

Sylvia Riley

From 1962 the small International Group, founded by Pat Jordan, Ken Coates and Peter Price, had been based at the shop. Locals knew it as a second-hand bookshop, with books for sale or exchange, but trusted punters were given access to the complete works of Marx, Lenin, Engels, Trotsky and Castro, their books held back and half-wrapped, like pornography.

Dane Street, and most of St Ann's, was subjected to a huge clearance project in the late 1960s and early 1970s, involving the demolition of its houses, shops, churches, pubs and businesses, and the rehousing of some thirty thousand people. Most of the old houses had been built in the 1800s and, as such, had no internal toilets, while eighty-five percent of homes had no bathroom. There were also problems of poor sanitation and damp, but the new housing would come at a heavy cost to the community.

In *St Ann's* Ray Gosling wrote of how places of 'sound construction and cherished homes' were to be pulled down, but also of the City of Nottingham's proposal to 'decant' its inhabitants. Gosling was concerned for the people waiting for improvements and facing large rent increases or having to move to another area.

'Will any councillor move his home into St Ann's?' he asked. Gosling also feared the new road plan which was 'dashing all thoughts of a pleasant new area.' He wrote, 'St Ann's is such a beautiful site and the life so varied – some of the finest shops in variety and quality anywhere in the Midlands – and the people, old and new, with such strength and spirit.' Nottingham should be 'treating St Ann's as the fine natural valley that it is.'

In his hopes for a new, mixed community of rich and poor, Gosling made demands of the council planners. The first of these: 'That the people living, working, using St Ann's to be told directly of proposals and plans as they progress: that their wish and their need be asked for and met.'

It was from this time that Gosling began his campaigning with the community of St Ann's against the city planners that were intent on flattening 340 of its acres. To save the better homes and shops, Gosling wanted selective demolition, and he helped set up the St Ann's Tenants and Residents' Association (SATRA), bringing people together to demand improvements and decent services for the new estate. Between 1967 and 1979 Gosling was chairman of SATRA, working closely with the retired engineer Arthur Leatherland, a conservative teetotaller who lived on Cromer Road where he had grown up. SATRA was a diverse group of people who initially met for free at St Catherine's Church Hall, later getting their own premises.

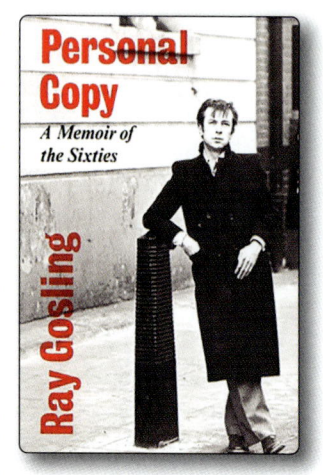

In *Personal Copy*, Gosling reflected on these 'most radical and amazing times.' He had been reviewing books, broadcasting and drinking, finding his way in the swinging sixties, when St Ann's began to occupy his mind. He had got to know the area and its fifty pubs, 'one of the most fantastic drinking places in the world...' A few years earlier, Gosling had developed a taste for campaigning having stood as an independent councillor, his "Vote for a Madman" slogan helping him to receive thirteen percent of the vote and inspiring the pop singer David Such to later form his Monster Raving Loony Party.

Gosling's agent during his 1963 run had been Richard Silburn. Together with Ken Coates, Silburn was running evening classes at the Workers' Education Centre about the sociology of the poor: poverty, deprivation and morale. It was in St Ann's that Gosling, Silburn and Coates had been drinking with Harold Wiltshire, Professor of Adult Education for the University of Nottingham, when the professor granted permission for a series of classes at the WEA. Coates and Silburn, researchers at the university, soon enrolled students to conduct a social survey in St Ann's.

Coates and Silburn's community study of 1966 looked at the living, social and working conditions in St Ann's, and the attitudes of people who lived in such conditions. The study informed two books, *St Ann's – Poverty, deprivation and morale in a Nottingham Community* (1967) and the more famous *Poverty: The Forgotten Englishman* (1970), which gave rise to a film directed by Stephen Frears.

The authors found that 'poverty is not so much a simple lack of wealth as a more basic lack of power.' St Ann's togetherness comes across as a mixed blessing, privacy not being easy when living in such close proximity. There are chapters on schools, housing, poverty and expectations.

Gosling may have led the people of St Ann's but he acknowledged that 'Ken Coates was the intellectual leader.' Coates had founded the monthly trade union paper *Union Voice*, which showed how the rich few milked the poor many, and Gosling had great respect for him, yet he never forgave Coates for the way that the St Ann's survey was done, making poverty the issue.

Coates and Silburn were writing from an outsider's perspective. In 2015, another writer was to bring the academic world and local community together, this time from an insider's view. Lisa Mckenzie's *Getting By: Estates, Class and Culture in Austerity Britain* was written to tackle prejudice and stereotype, and to explain the complexity of working-class life, and life on council estates. She collected nine years' worth of stories and narratives from St Ann's, academic research that complemented her own experience of living on the estate.

Mckenzie tells of working-class families from a working-class perspective. It's a story of a resilient and creative community, battling for survival against austerity whilst being blamed for society's ills. Mckenzie is the daughter, granddaughter, and great-granddaughter of Nottinghamshire miners. She left school in 1984 during the miners' strike, a strike that hit her family hard. As the loss of mines and factories devastated her community, she moved to St Ann's, where she had her son.

After finding *Poverty: The Forgotten Englishman* in the library, Mckenzie changed her direction, enrolling on an access course in 2000. She had discovered that it was possible to study your own area and by 2009 she had her PhD. Mckenzie is now a research fellow in the Department of Sociology at the London School of Economics and Political Science, working on issues of social inequality and class stratification. She dedicated *Getting By...* to Coates and Silburn. Her University of Nottingham supervisor, Nick Stevenson, is something of an expert on David Bowie, the subject of one of his own books.

Peter Richardson's photobook, *St Ann's, The End of an Era* (2020), provides a snapshot of life during the upheaval of fifty years ago. At that time, with many residents living among the demolition work, Richardson was at Derby College of Art on a photojournalism course and working on the new estate as a summer labourer with Wimpey. The young man was inspired to photograph the site and used his skills to capture the demise of the community, a way of life gone forever. He merely captured what he saw around him, the cobbled streets, the people, pubs, backyards and alleyways, with some residents' comments and memories featured alongside his ninety-eight images, split into sections such as "Wash Day".

In *Animal QC* (2016), Gary Bell writes of his family's small terrace house in 1960s' St Ann's having access to a toilet block shared with six other families. Bell's teenage parents – his father was a coalminer, his mother worked at Players – rented in what is described as a noisy and lively area. Gary Bell is the author of the Elliot Rock legal series. A leading criminal barrister, Bell has lived a colourful life, having been a football hooligan and imprisoned for fraud before reinventing himself.

During the redevelopment, Ruth L Johns knew St Ann's well and, in 2002, she compiled *St Ann's Nottingham: Inner-city Voices*, written together with the people of St Ann's. The impressive book is a large social history of St Ann's in living memory, with nine hundred and forty images and countless contributions. Johns' previous book, *Life Goes On* (1982), outlined the philosophy and practice of the first ten years of Family First, a pioneering Nottingham housing association and community self-help organisation that she founded in 1965; while her case study, *The Job Makers* (1984), focused on Nottingham's working community of small firms.

Joan Downer, a librarian turned teacher turned poet, wrote "St Ann's Estate" (1978), a poem for the excellent but short-lived literary magazine *Nottingham Quarterly*. Downer describes the new homes as being:

> Strung out like bacilli
> on the gentle slopes the new
> houses glint and run
> confusedly alike
> yet different...

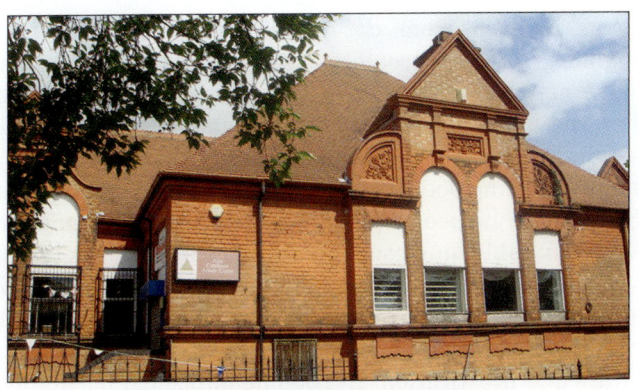

Afro-Caribbean National Artistic Centre,
Hungerhill Road, St Ann's.

Established in 1971, the Afro-Caribbean National Artistic (ACNA) Centre, moved to Hungerhill Road, St Ann's, in 1978, where it became an important community facility for creatives. Among the many groups based there has been a creative and professional writing group, led by the poet Panya Banjoko. Together with the Engagement Curator Bo Olawoye, Banjoko also worked with The

Renewal Trust to put together a free publication all about St Ann's. This involved a series of creative writing workshops run by Banjoko.

Another writer and performance poet associated with St Ann's is Michelle "Mother" Hubbard, who moved to the area in 1983 and lived on Brewsters Road. There are many sons, daughters and grandchildren of Jamaicans who arrived in Britain at the time of Windrush who have lived in St Ann's. The Nottingham-born playwright and former Cottesmore School pupil Jenny McLeod began writing plays in the middle of her A-levels after she saw an advert in the *Evening Post*. McLeod won the Writing 87 workshop at the Playhouse with *Cricket at Camp David*, then wrote *Island Life*, a play that began in Nottingham before touring nationally. Other plays and TV work followed, plus a stint as writer-in-residence at the Playhouse (1991–92). In 1998, she wrote her first novel, *Stuck Up a Tree*, commissioned by Virago after the editor read an interview of McLeod's for the *Independent*. The story's protagonist is Ella, a successful London caterer who returns to her hometown (a fictional setting) and her larger-than-life Jamaican family. McLeod set up the writers' group Scribblers Inc.

Pitman Browne from St Ann's has been a presence on Nottingham's literary scene since his arrival from Jamaica in 1962. He may have come here feeling 'cheated because of the weather and living conditions,' but Browne has become a valued, award-winning member of the community, mentoring emerging writers, performing poetry and initiating events. As a key member of CHROMA he helped to put Black writers on the map, and he runs his own publishing company. Browne's six books, about culture and philosophy, include *Children Get Out of the Ghetto Mentality* (2000), which explores Nottingham's youth subculture, covering case histories and conversations about drugs, truancy, gang wars and prostitution. In 2005 he published his autobiography *What Is My Mission?*

Nottingham-based Mufaro Makubika wrote a play about St Ann's, its Caribbean community and their history, entitled *Shebeen*. It's about the Windrush generation, questioning their lives, values, and aspirations against the hostility of the society that had invited them to come to Britain. 'The characters in the play are all working class,' said Makubika, 'either immigrants or from the local community, but the play's themes, like having dreams, apply to everyone.'

Makubika's central characters, George and Pearl, hold a shebeen to try to bring relief from the summer heat, from social oppression and from their relationships. Shebeens, later to be known as blues parties, were meeting places, usually at someone's house, where people could get together. They often involved music and drink. In *A Centenary History of Nottingham*, John Beckett records that shebeens existed because the colour bar meant that alcohol licences were not granted to the Caribbean community. For Makubika,[1] 'A shebeen is about companionship and relating. Yes, there is partying, but ultimately it's about people trying to commune.'

Shebeen was awarded the Alfred Fagon Award for Best New Play in 2017. It was with the support of Nottingham Black Archive that the playwright, who has African heritage, initially researched the race riots and how St Ann's became an estate.

The story of St Ann's continues to be reflected in its residents' written words.

---

[1] Udeh, 2018.

Chapter 46
32 Victoria Crescent –
When Bertie met Frieda

'I love your wife and she loves me.' DH Lawrence

32 Victoria Crescent, Mapperley Park.

In 1912, DH Lawrence walked along Private Road in Mapperley Park. Turning up Victoria Crescent, he located his destination, the first house on the left, the home of his favourite professor, Ernest Weekley, who had been Lawrence's teacher of modern foreign languages at University College. Weekley had invited Lawrence for lunch after being asked for assistance in finding work abroad as a language instructor. Only, the professor was not home. Instead, Lawrence was met by a boy.

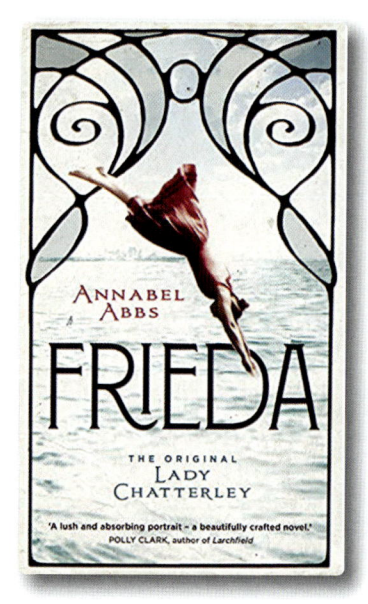

'Mr Lawrence, we've been expecting you,' the boy might have said, leading Lawrence through to the rear of the house where his sisters and mother were waiting to receive him. Lawrence was instantly impressed by Mrs Frieda Weekley. Her beauty and foreignness surprised him and they spoke with spontaneity, carelessness and directness. She talked of sex from a Freudian perspective and of her thoughts on free love. With her children upstairs, Mrs Weekley and Lawrence became close (rumour has it, very close). In Annabel Abbs' 2018 book *Frieda*, Mrs Weekley is captivated by the young poet, this stranger with the vim and spirit of a wildcat, and her hand is smoothing a lock of hair from his eyes as they notice Ernest Weekley appear in the doorway.

Before leaving, Lawrence arranged a return visit for the following Sunday to have Frieda check over his grammar, at a time when her husband would be in Cambridge. Back in Eastwood, Lawrence was unable to free himself from thoughts of Frieda, and he posted her a letter. One line, unsigned. It stated, 'You are the most wonderful woman in all England.'

Frieda had been married for thirteen years and, whilst extra-marital liaisons were not new to her, she was aware that the adventure and future prescribed for her by Lawrence would mean leaving England and leaving her children, in addition to her husband, her mother, a father to whom she was devoted, two dear sisters, nephews and nieces, her parents-in-law and a beloved nanny – all with great emotional pain.

The lovers met several times over the next few weeks, including a trip to the theatre. Accepting that she was throwing her life away if she stayed in Nottingham, Frieda Weekley took off with Lawrence, leaving behind her comfortable existence and three children. It was within a month of their meeting. She may have been the daughter of minor German aristocrats but she was not wealthy, and her family made clear their opposition to the abandonment of her marriage and children for the love of a penniless poet.

Lawrence insisted that she tell her husband about them but she repeatedly failed to do so. Lawrence wrote to his former teacher, declaring: 'I love your wife and she loves me...'

Ernest Weekley divorced Frieda and in 1914 she became Mrs Lawrence. From *Sons and Lovers* onwards Frieda influenced Lawrence's novels, especially their psychological nature.

On splitting with Frieda, Ernest Weekley became a successful writer in his own right. His debut non-fiction book, *The Romance of Words* (1912), was an instant hit. Ten more books followed, all on etymology, most of which were published in the 1920s and 1930s, including the much-cited *An Etymological Dictionary of Modern English* (1921).

Chapter 47
The White Horse, 313 Ilkeston Road, Radford – Down the Local

'We can go to the White Horse on Saturday night. They've got good ale there, and you can sing if you like.'

Alan Sillitoe, *The Broken Chariot*

The White Horse, Ilkeston Road, Radford.

The White Horse is where Arthur Seaton and his creator made their memorable first impression. Several pubs feature in Alan Sillitoe's *Saturday Night and Sunday Morning* (1958), but The White Horse is the most noteworthy. It's where the novel's memorable opening is set, in which it's not only Saturday night, it's Benefit Night and Notts County have just won. The floors are shaking and the windows are rattling. The week's monotonous graft at the Raleigh factory is being swilled out of systems and, with eleven pints and seven gins in his belly, Arthur Seaton is about to fall down the stairs.

The origin of the scene was Sillitoe's short story of 1954 called *Once in a Weekend*, featuring a young factory worker who, after his Saturday night in The White Horse, wakes up the following morning in bed with his workmate's wife. The story opened "With eleven pints of beer and seven small gins inside him, Arthur fell from the top of the stairs to the bottom." *Once in a Weekend* was rejected by several magazines before becoming the first chapter of Sillitoe's bestselling novel.

The White Horse was just round the corner from where Sillitoe lived and it makes its way into a number of his stories, such as "The Firebug" from *The Ragman's Daughter* (1963). Sillitoe's former home at 5 Beaconsfield Terrace, off Salisbury Street, is featured in the film adaptation of *SN&SM;* Sillitoe's mother, Sabina, was living there at the time. A studio set was used for the interior shots of The White Horse for the 1960 film, which features the drinking game that ends with Albert Finney's stunt double descending the stairs. Those stairs still exist, as does the building, but the pub is now The White Horse Café, although this seems to be using the back of the building with a taxi company in the former pub lounge. No ale will be swilled there nowadays though, as the café is Muslim-owned.

Other locations mentioned in *SN&SM* include the Old Market Square, Goose Fair, the River Trent, The Peacock pub on Mansfield Road and The Trip to Jerusalem. The Eight Bells pub on St Peter's Gate, which closed in 1960, saw its interior used in the film. Many of the locations in the book have since been demolished, as have most of the properties lived in by the Sillitoe family. The poverty-stricken family of six regularly moved, sometimes dodging rent collectors, transferring all their possessions in a handcart to the next poor housing. The whole family often lived in one room, with other families sharing the hall, landing and outside lavatory.

Alan's father Christopher was often unemployed and violent. Sabina was known to make herself the target of his rage to spare her children. In the mid-to-late 1930s, when they lived in a terraced house adjacent to the Raleigh factory, the Sillitoe siblings would huddle up in bed hearing stories about the Hanleys, characters invented by Alan for their entertainment. Brian and Michael, the baby of the family, 'treated Sillitoe with the affectionate respect normally afforded to an uncle, even a parent, and some of this endured into adulthood,' wrote Sillitoe's biographer, Richard Bradford, in 2008.

Alan Sillitoe attended two schools nearby, Forster Street School, where Ada Chance was the drill sergeant of a teacher who taught him the importance of correct spelling, and Radford Boulevard School (designed by George T Hine) at the crossroads where the Boulevard meets Ilkeston Road, known as "Damnation Corner". The school was actually two, the girls and boys separated, with no mixing. Sillitoe failed the entrance exams for Nottingham Boys' High School, but he probably would have hated the regimentation and conformity.

Raleigh, at different times, employed each member of the Sillitoe family. In *SN&SM* Arthur Seaton reflected on his work as a lathe operator:

> The thousands that worked there took home good wages. No more short-time like before the war, or getting the sack if you stood ten minutes in the lavatory reading your *Football Post* – if the gaffer got on to you now you could always tell him where to put his job and go somewhere else.

When Sillitoe worked at Raleigh, his first full-time job after leaving school, he was told that it was "the law" to join the union. Forcing him to join any organisation was not going to work. Rebelling against authority was as much part of the author as it was of his most famous novel. In Sillitoe's case, this attitude may have begun with how he felt about his violent father.

With his formal education completed in 1942, the small and skinny Alan Sillitoe enrolled on the local wing of the air Training Corps using a fake ID. He joined up with his mate Arthur Shelton, a likely inspiration for the name Arthur Seaton. Seaton's character comes from a mixture of sources: Alan's brother Brian for one, and perhaps Nicholas Penny, who had been a recent protagonist of Hilda Lewis's (1957), and who said, 'My job – as I see it – is ter look fer mysen first!' (very Arthur Seaton).

Not far from The White Horse is the University of Nottingham's Raleigh Park halls of residence, on Sillitoe Way, a self-catering hall located close to Jubilee Campus. One of its five courts is Sillitoe Court, named in 1990, other courts include Byron and Chatterley. Students may have enjoyed The White Horse pub had their halls been there in Sillitoe's day.

The White Horse has been home to the Radford Boys' Boxing Club. Alan and Roy Smith of Sneinton set up the club and coached young fighters under the big glass roof above the pub before it took over the building to the rear. Nottingham-born Herol "Bomber" Graham and Jason Booth learned their trade at the club before going on to become European Middleweight and Commonwealth Flyweight champions respectively. It's fitting that boxing has a connection with The White Horse, as Arthur Seaton was "handy" despite taking a beating at the hands of squaddies.

Of course, Seaton's fights were not just of the physical kind. From *SN&SM*:

> And trouble for me it'll be, fighting every day until I die. Why do they make soldiers out of us when we're fighting up to the hilt as it is? Fighting with mothers and wives, landlords and gaffers, coppers, army, government. If it's not one thing it's another, apart from the work we have to do and the way we spend our wages. There's bound to be trouble in store for me every day of my life, because trouble it's always been and always will be.

Boxer Lee Froch has something of the Arthur Seaton about him, and at one time he was landlord at The White Horse. Lee Froch has always considered himself a drinker and has been no stranger to falling down drunk. As a functioning alcoholic, now sober for years, Froch said, 'My children now don't remember me as the person who once fell down the stairs.'

The White Horse is still standing and its exterior still looks fighting fit.

Not everyone in Nottingham welcomed *SN&SM*. A Labour councillor tried to get the book removed from local libraries, whilst the Nottingham Watch Committee wanted the film banned, even citing its reference to 'Slab Square' as an obscenity.

Sillitoe isn't the only writer to have written about Radford, or lived there. Young Pat McGrath's novel *The Green Leaves of Nottingham* (1970) – which has an introduction by Sillitoe – and his short story collection *People in the Crowd* (1978), are both set in and around Radford. Sillitoe called McGrath's *Daybreak* (1979) 'An absorbing, vividly written novel on today's jazz – drug – dole – hitching – squatting scene.'

Ray Gosling lived on Radford's Hartley Road; Thomas Bailey and his son Philip James Bailey lived at 16 and 18 Denman Street (Philip moving to 449 Alfreton Road); Jane Jerram, author of *The Child's Own Story Book* (1837) was born in Radford. Then there's the great thinker, Herbert Spencer.

Herbert Spencer (1802–1903) was born in Derby but moved to Radford after his father gave up teaching. '[My father] took a house at New Radford, near Nottingham, on what was then known as the Forest Side – a suburb adjacent to a tract of wild land,' wrote Spencer in the first volume of his autobiography (1904). 'Here I spent the remaining part of my childhood.' Their house is now better known as the Spread Eagle Inn, Aspley Terrace, on Alfreton Road.

After early struggles at home and school, Spencer took great delight in his days rambling in Nottingham. He wrote:

> I have still vivid recollections of the delight of rambling among the gorse bushes, which at that early age towered above my head. There was a certain charm of adventure in exploring the narrow turf-covered tracks running hither and thither into all their nooks, and now and then coming out in unexpected places, or being stopped by a deep sandy chasm made by carts going to the sand-pits.

Spencer's father took work in the lace industry at a time when the production of lace by machinery was a novelty. Spencer wrote, 'Great profits were being made, and a mania resulted.' Before leaving Derby his father had bought a lace-machine and 'as Nottingham was the seat of the new industry, this enterprise was probably influential in determining his removal to Forest Side, which was, however, recommended for its salubrity.'

It wasn't long before 'the production of lace became excessive; the profits fell very greatly; and he eventually lost a considerable sum,' wrote Spencer.

Spencer became a prolific writer and authored many philosophical books. His second, *Principles of Psychology* (1855), made the argument that natural laws govern the human mind, and his major work, the ten-volume *A System of Synthetic Philosophy*, had him apply evolution to psychology, sociology, and the study of morality. It was Spencer that coined the term 'survival of the fittest' as a phrase for Darwin's theory of evolution. A year before his death, Spencer was nominated for the Nobel Prize for Literature.

Equally outspoken was Charles Sutton (1765–1829), a printer and proprietor of the liberal *Nottingham Review* who built Forest House in Radford, where he lived. Sutton was imprisoned in Northampton for political libel after using the *Review* to criticise the conduct of British troops during the war with the USA. He also acquired Radford Grove (built by WE Elliott) – also known as Radford Folly – where his son and business partner Richard Sutton (1789–1856) lived.

Book Three:
Nottinghamshire

Chapter 48
All Hallows Church, Arnold Lane, Gedling – Gandalf of Gedling?

'All's well that ends better.'
JRR Tolkien, *The Lord of the Rings*

Edwin Neave in All Hallows Churchyard.

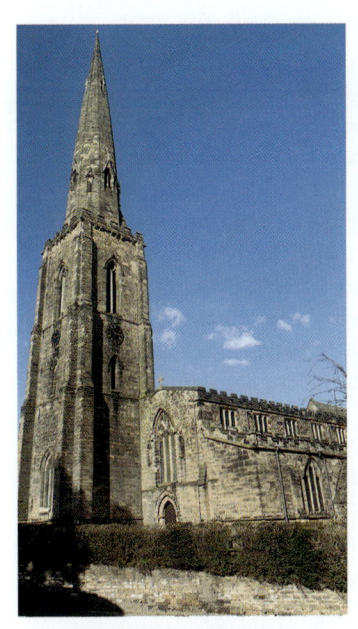

All Hallows Church.

Gedling's All Hallows Church, with its fourteenth-century spire (the second highest in Nottinghamshire), is recognisable from miles around. In its churchyard is the gravestone of Edwin Neave (1872–1909). Newly married, Neave had moved to Gedling in 1905, having worked himself up the insurance ladder – from clerk to inspector, to resident secretary, to branch manager – all for the Guardian Assurance Company. The sandy-haired gent enjoyed nothing more than drinking in Nottingham's pubs, playing his banjo and singing music hall songs.

It is a postcard that brings him to our attention, one that features a pencil drawing by a twelve-year-old

JRR Tolkien which he titled "They Slept in Beauty Side by Side", a phrase Tolkien had probably borrowed from Felicia Dorothea Hemans' poem *The Graves of a Household*. Tolkien's drawing depicts two figures in bed together, one of whom is Gedling's Edwin Neave.

It is thought that this drawing is of Neave and his partner (Emily) Jane Suffield, Tolkien's aunt. Alternatively, as Edwin and Jane were only living together at the time – they married the following year – it may actually be a self-portrait, with a young Tolkien on one side and Edwin Neave on the other. Either way, the picture was drawn by Tolkien in early 1904 when, with his mother Mabel gravely ill with diabetes,[1] he had been staying in Hove at the home of his aunt. Later that year Tolkien became an orphan.

When Edwin and Jane Neave arrived in Gedling, they lived in a cottage on Shearing Hill. They were both thirty-three-years old. Within four years Edwin Neave had died. Using money left by her husband, Jane and her friend Ellen Brookes-Smith bought Church Farm in Gedling, close to All Hallows Church on the other side of Arnold Lane. They renamed it Phoenix Farm and between 1912 and 1922 they worked there.

The Neaves had had no children of their own and Tolkien had been fond of them both. Jane Neave became something of a mother figure to Tolkien, who visited Gedling three times between 1913 and 1916, staying with his aunt at Phoenix Farm (now Jessops Lane) where his younger brother Hilary worked as a horticulturalist before joining the army. Tolkien also helped out around the farm.

It was during a visit to Phoenix Farm in 1914 that a twenty-two-year-old Tolkien wrote the first draft of "The Voyage of Éarendel the Evening Star". He later stated to friends that he had experienced 'a tremendous opening up of everything for me,' when working on the poem. Éarendel, who first appears here, later becomes 'an important element in the mythical background of *The Lord of the Rings*,' according to Gedling-born Andrew H Morton in his book *Tolkien's Gedling* (2008), written with John Hayes. Their book is about Tolkien's link to the area and how his seminal poem opened up his whole subsequent mythology.

In another of his drawings, Tolkien drew his aunt's farm, a picture he titled "Phoenix Farm Gedling". The farm was demolished in the mid-1950s but his picture survives, as does another of his drawings, entitled Lamb's Farm (Church Farm had belonged to a

Mr Lamb before Jane Neave bought it at an auction in 1911 and changed its name).

Growing up, Tolkien's aunt Jane had been surrounded by literature and drama, and the Suffields continued to perform their own plays, some of which were written by Tolkien. His maternal grandfather was an active member of various literary clubs and associations and he passed his love of literature, and collection of books, down to Jane, whose knowledge of English literature was impressive. Jane Neave also had a strong interest in science and her years working on farms were a lengthy interlude from her academic work. She was a science teacher for over two decades and gained a university degree in the subject.

Tolkien considered his aunt a most remarkable woman, and Morton and Hayes (2008) suggest that his famous wizard Gandalf may have been based on her. Jane Neave had a strong imposing physical presence, mystical tendencies and a great intellect. She also possessed a Gandalf-style long cloak, wide-brimmed hat and alpenstock, souvenirs from walking in the Swiss Alps.

In 1961, when she was eighty-nine years old, Jane Neave asked her nephew, by now the world-famous author of *The Hobbit* (1937) and *The Lord of the Rings* (1854), to write a book featuring his character Tom Bombadil. Tolkien agreed and wrote *The Adventures of Tom Bombadil* (1962). The book appeared just months before his aunt's death.

As for the long-departed Edwin, Tolkien may have written him into *The Notion Club Papers*, an abandoned novel, written at the same time that *The Lord of the Rings* was being developed. In the book, published posthumously, Erundel is mentioned, and Tolkien's main character is given the surname Lowdham (a neighbouring village to Gedling). Arundel Lowdham's father is called Edwin Lowdham.

---

[1]Hammond and Scull, 2001.

Chapter 49
Annesley Hall – The Forsaken

'...once the abode of a prosperous old family but a blight and a sorrow have fallen here.'

William Howitt.

Annesley Hall, situated between Mansfield and Nottingham, is a mansion that dates back to the mid-thirteenth century. Once the seat of the Annesley family, the hall passed to the Chaworths – their family name anglicised from Chaources – after George Chaworth acquired the estate by marriage. Its grounds bordered those of the Byrons of Newstead Abbey. Rivalry between the neighbours came to a head when the much-loved William Chaworth fought with his cousin, the Fifth Lord Byron, at a club dinner of Nottinghamshire gentry at the Pall Mall tavern, the Star and Garter.[1] The proprietors of Annesley Hall and Newstead Abbey were arguing over estate boundaries when Byron challenged Chaworth, an expert swordsman, to a rapier duel. They retreated to a back room where Byron promptly ran a sword through Chaworth's gut. Lord Byron was charged with wilful murder and sent to the Tower. Tried before his fellow peers, Byron claimed exemption, pleading Benefit of Clergy, and his verdict was reduced to manslaughter, allowing him free to scuttle off back to Newstead. The "Wicked Lord Byron", as he became known, lived in seclusion and died in 1798. Newstead Abbey passed to his young grandnephew George Gordon, the poet Lord Byron (1788–1824).

William Chaworth lies in the ruined old church at Annesley. As he was unmarried, his estate passed to his cousin, George, whose daughter Mary became heiress to the Annesley estate. The new Lord Byron was fifteen when he met his niece, the seventeen-year-old heiress. He feared the ghosts of the Annesley dead might come down at night from their picture frames and exact their revenge on him, but he soon had other things on his mind. In Byron's words, his 'heart had far outgrown his years,' and he kept returning to Annesley to see his bright morning star, riding over from his semi-ruinous home to give Mary jewellery, to hear her sing, to walk with her down the steps of the terraced garden, and to fall in love.

Byron's mother wrote to the family lawyer John Hanson:

You may well be surprised (...) that Byron is not returned to Harrow. But the Truth is, I cannot get him to return to school, though I have done all in my power for six weeks past. He has no indisposition that I know of, but love, desperate love, the worst of all maladies in my opinion. In short the Boy is distractedly in love with Miss Chaworth, and he has not been with me three weeks all the time he has been in this county, but spent all his time at Annesley.

It was an adolescent passion that could have healed a family feud, but Byron's feelings were unrequited. His poem, *The Dream*, captured their meeting on Diadem Hill, part of the Annesley estate, Mary Chaworth being the "Maid". It was on Diadem Hill that they often met and finally parted in what Byron described as being the most romantic period of his life. In "To My Dear Mary Anne" (1804) he wrote:

> The flame that within my breast burns,
> Is unlike what in lovers' hearts glows;
> The love which for Mary I feel,
> Is far purer than Cupid bestows.

The flame died with Byron's return to his studies. Mary Chaworth had not given him reason to believe she loved him. And after overhearing her speaking to a maid of 'that lame boy' he bade her farewell.

With Byron but a memory, Mary Chaworth looked down from the top of Annesley Hall, watching a society gathering as it took place. Leading the fox hunt was John Musters, a dashing and skilled horseman who owned much of West Bridgford. He later pursued her and she agreed to marry. They moved to Musters' seat at Colwick Hall in 1805 and had seven children. Byron visited her there when she was a young mother. Musters was unfaithful to his wife, causing her great stress, and they separated in 1814, at which time she began writing to the now-famous poet, in whom she'd previously declared no romantic interest. After an unsuccessful attempt to meet Byron in Hastings, Mary returned to her hard-drinking husband. Today, Byron and Mary Chaworth are featured on some nice wall art inside Colwick Hall, one of England's largest and most complete Georgian mansions.

It wasn't until after Lord Byron's death that Mary Chaworth first read a selection of poems that he had written for her. The pang of regret fell hard.

'Had I married Miss Chaworth,' wrote Lord Byron, 'perhaps the whole tenor of my life would have been different.'

As a young woman, the writer Mary Howitt was returning home from riding in Sherwood Forest when she passed Annesley and came face to face with Lord Byron. In *Mary Howitt, an Autobiography* (1889) this occasion is recounted:

> I saw a young gentleman approaching, leading his horse. Looking attentively at him, I observed that he limped on one foot, and it instantly occurred to me – Lord Byron! As he came up I took a close survey of him, and saw that it was really he. I could recognise him, not only by his limp, but by the portrait I had seen at the abbey. He was coming from the direction of Annesley, and he had probably been indulging in some sad remembrances by a ride round the residence of Mary Chaworth. He had now published his first Cantos *Childe Harold*, and was in the zenith of his fame.

After Byron's death, Thomas Moore found the following lines written, but not published, shortly after the marriage of Miss Chaworth (1805):

> Hills of Annesley, bleak and barren,
> Where my thoughtless childhood strayed,
> How the northern tempests, warring,
> How thy tufted shade!
> Now no more the hours beguiling,
> Former favourite haunts I see,
> Now no more my Mary smiling
> Makes ye seem a heaven to me.

Colwick Hall.

The Chaworth-Musters family became one of the most powerful in Nottinghamshire but Mary never recovered from her regret. In 1831 Colwick Hall was sacked by rioters on their way to burn down Nottingham Castle following the failure of the Second Reform Bill. Forced to hide from invaders, Mary and her servants took to the fields behind the hall as the fires raged. Already in bad health, she died a few months later. That same year, Chaworth-Musters' son, Charles Musters, died of malaria on Charles Darwin's voyage on the HMS Beagle.

Two years after their death, Mary Ann Chaworth-Musters' good friend Mary Ann Cursham (1794–1881), dedicated her poetry collection *Poems: Sacred, Dramatic & Lyric* (1833), to her sister muse, a 'Departed Spirit'.

As for Annesley Hall, it soon became, in the words of Mary Howitt's husband, the writer William Howitt, 'forsaken, neglected, and ghostly, by reason of the deep desolateness which possessed its grey walls, silent courtyard, and unkempt gardens.'[2] Annesley Hall remained with the Chaworth-Musters until it was sold in a state of disrepair in the early 1970s, at which time the Church Commissioners were happy to receive one pound from Ashfield District Council. Two devastating fires later and the historic building is in a precarious state of abandonment. English Heritage has listed the site and there's been some restoration but any visitors are likely to be enthusiastic ghost-hunters.

There's a memorial to the memory of Mary Ann Chaworth-Musters in New Annesley's All Saints Church. The old church is now a roofless and disused ruin which stands on a mound near Annesley Hall. In 2012 the church's remains were conserved and consolidated.

DH Lawrence describes the church and hall in his first novel *The White Peacock* (1911), this abandoned ruin of 'ghostly disorder' with 'prayer books scattered on the floor in the dust and rubble, torn by mice and birds.' Annesley Hall is reputed to be the most haunted place in Nottinghamshire and it featured on the TV show *Most Haunted*, with Yvette Fielding and the late psychic/charlatan Derek Acorah. Pay it a visit, if you dare.

All Saints Church, New Annesley.

---

[1]Grandby, 1942.
[2]Jacks, 1881.

Chapter 50
Aslockton – The Book of Common Words

> 'What the heart loves, the will chooses and the mind justifies.'
>
> Thomas Cranmer

Aslockton's most famous son is a man known for his role in history and his ultimate martyrdom, but he was also a writer whose work has had a lasting impact on the English-speaking world.

As quotable as any novelist, Thomas Cranmer has written the script for many a ceremony. Recognise this triplet? '...Earth to earth, ashes to ashes, dust to dust...' or this? '... to have and to hold from this day forward, for better for worse, for richer for poorer, in sickness and in health...' that's Cranmer. Take the familiarity of 'ashes to ashes' alone, which has been used as a title by Harold Pinter for a play (1966), David Bowie for a song (1980), Tami Hoag for a novel (1999) and a BBC TV police drama (2008–2010). They are perhaps the most quotable words by a Nottinghamshire writer! And there are many other examples of Cranmer's phrases permeating our lives. When Neville Chamberlain and Barack Obama each declared 'peace in our time,' they were quoting Cranmer.[1] Our entire language owes much to the man from Aslockton.

Thomas Cranmer was born in 1489 into a traditional Roman Catholic family. He spent his first fourteen years in Aslockton and lived in a cottage on Abbey Lane. He may have attended the Collegiate Grammar School at Southwell before heading to Jesus College Cambridge. After he married the daughter of an innkeeper, his fellowship was suspended, but within a year his wife had died and he had resumed his path, becoming ordained in 1520.

Henry VIII appointed Thomas Cranmer as his chaplain and then Archdeacon of Taunton. In the 1530s he was sent to Europe in an attempt to gather support for the annulment of Henry's marriage to Catherine of Aragon (the king already had his eyes on Anne Boleyn). Now a highly-valued advocate to the king in his desire for divorce, Henry appointed Cranmer his first Archbishop of Canterbury. Henry's marriage to Catherine was immediately pronounced null and void thanks to Cranmer's arguments for the annulment, proving that the king, and not the pope, had supreme jurisdiction over matters concerning his kingdom.

Two years after Henry's death in 1547, Cranmer produced *The Book of Common Prayer*, his greatest achievement. As editor, Cranmer borrowed and adapted material from other sources (mostly Latin), but he also provided liturgical vernacular that was to be read aloud, poetic prose that would ring out through all the parishes of the Church of England. Focusing on prayer, praise, and study, Cranmer brought to the people activities that were usually a matter for the clergy. It is a work of literary genius that not only had a simplicity that meant it could be understood by the barely literate, it flowed with idioms, imagery, repetitions and rhythms, and for this, Cranmer can assume the credit. Countless novelists, screenplay writers and poets have "loved and cherished" Cranmer's prose and been influenced by it, including William Shakespeare.

The book provoked much resistance but after the House of Lords passed The Act of Uniformity, Latin mass was abolished in England and all services had to be conducted in English using the book. Loyal Catholics burned the prayer book. Cranmer later produced a new and more radical version, but with the sudden and premature death of the new king, Edward VI, his plans were left in ruin as Mary Tudor rose to the throne.

When Mary, a committed Catholic, became Queen, Latin mass was back, and Cranmer was arrested, imprisoned and tried for treason. He recanted his beliefs but when called upon to do so in public he refused and was burnt at the stake in 1556. He held the hand that had signed the recantation in the flames until it was consumed.

After Mary died in 1558, Elizabeth, a Protestant, became Queen. The Act of Uniformity was adopted and it was stated that everybody had to attend the Church of England and use the Book of Common Prayer. Those not doing so were to be punished. Opposition continued and the feelings of discontent contributed to the English Civil War.

In Aslockton there are several places carrying Cranmer's name. The village pub is the Cranmer Arms, Aslockton Castle motte is known as Cranmer's Mound, the Primary School is the Archbishop Cranmer Church of England Academy, there is the Cranmer Preschool, and the Thomas

Cranmer Arms, Aslockton.

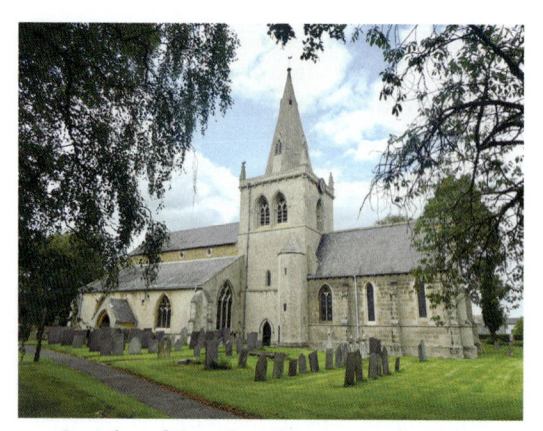

St. John of Beverley, Whatton-in-the-Vale.

Cranmer Centre, a large 2010 extension to St Thomas Church. In St. John of Beverley, Whatton-in-the-Vale, is an incised floor stone commemorating Cranmer's father, also named Thomas Cranmer, and it was in this church that the writer worshipped as a boy.

The 1662 version of *The Book of Common Prayer* is still widely used today. Acknowledged as a literary masterpiece, it has deeply influenced the English language and thought.

Thomas Cranmer Centre, Aslockton.

---

[1]Von Staats, 2016.

Chapter 51
Bingham – Shakespeare's Nottingham Knight

'I were born an' bred i' th' forest, and lay mysen to die here...'
James Prior, *Forest Folk*

The attractive market town of Bingham, once a great meeting point, houses much history in its oldest building, the parish church of St Mary and All Saints. Replacing a Norman church, much of the current St Mary's was built between 1220 and 1320, an impressive achievement by Bingham's small community. Support came from the Lord of the Manor, Sir Richard de Bingham, who was from a family of wealthy Nottingham wool merchants. Knighted by King Edward I, Richard de Bingham served as Sheriff of Nottinghamshire and Derbyshire in 1302 and was later appointed to survey Nottingham Castle. Inside the church is his fine stone tomb carved in Normandy and marked by the effigy of a cross-legged knight.

After the de Bingham family fell into poverty, the Rempstones became the new lords of the manor, continuing to improve the church. John Rempstone's son, Thomas, is an important historical figure, and Shakespeare's Nottingham knight.

Sir Richard's tomb, St Mary and All Saints Church.

Sir Thomas Rempstone was Knight of the Shire for Nottinghamshire, which he also represented in Parliament, but he is best known for his service to his close friend, John of Gaunt's son Henry Bolingbroke, Duke of Lancaster. King Richard II had exiled his cousin Henry and, after John of Gaunt died, confiscated his inheritance. Sir Thomas joined Henry in France and was one of the fifteen lances that returned to England to set about reclaiming his land and fortune. After capturing King Richard in 1399, Henry appointed Sir Thomas Rempstone as Constable of the Tower of London, and he

St. Mary and All Saints, Bingham.

was there to oversee the royal prisoner and witness his abdication, resulting in Bolingbroke taking the crown to become Henry IV. Rempstone was made a Knight of the Garter and member of the Privy Council, contributing towards his wealth and extensive land which included Bingham Manor. This story is recounted in William Shakespeare's *Richard II*, but in act II. scene i., the bard's Sir Thomas Rempstone is named Sir John Ramston.

Sir Thomas, who had been titled Admiral of the Fleet, accidentally 'drowned through the upsetting of a boat in the Thames in 1406.'[1] His body was brought back to Bingham's church for burial and he is to be found in the chancel. There is a worn floor-stone on which part of the engraved portraits of Sir Thomas and his wife remain.

Shakespeare's *Richard II* portrays the king's misrule and deposition by Bolingbroke as being responsible for the Wars of the Roses. Sir Thomas Rempstone (as Sir John Ramston) appears in the famous and much-quoted speech by John of Gaunt, regarded as an invocation of English patriotism. Shakespeare's 'this sceptre'd isle... [t]his blessed plot, this earth, this realm, this England,' precedes the moment that Sir John Ramston is mentioned as one of the knightly lances.[2]

In the late nineteenth century Oscar Wilde (1854–1900) was in Bingham. Wilde had a relationship with the son of the rector, George Francis "Frank" Miles, a colour-blind portrait painter who had met Wilde at Oxford in the mid-1870s. The rector's wife, Mary

Miles, was also a well-known painter. Frank Miles and Oscar Wilde lived together for a few years and it was Miles that introduced Wilde to Lillie Langtry and Lord Ronald Charles Sutherland-Leveson-Gower, the latter being the likely inspiration for the hedonistic aristocrat Lord Henry Wotton in *The Picture of Dorian Gray* (1890). Lillie Langtry and Oscar Wilde visited the Miles family at Bingham Rectory. Miles reluctantly ended the affair after his father had read Wilde's poetry and threatened to cut off his allowance.

There's another writer of that era who had a much stronger connection with Bingham: James Prior (1851–1922). James Prior Kirk is buried in Bingham's cemetery. His headstone reads:

> In loving memory of James Prior Kirk
> better known as James Prior
> Died Dec 17th 1922 aged 71
> Also his wife lily, died Mar 9th 1914 aged 48
> Also of their sons, Walter, died of wounds in France,
> Aug 17th 1918 aged 26,
> and Harold, died Apr 25th 1931 aged 23

James Prior lived in Bingham from 1891 to 1922, first at 19 Fisher Lane, a home called Lushai Cottage (previously named Brusty Cottage), then at the neighbouring Banks, at Banks Cottage, where he died. Much of his time in Bingham was spent as a social recluse, his eyesight failing him. Prior's daughter, Dorothy, continued to live at Banks Cottage until 1978 when she died aged eighty-seven.

It was on Mapperley Road near the centre of Nottingham that Prior was born. His parents had a millinery business on Peck Lane, Hounds Gate and Pelham Street, but Prior rejected hat-making and law (after leaving school he had become a solicitor), preferring to study language and literature, a decision that angered his father. By the age of twenty-seven Prior had little to show for his literary efforts so he took a teaching position at a boarding school. After his father died, he became involved with his uncle in a farming

Lushai Cottage, Bingham.

business but the money dried up. As it turned out, this would not be a wasted five years, as the experience would inform Prior's novel *Forest Folk* (1901).

After marrying his cousin Lily Kirk, Prior returned to Nottingham, living in Radcliffe-on-Trent before heading to Bingham, and it was here that all of his best work was written. His first published novel, *Rennie*, was followed in 1897 by *Ripple and Flood*, about the Trent. Then came *Forest Folk*, set during an eventful period of history that covers the Napoleonic Wars and Luddite riots. The all-important follow-up to this success was the disappointing *Hyssop*. Arguably his best book, *A Walking Gentleman*, arrived three years later, but by then his reputation had waned. Prior's last published work was *Fortuna Chance*, set in the 1720s. The author was granted a small pension in recognition of his services to literature.

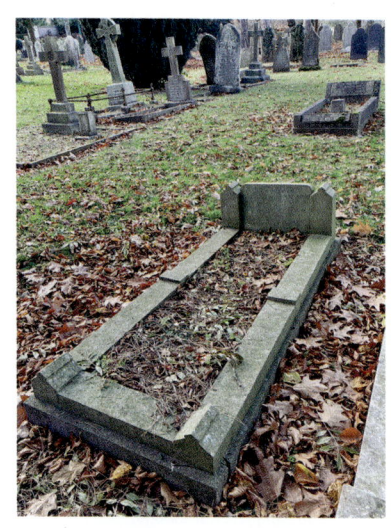

James Prior's headstone, Bingham Cemetery.

James Prior has been called the 'Thomas Hardy of Nottinghamshire' and comparisons can even be made to DH Lawrence, who shared a publisher with Prior and rated, if pitied, the author. Lawrence wrote, 'What a curious man James Prior is!' and wondered why Prior was a 'failure.' A good decade before Lawrence, Prior was writing about Nottinghamshire (its people and countryside), England's changing landscape (natural and political) and class differences, and often with the local vernacular. JM Barrie commented that James Prior was a 'fine writer,' but Prior never got the recognition his talent deserved, despite a pub being named The Forest Folk in honour of his book. The Forest Folk pub/hotel was in Blidworth – a setting for the book – and it had a space in its entrance room dedicated to Prior. The pub housed Prior memorabilia and thematic stained-glass windows. Near the spot where the pub once stood is Forest Folk Corner, where there is a planter with a gold-plated plaque which includes a quote by Prior:

In commemoration of
James Prior Kirk
1851–1922
Poet and author of 'Forest Folk'
A tale of Blidworth and Blidworth folk.
"I have put the best of myself into my books,
they are me and nobody else"

Five of the pub's *Forest Folk* stained-glass windows were salvaged in 2005 and are now inside Blidworth's St Andrew's Mission Hall. The windows have bars on the outside, but inside the hall you can clearly see the local animals and rural environment that the windows depict. *Forest Folk* was republished in 2017 by Spokesman Books.

---

[1]Brown, 1896.
[2]Mee, 1938.

Chapter 52
68 Bridgford Road, West Bridgford –
The Genre-hopping Allrounder

'He would never fulfill the glory of his promise.'

JC Snaith, *Thus Far*

68 Bridgford Road, West Bridgford.

John Collis Snaith (1876–1936) grew up in West Bridgford where he'd been born. He was educated at High Pavement School and University College. As a writer, he was unique, a jack-of-all genres. His forty-plus books include works of historical romance, fantasy, sci-fi, whimsical comedy, crime thrillers, poignant satire, psychological and visionary works; often holding eccentric ideas that made him too original, his output too varied, for either his readers or the critics to pin him down.[1]

Snaith was known in Nottingham for his cricket. He went from playing on the Forest to walking out at Trent Bridge, playing first-class for Nottinghamshire in 1900. He is thought to have lived at 68 Bridgford Road. A year before he turned out for Nottinghamshire, Snaith wrote *Willow the King: The Story of a Cricket Match*, described as 'the best cricket story ever written.' This humorous novel, with a romance at its heart, is about the annual two-day cricket match between Little Clumpton and Hickory. Snaith dedicated the book to his colleagues back at the Nottingham Forest Cricket Club.

Another team he played for was the Allahakbarries, named in the mistaken belief that "Allah akbar" meant "Heaven help us" in Arabic (it actually means God is great). The "barries" part of the name comes from the man that set up the side, JM Barrie. Between 1890 and 1913 the team of authors saw a number of famous writers turn out for them, including Arthur Conan Doyle, PG Wodehouse, Jerome K Jerome and AA Milne.[2] Barrie privately published a humorous booklet about his celebrity team called *Allahakbarries C.C.* (1880), a revised edition appearing in 1899 (reprinted in 1950 with a foreword by Don Bradman). The nineteenth century copies are much sought-after. During one of their "friendly" matches, Barrie's wife took to the crease and was promptly struck on the ankle by a yorker from the left-hander Snaith, who didn't know whether to appeal for forgiveness or lbw.

The Oxford English Dictionary credits Snaith with the earliest use of the expression "street person". Snaith's everyday street people encounter an unusual father and son in his novel *William Jordan Junior* (1907). The peculiar story follows the father, a scholar and bookseller, and son, a highly-strung poet and dreamer, as they struggle to negotiate contemporary life. Both characters are visionaries and neither is equipped for the real world. AE Russell was 'moved' by the novel, and *The New York Times* quoted its 'peculiar charm and rare quality' and 'psychological loveliness, half mystic, half human.'

This humorous and poignant novel may also be the one that James Elroy Flecker described as a masterpiece. It was in *The English Review* that Flecker wrote of Snaith: 'Three of his books are near literature and one is unique, a masterpiece, and it is all but unknown.'

In 1912 Flecker declined a lectureship at Nottingham University College, writing 'Nottingham is a deadly prospect.' Had he come here he would have been an assistant to Professor Ernest Weekley in the same year Weekley's wife left him for DH Lawrence.

Snaith's first sci-fi novel, *An Affair of State*, appeared in 1913. It was set in a near-future England under a cloud of social unrest. There's local interest in his acclaimed 1916 novel *The Sailor*, illustrated by WA Hottinger. The story opens in a rough part of town where Henry, a small boy, is crouched in desperate terror against the wall of a blind alley, while his drunken and terrible old aunt stands over him, heavy lash in hand, taunting the child before striking him. After escaping, Henry experiences an extraordinary life, becoming a mariner. From *The Sailor*: 'A large woman in a torn dress stood at the gate of a rag and bone dealer's yard. The season was November, the hour midnight, the place a slum in a Midland textile town.'

Snaith turned to fantasy in 1917, writing *The Coming*, about the second coming of Christ. In 1921 came his dystopian *The Council of Seven*, a novel about a totalitarian system of government that imposes a strict regime on anyone who challenges its vision for world peace. In *Thus Far* (1925), Snaith questions whether science has gone too far, in a story that features a powerful, amoral, telepathic superman, created with rays, chemicals and elements from the "missing link" in our evolution.

From sentimental romance to satire and works of great imagination, Snaith was a talented all-rounder, and not just on the cricket field.

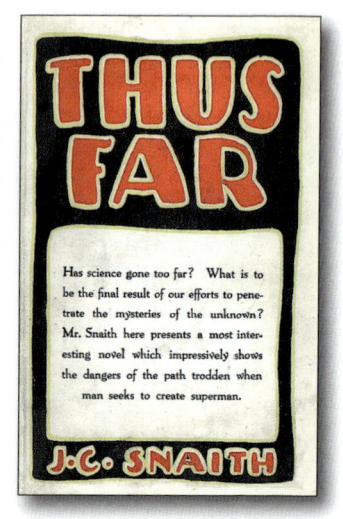

---

[1] Valentine, 2009.
[2] Telfer, 2010.

Chapter 53
Car Colston – The First History of Nottinghamshire

'The thorough Dr Thoroton'
Arthur Mee, *The Midland Stronghold*

St Mary's Church, Car Colston.

Nottinghamshire's principal historical and archaeological group, The Thoroton Society, was established in 1897. The society was named in honour of Dr Robert Thoroton, who published the first history of Nottinghamshire in 1677. Thoroton is strongly associated with the Nottinghamshire village of Car Colston where he worked as a doctor and magistrate, with a keen interest in genealogy. On visiting friends in Thrumpton he was told about a manuscript on the history of Nottinghamshire which his father-in-law Gilbert Bohun had begun writing. Thoroton, known for his record keeping, was encouraged to complete the work.[1] He took up the challenge and, after a decade of research, produced a folio of data which he titled *The Antiquities of Nottinghamshire*, making Thoroton the chief authority on the county.

Chronicling some 600 years of local history, this work of huge labour and detail recorded the landowners of each parish dating back to the Domesday Survey. It is said that Thoroton paid many assistants to gather information for him, enabling him to produce this first history of its kind. He dedicated the book to his friend Gilbert Sheldon, Archbishop of Canterbury, who lived in East Bridgford.

The present Old Hall in Car Colston is a rebuild, but it occupies land near where the Thorotons lived at Old Church Farm. Robert Thoroton was born in 1623, a year after his parents married at St Mary's Church in Nottingham. As a first-born, he was named Robert after his father, a tradition that dated back through six generations of Thorotons. The family had taken their name from the neighbouring village of Thoroton (or Thurverton) where they had owned land as far back as the thirteenth century.

Thoroton received a BA degree at Christ's College Cambridge, later becoming an MA and a Licentiate of Medicine. It was around this time, in 1646, that Robert's grandfather died and the family hall, grand but dilapidated, passed to Robert's parents. By 1660 Robert himself would be living in the hall with his wife Anne. They had three children, all daughters. The family remained in Car Colston having their home razed and rebuilt.

It was in 1678 that Thoroton died, just months after his great *Antiquities* was published. He had prepared his stone coffin six years earlier, which had been inscribed with his ancestral heraldic emblems. In 1845, during restoration work on the church, the coffin was found and opened. Schoolchildren were said to have witnessed Thoroton's remains, and his skull was displayed in the village shop as a local curiosity. Outraged, Rev John Girardot demanded that the remains were collected and reburied, only for workmen to unearth them again in 1863. This time the coffin was moved to its present position at the west end of the south aisle. I'm told that there are plans to make much more of Thoroton in Car Colston, including finding a better position for his stone coffin, which currently looks abandoned and unloved. As some consolation, there is a nice plaque on wall of the south aisle that reads:

Robert Thoroton's coffin, St. Mary's Church, Car Colston.

This Tablet was erected in the year 1908 by a few Members of the Thoroton Society in memory of Robert Thoroton, of Car-Colston, Doctor of Physick, & a Justice of the Peace for this County, who died here in the year 1698, and whose body was buried in the stone sarcophagus now preserved in this Church. In the year 1677 he published "The Antiquities of Nottinghamshire", a work of great labour and erudition.

In honour of Robert Thoroton, Bromley House Library keeps its local history books and local writers' special collections in the Thoroton Room.

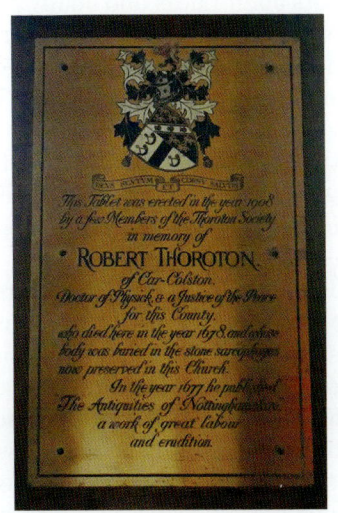

Robert Thoroton's plaque, St Mary's Church, Car Colston.

---

[1]Blagg, 1908.

Chapter 54
Devonshire Avenue, Beeston – A Place of Poetry

'There are some days when the only thing that makes any sense of the world, is poetry.'

Jenny Swann.

Nottingham, city of a thousand poets, is perhaps home to more poetry publishers per head than any comparable city in the world. Two of them are neighbours on Devonshire Avenue in Beeston, the distinguished poets John Lucas and Jenny Swann, who have been key players on Nottingham's poetry scene for years.

It was back in 1964 that John Lucas moved to Beeston for a lecturing job at the University of Nottingham. There, he started The Byron Press, which published BS Johnson, among others. The press ran until the mid-1970s, when Lucas left the university to set up Loughborough University's Department of English. In 1994 he started Shoestring Press, which celebrated its twenty-fifth anniversary in 2019.

John Lucas has taught English at universities throughout the world, spending his last few lecturing years as a professor at NTU, and he is Professor Emeritus at the Universities of Loughborough and NTU, where he finished his lecturing career. One of his own recently published novels is *Remembered Acts* (2020), about the aging process. In the novel, a character passing through Beeston refers to it as a 'small, and as far as he could see, non-descript town.'

A biographer and literary historian, Lucas has written and translated over forty books, including critical studies of Charles Dickens, John Clare and Arnold Bennett, in addition to his own poetry and prose in which Nottingham features prominently. Lucas' first pamphlet-collection of poems was entitled *About Nottingham* (1971), and his first full collection *Studying Grosz on the Bus* (1989) included poems about the city. In fact, Nottingham makes its way into all of his poetry collections, including *Portable Property* (2015).

In 2005 Lucas edited *Poetry: The Nottingham Collection*, a book in which each of its fifty-two contributors has a connection with Nottinghamshire. In NTU's archives there's a box of papers relating to literary figures with whom Lucas has engaged with and papers generated by Shoestring Press. Less well-documented is his support for local spoken poetry. For ten years Lucas ran a series of successful poetry readings at the Flying Goose in Beeston, events that attracted poets with national, and occasionally international, reputations, alongside local poets. The Flying Goose even hosted the Beeston International Po Fest. Lucas's most recent book, *Closing Time at the Royal Oak* (2021), features another local boozer. It is a fond look back on a time when pubs were at the heart of their community – and were serviced by a local brewery (in this case Shipstone's) – and at the fate of "the local".

Beeston's reputation for poetry has endured. In its halcyon days, between 1983 and 1993, there were annual poetry readings at Beeston Library, a series called "Poets in Beeston" which was organised by Margaret MacDermott and library manager Robert Gent, the latter also editing an anthology of modern poetry that came out of the readings called *Poems for the Beekeeper* (1996). "Poets in Beeston" brought many respected poets to the town including Sarah Maguire, Sheenagh Pugh, Carol Ann Duffy, Roger McGough, Ian McMillan, Catherine Fisher, Wendy Cope, Michael Rosen, Benjamin Zephaniah, Henry Normal, Tom Paulin, Nigel Planer and Jackie Kay. The town remains a hive of poetic happenings, and Devonshire Avenue's Jenny Swann is playing a key role.

John Lucas's house on Devonshire Avenue.

Jenny Swann moved to Nottingham in 2004 just as her poetry collection *Stay* had been published by Lucas' Shoestring Press. She had been living in Manchester when her husband secured a job at the University of Nottingham. It was a stroke of fate that the house next to John Lucas – one of only two people she knew in Nottingham – was up for sale. Swann had previously studied English Literature and the History of Art before working in museums like the V&A, and running poetry workshops in libraries and galleries.

After working as a freelance author and lecturer she arrived in Nottingham and was soon working as Poetry Editor for Five Leaves Publications, a role that reaffirmed her love of poetry pamphlets and publishing. Fully aware of the support in Beeston for its poets and writers, she set up Candlestick Press in 2008, receiving a Cultivate award a year later for her publishing.

Candlestick's poetry pamphlets are well produced and commercially successful, appealing to poetry lovers and people in the market for a gift or greeting card. Each pamphlet arrives with a matching envelope and bookmark, and they are all themed and introduced by a high-profile editor who has selected the poems, contemporary and historical. With themes like mothers, gardens, love, friendship, football, baking and walking, there's something for everyone. Jenny Swann ran Candlestick Press until 2016. In recent years, she has set up the consultancy and poetry card company One Plum Poem as she continues to explore the impact a single poem can make.

Back in 2015, the year Nottingham became a UNESCO City of Literature, John Lucas and Jenny Swann collaborated on *Ten Poems About Nottingham*, a collection that celebrates the city they love. 'Nottingham is a fantastic place for encouraging and supporting, a great place to make things happen,' said Swann, whose Candlestick Press published *Ten Poems About Nottingham* as a thank you to the city. Lucas introduces the ten poems that he personally selected, poems which provide a historical narrative that runs through the pamphlet. Opening with Derrick Buttress' poem on working at Raleigh and closing with Wayne Burrows' take on Nottingham's vibrant nightlife, the collection brings together a range of rural and urban verse from Henry Kirke White and DH Lawrence to fine contemporary poets.

The next-door neighbours have certainly made a strong contribution to Nottingham's reputation as a seat of poetry.

Nearby Chilwell has its own poetry publisher, Alan Baker – himself a poet – who runs Leafe Press and the online journal *Litter,* which specialises in experimental poetry. Among his latest publications is a pamphlet from local poet Kathleen Bell, *Do You Know How Kind I Am?* (2021). Bell followed this up with her first full collection, *Disappearances*, published by Shoestring Press. Shoestring has published three full collections from Neil Fulwood whose poetry regularly appears in the small press world. When not writing poetry Fulwood drives Nottingham City Transport buses and proudly writes from a working-class sensitivity.

Chapter 55
Eastwood – The Country of My Heart

'In this queer jumble of the old England and the new, I came into consciousness.'

DH Lawrence

DH Lawrence's early years in Eastwood were crucial to his development as a writer and as a man. Surrounded by the beautiful countryside he described as 'The country of my heart,' Eastwood is a charming town. It has its own blue line Lawrence tour which begins at the DH Lawrence Birthplace Museum, inside 'the flat fronted red brick house in Victoria Street,' as Lawrence described it.

DH Lawrence's Birthplace Museum.

Founded in 1976 by local enthusiasts, and converted by Broxtowe Borough Council in 1980, the Birthplace Museum incorporates a former grocer's and its neighbour, 8A Victoria Street, the two-up two-down terrace that was the first of the Lawrence family's homes in Eastwood. Built for miners in around 1850, the Lawrences lived here between 1883 and 1887. Their fourth child, David Herbert Richards Lawrence, was born on the 11th September 1885.

The museum is full of Lawrence art and artefacts, including a trunk with D. H. L inscribed on the side, a trunk that had travelled the world with Lawrence and his wife Frieda. The trunk is offered as visual evidence of Lawrence's 'absolute necessity to move.'[1] It was one of four trunks, 'one household trunk, one book trunk, F's and mine...' said Lawrence.

Inside 8A Victoria Street is the room in which Lawrence was born and, as a baby, may well have slept in the bottom drawer of a chest. The kitchen would have been the hub of the house with the front "best" room seldom used. It was Lawrence's mother, Lydia, that would have played the piano here. She didn't want her children to be 'condemned to manual labour' and valued education. Sons born in Eastwood in the 1880s were destined for a life down a mine, and the Lawrences lived within walking distance of ten pits. Yet none of the five Lawrence offspring ended up as a miner or married to one. Lawrence's father, Arthur, took a different view on education. He hated books, even the sight of anyone reading or writing. Lawrence had a difficult relationship with his father. In 1910 he wrote, 'I was born hating my father (...) I shivered with horror when he touched me.'[2] Lawrence would come to love him in later life, and it was from his father that Lawrence inherited his great love of nature.

From the home on Victoria Street, the Lawrences moved to a slightly better house, something they repeated with each move. 'It was a little less common to live in the Breach,' wrote Lawrence (1929), who was two years of age when he moved to Breach House (now 28 Garden Road). The Breach was a row of brick colliery houses built c1880. Breach House was a typical miner's cottage of the time, but with the extra space, porch and side garden offered by an end terrace. Breach House is known to readers of *Sons and Lovers* (1913) as The Bottoms, the home that Paul Morel's newly-married parents move to at the start of the book. From *Sons and Lovers*:

> The Bottoms consisted of six blocks of miners' dwellings, two rows of three, like the dots on a blank-six domino, and twelve houses in a block. This double row of dwellings sat at the foot of the rather sharp slope from Bestwood, and looked out, from the attic windows at least, on the slow climb of the valley towards Selby.

Lawrence was here until 1891. The house had belonged to the colliery owners that Arthur worked for, and it cost sixpence more a week to rent than their former abode. As Arthur was a butty, overseeing a team of miners, the family could afford it. The house was sold by the Coal Board in the 1940s, later to be left empty, fire-damaged and taken over by nature. It's since been restored sympathetically and is now run by volunteers. Upstairs is a library of over 200 books by and about Lawrence.

The Lawrences moved to a brand-new rented house on Walker Street, one not belonging to the colliery company. With its elevated position they didn't have to walk far for the great view Lawrence knew 'better than any in the world...' The houses were known locally as Piano Row due to the prosperity of the occupants. It was in the Walker Street home that Lawrence's brother died.

Lawrence's poem, "The Piano", from *Love Poems and others* (1913), captures a sense of nostalgia, 'weeping like a child for the past,' when, as a young boy, he would sit under the piano, at his mother's feet.

The family moved to Lynncroft in 1905, their final Eastwood home where they lived until 1911. It was here that Lydia died, leaving the bereft Lawrence without his 'love of loves.'

Eastwood is awash with Lawrence locations. Arthur Lawrence's favourite local pub was The Three Tuns, on Three Tuns Lane, where he would call in on his way home from Brinsley Colliery. The pub appears in *Sons and Lovers* as the Moon and Stars and hosts the wakes in the novel.

Lawrence used to collect his father's wages from Durban House on Mansfield Road, one of Eastwood's most impressive buildings (c1876). It was built for Barber, Walker & Co as their offices, the company that built the Breach. In 2016 Durban House ceased being a Lawrence Heritage and Exhibition Centre after it was closed by Broxtowe Borough Council. It has since been a spa but on last glance was empty. Of the building, Lawrence wrote (in *Sons and Lovers*):

> These offices were quite handsome: a new, red-brick building, almost like a mansion, standing in its own well-kept grounds at the end of Greenhill Road. The waiting room was a hall, a long, bare room paved with blue brick, and having a seat all round, against the wall.

Another building to feature in *Sons and Lovers* is the one now used by Phoenix Snooker. It was the Mechanics Hall and housed a library frequented by Lawrence at a time when it was the largest library in Eastwood. The town's Mechanics Institute was an adult education centre for workers wishing to improve their minds, and young Lawrence visited the library on a weekly basis. A friend of his, Enid Hilton, recalled the library opening every Thursday evening, and, in *A Nottingham Childhood with DH Lawrence* (1993), she wrote, 'Once I [picked] up a novel that was considered "not quite nice". The librarian made no comment, but my parents were at once informed.'

The room once used as a library is now an acoustic lounge bar called The Library. Before becoming Phoenix the venue had fallen into ruin, having sat idle for twenty years after being used as a Miners' Welfare building.

The former Mechanics' Institute, Eastwood.

Eastwood's The Lady Chatterley Pub offers a couple of tributes to Lawrence and it's not far from here that the British School was located, where Lawrence attended readings and literary society meetings, and taught between 1902 and 1905, 'Three years savage teaching of collier lads.' Next to the pub was the Congregational Chapel (demolished in 1971 and now a branch of Iceland) that Lawrence attended.

Alan Sillitoe recognised the landscape Lawrence wrote about, but not his characters which, Sillitoe thought, weren't like those he'd grown up with. In the early 1950s, Sillitoe and Ruth Fainlight took a bus ride to Eastwood, to visit Lawrence's birthplace and meet with an old friend of Lawrence's. The trip to Eastwood is a literary pilgrimage that thousands have followed. The residents of Eastwood may have changed since Lawrence's day, and indeed since Sillitoe visited, but there's no escaping his legacy's influence on the town, with many of its businesses having a Lawrencian name. Sillitoe noted, in 1987, that '"Lawrence Industry" is replacing that of the coalmines which once surrounded the place.'

It may have lost Durban House, but with its blue line tour, fine museum and many nods to Lawrence, Eastwood is keeping the Phoenix rising. I met a local woman there called Evelyn, a ninety-five-year-old active member of the DH Lawrence Society. She told me about the society's regular guest speakers, saying, 'These experts know what Lawrence was doing on 15th October 1907 at 6pm, but all I really want to know about are the stories.'

Evelyn would probably have enjoyed *Jobey* (1983) by Leslie Williamson (1922–2006). Billed as 'A time of struggle, a time of love, a time of tragedy,' *Jobey* is set during the general and then miners' strike of 1926. Jobey is in love with the daughter of the local colliery's boss, the community's biggest employer. As with many stories of strikes, the protagonist is conflicted, his allegiances tested. The plot features an underground explosion, and the plight of the miners stuck below ground is powerfully told. The working-class characters and their dialects are authentically depicted and the book came out at a prescient time, with the miners' strike of 1984–5 just around the corner. Like his hero DH Lawrence, Williamson was born in Eastwood and was a founder of the Eastwood Writers group. At his very well-attended funeral it was announced that Williamson also played another role – as an on-screen body double/lookalike for Robert Maxwell. He didn't mention that one much to anyone when he was alive!

---

[1]Lawrence, 1921.
[2]Moore, 1962.

Chapter 56
Elston Hall, Top Street, Elston –
An Evolved Man

'Owing to the imperfection of language the offspring is termed a new animal, but it is in truth a branch or elongation of the parent.'

Erasmus Darwin, *Zoonomia*

Elston Hall.

Erasmus Darwin (1731–1802), the Da Vinci of the Midlands, is a man whose philosophical poetry has been called dangerously radical. The Darwin family's long association with Elston, four miles south-west of Newark, began in 1680. Two years after inheriting Elston Hall, Robert and Elizabeth Darwin moved in and had seven children in as many years. Their youngest, Erasmus Darwin, was born there in 1731.

It was at Chesterfield School that Darwin became a prolific poet, often communicating in verse with his eldest brother Robert. At St John's College Cambridge, Darwin first had a poem published, an elegy for Frederick, Prince of Wales, before he rode horseback to Edinburgh to train as a doctor. In the summer of 1756 Darwin returned to Elston Hall before starting a medical practice in Nottingham, where he lodged with the upholsterer Mrs Burden on Long Row. It was in Nottingham that Erasmus Darwin wrote down his first invention, shock absorbers for wheels.

Qualified (or not as the case may be) as a medical doctor, his first patient was a shoemaker who had been stabbed in the gut by another shoemaker. He treated the victim but was unable to keep him alive. In fact, there are no records of Darwin having any surviving patients in the two months he was living in Long Row. And as the dead don't pay, or recommend you to any new clients, Darwin had to leave Nottingham and try his luck in Lichfield, where his unconventional methods and friendly manner proved more popular. So much so that Darwin became the most famous doctor of his time. Advocating exercise, herbs, fresh air, opiates and sex, he soon became recognised and was invited to become the Royal Physician to King George III. Darwin declined the offer,[1] preferring to stay in Lichfield where he was successful enough to be able to treat the poor and mentally ill for free.

As a boy at Elston Hall, Darwin would have been aware that his father had belonged to a group that would meet to share and create knowledge. This Gentleman's Society of Spalding was an early literary-antiquarian society whose members included Alexander Pope, Richard Bentley and Sir Isaac Newton. Inspired by this, Darwin co-founded a similar group in Lichfield. Meeting under each full moon, they became known as the Lunar Society. With members Matthew Boulton, Josiah Wedgwood and James Watt, the society offered Darwin the opportunity to share his creative and practical mind. His unpatented inventions include a flushing toilet, weather monitoring machines, a lift for barges, an artificial bird, a copying machine, a speaking machine able to recite the Lord's Prayer, and a steering wheel for his carriage, a mechanism adopted by cars a hundred-and-thirty years later. But it was through his verse that Darwin made his greatest impact.

Turning to didactic poetry, Darwin had a purpose, '...to enlist imagination under the banner of science.' It was an inventive mix; poetry that contained science and radical ideas that included a new theory of biological evolution. One long poem "The Botanic Garden" (1789), structured in rhyming couplets of four thousand lines, consisted of two parts, "The Economy of Vegetation" and "The Loves of the Plants". The former attacked political tyranny and religious superstition, the latter contained the first record of his theory of evolution. Produced by the radical publisher Joseph Johnson – a man later imprisoned for a "dangerous" publication – Darwin became a leading poet of the age, inspiring many of the early romantic poets. Mary Shelley's idea for *Frankenstein* (1818) came as she overheard a conversation between her husband (Percy Shelley) and Lord Byron in which they discussed Erasmus Darwin.

Popular poetic taste began to turn away from Darwin after establishment-backed critics ridiculed his political ideas and attacked his heroic couplets. Even Samuel Coleridge, who thought of Darwin as 'the first literary character of Europe, and the most original-minded Man' now commented, 'I absolutely nauseate Darwin's poem.' His poetry was parodied, linking him with the French Revolution, and he was labelled unreligious. The publication of his 200,000-word *Zoonomia, or The Laws of Organic Life* (1794–96) didn't help. By then Darwin claimed to be 'too old and hardened to fear a little abuse.' However, his reputation was shattered after he expanded upon his theory that life could develop without the guiding hand of a Creator.

In *Zoonomia* Darwin noted that mutations are often inherited, and that lust, hunger and security are the controlling forces of change, stating that the 'strongest and most active animal should propagate the species, which should thence become improved.' He later expressed a vivid picture of life's struggle for existence and offered the view that life developed over millions of ages, from microscopic specks arising spontaneously in primeval seas, through fishes and amphibians, to land animals and, eventually, humankind. One might easily say that Erasmus Darwin devised the theory of evolution his grandson, Charles, would publish sixty-five years later. 'The younger Darwin wrote in prose, and the elder imagined in poetry,' said Simon (2019); while Martin Priestman, in his book

All Saints Church, Elston.

The Poetry of Erasmus Darwin: Enlightened Spaces, Romantic Times (2013), wrote that, 'few writers can be so burdened with a surname which so clearly belongs to someone else.'

Charles Darwin (1809–82) was reluctant to align himself with his grandfather's views, perhaps trying to avoid the derision Erasmus had faced. Bishop Wilberforce joined the dots, accusing Charles of reviving the ideas of his 'ingenious grandsire,' but Erasmus Darwin has never been given due credit. In *Evolution, Old and New* (1879), Samuel Butler (1835–1902) accused Charles of borrowing heavily from Erasmus, and chastised him for not sufficiently acknowledging his grandfather's contribution to his theory. Charles Darwin's 1878 biography of his grandfather, *The Life of Erasmus Darwin* (1879), was even subjected to a harsh edit from his daughter Henrietta, with Charles' permission, his final tribute to Erasmus among the text cut from the published work, revealed in an unabridged edition (2002), edited by Desmond King-Hele.

Undaunted in his commitment to progress, Erasmus Darwin had offended political and religious conservatives equally. He was ridiculed for suggesting that electricity might one day have practical uses; he was criticised for his belief that women should have access to education, expressed in *A Plan for the Conduct of Female Education* (1797), he was lambasted for his prodemocracy stance, his abolitionist position, and his argument that not just the owners of property should have the right to vote; and above all, he was hated for his views on creation, not helped when he added to the family's coat of arms the Latin phrase *E conchis omnia* ("Everything from shells").

His final long poem, composed of rhyming couplets, "The Temple of Nature" (1803), came out a year after his death. The poem, originally titled "The Origin of Society", is widely considered his best poetic work, and it captures his view of life's journey of struggle for existence, from specks in the sea to civilized human society, confirming his belief in shared ancestry. Here's a taste:

> Organic life beneath the shoreless waves
> Was born and nurs'd in Ocean's pearly caves;
> First forms minute, unseen by spheric glass,
> Move on the mud, or pierce the watery mass;
> These, as successive generations bloom,
> New powers acquire, and larger limbs assume;
> Whence countless groups of vegetation spring,
> And breathing realms of fin and feet and wing.

Charles Darwin wasn't born until after his grandfather's death, but he would have visited Elston Hall, the Darwin family seat. With *On the Origin of Species* (1859), *The Descent of Man* (1871) and *The Expression of the Emotions in Man and Animals* (1872) Charles was abused and satirised in much the same way as his grandfather.

After Erasmus Darwin had left Elston Hall, his favourite poetry-loving brother Robert took over the estate, dying there a bachelor at the age of ninety-two. Robert published the popular *Principia Botanica* in 1787, and Elston Hall remained in the Darwin family until 1954, undergoing much modernisation whilst retaining the central stone house built c1700. A mismatch of styles and dates, the building is now used as flats. Across the road from the hall is All Saints Church. Near the altar is a memorial and bronze bust, by Dallas Collins, to Erasmus Darwin erected in 2002, and there are other fine marble and brass monuments to members of the Darwin family.

Erasmus Darwin's bust, All Saints' Church, Elston.

Erasmus Darwin's poetry influenced the work of Blake, Wordsworth, Coleridge and Shelley, but it was as a man of ideas that he was a genius. He was the first to explain how clouds are formed and to describe the process of photosynthesis in plants. He also proposed a big-bang-like origin of the universe and a black-hole-like end for Earth. But it was his theory of evolution that has the greatest legacy. As he observed, 'All nature exists in a state of perpetual improvement.'

---

[1]Duffin et al, 2013.

Chapter 57
Gonalston – Twist in the Tale

'I am running away. They beat and ill-use me...'
Charles Dickens, *Oliver Twist*

Gonalston Mill.

Between Gonalston and Lowdham is Gonalston Mill, a large three-storey red brick house built in 1769. The Grade II listed private home and footbridge used to be the water-powered Cliff Mill (also known as Lowdham Mill) – a notorious place.

Journalist John Brown was investigating the effects of factory life on its workers' health when he met Robert Blincoe, and heard about the terrible suffering endured at the mill. Blincoe's memories of child labour compelled Brown to record them, leading to one of the first English working-class biographies. This account of brutality and poverty in the Industrial Revolution had a significant political impact inspiring Charles Dickens and Frances Trollope.

Brown captured the illiterate orphan Robert Blincoe's horrendous story in detail but, affected by the story, before its release the writer had taken his own life. His manuscript was retrieved from a pawnshop and acquired by Richard Carlile, a radical campaigner and friend of the Nottingham bookseller Susannah Wright. Carlile serialised Blincoe's ordeal without his knowledge in *The Lion*, a two-penny paper, and in 1832 his words appeared in one volume by John Doherty as *The Memoirs of Robert Blincoe*. Doherty was a trade union leader-come-small-publisher who hoped Blincoe's memoirs would help his campaign for a shorter working week.

Abandoned at a St Pancras poorhouse, Blincoe was given hope of a new life when, in 1799, aged seven, he was told he'd be heading north to work in a cotton-mill. He and eighty others were expecting meals of roast beef and plum pudding, horse riding, decent pay and an education. Filled with pride and delusion the paupers were dressed in new clothes and sent north, cheering as they mounted their wagons for the bumpy four-day journey to Nottingham.

As they crossed Trent Bridge and approached the centre of town, the children marvelled at the scene: fields and meadows like a carpet of crocuses laid out beneath an elegant Georgian skyline of windmills and church spires. Blincoe and his fellow parish apprentices headed up to a large warehouse in St Mary's churchyard and heard the pitying voices of local onlookers as the 'live-stock' from London arrived. Their new bosses were the three Lambert brothers, cotton-spinners, hosiers and lacemen. The young boys were to become stocking weavers, the girls lace-makers. The children rested up and even visited Nottingham Castle before heading to Gonalston Mill. They arrived at their apprentice house, halfway between Lowdham and Gonalston, and were told they'd be remaining there for the next fourteen years, working an average of fifteen hours a day, six days a week, with Sundays off for church.

The house was cramped, two to a bunk, with poor sanitation and revolting food, but it was nothing compared to life inside the mill. The children awoke at 5am to a loud bell and the governor's ready whip. The cotton-mill met them with a nauseating smell of untreated cotton, not helped by the oppressive heat. Blincoe's first job was to pick loose cotton from spinning frames. He lost half his index finger to the machine but was forced to continue. These machines could be deadly. Blincoe witnessed one girl being dragged into one by her apron, her bones shattered and skull crushed.

If the children didn't work quickly, they could expect to be beaten with a stick or hung up by their wrists. Desperate, Blincoe came close to throwing himself from the highest window. Instead, he decided to escape and got as far as Burton Joyce before being recognised and dragged back to the mill. The abuse was unrelenting, but Blincoe was a fighter, determined to remain strong. He was the kind of kid to ask for more.

With England at war with France, many continental ports were closed to British exports. Together with failed harvests and a steep rise in taxes, this meant that the Lamberts needed to adapt and switch to steam, but they couldn't afford the costs. In 1803 the mill closed. The apprentice children were sold to the owners of Litton Mill in the Peak District. If they had been expecting a better way of life they were mistaken. The hours, rations, beatings and injuries were even worse. The apprentices were expected to work until they were twenty-one, but many didn't make it. The young dead were buried across several churchyards to hide the true extend of the horrors.

Blincoe survived to tell his tale and, many academics have speculated, his memoirs inspired Charles Dickens to write *Oliver Twist* five years later. This idea is best presented by John Waller in *The Real Oliver Twist* (2005), a history of the lives of workhouse children in the industrial revolution. Dickens had been a young reporter on *The Mirror of Parliament* when Blincoe's memoir had been quoted there. Parliament was rife with debate about working hours and conditions and Blincoe's testimony was a significant one.

The opening of *Oliver Twist* begins in a parish workhouse where the children are part-raised and subjected to the brutality of its greedy officers. Twist, like Blincoe, narrowly avoids being sent to a master sweep. There is an offer for his ownership – of five pounds, more than the one pound ten shillings paid for Blincoe by the Lamberts – in a host of similarities. For example, both Twist and Blincoe are given fictional names by their overseers (Blincoe was called Parson).

The Memoirs of Robert Blincoe didn't just inspire Dickens, they also provided the basis of Frances Trollope's controversial novel, *The Life and Adventures of Michael Armstrong, the Factory Boy* (1840). Trollope had consulted with the campaigners of factory reform and met the publisher of Blincoe's memoir, before describing the plight of the children of the cotton trade. A real fillip for those reformers, Trollope relayed passages of Blincoe's struggle, including the time he crept out under the cover of night to steal food from the well-fed pigs.

Oliver Twist and Michael Armstrong aren't the only famous literary waifs to possess a Nottinghamshire connection. There's Tom, the illiterate chimney-sweep who earned money for his master to spend in *The Water-Babies* (1863), whose author Charles Kingsley moved to Nottinghamshire as a toddler when his father became vicar at North Clifton, and there's Peter Pan, said to be inspired by the sight of an urchin strolling through Clifton Grove.

In more recent times, the late great Nottingham storyteller Pete Davis, a huge Dickens fan, recounted the life and trials of Robert Blincoe in a one-man spoken show.

Chapter 58
Haggs Farm – Sowing the Seeds

'Whatever I forget, I shall never forget the Haggs – I loved it so.'

DH Lawrence

Haggs Farm, Underwood.

In Underwood, three miles from Eastwood, is a long house with farm buildings called Haggs Farm, a place where DH Lawrence got his initial incentive to write.

Lawrence was fifteen when he first visited Haggs Farm and the Chambers family. Mrs Chambers knew Lawrence's mother, Lydia, through Eastwood's Co-operative Women's Guild, and she invited her for tea. Joining Mrs Lawrence was her youngest son, who struck up a friendship with the family, sharing their enthusiasm for reading and learning. Whilst the Chambers struggled financially, they were rich in literature and they'd often read aloud books and plays and discuss them. Lawrence enjoyed the novelty of ease and freedom at Haggs and he was soon a regular returnee, where he could display the more confident and happier side of his personality, an eagerness and creativity that had been stifled at home. Lawrence's mother and sisters began to resent the amount of time he was spending there, sometimes working on the farm or in the kitchen.

Haggs Farm was about a mile from the nearest village. To the front was a wood which Lawrence walked through from his Walker

Street home in Eastwood. To the rear of the house was a large garden with fruit trees and bushes. The landscape in and around Haggs appealed to Lawrence, who was so inspired by the natural world. Haggs Farm became his second home and the Chambers family were supportive of his literary ambition, especially Jessie Chambers (1887–1944), a shy fourteen-year-old when Lawrence had first visited, an occasion that is retold in *Sons and Lovers* (1913):

> ... in the doorway suddenly appeared a girl in a dirty apron. She was about fourteen years old, had a rosy dark face, a bunch of short black curls, very fine and free, and dark eyes; shy, questioning, a little resentful of the strangers, she disappeared. In a minute another figure appeared, a small, frail woman, rosy, with great dark brown eyes.

Lawrence had known Jessie from the Congregational Chapel at Eastwood and by 1902 they had become close friends. 'The chief friend of my youth' is how he later described her in *Autobiographical Sketch* (1929). They inspired one another and both planned to be schoolteachers. Together at Haggs they would read, often in an alcove in the kitchen, and Lawrence helped Jessie with maths, geometry and French, although at times he was rather sharp with her, according to Jessie's brother John (David). Jessie was hugely important to Lawrence, who credited her with launching his literary career.

In *Lawrence: A Personal Record* (1935), initially published under a pseudonym, Jessie wrote:

> We had a right of way through the Warren and across the meadow which brought us to the high road just above the reservoir, and this was the path Lawrence usually took when he came to see us ... Lawrence and I would set off for my home literally burdened with books ... The characters interested us most, and there was usually a more or less unconscious identification of them with ourselves, so that our reading became a kind of personal experience.

Jessie's sister May said, 'Bert was always eager to talk about books and poetry...' and Jessie knew of his ambition to become a writer. By 1906, after mainly writing poetry, Lawrence had started his first novel, *Laetitia*, which became *The White Peacock* (1911). Set in countryside around Haggs Farm, the book took four years of writing and rewriting, alongside his studies. The character Emily was inspired by Jessie.

Haggs Farm and the Chambers had earlier made their way into Lawrence's first published story, "A Prelude" (1907), submitted to the *Nottingham Guardian* under Jessie's name. Recognising his talent, Jessie collected his early writing and poetry, and, when Lawrence was teaching in Croydon, she sent copies to Madox Hueffer (later Ford Madox Ford), editor of *The English Review*, to which the Chambers subscribed. Madox Hueffer agreed to publish the 'very interesting' pieces in 1909 and recommended *The White Peacock* to a publisher.

Jessie Chambers not only read all of Lawrence's early work, she offered him her considered thoughts, writing suggestions and corrections in the margins. She suggested that Lawrence should write more honestly about his life and past, believing the truth to be more poignant and interesting than the situations he had invented.

In 1910, the Chambers family moved from Haggs Farm to Arno Vale Farm. In *A Personal Record* Jessie wrote of that summer:

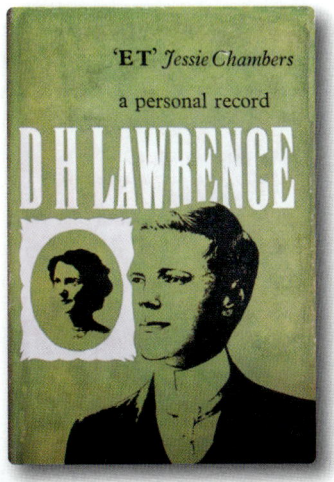

> When the August holiday came Lawrence suggested that he should spend some days with the family at the new farm, which he had scarcely seen, and we prepared a room for him. He went home first, however, and when I met him several days later, instead of returning with me as he had planned to do, he broke off our engagement completely.

Despite this, and subsequently feeling shy at facing Mr Chambers, Lawrence did return to see the Chambers family. One Sunday he went round for tea and they all stood round the piano singing hymns and folk songs. The location of Arno Vale Farm was described in *Sons and Lovers* when Paul Morel clashes with Baxter Dawes.

David Chambers remembered seeing Jessie read the manuscript after Lawrence had deserted her. 'She had to read it all,' he said. 'She had to read what he had done to her,' before making her considerable comments. 'Lawrence was ruthless,' he added. 'He would make use of anybody. My sister felt that Lawrence had betrayed himself. She felt that he had allowed the animal side of his nature to come to the top.'

On reading a subsequent draft of *Sons and Lovers*, Jessie was hurt and bewildered by Lawrence's depiction of Miriam, a character based on her, and his representation of their relationship, claiming it to be false and self-serving. In the novel, originally titled *Paul Morel*, the conflict between Paul and Miriam shadows the real-life relationship between Lawrence and Jessie, whose troubled love affair included a brief and unsatisfying sexual relationship. Despite Jessie's requests, Lawrence retained his fictional version, leaving Jessie feeling 'a terrible inner injury.'

Mirroring life, Paul falls into a relationship with Miriam, a farmer's daughter who attends his church, and they take long walks together conversing about books. Paul's mother disapproves, disliking Miriam and the time they spend together, and fearing that she will take Paul from her.

Jessie cut off all contact with Lawrence after he sent her the galley proofs of *Sons and Lovers*. She wrote her own version of the Miriam and Paul story in a novel entitled *The Rathe Princess*. When this was rejected, she burnt the manuscript and all the letters Lawrence had sent her.

In between drafts of *Sons and Lovers* and its publication, Lawrence had ended his long relationship with Jessie Chambers, become engaged with and parted from another girlfriend, Louie Burrows, and met and travelled with his future wife Frieda Weekley (née von Richthofen).

Towards the end of his life, Lawrence nostalgically wrote of his time at Haggs Farm in a letter to David Chambers, by then a lecturer in History at Nottingham University College:

> I loved to come to you all, it really was a new life began in me there ... Tell your mother I never forget, no matter where life carries us ... Oh, I'd love to be nineteen again, and coming up through the Warren and catching the first glimpse of the buildings. Then I'd sit on the sofa under the window, and we'd crowd round the little table to tea, in that tiny little kitchen I was so at home in ... If there is anything I can ever do for you, do tell me. – Because whatever else I am, I am somewhere still the same Bert who rushed with such joy to the Haggs.'[1]

In *Sons and Lovers*, Haggs Farm appeared as Willey Farm and the Chambers were the Leivers. There is no name change when the farm is mentioned on the final page of *John Thomas and Lady Jane*, the second version of *Lady Chatterley's Lover*, in which Mellors is named Parkin, Lawrence writing: 'Connie and Parkin went slowly down the tussocky hill, above the grey-green country. Across was Haggs Farm, and beyond Underwood, the mining village, and the mines.'

For more about Haggs Farm, Lawrence and the Chambers family, read *Miriam's Farm*, a book of essays edited by Clive Leivers, Honorary President of the Haggs Farm Preservation Society.

In 1915 Jessie married Jack Wood, a farmer's son and fellow teacher, later a headmaster. Whilst working as a teacher, Jessie continued her own studies and she remained an active socialist and pacifist. Arno Vale Farm stayed in the ownership of the Chambers family, until the late 1930s when the land was sold for housing development. At the time of Jessie's death in 1944, the Woods lived at 43 Breckhill Road, Woodthorpe, a short walk from Arno Vale and under a mile from where Lawrence first met his future wife Frieda.

---

[1]Fussell, 1980.

Chapter 59
Halam – A Little Village of Words

'Certain books (...) like certain landscapes, stay with us even when we left them, changing not just our weathers but our climates.'

Robert Macfarlane, *Landmarks*

St. Michael the Archangel's Church, Halam.

About a mile and a half from Southwell is Halam, a picturesque village of around 400 people, and an unlikely hotbed of literature.

Legend has it that Halam's church was built in the eleventh and twelfth century with stone intended for Southwell Minster, which was being built at the time. Apparently, the carts would come to rest at the foot of a steep hill near Halam, allowing the carters a chance to refresh at the inn. Seizing their opportunity, locals would steal stones that they then used to build their own church. Today, Halam's inn, the Waggon & Horses, is the first carbon-neutral pub in the UK, and home of the Nottinghamshire Pie, a beef and stilton combo.

After returning from Australia, the poet Richard Howitt (1799–1869) took a small farm at Halam, no doubt attracted to its rural setting. As the author Stephen Haddelsey told me, Halam is a 'peaceful farming village, with plenty of very pleasant countryside walks – ideal for thinking and writing.'

A resident of Halam for over twenty years, Haddelsey has written seven books whilst living in the village. Through his writing he champions subjects and individuals that have been overlooked or shunned by history. Highlighting stories that deserve to be told, his books include *Charles Lever: The Lost Victorian* (2000), about the gifted but maligned Anglo-Irish novelist, and *Born Adventurer: The Life of Frank Bickerton* (2005), who led an extraordinary life of adventure, playing a leading role in one of the key expeditions of the Heroic Age of polar exploration.

The novelist Carolyn Kirby spent fifteen happy years living in Halam and recently returned to speak to Halam's reading group about her novel, a visit that 're-kindled my love for the place and its people,' she told me, adding, 'I really felt folded once again in the warmth of their spirit and the beauty of the landscape.' A product of the village's reading group, Kirby's award-winning historical thriller, *The Conviction of Cora Burns* (2019), had the crime critic Barry Forshaw writing of the book being one of the standout novels of the year.

Kirby recalls a young Robert Macfarlane walking past her house in his high school uniform. During Macfarlane's time at the Nottingham High School for Boys, GJ Martin was a teacher there. Martin is the author of several books including *The Sane Asylum* (2017) and he now considers Macfarlane a friend.

Robert Macfarlane lived in Halam until the age of eighteen when he left for Cambridge. According to the *Halam News*, he used to sing in the church choir. Former *Halam News* editor, Karin Lindley, recalls that the Macfarlanes lived over the beck and up to the top of the hill where it runs out of road at the end of Gray Lane. The family were keen walkers and pursuers of outdoor activity. Beyond rural Nottinghamshire Robert Macfarlane would be taken up to Scotland and the Lakes; climbing, swimming and photographing the landscape (Robert's mother was the photographer). Macfarlane recalls 'sighing when Mum said, "take the dog for a walk," but his parents' love of the outdoors has influenced his writing. He acknowledges that his rural upbringing offered him an 'extraordinary childhood' and it's perhaps no surprise that he would go on to explore the fields, moors, rivers and woods of England for his writing.

Macfarlane recently said that he was, 'aware of walking above stories of space that extended beneath me.' Some of those stories were those of the miners from the nearby mining country. The author remembers the headworks and the slagheaps, and the damage mining inflicted on its workers. His father, a respiratory physician, treated their illnesses and showed him x-rays of their lungs – damage the underworld could do.

Were it not for Halam, and Robert Macfarlane's schooling in the City of Caves, he wouldn't have been able to write *Underland* (2019) in which he ventures below our feet, exploring the area where we 'shelter what is precious ... yield what is valuable ... dispose of what is harmful.'

Underland poetically describes our underground networks, a living world which charts our past and points to our future. Nature and place have always been at the heart of Robert Macfarlane's books. His previous works, *Mountains of the Mind* (2003), *The Wild Places* (2007), *The Old Ways* (2012), *Landmarks* (2015) and *The Lost Words* (2017, with Jackie Morris), all feature nature and landscape, and our relationship with them.

A Fellow of Emmanuel College Cambridge by day, Dr Macfarlane continues to combine his adventure with academia, delivering important work, beautifully written. At Nottwich, a global gathering of UNESCO Cities of Literature, Robert Macfarlane spoke about how culture and literature can be used to strengthen and protect efforts to safeguard cultural and natural heritage.

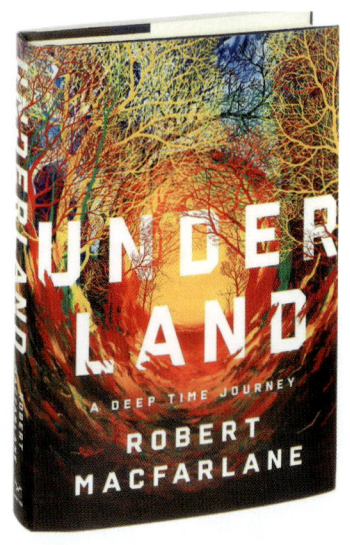

Chapter 60
The Hemlock Stone – Inspiring Legend

'What tempest sculptured thee? What demon hurled thee here, a lonely rock?'

Henry S Sutton

The Hemlock Stone, Bramcote.

The Hemlock Stone is a thirty-foot-tall outcrop of red sandstone near Bramcote dating back to the Triassic period some 200 million years ago. It's said that the stone was hurled here by the devil from a hill above Castleton in Derbyshire, attempting to silence the annoying church bells at Lenton Priory and missing his target. The stone has Christian and pagan associations and its striking and curious nature invites speculation, putting it on the radar of many a Nottinghamshire writer.

In his book *Bypaths of Nottinghamshire History* (1905) the librarian John Potter Briscoe, wrote: 'The Hemlock Stone at Bramcote is one of the enigmas of the County, not only to the rank and file of its inhabitants but to the generally well-informed portion of our community.'

The eighteenth-century poet Dr Spencer Timothy Hall (1812–85), who went by the name "The Sherwood Forester", believed the stone to be of natural origin but improved by man through artistic quarrying. William Stukeley (1687–1765) had been of a similar belief, writing, 'A little Beyond Wollaton Hall, in the road, upon the brow of the hill, is a high rugged piece of rock, called Hemlockstone, seen at good distance: probably it is the remains of a quarry dug from around it.'

The Hemlock Stone may have been part-crafted by man but nature also continues to shape its look. As the lower half is eroding more quickly it's becoming top heavy, the higher section retaining its darkened stain from the Industrial Revolution.

DH Lawrence visited the stone in 1901. In *Sons and Lovers* (1913), Paul Morel and his pals were unimpressed by it:

> They came to the Hemlock Stone at dinner-time. Its field was crowded with folk from Nottingham and Ilkeston. They had expected a venerable and dignified monument. They found a little, gnarled, twisted stump of rock, something like a decayed mushroom, standing out pathetically on the side of a field. Leonard and Dick immediately proceeded to carve their initials, "L.W." and "R.P.", in the old red sandstone; but Paul desisted, because he had read in the newspaper satirical remarks about initial-carvers, who could find no other road to immortality. Then all the lads climbed to the top of the rock to look around.

Henry S Sutton (1825–1901) had gone one better than Lawrence in writing a long poem about the stone. Sutton was the son of the Nottingham bookseller Richard Sutton and the brother of the author Eliza S Oldham (1822–1905). Sutton's poem reflects upon the years of visitors from 'lovers and maidens' to soldiers, knights, cavaliers and roundheads and village fools. Sutton writes of sacrificial ceremony and blood sacrifice at this 'altar cut by Nature's hand'. He wrote:

> What eye innumerable, O aged stone,
> Have gazed, and gazed, thine antique form upon!

Sutton's poem is a fitting ode to this large pillar of rock on a hillside near Bramcote.

Chapter 61
Keyworth Cricket Club, Platt Lane –
Read All About It

'I'm a lame duck, a desk-jockey now, a paper-pusher...'
Frank Palmer, *Final Score*

From Dickens, Twain, Hemingway, Wodehouse and Orwell, to Ken Follett and Will Self, many journalists have gone on to become renowned authors, and Nottinghamshire has more than its share. Stephen Booth, Mhairi Macfarlane, TM Logan, Cecil Roberts, Graham Greene and JM Barrie are all amongst the journo-come-authors with connections to our county. As is Frank "Baggy" Palmer (1933–2000), a man who bagged a British Press award for breaking a sensational case, and even shaped British politics, before turning to detective fiction.

At Keyworth Cricket Club, on the opposite side to the pavilion, is a memorial bench bearing the greeting 'Ey up sunshine'. Unveiled by the Nottingham branch of the National Union of Journalists, it's dedicated to the late Frank Palmer and reads:

'Ey Up Sunshine'
Frank Palmer 1933–2000
Journalist and Author
From his friends in the N. U. J.

Before settling in Keyworth and writing crime novels, Palmer had been an acclaimed journalist, a dogged old-school reporter, exposing corruption and hypocrisy. After National Service, during which he worked in Paris as a military shorthand writer, Palmer set up and ran Eastern News Service in the front room of his mother's Lincolnshire home. His newspaper career began in the 1950s with the *Lincoln Chronicle* and *Lincolnshire Echo*.

Moving to Manchester, he joined the *Daily Express* and was the first journalist to interview Matt Busby after the Munich Air Disaster. For this story he achieved the rare feat of writing the front and back page leads for a major newspaper on the same day.

He then joined the *Daily Mirror*, becoming their man in the East Midlands for more than twenty years. During this time, Palmer helped many a young journalist. One such beneficiary was Alastair Campbell (yes, that one), who said: '[Frank] taught young journalists like me everything about good, old-fashioned journalism.'

Frank Palmer was named a Reporter of the Year at the British Press Awards for his scoop on 1978's most sensational trial, which came to be known as "the sex-in-chains case". He broke the story of Joyce McKinney, who had kidnapped a Mormon missionary with whom she was obsessed. McKinney had come to Britain in pursuit of the man and ended up chaining him to a bed. She later jumped bail and fled to the US, dressed as a nun.

'Frank was a really fine, good, old-fashioned reporter,' said Richard Stott, former editor on the *Daily Mirror*. 'He was the one who would always walk that extra mile to answer that one question which needed to be asked ... who would make that extra phone call and knock on just one more door.'

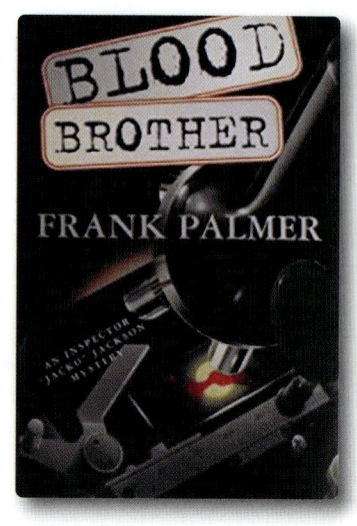

Bob Turner, former News Editor of the *Nottingham Evening Post*, said of Palmer that 'He was loyal to his profession, loyal to the *Mirror* and loyal to his colleagues. He was a remarkable man.'

Dedicated to the *Mirror* he might have been, but Palmer became disillusioned during the paper's Maxwell era and, in 1991, he took early retirement to write a detective novel that had been in his head for years. That novel, *Testimony*, was published in 1993. It was the first of eight books in the Detective Inspector "Jacko" Jackson series. Palmer's son Nick told me, 'Dad and indeed all of us were so chuffed when he got it published, after trying very hard for a number of years.'

An admirer of Raymond Chandler, John le Carré, Ian Rankin and Val McDermid, Palmer was a master at keeping the reader guessing, something he continued to achieve with his second series, set in Nottingham. His nine Phil "Sweeney" Todd books featured a Nottingham cop of humour and humanity, introduced in 1996's *Dark Forest*. By the time of his last book, *Todd's Law* (2000), Palmer was one of Nottingham's most popular authors, if library borrowings are anything to go by.

Local photographer Robert Rathbone worked on Palmer's dust jackets and publicity photos. A good friend of his, Robert describes him as a 'wonderful, bubbly character who was fabulous company.' He told me:

> We used to meet other journalists in the Blue Bell pub on a Friday evening to catch up on the latest gossip. Frank would hold court while he collected all the stories. A lot of his ideas [for his crime novels] came from stories we had worked on. He used bits and bobs that we had witnessed, blending them together to make his stories. He also based a lot of his characters around his friends and acquaintances. We went to various events so Frank could take in the atmosphere including a return to Old Trafford for a night match which brought back memories of his coverage of the Munich Air Disaster.

It was the village of Keyworth that Frank Palmer made his home, and it's been said that his hospitality there was legendary. Amongst his loves were football, classical music, and The Peacock pub on Mansfield Road, but cricket had a special place in his heart. A big follower of Notts CCC, he was also vice-president of Keyworth Cricket Club.

Frank Palmer died at the QMC, aged sixty-six, following a heart attack after having an operation on a burst appendix. Former colleagues and friends packed Keyworth's St Mary Magdalene Church for his funeral. Funny and warm, Palmer was a true character, and he would not have looked out of place in one of his books.

Other local NUJ writers include the broadcast journalist John Holmes and the former *Post* worker Chris Arnot. Holmes has published a large, chatty, name-dropping volume *This Is the BBC Holmes Service* (2021) which proved the value of keeping a detailed diary during his long BBC career. Chris Arnot has made a career out of writing books on his interests – cricket and football grounds, and beer, as well as a book on The Archers.

Of the current authors with a journalistic past, the biggest seller with a Nottinghamshire link is the thriller writer Robert Harris, who grew up in Sherwood and Carlton, spending his early childhood on a Nottingham council estate where his father worked as a printer. Aged six, Harris wrote an essay entitled "Why me and my dad don't like Sir Alec Douglas-Home".

Chapter 62
Langar House, Church Lane –
The Butler Did It

'Books are like imprisoned souls till someone takes them down from a shelf and frees them.'

Samuel Butler, *The Note-books of Samuel Butler*

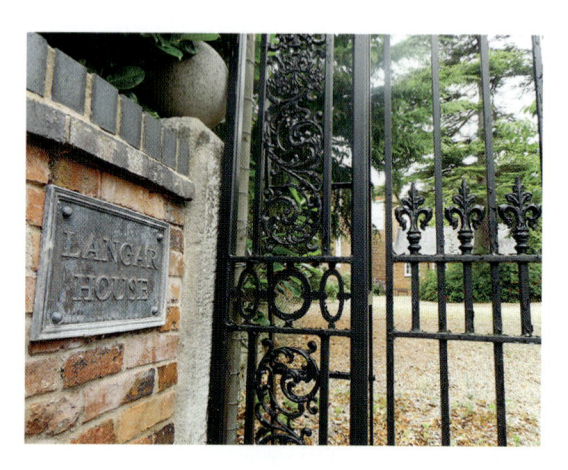

Samuel Butler (1835–1902) was born at Langar Rectory, just outside the village of Langar, near Bingham. Now known as Langar House, the 1722 building of Queen Anne style was sold by the church commissioners in the 1950s after it became too impractical and expensive to be used by the parish. The Grade II listed house boasts a fine staircase with twisted balusters and eight bedrooms, plus a separate cottage, and it sits within five acres of land. It is positioned at the end of a tree-lined driveway near the medieval, Grade I listed St Andrew's Church.

Samuel Butler's father, Thomas Butler, was Rector of St Andrew's between 1834 and 1876, during which time he rebuilt the run-down church and tower. He also provided a school for the village and oversaw the restoration of another local church, St John of Beverley.

Reverend Thomas had been pushed into the clergy by his father, a doctor who had worked his way to Cambridge University before becoming headmaster of Shrewsbury School and later Bishop of Lichfield. Thomas wanted Samuel, his eldest son, to follow him into the church, but the young rebel had other ideas. He longed to escape the suffocating moral atmosphere of Langar Rectory where he had received his early education and been beaten and bullied by his severe father who 'never liked me, nor I him; from my earliest recollections I can call to mind no time when I did not fear him and dislike him...' wrote Samuel Butler. He frequently 'sought solace in the kitchen talking to the cook, the footman and the housemaid'.[1]

Aged twelve, Butler was dispatched to the Shrewsbury School where his grandfather had been the head.[2] Neither of the strict regimes suited Butler's independent and heretical nature, but he went on to attend St John's College, Cambridge, where he graduated with a First in the Classical Tripos.

'My most implacable enemy from childhood onward has certainly been my father,' wrote Butler, and a year after his graduation, after one final altercation with his father, he set sail aboard the Roman Emperor ship for the five-month journey to New Zealand. He was getting as far away from Langer Rectory as he could, rejecting everything his father stood for and the constraints of Christianity.

On arriving in New Zealand Butler sought unclaimed land. A leading cross-country runner at school, he required all his stamina, courage and initiative as he explored the mountainous terrain through a series of demanding expeditions, eventually settling in fifty-five-thousand acres where he built a sod and cob cottage which he filled with books and pictures. He even managed to get a piano carted up in a bullock dray to this remote home.[3] Despite his inexperience he worked the land as a sheep farmer, establishing a successful sheep run that employed seven men. Butler made many friends and was able to share his interests in art and music with the community of Christchurch, where he was increasingly spending his time. It was in New Zealand that he began his literary career with publications that included several commentaries on Charles Darwin's *On the Origin of Species* (1859). Darwin's book had a great influence on Butler, who had renounced Christianity for evolution, a position he would later question with his own theory.

It's claimed that he proposed marriage in 1864 to Mary Brittan, who rejected his love,[4] and that this led to his abrupt move from New Zealand. He had been urged to return to England by Charles Pauli, an Oxford-educated accountant who Butler had come to know intimately. After selling his sheep station and returning to England with Pauli, Butler continued to provide him with a substantial financial support in the form of a regular allowance that lasted a further thirty-four years. Butler had close relationships with men and women but never married. For many years he patronised female prostitutes, at a rate of one visit a week.

Wealthy, healthy and stimulated by his experiences in New Zealand, Samuel Butler settled at Clifford's Inn near Fleet Street, London, and was inspired to create. He trained as an artist, exhibiting oil paintings at the Royal Academy between 1869 and 1876. He also became an innovative photographer, a composer of music, and a prolific writer.

In his oil painting, "Family Prayers", Butler encapsulates his attitude to Victorian piety and life at Langar Rectory. He painted it in 1864 just after his return from New Zealand, and it hangs in St John's College Cambridge.

During his lifetime, one piece of work established Butler's reputation as a writer. That was *Erewhon* (1872), its title an anagram of "nowhere". The first draft of this satiric fantasy of modern civilisation was written in New Zealand and the country informs its setting and content. Likened to *Gulliver's Travels* (1726), the inventive, prophetic and provocative dystopia, published at the author's expense, was acknowledged by Aldous Huxley to have influenced his *Brave New World* (1932).

Despite the success of *Erewhon*, by 1876 Butler was struggling for money as a result of bad investments and the continuing funding of Charles Pauli, a one-sided devotion. Butler gave lectures to working men's clubs and focused on his literature, producing a range of books and essays, even attempting to prove that *The Odyssey* was written by a young Sicilian woman. His provocative *Evolution, Old and New* (1879) led to a bitter relationship with Charles Darwin, the man whose work had previously saved him from the doctrine of Langar Rectory. Butler had rejected Darwinism after finding his own relationship with God. He was not anti-evolution but, unlike Darwin, believed that creatures transmitted their acquired habits to their offspring as unconscious memories: views on evolution that were more aligned to those of Erasmus Darwin (Charles' grandfather).

Butler's work succeeded in uniting much of the academic and scientific community against Charles Darwin but, after rejecting both religion and Darwinism, Butler became a rather isolated figure.

Butler didn't return to Langar. His fractured relationship with his parents further deteriorated after the second publication of *Erewhon* which, unlike the first edition, named Samuel Butler as the author. Between 1872 and 1884 he wrote *The Way of All Flesh*, 'one of the great time-bombs of literature,' said VS Pritchett. 'One thinks of it lying in Samuel Butler's desk for thirty years, waiting to blow up the Victorian family and with it the whole great pillared and balustraded edifice of the Victorian novel.'

Dissatisfied with his manuscript, and rightly fearing it would cause outrage within his family and the reading public, Butler delayed its publication, intending to later revisit it. On his deathbed in 1902, he instructed that it be published in its present form.

The Way of All Flesh (1903), a story of English domestic life, is his masterpiece. Largely autobiographical, the book influenced the anti-Victorian reaction, helping to challenge Victorian values and conventions. A stinging satire on parental and religious hypocrisy, *The Way of All Flesh* follows four generations of the Pontifexes, a tormented family bound together by illusion and hatred. The character of Ernest Pontifex is formed from the author's early self, whereas Overton, the story's narrator, is the mouthpiece for the older writer. Theobald and Christina are based on Butler's harsh, unjust and objectionable parents, old George is Butler's grandfather, and his harsh schoolteacher Dr Kennedy appears as Dr Skinner, a man who has '...the harmlessness of the serpent and the wisdom of the dove'. When Theobald is teaching his two-year-old son Ernest to read, Butler writes, 'He began to whip him two days after he had begun to teach him.' Later in the story he bemoans the fact that his father has no office to go to: 'One reason why clergymen's households are generally unhappy is because the clergyman is so much at home or about the house.'

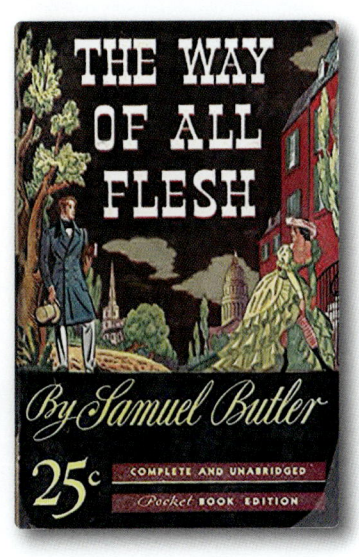

The story takes much from Butler's time at Langar, which he calls Battersby-on-the-Hill, where he had to steal his own birthright. The novel's conflict between father and son is prominent, as is the theory of evolution. Narrated with a cutting wit and lack of sentiment, the Modern Library ranked *The Way of All Flesh* twelfth on its list of the hundred best English-language novels of the twentieth century.

Intensely concerned with religion and evolution, Samuel Butler was a nonconformist. Taking his own unconventional stance he spent his life battling the institutions and morality of his age. His many admirers included EM Forster and George Bernard Shaw, who said, 'The English do not deserve to have great men. They allowed Butler to die practically unknown.'

---

[1]Brown 1990.
[2]Stillman, 1932.
[3]McLintock, 1966.
[4]Robinson, 1990.

Chapter 63
Lowdham – A Literary Lowdown

'The Greatness of a Culture can be found in its festivals.'
Siddharth Katragadda, *Dark Rooms*

The Bookcase, Lowdham.

On Main Street in the village of Lowdham is The Bookcase, a small independent bookshop that was established by Jane Streeter. A former bookseller in London, Streeter had moved back to Nottinghamshire in 1987, buying a house in Lowdham. When a shop came up for lease in 1996, she made the life-changing decision to open a bookshop, and in its first year The Bookcase won the prestigious Independent Retailer Excellence Award.

True to its slogan, "more than just a bookshop", The Bookcase supports around forty local schools by supplying books and advice and arranging author visits. The shop also has a good relationship with local authors, not just stocking a selection of their books but hosting events too, with Catharine Arnold, Elizabeth Baguley, Duncan Hamilton, Eve Makis, Jon McGregor, Stanley Middleton, Nicola Monaghan and Alan Sillitoe all having launched books there. Nottinghamshire writers have a dedicated page on the bookshop's website and there's a separate website exclusively for local books called Nottingham Books which was set up in 2008.

Jane Streeter was appointed President of the Booksellers' Association of the UK and Ireland from 2010–2012, only the second woman to undertake the role and the first person from an independent bookshop. In 2016/17 she was Chair of World Book Day and, as the UK representative on the European and International Booksellers Federation, she develops important relationships with booksellers around the world. Despite all this, The Bookcase holds a busy events programme and has recently added a YouTube channel showing a series of interviews. Their "The Bookcase Presents..." videos include Catharine Arnold talking about her book

Pandemic 1918 (2018) and Kadiatu Kanneh-Mason on *House of Music – Raising the Kanneh-Masons* (2020).

Under their own publishing arm, Bookcase Editions Ltd, The Bookcase has published seven titles, all from local authors. Among them is the late Nigel Pickard's debut novel *One* (2005), a 2004 reissue of *Leading the Blind* by Alan Sillitoe, and a cookbook containing all the favourite recipes from the Lowdham Book Festivals, written by the festival's chef Jackie Skinner.

Streeter and her bookshop have played a leading role in the Lowdham Book Festival since its inception in 1999. The festival began after Ross Bradshaw, then Literature Development Officer for Nottinghamshire County Council met up with Streeter. At their first meeting they decided to run a book festival, both having previously run successful literature events.

Lowdham Book Festival, in the village hall.

Photo: Clare Dudman

Lowdham Book Festival became the flagship literary event for the whole county and in 2019 it celebrated its twentieth year. Whilst the festival traditionally takes place in the last full week in June, it spawned monthly "first Friday" talks and film events, a winter weekend, and ventured beyond Lowdham with the Nottingham Playhouse, Southwell Library and the Minster School all hosting events.

Typically, Jane Streeter would organise the main events while Ross Bradshaw arranged some of the programme and the "last Saturday" when the festival would take over the village. Centred around the Village Hall and its onsite cafe, the book fair and many events spilled into the grounds where there would be a children's storytelling tent, countless stalls of writers' groups, and the chance to buy some unusual new releases and old out of print paperbacks. The last Saturday's busy round of free talks added Lowdham's Methodist Chapel and WI Hall to its venues, and with seats being allocated on a first-come-first-seated basis there was often a rush to get from one venue to the next.

You never really knew what to expect sweltering inside the marquee behind the Village Hall or crammed inside the Committee Room. I have heard John Lucas on how, years after a man died, generations of birds would still sing the tune he used to whistle in his garden, and Nigel McCrery tell of the time he had the Russian Royal Family's bones in an old travel bag in the boot of his Volvo. Quirky was often the word, but Lowdham never failed to celebrate the art of storytelling in its varied forms.

Lowdham attracted writers and poets from around the country, and even as far as New Zealand (Trish Nicholson). Here are just some of those to have appeared: Joanne Harris, Joanna Trollope, Rachel Joyce, Victoria Hislop, Jonathan Meades, Caitlin Moran, Sophie Hannah, Peter James, Elly Griffiths, Rebecca Tope, Jasper Fforde, David Almond, Roger McGough. Carol Ann Duffy, Simon Armitage, Ian McMillan, Jackie Kay and Michael Rosen. And there have been so many Nottinghamshire writers who have spoken at the festival over the past two decades that it might be easier to name those that haven't. These occasions usually coincided with the promotion of new books; one of them being *These Seven*, launched in 2015 at the Methodist Chapel with local contributors Shreya Sen-Handley, John Harvey, Alison Moore, Paula Rawsthorne, Megan Taylor and Brick, all in attendance.

Jane Streeter's fondest memory is of one of the festival's first gatherings, when Alan Sillitoe was interviewed in the Village Hall. 'We sold out and I remember sitting at the back,' she said,[1] 'looking round at all the people and feeling an incredible sense of pride in this community.'

Sillitoe returned to Lowdham several times and in 2011, the year after his death, there was an exhibition of memorabilia, books and photos celebrating his life and work, all part of the campaign to raise the money needed to commission a statue of the writer.

---

[1] *LeftLion*, 2010.

Chapter 64
Newark – Pieces of History

'The library in Newark-on-Trent. The one place I could go back in the '80s and '90s to sit and absorb books after a crap day at school.'

Matt Haig

GH Porters, Newark.

There's a plaque on the outside of GH Porters on the corner of Market Place and Ridge Street in Newark that marks the spot where S and J Ridge of Newark ("Ridge's") printed the first volumes of Lord Byron's poetry. Successive generations of the Ridge family were stationers, booksellers and printers. When the firm was founded, by Allin and Ridge, they set up Newark's first circulating library around 1775, but it's for Byron's poetry that they are most famed. As a plaque boasts:

> Here were published Lord Byron's first poems
> "Fugitive Pieces" Nov. 1806 [and]
> "Hours of Idleness" July 1807

In 1806, with his mother living in Southwell, an eighteen-year-old Lord Byron took a collection of his poems to the firm of Newark printers. He had decided to have them published anonymously for private circulation. While his words were being printed, Byron stayed nearby at The Clinton Arms.

A proof copy was presented to his Anglican friend, Reverend JT Becher, who recommended, in verse, that all issues be withdrawn immediately, the lines under the title "To Mary" being unsuitably outspoken. Byron had already removed a couple of poems at the final hour and, post-publication, he quickly gave orders to destroy the whole impression. From that print run of no more than a hundred slender copies, four remain in existence.[1]

Fugitive Pieces was peppered with errors and revealed information that could prove problematic for those named. The work was a product of Byron's time in Southwell, but whatever antics he could get away with in person, it seems he couldn't in print. His references to certain young residents would have not been sufficiently disguised as to spare them scandal.

Byron's second volume, *Poems on Various Occasions*, issued without "To Mary", contained more poems and fewer misprints. It incorporated much of the first work and was once again published anonymously by Ridge's. The collection was printed no later than the 13th January 1807, with alterations made to limit any offence caused back in Southwell. When a further edition, *Hours of Idleness*, was published that same year, it was the first of Byron's volumes offered for sale, the title page including the author's name, 'George Gordon, Lord Byron, a minor.'

The printing press on which Byron's first volume was printed has been exhibited at Newark's Millgate Museum. For more on Newark's rich printing heritage read *Newark as a Publishing Town* by TM Blagg.

The Clinton Arms, Newark

When Byron was in Newark he usually visited The Clinton Arms, formerly known as The Kingston Arms when it was a coaching inn with ninety horses. A plaque on its façade includes the words:

> Lord Byron stayed in this building during 1806 and 1807 when two volumes of his poems were being printed in Newark.

Back when it was The Kingston Arms, in 1771, the Newark Book Society was founded there, a group of well-to-do diners who would discuss and exchange books. The society survived nearly a hundred years. To the left of The Clinton Arms was The Saracen's Head, another literary location. The Saracen's Head closed in 1956 after a long and colourful history. The inn is mentioned by Sir Walter Scott in his historical novel, *The Heart of Midlothian*, written in 1817 and published a year later. It's at The Saracen's Head that the dairymaid Jeanie Deans stays during her journey from Edinburgh to London. Set in the 1730s, *The Heart of Midlothian* is perhaps the finest of Scott's hugely popular "Waverley" novels.

It may now house branches of WH Smith and Barclays, but the building maintains a link to its past with a bust of a Saracen's head above a plaque which states:

> Licensed in the reign of Edward III. This is the 18th cent. building at which "Jeannie Deans" ("Heart of Midlothian") by Scott stayed on her way to London about 1733. An important posting inn during coaching days.

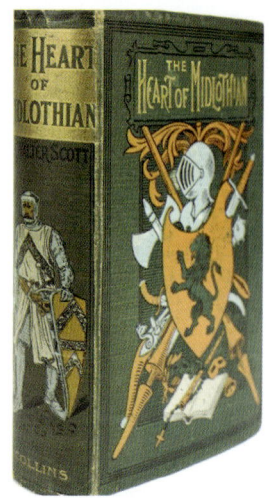

Jeanie's name may be misspelt, but the plaque is prominently positioned and The Saracen's Head's role in the novel is worthy of record as it receives more than a passing mention. The relevant section begins, 'At noon the hundred-armed Trent, and the blackened ruins of Newark Castle, demolished in the great civil war, lay before her.'

The prose continues with Jeanie Deans, after entering Newark, heading straight to The Saracen's Head, where a wench serving refreshment inquires if she's not a Scotchwoman going to London upon justice business. Two women with Scottish accents had passed by that morning asking about her.

Walter Scott visited The Saracen's Head several times and mentions the inn in his diary. The Saracen's Head and The Clinton Arms – with their plaques for Walter Scott and Lord Byron – sit side by side, and the two men were also well acquainted. When Scott read Byron's *Hours of Idleness*, he thought the young poet had been treated unfairly by the critics, writing that, 'Like all juvenile poetry,' it had been written, 'rather from the recollection of what had pleased the author in others than what had been suggested by his own imagination; but, nevertheless, I thought they contained some passages of noble promise'.[2]

Scott was already known as a poet when he published his first novel, *Waverley* (1814), the forerunner of his successful series. His subsequent books were listed as being 'by the author of Waverley.' A year after his debut, Scott and Byron first met, in John Murray's drawing room. Byron had earlier satirised and criticised Scott and other contemporaries in his book *English Bards and Scotch Reviewers*, written when he was twenty. Originally titled "British Bards", Byron had Ridge's set it up in type before deciding to enlarge its scope to include critics, satisfying his desire for revenge, having been told by a critic to abandon poetry. The scathing satire underwent several revisions, being last published in 1809.[3]

Byron was twenty-seven when he met Walter Scott, who was sixteen years his senior and primed to meet a man of peculiar habits and a quick temper. Scott found Byron to be considerate and kind, though almost gloomy, and very animated when in conversation. They got on well and had lots to say to each other.

John Murray, Junior wrote that:

> After Scott and [Byron] had ended their conversation in the drawing room, it was a curious sight to see the two greatest poets of the age – both lame – stumping down-stairs side by side. They continued to meet in Albemarle Street every day, and remained together for two or three hours at a time (Smiles, 1891).

The men found much agreement, except upon the subjects of religion and politics. Scott was a Tory, Byron an anarchistic Whig. With such different ideologies and lifestyles, Scott and Byron may never have been destined to become close friends, but they later corresponded in letters and exchanged gifts, Scott giving Byron a dagger mounted with gold, Byron responding by sending Scott a large vase full of Athenian men's bones. Their letters show good wishes and mutual affection. Scott displayed concern for the young man whose talent he rated highly, and Byron maintained a deep respect and appreciation for the older novelist whose Waverley novels he would reread.

It's been claimed that Scott gave up writing poetry because he couldn't match Byron's success and, according to Roderick Speer in *Byron and Scott* (2009), it's due to Byron's awe at Scott's achievement with his Waverley novels that our poet put so much historical weight behind *Don Juan* (1819–24).

Another highly regarded poet was Newark's Henry Constable (1562–1613), best known for *Diana* (1592), one of the first English sonnet sequences. He also contributed to *Englands Helicon* before he died in exile at Liège. Constable's *The Sheepheard's Song of Venus and Adonis* was critiqued by W Carew Hazlitt, who wrote, 'A more beautiful specimen of early English lyric poetry (...) could hardly be found in the whole circle of Elizabethan poetry.' Ben Jonson also pays tribute to Constable's verse in his collection *Underwood* (1640).

Better known in America, Winifred Marshall Gales (1761–1839) was born in Newark. From early life she exhibited literary talent and by the age of seventeen had published a romantic novel. After marrying Joseph Gales, a printer, they moved to Sheffield where they founded the *Sheffield Register*,[4] a liberal paper that they used to advance the calls for political and religious reform. For this, Joseph was forced to flee to Hamburg, leaving Winifred to look after the business of running a bookshop and publishing the *Register*. She later joined her husband in Germany before they left for America, setting up *Gales' Independent Gazetteer* in Pennsylvania and then the *Raleigh Register* in North Carolina. In 1804 they released *Matilda Berkley or Family Anecdotes*, the first novel published in North Carolina to have been written by a resident of the state. Amid North Carolina's growing orthodoxy they headed to Washington DC. where Winifred ended her days and her eldest son edited the *National Intelligencer*.

Another Newark-born writer of significance was the playwright Thomas William Robertson (1829–71). He has a blue plaque on Middle Gate which he shares with the town's first theatre, now a branch of Millets:[5]

Site of Newark's first theatre
1773–1895
Birthplace of Playwright
Thomas William Robertson 1829–1871

Robertson was a failed actor before he earned a living writing newspaper articles and translating and adapting foreign plays. He then wrote plays of his own and landed a hit with *Society* in 1865. At a rate of a play a year, he provided five more for the Prince of Wales Theatre in London, tackling the social issues of the day. Robertson achieved box-office success and influenced other playwrights. He was a pioneer of modern stage directing and was able to improve the financial condition of dramatists by establishing payment per performance. He died at the height of his fame, aged forty-two.[6]

Today, Newark's best theatre is the hundred-year-old Palace Theatre. The bestselling author Matt Haig used to live a five-

Palace Theatre, Newark.

minute walk away and, as a fifteen-year-old, he spent a week there on work experience. During this time, Haig remembers having to look after a donkey that was starring in a production of *Joseph and the Amazing Technicolor Dreamcoat*. Haig spent most of his childhood in Newark, and as a teenager in the 1980s and '90s it was a place he wanted to escape. His parents still live in Newark and his own feelings for the town have warmed. He has said, 'The town I wanted to leave behind – and did leave behind – is now one I love to visit. It's the town that made me, and I recognise myself in its crags and imperfections.'[7]

A young Haig found refuge in Newark's library where he 'experienced the magic paradox of books: that they were a place of escape and return.' He would spend a lot of time there, being taken to another world where he could find himself. The library was a safe space, and as Haig recalled, 'non-judgmental, where you were relatively unlikely to get into a fight or be laughed at because of your hair.'

Haig's second novel, *The Dead Fathers' Club* (2006), is a quirky update of *Hamlet*, set in Newark. The eponymous club is made up of the ghosts of dads, who meet near a pub most of them had frequented in life. The story is narrated by eleven-year-old Philip Noble whose pub landlord father has died in a road accident, and his mother is succumbing to the greasy charms of her dead husband's brother, Uncle Alan. The remaining certainties of Philip's life crumble away when his father's ghost appears in the pub and declares that Uncle Alan murdered him.

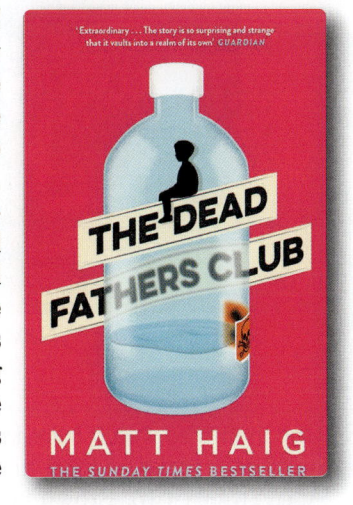

In the 1960s Alan Fletcher lived in Newark and the town was a setting in his *Mod Crop* trilogy published in the 1990s. Fletcher was a story consultant on the cult film *Quadrophenia* and wrote the novel of the same name.

Also set in Newark is Helena Pielichaty's YA book, *Accidental Friends* (2008), in which four sixteen-year-olds from different backgrounds meet in a broken-down lift at Hercules Clay College. Pielichaty was born in Sweden to a Polish-Russian father and English mother. She settled in Newark in 1985. The book's college is fictional, but Hercules Clay existed. The seventeenth-century town alderman lived in a house in the corner of the Market Place, destroyed by Cromwell's Parliamentary forces. Fortunately for Clay and his family, he'd just moved them to the premises next door after dreaming three times that his house was on fire. A plaque tells the story:

> Here stood the house of Ald. Hercules Clay. Destroyed March 11th 1643 during the second siege of Newark by a bomb aimed at the Governor's Residence. The Alderman thrice dreamed of the destruction of his home, and consequently removed his family to a place of safety. As a thankoffering he bequeathed a legacy in perpetuity to benefit his poorer townsmen.

Newark Market Place.

One man who would have known all about the siege was Newark's most distinguished local historian, Cornelius Brown (1852–1907). Aged twenty-two, Brown became editor of the *Newark Advertiser*. He lived at 4 Magnus Street and wrote seven major works, including a two-volume *History of Newark* (1904–07).

There's always plenty of local interest at the annual Newark Book Festival, founded in 2017 by Sara Bullimore, who took the project on from Books in the Castle. Newark and its book festival are well worth a visit. So too is Newark's newest bookshop, Neverland Bookshop, which has opened on Carter Gate. The shop has a large children's section and a Neverland theme.

---

[1]Gray, 1950.
[2]Cochran, 2010.
[3]Barber, 1939.
[4]Eaton, 1944.
[5]Warner, 2013.
[6]Booth, 2004.
[7]Haig, 2018.

Chapter 65
Newstead Abbey – A Resplendent Home

'Newstead Abbey is one of the finest specimens in existence of those quaint and romantic piles, half castle, half convent, which remain as monuments of the olden times of England.'
Washington Irving, *Abbotsford and Newstead Abbey*

Newstead Abbey.

In the rolling acres of Robin Hood country, in the heart of Sherwood Forest, is Newstead Abbey, surrounded by woodland, lakes, waterfalls and walled gardens. It is located close to the ancient road between Nottingham and York, along a mile and a quarter of tree-lined road.

The Augustinian priory was built by Henry II between 1163 and 1173 to atone for the murder of Thomas Becket. Tales of Robin Hood associate themselves with the Abbey, as King John stayed here and outlaws ransacked its riches. It was hoped that the then new Nottingham Castle would curtail the thieving but, after it opened, that too came under attack. A small number of Black Canons – so named for their black cape and hood – lived at Newstead until 1539, and it's thought that the character Friar Tuck is based on a canon from there. Somewhat rebellious, some of the canons drank excessively and didn't stick to their strict order, leading the Archdeacon of Canterbury having to travel to Newstead Abbey to admonish them.

Many reigning kings chose to stay at Newstead and use Sherwood's royal hunting park. Following the Dissolution of the Monasteries in 1540, Henry VIII presented Newstead Abbey to one of his commissioners, Sir John Byron of Colwick Hall, for the sum of £810 (he was the father of Little Sir John with the great beard). Sir John, who was Constable of Nottingham Castle and Lieutenant of Sherwood Forest, turned the monastic buildings into a mansion.

As instructed by Henry VIII, Sir John pulled down the priory's church, using the rubble to extend the accommodation. For nine generations and nearly 400 years, Newstead would be in the ownership of the Byron family.

It was during the Civil War that the grandson of the first lay owner of Newstead was created a peer and the Abbey was looted by Parliamentarians. By the early eighteenth century, under the ownership of William, the fourth Lord Byron, it was among the most admired aristocratic homes in England. A gentleman to the bedchamber of Queen Anne, the creative Byron wrote music and painted. He also collected art, amassing work by Rubens, Titian and Van Dyck.

His son, another William, then got his hands on the property, the so-called "wicked" fifth Lord Byron, who killed his cousin, abducted a teenage actress, and dined with loaded pistols upon his table. After leaving the Navy, the wicked Lord led a life of expense and excess. He bought a fleet of ships for Newstead's upper lake and staged mock battles with live cannon.[1] After being found guilty of killing William Chaworth in a duel, he escaped punishment but was consumed by debt. He sold most of the Abbey's contents in 1778, including livestock, statues, his father's fine art collection and a marble fireplace. Many trees were felled, their timber sold to ease his mounting debts. It's thought that the misanthrope enabled the Abbey's deterioration in order to spite the son he assumed would inherit it, but this, and the claim that he trained racing crickets, may be nothing more than a myth. After suffering physical and mental illness he died alone in his empty mansion in 1798.

George Gordon, the poet Lord Byron, was a small, ten-year-old boy from Aberdeen when he inherited the estate and title in 1798. Never laying his eyes on his wicked great-uncle, he left to attend school at Harrow after first seeing Newstead. His new home was leased to Lord Grey de Ruthyn.

A poem entitled "On Leaving Newstead" appeared in Byron's first volume of poetry, *Fugitive Pieces* (1806). The poem begins:

> Through thy battlements, Newstead,
> the hollow winds whistle;
> Thou, the hall of my fathers, art gone to decay.

A more polished version of the poem appeared in future volumes.

Until the summer of 1808, Byron's new home had been leased. Its final lodger, Lord Grey, kept the place in a 'beastly state,' according to Mrs Catherine Gordon Byron, the poet's mother. Byron himself moved to Newstead Abbey later that year, a few months before his coming of age. He kept his quarrelsome mother in Burgage Manor, Southwell, preventing her from visiting by continually repairing the Abbey.

'Newstead and I stand or fall together,' he wrote to his mother in 1809, adding:

> I have now lived on the spot, I have fixed my heart upon it, and no pressure, present or future, shall induce me to barter the last vestige of our inheritance. I have that pride within me which will enable me to support difficulties. I can endure privations, but could I exchange Newstead for the first fortune in the country, I would reject the proposition.

His intended thorough repair of the mansion began with the rooms that were for his own use, behind the hall in the north-west angle of the Abbey, private apartments that were separated from those in the south-east wing intended for guests. Using borrowed money, Byron could only make part of the Abbey habitable, so whilst smaller rooms were furnished with velvet curtains and new carpets, the rest of the building remained in a semi-ruinous state.

The damaged, rain-affected roof was not repaired, but Byron at least had rooms in which to entertain several of his friends who, after finishing their education, had joined him at Newstead. Dressed as monks, they would stay up late, emptying the wine cellar of its claret, burgundy and champagne, Byron supping from a skull found in the grounds.[2] The abandoned Great Hall witnessed some of their high jinks, including pistol-shooting, with empty bottles as a target, and the Great Dining Room was used for reading, fencing, boxing, singlestick and shuttlecock. It was also here that Byron kept his bear. A person was lucky if they could walk from one end to the other without being mauled by a bear, bitten by a dog or shot by a pistol.

From his digs at Trinity College, Byron had brought with him his tame bear, which would roam the estate with his other animals, including a docile wolf, hedgehogs, geese and turtles. His favourite and most famous pet, was Boatswain, a Newfoundland dog 'who possessed Beauty without Vanity, Strength without Insolence, Courage without Ferocity, and all the virtues of Man without his Vices,' as reads his impressive monument in the Abbey's grounds – on the spot of the Priory's church altar – built after Boatswain died of rabies. Also etched upon it is the poem, *Epitaph to a Dog*, which contains the words:

> '...the poor Dog, in life the firmest friend,
> The first to welcome, foremost to defend,
> Whose honest heart is still his Masters own,
> Who labours, fights, lives, breathes for him alone...'

Boatswain would swim with Byron in the upper lake. The poet had wanted to be buried with Boatswain's remains, as his original will requested:

> I Desire that my body be buried in the Vault of the Garden of Newstead without any ceremony or burial service whatever and that no Inscription save my name and age shall be written on the Tomb or Tablet and it is my Will that my faithful Dog may not be removed from the said Vault...

Boatswain's Tomb, Newstead Abbey.

The access to Boatswain's vault was opened in 1987. Beneath his memorial was enough space to house a coffin large enough for a small human. But, despite Byron's wishes, his own remains are not there. Denied burial at Westminster Abbey, most of him is inside the family vault in Hucknall.

Newstead Abbey had a library that Byron would make use of, as he spent much of his time reading. He also wrote his satire *English*

Bards and Scotch Reviewers (1809), mentioned earlier, at Newstead, produced in response to the adverse criticism generated by his early poetry.

In the June of 1809, Byron left for a foreign tour, returning to England from Greece in 1811 when he learned of his mother's ill-health. She had been living at the Abbey, having moved there from Burgage House, when she suffered a heart attack, perhaps brought on from the stress of a Nottingham upholsterer fixing a notice to the gate, demanding payment of debt. Mrs Byron had little money and, knowing that her son had left a mountain of unpaid bills, she had been, perhaps literally, scared to death of the bailiffs turning up.

Byron had already written to his mother, saying he'd be visiting her at Newstead Abbey. On hearing of her illness, he returned home immediately, only to arrive too late to see her alive. He refused to attend her funeral. Instead, as the procession left the Abbey, he put on his boxing gloves and began sparring.

Several of Byron's friends had also died that year, leading him to write, 'Some curse hangs over me and mine. My mother lies a corpse in this house: one of my best friends is drowned in a ditch. What can I say, or think, or do?'[3]

Byron's final visit to Newstead was in the September of 1814, accompanied by his half-sister Augusta, perhaps the only woman he truly loved. It was at this time that Byron proposed to Annabella Milbanke, who accepted. In a letter to her aunt, Byron wrote, '...if she has nothing I had better sell N[ewstead] again...' Byron had decided to barter his inheritance, needing the money to ease his financial woes.

For Byron, Newstead had also become a symbol and a reminder of his family's fate and misfortune. By 1816 he was, reluctantly, seeking a buyer for his, 'Newstead! fast-falling, once resplendent dome!'

It was in this year that Caroline Lamb's scandalous first book, *Glenarvon*, was published, a gothic novel that caricaturised her friend Jane Harley, Countess of Oxford, whom Byron had had an affair with in 1812–13. Lamb, who famously called Byron, 'Mad, bad and dangerous to know,' had previously engaged in her own very public affair with Byron. Her husband, William Lamb, later became the British Prime Minister.

Newstead Abbey was not sold until after Byron and his wife had separated and he had gone to Italy. It took an old school friend,

Colonel Thomas Wildman (1787–1859), to agree to buy it. In 1818, Wildman paid £94,500 for the estate (£5,659,977 in today's money), spending double that amount over the next thirty-four years on restoring and rebuilding the house and gardens. It was Wildman that introduced peacocks to the estate.

Wildman had wanted to chop down a lone tree that seemed out of place, until a servant, who had worked for Byron, informed him that his lord had been especially fond of it, the poet having planted it himself as his very first act on his first visit to Newstead. Wildman spared the tree, now known as Byron's Oak. Its stump remains in situ on the south lawn, marked by a plaque.

As a boy, Byron had written of the tree, 'As it fares, so will fare my fortunes.' Revisiting the Abbey in 1807, his neglected tree was not faring well, prompting him to write his poem, *To an Oak at Newstead*, which begins:

> Young oak, when I planted thee deep in the ground,
> I hoped that thy days would be longer than mine...

Byron saw the tree as a metaphor for the ruined splendour of his own family and, after his death, it became a place of pilgrimage for visitors to Newstead.

Wildman gave the author Washington Irving (1783–1859) a guided tour of Newstead Abbey on his visit to England. Irving spent three weeks there and wrote about it in his book *Abbotsford and Newstead Abbey* (1835), in which Irving tells of the infamous Byron family – contributing to the notoriety – and Newstead's connections to Robin Hood. Of the Abbey he wrote:

> It stands (...) in the midst of a legendary neighborhood; being in the heart of Sherwood Forest, and surrounded by the haunts of Robin Hood and his band of outlaws, so famous in ancient ballad and nursery tale.

Washington Irving was the first American writer to gain fame in Europe. Known for *Rip Van Winkle* (1819) and *The Legend of Sleepy Hollow* (1810), it was Washington that gave the nickname Gotham to New York City. By the end of the nineteenth century, Irving was particularly popular with Nottingham readers. Both the public Central Library, and the subscription Bromley House Library, hold complete collections of his books.

Colonel Wildman died childless and, in 1861, his widow sold the Abbey to William Frederick Webb for £147,000 (£12,235,000 in today's money). At that time it was stated that the Prince of Wales was in treaty for the estate, with Queen Victoria being interested in buying it until Webb outbid her. Known in Africa as "the Giraffe" on account of his height, Webb was an African explorer and big-game hunter. Ten years earlier he had fallen ill and been assisted by Dr David Livingstone, the Victorian missionary and explorer, most remembered for being found by HM Stanley who uttered, 'Dr Livingstone, I presume?'

Webb came to know Livingstone well and the doctor made several trips to Newstead to stay with the Webbs.[4] It was at the Abbey in 1864–65 that Livingstone wrote part of his book *Narrative of an Expedition to the Zambesi and Its Tributaries* (1865). The room in the Sussex tower, in which Livingstone wrote, is named after him. Livingstone's days at Newstead were some of his happiest, as it was here that he got to know his daughters, Agnes and Anna May.

In 1865, Webb became High Sheriff of Nottinghamshire. By this time his wife had accumulated a fine collection of Byron artifacts that included a rare copy of his first volume of poetry. After her husband's death, the estate passed through their surviving children before their grandson, Charles Ian Fraser, took ownership, inheriting the Abbey from his mother's side of the family. Under the Webbs, the main rooms had been opened up to the public and Fraser kept up that offer. Living in Scotland, he had little interest in the Abbey, and sold off much of the land to the Nottingham Corporation (City Council) during the 1920s. He also had part of the Abbey converted into flats. But what to do with the historic public rooms? This problem was given to an associate, Harry German, to solve, and he asked his friend, Sir Julien Cahn, for help.

Cahn was an eccentric who, having built the largest furniture empire in England, used his wealth to fund his extraordinary hobbies.[5] 'The opportunity of a lifetime should be seized in the lifetime of the opportunity,' said Cahn, and Newstead Abbey presented an opportunity he had been looking for. He had been wanting to erect some sort of dedication to Byron, and was considering a statue, when the Nottingham writer Cecil Roberts suggested to Sir Julien that he bought Newstead Abbey and presented it to the Nottingham public. Sir Julien was persuaded to buy all the outstanding land from Fraser too: twelve acres and the lakes.

Sir Julien Cahn was a known wealthy benefactor, who also paid for the lions outside the Council House, and he agreed to buy the property in 1930. Having offered it to the National Trust, who were indifferent to the idea, he decided that the corporation could have it, if they agreed to take care of it, forever. Fraser also agreed to donate many invaluable relics including Byron's furniture. A grand handover ceremony was arranged, with the Prime Minister of Greece, Eleftherios Venizelos, as a guest of honour. The Greek PM was met at Hucknall Market by 750 pupils from the local National School. He said he had:

> come to bring to Byron the deep and sincere homage and the gratitude and remembrance of his whole nation. Nobody, could think of a free Greece, without thinking at the same time of Lord Byron.

Venizelos' impressive speech, given at the handover ceremony in front of Newstead Abbey, expressed what Byron meant to the people of Greece:

> Byron laboured for Greece, but died for Europe. Childe Harold dies as a crusader, and his death had been a precious and an unforgettable contribution to the struggles by which the holy places of human ideals should be restored to the sacred role of freedom. You realise, therefore, how deep and rich are the sources from which the devotion of Greeks to the memory of such a man sprouts and sparkles. His name spreads round on the lips of millions of Greeks, men, women and children, as that of a most cherished person, and it became a Christian name for hundreds of Greek boys. The statue of the poet adorns more than one Greek city. A new town built near Athens has been named after him – Byronia.

It was in this decade that the popular author Dorothy Whipple and her husband rented one of the cottages in the grounds of Newstead Abbey, spending weekends there. In her novel, *The Priory* (1939), Whipple used the Abbey as inspiration for her decaying country house, Saunby. Copies of her novel are available from the Abbey's shop.

The old priory's original façade and medieval cloisters stand to this day, surviving earthquakes and a civil war. Visitors can see the poet's furniture, letters, handwritten manuscripts and portraits, and also his gilt wood bed, his pistol and his writing desk, plus the circular table on which a portion of *Childe Harold* was composed. Boatswain's portrait by the famous Nottingham animal artist Thomas Sanders is also on show.

Even if the building itself is closed, it's worth a trip to explore Newstead's wonderful grounds. Bryan recalls visiting with Tony in BS Johnson's *The Unfortunates* (1969), and:

> ...walking the mile or more up the long rhododendron-lined drive, towards the house, the Abbey, that Byron so loved, and sold, the house butted up against the single standing west front of the Abbey, so arrogantly intimate with it...

The Writers' Garden, Newstead Abbey.

A writers' garden has recently been added. The plinths and busts on display represent six Nottinghamshire writers, taken from the eight that were previously at the entrance to Nottingham Castle. They are: Henry Kirke White (1785–1806), William & Mary Howitt (1792–1879 & 1799–1888), DH Lawrence (1885–1930), Philip James Bailey (1816–1902) and Lord Byron (1788–1824).

In his supreme poem, *Don Juan*, written a few months before his death, Lord Byron was thinking of Newstead Abbey. In Canto 13, Byron has his Spanish hero and other guests visit an unnamed Norman Abbey for a house party. 'Before the mansion lay a lucid lake, Broad as transparent,' wrote Byron from Genoa, his mind back at Newstead.

In the epic poem, Don Juan encounters a phantom. In writing this, the most famous poet in the world was perhaps recalling his own meeting with a "ghost", the Black Friar of Newstead Abbey, also known as the Goblin Friar. Byron had seen the friar shortly before his disastrous marriage to Anne Milbanke.

Byron's memory of, 'my own county of Nottingham,' was never far from his thoughts, and when people think of Newstead today, Byron is rarely far from theirs.

Byron's bust, Newstead Abbey.

---

[1] Brand, 2020.
[2] Gray, 1950.
[3] Marchland, 1975.
[4] Brown, 1896.
[5] Rijks, 2008.

Chapter 66
Old Church Farm, Eakring – Cresswell Country

'I am an idle devil. But at least I work at it.'

Helen Cresswell

Old Church Farm, Eakring.

Helen Cresswell (1934–2005) was a prolific writer of children's books, more than a hundred of them, insisting that children 'deserve the best.'[1] She also wrote for television, producing a mix of fantasy and anarchic humour that contributed to the golden age of British children's drama.

Bang in the centre of Nottinghamshire, between Ollerton and Southwell, is the small village of Eakring, put on the literary map by Helen Cresswell's *Lizzie Dripping*. Cresswell lived at Old Church Farm, a handsome Georgian house on the corner of Newark Road and Kirklington Road. She wrote at a desk that had previously belonged to TS Eliot.

A keen gardener, one day she was pottering on her back lawn when she overheard her next-door neighbour, Mary Stokes, telling her daughter, 'You're a right Lizzie Dripping, you are.' Lizzie Dripping is a slang term given to a "dreamy" girl who struggles to differentiate between fact and fiction. On hearing the name, Cresswell's character was born. The author said, 'I write a title, then set out to find where that particular road will take me.'

Lizzie Dripping is set in the fictional village of Little Hemlock, which is really Eakring. The author's house was three houses down from the village church, St Andrew's and its churchyard, a key location in the stories, and where Lizzie's "imaginary" friend lives and would sit on a flat gravestone knitting. It was at Cresswell's insistence that the TV series' location shots were filmed in Eakring, and some of the local children had cameos, including the author's young daughter.

Lizzie is a loner, a mischievous twelve-year-old, who meets a local witch (played by Sonia Dresdel), who only Lizzie (and the TV viewers) can see. Lizzie, whose real name is Penelope Arbuckle, has a reputation for being an imaginative liar, making it impossible to convince people that her witch exists. Initially created in 1972 for a Jackanory Playhouse presentation, *Lizzie Dripping and The Orphans* led to a full series being commissioned by the BBC, and *Lizzie Dripping Again* hit our screens between 1973 and 1975. It attracted more viewers than the BBC's flagship childrens' show *Blue Peter*.

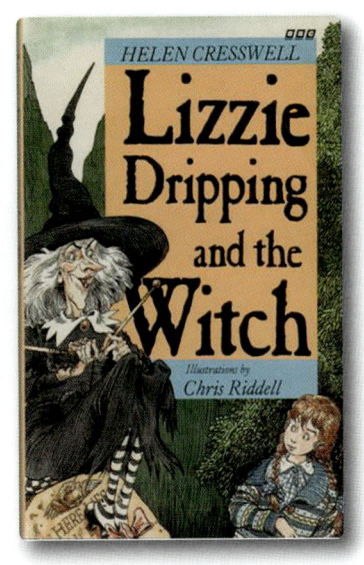

It was a future *Blue Peter* presenter, Tina Heath, who played Lizzie and provided her first-person narration, taking over from Hannah Gordon who had voiced the pilot. Nine episodes were made, of twenty-five minutes each, and there were six Lizzie Dripping books. The series ended with Lizzie saying goodbye to her friend, a metaphor for her growing up. Cresswell later wrote a Lizzie tale for Jackanory's twenty-first anniversary, read on-screen by Patricia Routledge, and an omnibus appeared in 1994. Heath also reprised Lizzie in 1987 for a BBC audiobook.

Cresswell never plotted and barely edited her work. The fantasies arrived spontaneously, from everyday life, literature and motherhood. Her stories were all set in an undefined, imaginary era, limiting the need for research. 'I do not particularly believe in what most people call reality,' she said. 'I only really believe in truth of the imagination.'

St. Andrew's Church, Eakring.

Born in 1934 in Kirkby-in-Ashfield, Helen Cresswell was the middle child of three. As a child she wrote many poems, one of which, "The Seagull", was published in the *Mickey Mouse Comic*. The young poet went on to read English at King's College London where she was nearly thrown out for not attending lectures. She spent most of her time in the students' union, partly because she was already familiar with the books being studied. After university, Cresswell had brief spells as a literary assistant, a fashion buyer and a teacher, before writing her first book, *Sonya-by-the-Shore* (1960). Assuming she would be a poet, she was surprised by how well her story was received, and a career as a children's writer ensued.

Cresswell married her childhood sweetheart, Brian Rowe, in 1962, and their two daughters followed. As did *The Piemakers* (1967), one of the year's best children's books, a story based on the pies made in Denby Dale. It tells of how members of the Roller family win a prize for the biggest and best pie ever created. *The Night-Watchmen* (1969), was another success, following two elderly wanderers, Josh and Caleb, who adopt a disguise and enter into hiding, until their cover is blown. Following *Up the Pier* (1971) and *The Bongleweed* (1973), was one of Cresswell's personal favourites, *Winter of the Birds* (1975), a haunting work of science-fiction in which a boy discovers the power of imagination when his neighbourhood is threatened by flocks of steel birds.

Cresswell's best-known book is *Moondial* (1988), a tale of magic and fantasy, also made into a hugely successful TV series. In the book, Minty goes to stay with her aunt in the village of Belton. On finding a moondial in the grounds of Belton House, Minty discovers that she can go back in time, leading to a rescue mission. The following year Cresswell won The Phoenix Award for her book *The Night Watchmen*.

For three decades Helen Cresswell was a mainstay of children's TV, writing *The Secret World of Polly Flint* (1987), and adapting E Nesbit's *Five Children & It*, a six-part series aired on the BBC in 1991. When rewriting Enid Blyton's Famous Five adventures,

Cresswell made sure that the scripts retained some of the original language such as "smashing", "gosh" and "wizard". In 1995, the author's dramatisation of Gillian Cross's book, *The Demon Headmaster*, had viewers in fear of the story's hypnotist teacher.

The Secret World of Polly Flint had Cresswell taking inspiration from the Nottinghamshire legend of the lost village of Grimston (or Grimstone). Legend has it that Grimston(e) previously stood on the site of Wellow, only to be swallowed up by the ground underneath. On Christmas Day, or any given Sunday, it's said that if you put your ear to the ground of the village green, close to Wellow's maypole, you can hear the bells of Grimston Church ring out and hear the village's former inhabitants.

To cheer herself up after losing both her parents in the same year, Cresswell wrote *The Bagthorpe Saga*, which ran to eleven books. These comedic adventures of an eccentric family began with *Ordinary Jack* (1977) and culminated with *Bagthorpes Battered* (2001). The stories were based on the author's own memories of family life, and she dedicated the fourth Bagthorpe book to herself, using her married name of EH Rowe. Paul Stone, who had directed *Lizzie Dripping* in the early 1970s, directed Cresswell's TV version of *The Bagthorpe Saga* in 1981.

After her marriage ended in divorce in 1995, Cresswell continued to live and write at Old Church Farm until her death ten years later, aged seventy-one. Over the years she contributed much to Nottingham's literary life, constantly attending book events and being a member of Nottingham Writers' Club. She also visited many local schools, inspiring children to read and teaching parents of the importance of reading to youngsters.

In 2000 Cresswell was awarded a BAFTA Children's Writers' Award.

---

[1]Brown, 2005.

Chapter 67
The Old Library, Edwinstowe – Festival in the Forest

'Happily, the working classes are now awakening to a sense of their own power!'
Christopher Thomson, *The Autobiography of an Artisan*

The Old Library, Edwinstowe.

Born in Hull on Christmas Day of 1799, Christopher Thomson was a strolling actor, artist and author, who helped his adopted Nottinghamshire village to become a hive of literary activity. His father was a Scottish sailor turned publican who subscribed to a circulating library, opening his son's eyes to Milton, Shakespeare and others. In his teens, Thomson saw *King John* at the theatre and began dreaming of becoming an actor. After following his father in working at sea, he returned to Hull and married Hannah Leaf. When work dried up, he performed in a play but, 'its first effect was to starve me: what, then, was to be my next adventure.'

Enwrapped in his desire for the stage, that next adventure was to be the life of a strolling actor. His pregnant wife and young child joined him on his travels through Humberside, South Yorkshire, Derbyshire and Nottinghamshire. Thomson and his various companies were struck by the different tastes found in adjoining villages and towns. Whilst one venue might have an utter contempt for everything associated with literature, its neighbouring population might display a love for it.

One thing these provincial towns did have in common was that their local theatres were mostly deserted which, for the Thomsons, meant a poverty-stricken existence. Thomson walked all the way to a Weekday Cross pawnbroker for a coat, accepted free milk from a Kimberley landlady, and he continued to act: in Long Eaton, Basford, Bulwell, Pleasley, Sutton-in-Ashfield, Calverton, Oxton, Arnold, Farnsfield, Blidworth and elsewhere, his group of players finding theatres in large barns or fitting them up as they went along, carrying props on their backs. Everywhere they walked involved a search for food and a place to stay. Their feet bled and their stomachs were often as empty as their pockets.

Early in 1828 Thomson moved to Edwinstowe, finding that 'a small knot of the reading and inquiring class in this village were constant play-goers.' This contrasted with Warsop village which he found large and populous, with extremely ignorant inhabitants. To supplement his meagre income, Thomson sought work as a painter, and his first grand job was painting a boarding school in Nottingham's St Peter's Gate. Thanks to the kindness of his new friends back in Edwinstowe – especially the local shoemaker Reuben Trueman, a zealous advocate for the onward march of society – Thomson landed work locally painting a house. Perhaps he could find a painting business here, he thought, in this village he was so taken with, where 'the remains of the old forest of Sherwood were within bow-shot of my home.'

After settling in Edwinstowe, Thomson continued to paint and act but said, 'I was not so comfortable on the stage as I had expected to be. My residence at Edwinstowe for a period of nearly three years had in some measure ruralised me.'

His wife's ill health, a growing family and the presence of supportive friends, kept the Thomsons in Edwinstowe and eased his decision to leave the acting profession he loved. Now painting houses for a living, it was another of his passions that began to consume him, his long-held belief in self-education. 'Ignorance is a living death,' he wrote, encouraged by the growing movement for accessible education, adding, 'In a few more years, the spread of Education and Science will break down the barriers that Bigotry, Prejudice, and Conventionalism have been studiously building up in years past.'

'It was my privilege,' he said, 'soon after settling in this village, to make the acquaintance of two or three right thinking men and thus early we pledged ourselves mutually to endeavour to banish crime from the village, and if possible, restore it to virtue and freedom.'

Locals were seen to be spending their leisure time in the beerhouse, favouring drunkenness over education, but in 1833 a few men set up a Lodge of Oddfellows. Thomson was unconvinced by the idea at first but, after visiting with his friend Trueman, he saw the benefits to his cause. Edwinstowe's Birkland and Bilhagh Lodge, 'raised the drooping spirit of the labourers,' said Thomson. The group met in local inns, but Thomson thought it better they had their own hall, something they achieved despite objection from the village publicans unhappy with the loss of trade.

Thomson's hope was to live to see education that was universal and free. In the meantime, he was set on doing his bit for a movement that steadily 'roused the sleepy mass to new action.' Over the next decade he assisted in the opening of forty to fifty lodges, travelling miles to deliver addresses and lectures, promoting the lodges' principles: the chance for the masses to socialise and receive education at the same time.

In 1836 Thomson encouraged a few subscribers to pay a penny a week for a reading room, and two years later Edwinstowe had a library, part of the Edwinstowe Artisans Library and Mutual Instruction Society. Open to men, women and children, within six months they had fifty members. Events were held to raise funds and the library eventually amassed a collection of five-hundred volumes, from Shakespeare, Byron and Scott, to periodicals such as *Howitt's Journal*.

Realising that many villagers were illiterate, Thomson set up night classes from October to March at the Jug and Glass Inn. Classes were free to all villagers, with members providing their own coal, candles and books. In

Ye Olde Jug and Glass, Edwinstowe.

addition to reading and writing, learners could gain instruction in arithmetic, music and drawing. There was also a conversation class, where any subject could be discussed. With a blackboard and piece of chalk, Thomson often taught this class, which could attract up to 200 people.

A "committee of fun" met in the Jug and Glass to make plans for the village feasts. Out of this came the Gathering of the Foresters event of 1841, a literary celebration, or early book festival. The poet Spencer T Hall (1812–85) was the chief guest. A close friend of Thomson's, Hall was known as the laureate of Sherwood Forest, and he was presented with a carved oak walking stick as a tribute of respect for his literary worth. There were also tributes to the memory of Byron, Ben Johnson, Robert Dodsley, Pemberton de Wanderer and other departed writers, with a special proposal made to the immortal memory of Robert Millhouse (1788–1839), who wrote the poem "Sherwood Forest".

Millhouse had known poverty all his life and been buried in an unmarked grave. In Hall's address to the gatherers, he said:

> I trust it will not be in the power of another generation to say, that the people of this day erected costly monuments to the wholesale butchers and robbers of humanity, while the peasantry of Sherwood Forest let the dead grass sigh over their sleeping bard, for want of a simple slab to guard his grave from the blast.

Penny subscriptions were requested as, with permission of the Nottingham Cemetery Company, plans for a monument to Millhouse were underway. Hall added, 'As one of his personal friends, one of his sincerest, too, when this object is carried out, I would beg of you one privilege, the melancholy but affectionate one of writing his epitaph.'

Loud cheers erupted, and from those words the money was collected for a monument to be erected over Millhouse's grave, complete with the epitaph:

> When Trent shall flow no more and blossoms fail,
> On Sherwood's plains to scent the springtide gale,
> When the lark's lay shall lack its thrilling charm,
> And song forget the Briton's soul to warm;
> When love o'er youthful hearts hath lost all sway,
> Thy fame, O Bard, shall pass – but not till then – away.

Many toasts followed Hall's speech with more writers honoured. Among them were the names of William, Mary, Richard and Godfrey Howitt, Thomas Miller, John Bridgeford, Samuel Plumb, Sidney Giles, Ephraim Brown, EG Pickering, and the memory of Joanna Williams, writer of the forty-seven-verse poem "Sherwood Forest". The next guest speaker, Charles Plumbe, postmaster of Sutton-in-Ashfield, was introduced as a man of refined intelligence and poetical ability. Edwinstowe was proud of its literary heritage, and people walked from miles around to join the festivities.

The following year they held a second Sherwood Gathering, in honour of literature, science, art, and moral worth, all under a tent within sight of the majestic oaks of old Sherwood.

In 1847 Thomson wrote *The Autobiography of an Artisan*, published by J Shaw and Sons, Wheeler Gate. 'What! a labouring man to think of writing books' he wrote. 'Shocking, truly! What next?'

The book was dedicated to 'the artisans and labourers of England, fellow workmen in the holy cause of self-elevation, and to the friends of the industry of England, of whatever rank or station.' Written to benefit his fellow labourers, Thomson's autobiography told of his life in poverty as an actor, of his family, of which he had seven children (one was a poet and others were singers and musicians), the magic of Edwinstowe village, where 'nowhere has that spirit [of Robin Hood] been more fondly nursed,' and of his role in educating the masses. 'However great the evils they endure, a knowledge of the disease is half the cure,' he wrote, believing knowledge and understanding could lift people out of oppression.

As the years passed, Thomson continued to support education and the power of the arts. His day-job led him to work on making improvements to Rufford Abbey, hired by the Earl of Scarborough, but, after his workload abated, the Thomsons left Edwinstowe and settled in Sheffield. After working as a newsagent, Thomson turned his attention to landscape art, adopting a successful career as a painter. As for Edwinstowe, it remained a place of inspiration for verse and prose, and drew Nottinghamshire's fine network of writers from across the county, a remarkable circle that Spencer T Hall recalled in his works *The Sherwood Forester* (1842) and *Sketches of Remarkable People* (1873).

Hall's writing and Thomson's autobiography honour our great writers of the mid-nineteenth century, but it's someone even closer to home that Thomson saved his greatest praise for, writing, 'I have a most kind, indulgent, and industrious wife, and to her I owe my happiness.'

Christopher Thomson died in Sheffield, aged seventy-one. His wife Hannah died a few days later.

Edwinstowe's night classes (and its library) moved to the Old Library (built in 1913) where they continued. There's a blue plaque on the wall of the Old Library stating:

Christopher Thomson
1799–1871
Sailor, Comedian, Social Reformer, Artist, Author and advocate for the local Oddfellows. He contributed much to supporting the community of Edwinstowe, setting up a 'Penny Library', Night Classes and lectures, as well as 'Self-Help' groups from 1838–1849. This building (formerly the Old Library built 1913) followed in a similar tradition.

Edwinstowe Historical Society, who have a vast cache of Thomson-related material, are in discussion with the BBC to make a short film about him.

Chapter 68
The Rancliffe Arms, Loughborough Road, Bunny – The Wrestling Baronet

> '...institution of annual wrestling matches held on a piece of ground, now in the gardens of the Rancliffe Arms.'
> Everard Guilford, *Nottinghamshire*

Rancliffe Arms, Bunny.

Every year between 1712 and 1811 wrestling took place at the Rancliffe Arms, with a gold-laced hat for the winner. The competition's instigator was Sir Thomas Parkyns, the second baronet of Bunny; known as "the Wrestling Baronet" on account of his devotion to the sport, to which he applied philosophy, art and science. His book on wrestling, entitled *Inn-Play, or the Cornish Hugg Wrestler* (c1713), was probably the first book printed in Nottingham.

Inn-Play was published by William and Anne Ayscough who, together with John Collyer, established Nottingham's first printing press between St Peter's Gate and Pepper Street (off Bridlesmith Gate). Not long after, the Ayscoughs and Collyer held rival businesses. The Ayscoughs produced the *Nottingham Weekly Courant* whilst Collyer printed the *Nottingham Post*. The Ayscoughs moved their printing press to Woolpack Lane in 1718 where, after William died, Anne continued the business. Nottingham's first printers are buried at St Peter's Church.

As for Parkyns' *Inn-Play*, it offers insight into the history of professional wrestling and is an early "how to..." with all the wrestling techniques explained. The author was hoping that the book would create a renewed interest in the sport and improve standards. Parkyns also used the book to promote wrestling as a sensible means of duelling, in preference to guns, thinking his book would save lives. The book may even be viewed as an early protest book, against the use of weapons.

Parkyns was educated at Westminster School and Trinity College, Cambridge. A classicist, man of letters, architect and builder, he studied mathematics under Sir Isaac Newton, and he read medicine in order to help his poorer neighbours. He was an able lawyer too, but is best-known for his eccentricities.

A short stroll from the Rancliffe Arms is a stunning monument to Parkyns inside St Mary's Church, the largest church building in south Nottinghamshire. This life-sized statue, erected by Parkyns during his lifetime, depicts the great man in wrestling pose. When he died in 1741, he was buried beneath it inside the family vault he had also had made. His coffin was one of many stone coffins he had collected during his lifetime. Part of his epitaph reads:

Parkyns' Monument, St Mary's Church, Bunny.

> That Time at length did throw him it is plain,
> Who lived in hope that he should rise again.

It was during the reign of Queen Elizabeth I that the Parkyns family came into possession of the manor of Bunny, and he did much for the village, practically rebuilding it. He restored the village hall, provided rooms for four poor widows, walled the park, and built a picturesque school for the village children, including apartments for the master. Here the children were taught science and Latin at Parkyns' request. He wrote *Introduction to the Latin*

St. Mary's Church, Bunny.

Tongue for his grandson, who attended the Bunny school, and a book grant was given to any apprentices who went on to university. Parkyns didn't hire an architect, he designed the buildings himself. His work included parts of the Rancliffe Arms, and Bunny Hall, built for himself in eccentric style. Sadly, only a wing survives.

Parkyns was a fine athlete and 'he never had a day's illness till he was seventy-eight, and even in middle life was a good runner and a tireless bellringer,' wrote Mee (1938). He employed many people and was one of the first bosses in Britain to introduce a minimum wage, some compensation for his staff who often had to grapple with him. It's said that he would employ no man on his estate unless he was a proficient wrestler.

Chapter 69
Retford – Our Friends in the North

'Retford, I am pleased to report, is a delightful and charming place.'

Bill Bryson, *Notes from a Small Island*

Retford.

The annual North Notts Lit Fest is becoming one of the county's leading book festivals, which shouldn't come as a surprise because Retford is a prime literary location. Presented by Bassetlaw District Council, North Notts Business Improvement District and Barrister's Book Chamber, the first North Notts Lit Fest took place in 2019 and by the following year it was delivering an eight-day programme of events.

The festival has played host to some of the county's top writing talent. The international bestselling crime writer Stephen Booth; BAFTA award-winning writer and TV producer Henry Normal; the historian and author of *The Fall of the House of Byron* (2020), Emily Brand; the author of *The Boy at the Back of the Class* (2018), Onjali Raúf; the author of *The Strangeworlds Travel Agency* children's series, LD Lapinski; and the powerhouse poet Paul Cookson have all appeared, as has photojournalist and author Sally Outram, North Notts Literary Ambassador Liz Carney-Marsh and publisher Angela Meads from Bookworm of Retford. The 2020 festival had a virtual plaque-finding trail around Retford and Worksop, with hidden authors popping up and reading first chapters.

There was also a storytime event at Barrister's Book Chamber on Churchgate. This unique independent bookshop, owned and run by a qualified barrister, relocated to Matlock. It had a sister shop in Retford on Carolgate called The Barrister in Wonderland, which reopened with the new name Wonderland Bookshop in 2021 under the ownership of Helen Tamblyn-Saville, who had worked at the previous shop. 'I knew that we couldn't let Wonderland go,' she told me, 'so I made an offer to take it over'. Tamblyn-Smith is also a district councillor and once bowled in the Tenpin Bowling World Cup. Wonderland Bookshop specialises in new children's books for all ages, from infants to young adults. 2021 also saw forty individually designed book benches placed throughout Retford and North Notts.

Wonderland Bookshop, Retford.

Bookworm of Retford operated as a bookshop for twenty-five years, but now offers publishing and book deliveries. Working from home, they continue to provide a bespoke ordering service, while their publishing arm has been in existence for over a decade and produces many genres, using all forms of publishing – traditional, assisted and self-publishing – depending on the nature of the books. One of their titles is *From Here We Changed the World* (2018) by Adrian Gray, which features several pages about East and West Retford's role in shaping Christian and world history. More can be discovered about the Mayflower Pilgrims in Retford at the Mayflower Pilgrim Visitor Centre inside the Retford Hub.

A number of authors and poets have strong links to the town. Catherine Grace Frances Gore (1798–1867) grew up in Retford.

The daughter of Charles Moody, a Retford wine merchant, Gore went on to become a prolific novelist and dramatist. The best-known of the so called "silver fork" writers, her work depicted the high society of the Regency period. Her books, often about women and for women, include the successful *Pin Money* (1831), *The Broken Hearts* (1823), a verse story, and her best-known novel *Cecil, or Adventures of a Coxcomb* and its sequel, *Cecil, a Peer*, both published in 1841. Gore mixed in affluent circles in London and Paris. Her novels have been compared to Jane Austen's.[1]

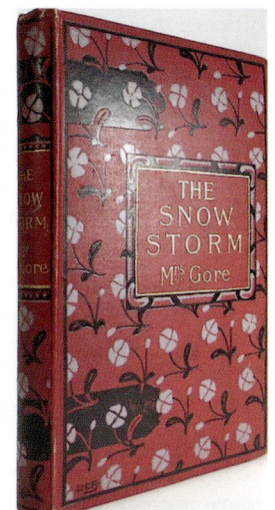

John Shadrach Piercy moved to Retford in 1822 to teach at the National School. Piercy was living here when he wrote *The History of Retford in the County of Nottingham* (1828), important for its references to material that has subsequently been lost.

The acclaimed poet, writer and performer Max Blagg was born in Retford in 1948. An established and respected figure on the New York literary scene, the city in which he's lived since 1971, Blagg is known for raising the dead in a series of interviews with famous deceased celebrities.

Current authors from Retford are Dr Robert Tansey, author of *The Melton-Uppbury Village Mysteries*, all written under the name Sebastian Blanchard; Barry Upton, whose novels include *The Academy* (2016); John Holmes, whose work includes the novel *Legacy and a Gun* (2019); Graeme Cumming, author of *Ravens Gathering* (2012); and Joyce Lesley Keating, who counts *Oath of the Dove* (2018) among her stories.

Retford also has a writers' group, the imaginatively-titled Retford Writers' Group, and an authors' group called, you guessed it, the Retford Authors' Group. A collection of the group's books can be found at The Glasshouse in Retford.

Stephen Booth lives in Laxton, a few miles south of Retford, and each year he launches his latest crime novel in the town. Booth came to live in Nottinghamshire in 1986 to work as the news editor on the *Worksop Guardian*. His award-winning crime series began in 2000 with *Black Dog*. In choosing to write about young police officers that age at a rate of four novels a year, Booth has allowed himself the luxury of a long series. The Peak Experience visitors' guides featured locations from Booth's Cooper & Fry books, recognising the interest in the locations featured.

Retford is the hometown of the photographer-come-author Nicola Davison Reed. Her book *Retford Through Time* (2012) uncovers secrets of the town's earlier prosperity and reveals the faces of the residents that once filled the Georgian and Victorian frontages and former coach inns, all of which can be compared to the Retford of today.

By the seventeenth century Retford had a parish library, and two centuries ago there was a circulating library. The current public library on Churchgate is one of Nottinghamshire's oldest (the earliest survivor is likely to be the small Epperstone Public Library, 1843). Retford Library has recently been refurbished, making it more accessible, whilst there's more space for performances and cultural activities. The new design is sympathetic to the original building, highlighting its historic features, and the children's library has been relocated to the rear, close to the outdoor area and new garden, ideal for families. It's another example of Retford establishing itself on the county's map as north Nottinghamshire's literary capital.

Retford Library.

---

[1]Wagner, 2020.

Chapter 70
Robin Hood Theatre, Averham –
Play by the River

'Pleasing not only locals but also *tout le monde.*'
Sir Donald Wolfit

Robin Hood Theatre, Averham.

Situated between Newark and Southwell and set around the crossroads of Staythorpe Road and the old Main Road is the small village of Averham, home to a theatre that can seat half its population. Cecil Day Lewis, Geraldine McEwan, Anthony Hopkins and Judi Dench have all played this little wooden countryside venue on the bank of the river Trent.

As a member of the Oxford Union Dramatic Society, Joseph Cyril Walker acted and produced plays when he wasn't painting the scenery. Back home in his village of Averham pronounced "Airam", he would put on performances at the local school hall, at first writing the librettos himself and playing the organ – his family making up the cast – before he had the idea of building a theatre.

In 1907 Walker had succeeded his father as rector of Averham, at the Church of St Michael and All Angels, but it didn't hold him back, and it was in the rectory gardens that local carpenter Robert Lee and a group of volunteers built his wooden hundred-and-fifty-seater Robin Hood Opera House west of the rectory. It opened in

1913. For one month in the summer and one month in the winter, the theatre played to appreciative audiences who marvelled at Rev Walker's set designs whilst enjoying his musicals, pantomimes and thrillers. The little wooden theatre became a place to be seen and local theatregoers were known to sport their best evening dress. The venue had a modest façade but its ornate interior of gold leaf and fine plasterwork thrilled audiences almost as much as the plays.

During the First World War the theatre was used to entertain the troops. Performed at each full moon, the shows drew full houses, the extra light enticing those from farther afield. A former Gilbert and Sullivan leading lady, Jessie Bond, now retired from the West End and living in Nottinghamshire, trod the boards, as did a fifteen-year-old Donald Wolfit, making his theatre debut in a musical comedy. Newark-born Wolfit would go on to become a renowned actor/manager and one of England's greatest Shakespearean actors. For this, and his wartime performances, Wolfit was knighted in 1957. He provided the inspiration for the protagonist, Sir, in the film *The Dresser* (1983), played by Albert Finney. A retired Wolfit was once asked if it was true that he'd played the legs of a panto donkey in Averham. 'Why yes,' he replied, 'all four of them.'[1]

After Rev Walker's death in 1942 his theatre company, The Country Bumpkins, continued to play but 1950s' fire restrictions scuppered their fun and the wooden theatre fell silent, save for the local youths that played football in the abandoned auditorium. The new rector, Bishop Mark Way, with the support of Valerie Baker and Gordon Kermode, helped revive the theatre and it reopened in 1961 under a charitable trust. Sir Donald Wolfit became a patron and gave a Shakespearean recital to help raise funds. He even composed an ode for the occasion which ended with the words:

> So here's to the venture – good luck from my heart.
> Many amateurs learn here to practice their art
> In memory of Walker and great Jessie Bond
> Pleasing not only locals but also *tout le monde*.

When the new Nottingham Playhouse was formed in 1963, the Robin Hood Theatre would lend the theatre furniture in return for the use of their wardrobe. It was at this time that the Cambridge Footlights first took to the Averham stage, with John Cleese, Tim

Brooke-Taylor and Bill Oddie starring in *Cambridge Circus*. The Footlights came back annually, one highlight was a 1968 BBC2 live show directed by Clive James. Other Footlighters to enjoy full houses at the Robin Hood Theatre include Germaine Greer, Eric Idle, Julie Covington and Graeme Garden.

The theatre has suffered many challenges, but with the generous support of locals it has survived. Now under the trusteeship of the Nottinghamshire County Council, it was refurbished and reopened in 2013. With a commitment to its youth group, the Robin Hood Theatre Company provides workshops and opportunities for young people to learn and showcase new skills. Like Wolfit before them, many actors have given their first performance on the Averham stage including Simon Ward (Young Winston), Isla Blair, Jeremy Clyde, Christopher Neame and Christopher Timothy.

There's also support for new writing. A script development group called Play Group meets monthly and the theatre gives East Midlands-based writers the chance to submit playscripts for selection, the best receiving a three-night run. All this because the local vicar loved a play.

---

[1]Baker, 1981.

Chapter 71
Rufford Abbey – A Secret World

'Polly Flint knows there is magic in the place. And she should know, because she is an unusual girl who can see things others can't.'

Helen Cresswell, *The Secret World of Polly Flint*

Rufford Abbey.

Near Ollerton, on the edge of Sherwood Forest, is the ruins of a remarkable twelfth-century abbey, one of the first in England to be converted into a country estate. Now a popular visitor attraction under the stewardship of English Heritage and Nottinghamshire County Council, the beautiful parkland offers many spots where the imagination can roam freely.

The grounds of Rufford Abbey play a prominent role in Helen Cresswell's children's book, *The Secret World of Polly Flint* (1984), later a Central Television series of the same name (1987). Cresswell's book, runner-up for the Whitbread Award, features Rufford's animal graves, the ice houses, the ford, the lake, the woods and the Abbey itself. In the book, young Polly escapes her loneliness by retreating to a magical parallel world, reached through her imagination.

Polly visits Rufford from nearby Wellow, arriving at the ford where she is promptly sprayed with water by a passing car before she embarks on a series of adventures. One destination is the animal graves. These cover the last years of the estate, from 1880 to 1938, when much of the land was sold to Sir Albert Ball, before the council bought it in 1952. The graves include the headstones of domestic and social animals.

'Animals' graves. Well that is posh,' says Polly, played in the TV series by Kate Reynolds (with a Nottinghamshire accent). The gravestone of Snuffy, 'deceased 1893,' is read aloud by Polly, who announces Snuffy as a 'snobby pet dog of Miss L Saville Lumley.' Another of the dogs afforded a grave is Boris, 'a funny name for a dog,' according to Polly, who adds, 'a faithful friend is hard to find,' before the black terrier comes back to life and joins her adventures.

Within Rufford's lake is its "tunnel bridge", an arched bridge that Polly names 'the secret tunnel.' It's through this that time gypsies travel from their lost world, meeting Polly in the process. The top of this folly bridge has been a curiosity since the middle of the eighteenth century, capturing many an imagination. When Polly stands looking at the lake, it's 'the biggest stretch of water she had ever seen.' The lake was introduced by Sir George Savile, Eighth Baronet, in 1750. Savile's decorative lake was filled by a stream from Rainworth Water.

Rufford's lake and its ducks have inspired another children's book, *The Ducks of Rufford* (2011), about five ducklings who spend their first year exploring Rufford's lake. A comment

Tunnel Bridge, Rufford Abbey.

on the changing seasons, Gavin and Oskar McIntosh's story proves that it's always nice weather for ducks. Rufford's famous ducks also feature in *Emma, Eddie and Jack Go To: Rufford Park* (2016), a story for young children by Nottinghamshire-based author Jackie Yelland. The retired primary school teacher told me that she chose Rufford as the setting for her book as she saw it as, 'a child/family friendly place where activities can happen in a beautiful setting.'

George, Memoirs of a Gentleman's Gentleman (1984), written by the eponymous George's daughter Nina Slingsby Smith and based on his diaries, tells of his early career in service at Edwardian Rufford Abbey. But of all the writing associated with Rufford, it is a folk song that carries the most fame: "The Rufford Park

Poachers". The ballad recounts the true story of a mass brawl between the poachers and gamekeepers in 1851. Depicting the poachers as brave heroes, the ballad is on the side of the men that assembled at Rufford Park to take action against the wealthy landowners' unfair control of the game. From the folk song:

> So poacher bold as I unfold
> Keep up your gallant heart
> And think about those poachers bold
> That night in Rufford Park

Many of the poachers faced imprisonment and deportation for their action.

In 1618, the poet and playwright Ben Jonson (1572–1637) visited Rufford Abbey and was taken hunting for game. He was met by Jane, Countess of Shrewsbury, who ran the household at Rufford, which was known for its free hospitality and generous provision. Jonson later wrote an epitaph for Jane on her death in 1625.[1]

The famed White Lady that is said to haunt Rufford is the apparition of Lady Arbella Stuart, whose parents were secretly married at the Abbey in 1574.[2] The noblewoman was tipped for the throne before she ended up being banished to the Tower of London, dying from starvation after refusing food. A talented Renaissance thinker, she left behind many letters expressing her anguish over her constricted life and yearning for independence. More than a hundred letters to relatives, royals and others were collected and published in the 1994 book, *The Letters of Lady Arbella Stuart*.

When the Abbey was founded, the local villages of Cratley, Inkersall, Grimston and Rufford were all emptied to make way for the new estate, the displaced locals moving to the new village of Wellow. The Cistercian monks arriving from Yorkshire needed a quiet monastery away from people and, although it took a century to complete, the Abbey became their place of solitude. A chequered 880 years later, and Rufford now attracts busloads of people, enjoying the grounds, the history and the ducks. No doubt there are some Helen Cresswell fans amongst them.

---

[1]Groundwater, 2013.
[2]White, 2020.

Chapter 72
Sherwood Lodge – Family Fortunes

'My father gave me the book on publication in 1934 when I was already sixteen years into a lifelong attachment to the horse.'

Sir Peter O'Sullevan, *Warrior*

Sherwood Lodge, Arnold.

Sherwood Lodge in Arnold, built c1790, became associated with the Seely family of politicians, industrialists, landowners and writers. It also has a connection to Warrior the War Horse who served in many key battles during the First World War and became known as 'The horse the Germans couldn't kill.' The image of a horse being entrenched in deep mud and dragged out by the soldiers around it will be familiar to fans of Spielberg's *War Horse*, but the story of Warrior is a true one, and it was written half a century before Michael Morpurgo's popular book on which the film is based.

The philanthropist and radical MP, Charles Seely (1803–1887), was one of the wealthiest industrialists of the Victorian era. In 1864 he hosted the Italian revolutionary General Giuseppe Garibaldi, inviting him to stay with him on the Isle of Wight to avoid the adoring crowds in London. Queen Victoria had requested that Seely urge Garibaldi to leave the country, and she registered her displeasure when he didn't.

Sherwood Lodge became home to Seely's son, Sir Charles Seely (1833–1915). In *The Great Houses of Nottinghamshire and the County Families* (1881), Leonard Jacks wrote of Sherwood Lodge that 'before Mr. Seely purchased the property, it was the residence of the Rev George Francis Holcombe, who was Vicar of Arnold, a county magistrate, the possessor of rare social qualities, and a very good judge of horse flesh.'

Like his father, Seely joined the Liberal Party and, from 1869, served two spells as an MP for Nottingham and Nottingham West. In 1895 he was the first person to be made a Freeman of Nottingham and a year later he was made Baronet of Sherwood Lodge and Brooke House. Seely made considerable improvements to Sherwood Lodge, doubling its size, including the addition of a library, and with these alterations and the chapel at the eastern edge, Sherwood Lodge became his main residence. He made large purchases of land in the area around the estate, taking his land in Nottinghamshire to some 3,000 acres. Toward the end of his life, when suffering ill heath, Seely lived on the Isle of Wight where he built Brook Hill House, later home to JB Priestley.

Inheriting the family estates at Sherwood Lodge was Sir Charles Hilton Seely (1859–1926), Second Baronet and Liberal MP for Mansfield. He was also a Justice of the Peace for Nottinghamshire and the Deputy Lieutenant. The third baronet was Hugh Michael Seely (1898–1970), who became the first Baron Sherwood. Another Liberal politician, he was also High Sheriff of Nottinghamshire.

Another son of the first baronet was Frank Evelyn Seely (1864–1928), who worked in the family business at Babbington Colliery. He also joined the army and served as a captain in the South Nottinghamshire Yeomanry. During the First World War he fought in Egypt and Gallipoli before reaching the rank of Lieutenant-Colonel. He was known for his philanthropic work throughout the county and made High Sheriff of Nottinghamshire. A councillor for Calverton, he was also known for his support to convalescent homes and the social services.

His name was taken by the main school in Calverton when it opened in 1957. The Colonel Frank Seely Academy can count the popular Olympian Christopher Dean and the current Chief Whip Mark Spencer amongst its former students. The writer Derrick Buttress used to teach there. As a year seven pupil at Colonel Frank Seeley, Aaliyah Neil (AS Neil) became one of the UK's youngest published crime writers. She was eleven years old when her book *Simon Dovers* (2018) was released. It's about a boy with an eye for crime who stumbles across a dead body.

Burntstump Seely Church of England Primary Academy was founded in 1902 by the Seely family of Sherwood Lodge. Apparently, it was after noticing a group of children struggling through the snow and ice on their way to school in Arnold, that the Seelys decided to build a local school for them. The Seely family "governed" the school, known as Sherwood Lodge School, until 1956.

One of Colonel Frank Seely's brothers, and the first baronet's youngest/seventh child, was John Edward Bernard "Jack" Seely (1868–1947). Born at Brookhill Hall, just over the Nottinghamshire/Derbyshire border, General (or Colonel) Jack Seely went to school with Winston Churchill and they became lifelong friends, Churchill becoming a godfather to one of Jack's sons. Jack Seely was awarded the Distinguished Service Order for his bravery in the Boer War and, returning to England, he was elected Conservative MP for the Isle of Wight. Later, like Churchill, he crossed to the Liberal Party. Seely was a member of Asquith's War Council and became Secretary of State for War in the two years before the First World War. Forced to resign as a result of the Curragh mutiny, he was sent to the Western Front in 1914 and was the only former cabinet minister to still be on the front line four years later.

Seely took his thoroughbred horse with him to war, and they survived the four years of bombs and bullets. Known to his soldiers as "General Jack", Seely made his name as a humane leader. His trusted mount, Warrior, remained with him throughout the war. Together they survived many dangerous situations before returning home after the Armistice. Physically unscathed, they lived on the Isle of Wight where they rode on to the combined age of one hundred.

General Jack remained haunted by his experience at war, and wrote of his life in *Adventure* (1930), *Fear and Be Slain: Adventures by land, sea and air* (1931), *Launch! A Life-Boat Book* (1932), introduced by the Prince of Wales, *For Ever England* (1932), described as 'a splendidly beautiful book for Britons of all ages,' and *The Paths of Happiness* (1938). As JEB Seely, General Seely or Lord Mottistone (in 1933 Seely was raised to the peerage as Baron Mottistone). His most famous book is *My Horse Warrior* (1934), both a memoir of his time as a soldier and a biography of his horse.

Seely's book is really the story of Warrior, from his birth on the Isle of Wight to his life as a famous and fearless war horse. It describes the twists of fate that saw him survive a war that took the lives of eight million horses. This moving true story is illustrated by Sir Alfred Munnings, who first painted Warrior at the front when he was the official War Artist to the Canadian cavalry, led by Seely.

Warrior lived until the middle of the Second World War, by which time he was thirty-three. In 2014 he was posthumously awarded the first Honorary PDSA Dickin Medal, the animals' equivalent of the Victoria Cross. The medal was accepted by John Brough Scott, MBE, Jack Seely's grandson. Brough Scott is a former jockey, horse racing journalist, radio and television presenter and an author. His *Henry Cecil: Trainer of Genius* (2013) won a 2014 British Sports Book Award in the Best Horse Racing Book category, one of ten books written by the author. Another is *Galloper Jack* (2003), a critically-acclaimed biography of his grandfather. In 2011 Brough Scott published *Warrior: The Amazing Story of a Real War Horse*. This is a new edition of Seely's story, complete with Munnings' original illustrations. The book is introduced by Brough Scott, with Sir Peter O'Sullevan writing the preface.

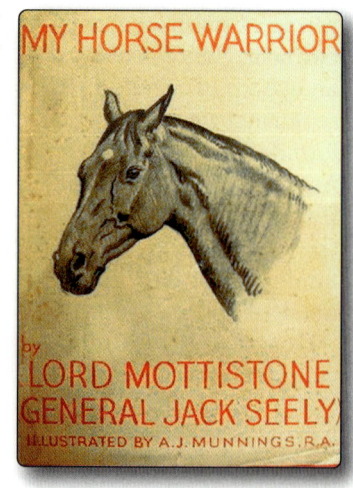

First editions of the 1934 illustrated hardback version of *My Horse Warrior* by Lord Mottistone are worth tracking down. As for Sherwood Lodge, it would no longer be recognisable to the Seely family, the grand old house having been demolished and replaced. Only the red-brick, pantiled five-bedroom farmhouse and barns, known as Dairy Farm, which used to provide milk to the Seely estate, remains.

A former headquarters of the National Coal Board, Sherwood Lodge has been home to the police since the 1970s and, appropriately, has been used for police horses. It now has a new three-storey building costing £18.5 million. A joint headquarters for the Nottinghamshire Police Force and Nottinghamshire Fire and

Rescue Service, the land also hosts a private hospital and Burntstump Country Park.

Stephen Booth's Detective Sergeant Diane Fry is no stranger to Sherwood Lodge in Booth's Cooper & Fry crime series, as Derbyshire's E Division are often required to cooperate with Nottinghamshire Police, meaning the venue remains a literary location.

Chapter 73
Southwell – A Literary Town

'Certainly I remember a bookshop (...) and going into it, perhaps I bought The Leaves of Southwell there...'

BS Johnson, *The Unfortunates*

Southwell Minster.

Many Nottingham writers have taken inspiration from their memories of Southwell, including DH Lawrence, Alan Sillitoe, and BS Johnson, whose experimental book-in-a-box, *The Unfortunates*, includes the narrator's recollections of visiting Southwell with June, seeing the town as 'a useful place to bring up children.' Johnson recalls 'the delicate, convoluted carving on the capitals, foliage...' of Southwell Minster's thirteenth-century Chapter House. 'And the stink of such dead places.'

BS Johnson was good friends with Alan Sillitoe, who features Southwell Minster in his short story collection *Men, Women and Children* (1973). In Sillitoe's "A Trip to Southwell", Alec and Mavis go there on a date, getting off the bus at the stop nearest to the Minster.

'He liked the Minster,' wrote Sillitoe, 'pleased it wasn't a city church but one placed on its own, an island among green lawns.

You could walk all around it, see every angle of its middle tower and two end pinnacles.'

Once inside the Minster, Alec tries to kiss Mavis, before they enter the Chapter House where 'He knew it was a beautiful place, the round room and arched ceiling, built so cleverly he couldn't think how and soon stopped trying to.'

Southwell Minster featured on the front cover of Nikolaus Pevsner's original guide to the buildings of Nottinghamshire, part of a series of forty-six volumes published between 1951 and 1974. The Minster and its leaves of Southwell were a main reason why Nottinghamshire featured so early in the series, being just the second volume (1951). The latest edition, revised by Clare Hartwell (2020), also features Southwell Minster on its cover. Pevsner had earlier written a short book for Penguin called *The Leaves of Southwell* (1945), referred to in *The Unfortunates*.

The first printed guide to the Minster was written by the novelist Elizabeth Glaister (1840–92). Her brother, Canon Glaister, was a curate there in the 1860s, prompting Elizabeth and her mother to move to Southwell's The Burgage. Glaister's first novel, *The Markhams of Ollerton: A Tale of the Civil War 1642–1647* (1873), is partly set inside the Minster and contains much local history. The author applied her extensive knowledge of architecture and embroidery to her writing. During Glaister's years in Southwell, the Minster had a lending library, with records of borrowing that go back over 200 years. She lived in the town until her death. Her grave and that of her mother, who outlived her, can be seen in the churchyard.

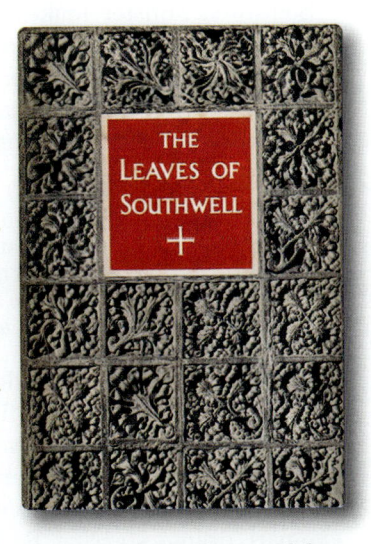

Another writer whose remains lie in the grounds of Southwell Minster is the suffragist Lady Laura Ridding (1849–1939), whose husband, George Ridding, was the first Bishop of Southwell. There is a large bronze statue of him by FW Pomeroy inside the Minster. Its base is by the lauded church architect WD Caröe. The Riddings took an active role in local education and social work. The Bishop's biography, *First Bishop of Southwell 1884–1904* (1908), was written by his wife. In addition to writing five biographies, Lady Laura Ridding wrote a historical novel, *By Weeping Cross* (1899), and she was President of the National Union of Women Workers, a group she co-founded at a conference in Nottingham.[1]

A former Vicar-General's only son, William Dickinson Rastall (1756–1822) was another literary Southwellian who, having left university, devoted himself to the study of the law, writing several legal works. Later living at Muskham Grange, near Newark, he was a Justice of the Peace for the counties of Nottingham, Lincoln, Middlesex, Surrey and Sussex. Dickinson, as he became known, wrote *The History of the Antiquities of the Town and Church of Southwell* (1787), which contained illustrations of the church and its history. This, and his *History and Antiquities of the Town of Newark* (1806), later formed half of a four-part collection.

Southwell Minster makes its way into DH Lawrence's related classics *The Rainbow* (1915) and *Women in Love* (1920), the author having visited Southwell when he was twenty-five. In Chapter Four of *The Rainbow*, about Anna Brangwen's youth, Will Brangwen thrills her with talk of churches, architecture and different periods:

> 'Have you been to Southwell?' he said. 'I was there at twelve o'clock at midday, eating my lunch in the churchyard. And the bells played a hymn. Ay, it's a fine Minster, Southwell, heavy. It's got heavy, round arches, rather low, on thick pillars. It's grand, the way those arches travel forward. There's a sedilia as well – pretty. But I like the main body of the church and – that north porch –'

In Chapter Thirteen, their daughter Ursula and Maggie cycle to Southwell, and other places, finding they 'had an endless wealth of things to talk about. And it was a great joy, finding, discovering.'

The Southwell-born screenwriter William Ivory adapted DH Lawrence's novels, *The Rainbow* and *Women in Love*, to produce a two-part drama starring Rachael Stirling as Ursula Brangwen, Rosamund Pike as Gudrun Brangwen, Saskia Reeves as Anna Brangwen and Rory Kinnear as Rupert Birkin. Ivory was educated at the Southwell Minster School, one of the oldest continuous educational foundations in England.

In Lawrence's *Women in Love*, in the chapter "Excurse", Birkin and Ursula return to the car after arguing. They are driving when:

> They dropped down a long hill in the dusk, and suddenly Ursula recognised on her right hand, below in the hollow, the form of

Southwell Minster.

'Are we here!' she cried with pleasure.

The rigid, sombre, ugly cathedral was settling under the gloom of the coming night, as they entered the narrow town, the golden lights showed like slabs of revelation, in the shop-windows.

'Father came here with mother,' she said, 'when they first knew each other. He loves it—he loves the Minster. Do you?'

'Yes. It looks like quartz crystals sticking up out of the dark hollow. We'll have our high tea at the Saracen's Head.'

As they descended, they heard the Minster bells playing a hymn, when the hour had struck six.

Once at the Saracen's Head they sit in the parlour by the fire, overwhelmed with mutual love. As they take tea, Birkin proposes that they both quit their jobs so that they can travel.

Lord Byron visited the Saracen's Head, Southwell's oldest pub, where Charles I is said to have spent his last night of freedom. As a teenager, Byron took part in an amateur production of *The Weathercock* at the Assembly Rooms next door (now the hotel side of the Saracen's Head – there's a plaque). His relationship with the town began in 1803 when his mother began renting Southwell's newly built Burgage Manor, with Newstead Abbey in need of repair. When on holiday from Harrow and then Cambridge, Byron spent much time here. Since 1990, Burgage Manor has been owned by Geoffrey Bond, author of Lord Byron's Best Friends (2013).

The Assembly Rooms.

In the March of 1804, Byron had been pleased to receive a letter from his half-sister Augusta. Their continued affectionate correspondence revealed his early impression of Southwell, as

Burgage Manor, Southwell.

in April, he wrote: '... this horrid place where I am oppressed with ennui, and have no amusement of any kind, except the conversation of my mother which is sometimes very edifying but not always very agreeable ... I sincerely wish for the company of a few friends of my own age to soften the austerity of the scene. I am an absolute hermit.' His wish for friends was about to be granted, as he wrote a week later: 'My mother gives a party tonight at which the principal Southwell Belles will be present, with one of which, although I don't as yet know whom I shall so far honour, having never seen them, I intend to fall violently in love...'[2]

The sixteen-year-old Byron might not have fallen in love, but he did make friends with one of the "Southwell Belles", twenty-one-year-old Elizabeth Pigot (1783–1866), and her brother John, who lived opposite Burgage Manor on the other side of Burgage Green.

Elizabeth Pigot wrote of her initial impression of Byron: 'The first time I was introduced to him was at a party at his mother's, when he was so shy that she was forced to send for him three times before she could persuade him to come into the drawing-room, to play with the young people at a round game. He was then a fat, bashful boy, with his hair combed straight over his forehead...'

Byron began seeing less of his quarrelsome mother and more of his new circle of friends. These included John and Julia Leacroft, the teenage children of Captain John Leacroft. The Leacroft family lived at Burgage House on King Street, near the top of the green, and Byron visited them many times.

Burgage House, Southwell.

In the summer of 1806 Burgage House became one of the barns and larger premises in Southwell to host theatrical performances. Byron and his friends converted the drawing room into a makeshift theatre where they performed amateur dramatics, Julia and Byron playing the lead roles. Their flirting continued long after the staged dramatics were over. Fifteen years later Byron wrote in his diary:

> When I was a youth, I was reckoned a good actor. Besides Harrow speeches, in which I shone, I enacted Penruddock in the *Wheel of Fortune*, and Tristam Fickle, in the farce of *The Weathercock*, for three nights, in some private theatricals at Southwell, in 1806, with great applause.[3]

Burgage House stayed in the Leacroft family until the 1870s. It was a council youth club in recent years.

By January 1807 it had been expected that Byron and Julia would marry, but Byron had no such intention. The Leacroft family were not happy, and may even have attempted to entrap the poet to force his hand in marriage. It's also rumoured that Julia's brother John challenged Byron to a duel.

After leaving Southwell for good, Byron wrote to John, 'If we must cut each other's throats to please our relations, you will do me the justice to say it is from no personal animosity between us.'

To Elizabeth Pigot, Byron wrote, 'Oh Southwell, Southwell, how I rejoice to have left thee, & how I curse the heavy hours I have dragged along for so many months, amongst the Mohawks who inhabit your Kraals.'

Until 1811, Byron regularly corresponded with Miss Pigot, who remained in Southwell for the rest of her life, moving from the family house on the Burgage after her mother's death in 1833. Pigot then lived at Greyfriars, 25 Easthorpe, where she died in 1866. Miss Pigot never married. Megan Boyes has written a biography of Elizabeth Pigot, *Love without Wings* (1988).

Greyfriars. 25 Easthorpe, Southwell.

Byron's theatricals and partying didn't interfere with his early poetry and, encouraged by the Pigots, his plans to publish were put into action. In his first volume, *Fugitive Pieces* (1806), Byron addresses his friends in Southwell, Elizabeth Pigot becoming Eliza, with Julia being the subject of "To Julia", later re-titled "To Lesbia", and then, "To a Lady" (1807). Much of the work can be viewed as a document of Byron's time in Southwell. As he wrote in the preface, it was printed 'for the perusal of a few friends to whom they are dedicated.'

In "To Julia", Byron communicated to Miss Leacroft that he no longer loved her, for which he takes all the blame. His scandalous poems, which included one about his own unrequited love at Annesley Hall, suggested that he had many relationships in Southwell. Byron wrote that Southwell's 'inhabitants are notorious for officious curiosity,' and this curiosity would fuel the scandal. It was Byron's friend, Rev John T Becher (1770–1848), a future Vicar-General of Southwell Minster, that insisted on the book's withdrawal. Becher later founded Southwell's workhouse and became known as the "wicked workhouse man", although Julie O'Neill's *The Life and Times of J T Becher* (2002) depicts him more as a social reformer and humanitarian.

Around the time Byron first arrived in Southwell, the poet Samuel Plumb (1793–1858) was leaving, having lived there as a boy. Plumb was one of the Sherwood Forest group of writers. As was Charles Plumbe (1813–99), who wrote of Southwell Minster in his poetry. The Plumb(e)s can be added to an illustrious list of writers to have written about Southwell, clearly one of Nottinghamshire's great literary towns.

At the turn of the nineteenth century several private venues in Southwell were hosting theatrical performances, and by 1816 Southwell had its own theatre, a building of two large rooms on the Market Place junction of King Street and Queen Street, formerly used for Southwell's arms. It all changed after Joseph Smedley was granted a licence to perform. Smedley, who would visit the theatre every other summer for six weeks until the mid-1800s, was a former actor who married an actress, and they formed a touring theatre company. In the mould of Mr Vincent Crummles in Charles Dickens' *Nicholas Nickleby*, Smedley managed a troupe of actors that featured members of his family. The Smedley Travelling Company of Actors toured market towns and listed the small theatres of Newark and Southwell amongst their thirty venues across five counties. Typical performances would consist of a domestic comedy or melodrama followed by a couple of songs and ending with a farce, the Smedleys playing most of the key roles in their repertoire of acts.

The theatre was reached via an alleyway which ran down the side of Manchester House. Southwell's theatre was said to be 'neatly fitted up and fully competent.' Three shillings would get you a box, half price for children, with two shillings for the pit. Tickets were bought in advance but, if you were lucky, a shilling on the door could secure a place in the gallery. The scenery was always elaborate and, by the late Georgian era, included mechanical devices, which helped to give the effect of stormy weather.

Similar theatres had a reputation for drunken rowdiness, but Smedley's insistence on sobriety and good behaviour, and his vision for a 'school of eloquence,' a 'Temple of the Arts,' helped Southwell's theatre maintain its respectability and quality. By 1837 Joseph Smedley had passed on the theatre's management to two actors, Rogers and Mosley, but Smedley's forty-year role as a theatre manager coincided with the venue's golden years. Nottingham-born Richard Smedley (there's no evidence of a family connection) used archived papers and playbills relating to Smedley's company for his 2018 book *The Life and Times of Joseph E Smedley*. Richard worked as a young backstage hand at Nottingham's Theatre Royal, making his way through a variety of roles before becoming Finance Director. After years of managing theatres in London, including the Victoria Palace, the Apollo, and the Palladium, he returned to the Royal Centre as General Manager.

Back in 1881, Southwell's theatre was inherited by the Loughton family. Alfred Loughton, a local celebrity, lived there until his death in 1953. Loughton was a skilled violin-maker, whitesmith, bell-hanger, moth collector, gas-fitter and inventor of the "Southwell Cycle",[4] but he was best known as a multi-award-winning photographer, and he published the book *Pictorial Southwell*. Loughton photographed George Bernard Shaw outside the theatre's entrance in 1930. There's now a blue plaque on the wall where the Irish playwright and Nobel Peace Prize winner stood. It states:

Southwell Old Theatre
Around 1812–16 James Adams, a whitesmith,
converted the first floor for use as a theatre.
It opened with performances by a travelling company,
managed by Joseph Smedley.
Playbills show the theatre had boxes, a pit and gallery.
In 1881 the Loughton family inherited the property.
Alfred Loughton became a well known photographer.

In recent years the Grade II listed building received a boost when it was restored by the Tinley family. They converted and reopened the premises as The Old Theatre Deli and they host the occasional performance in the large room upstairs. The Old Theatre is one of England's few remaining Georgian theatres.

Southwell now has its own theatre club, a community drama group founded in 1976. The Southwell Theatre Club usually perform in Southwell Library, where they're known for their murder mysteries and poetry readings. Between 1960 and 2006 Southwell Library had been on the corner where Burgage Lane meets Kings Street (what's now the Riverside Church). The most recent Southwell-set novel to appear in the library is Beth Moran's *I Hope You Dance* (2015). Southwell Library is famously up for anything, once staying open all night with a full arts programme throughout to while away the hours!

Since 2007, Southwell Library (now in the centre of the town) has been a driving force behind the Southwell Poetry Festival. A major part of Nottinghamshire's literary calendar but now subsumed under a wider Inspire/Nottinghamshire Libraries poetry festival. It started as a special event for the new millennium. Brought back in 2002 by popular demand, the event grew in scale thanks to the library's support. Southwell Minster and Southwell Minster School have also been involved and the festival has attracted many leading poets, such as John Hegley, Jackie Kay, Hollie McNish, Lemn Sissay, Jo Bell, Wendy Cope, Carol Ann Duffy, Andrew Motion, Simon Armitage, Ian McMillan, Maura Dooley, Kei Miller, Paul Farley, Daljit Nagra, Elaine Feinstein, Kate Fox and Helen Mort. There's been plenty of local talent on display too, with Matthew Welton, John Harvey, Rosie Garner, Henry Normal, Ben Norris, Mahendra Solanki, Andrew Graves, Georgina Wilding and Andy Croft all making an appearance. Croft, as the festival's writer-in-residence, even composed a poem to address the old question of Southwell's pronunciation ('South-well' or 'Suth-ull'?).

The poet and historian William Hutton (1723–1815) was a bookseller in Southwell. It was in 1749 that he opened his small bookshop, having taught himself bookbinding. Hutton had previously been an apprentice stocking maker for his uncle George in Nottingham.[5] After his bookshop proved unsuccessful, he moved to Birmingham where he is regarded as the city's first historian. A blue plaque on Birmingham's Waterstones bookshop, on High

Street, marks a spot where he lived. After walking the entire length of Hadrian's Wall, Hutton wrote an account of his journey in *The History of the Roman Wall* (1802). His last book was to be his autobiography, *The Life of William Hutton* (1815). His daughter was the novelist and letter writer Catherine Hutton (1756–1846).

---

[1]Boussahba-Bravard, 2007.
[2]Marchland, 1975.
[3]Herbert, 2007.
[4]Dobson, from *Folio*.
[5]Gordon, 1900.

Chapter 74
St Mary Magdalene Church, Hucknall – What Lies Beneath

'Death, so called, is a thing which makes men weep, And yet a third of life is passed in sleep.'

Lord Byron, *Manfred*

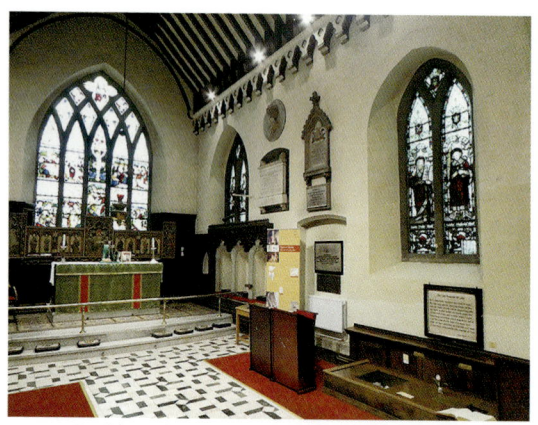

St. Mary Magdalene Church, Hucknall.

Hucknall, known as Hucknall Torkard until 1916, has a proud literary heritage spanning the past two centuries, from Lord Byron's resting place to the introduction of new literary events.

In 1988, after a bi-centenary celebration of Byron's birthday, the Newstead Abbey Byron Society was formed. The society's first Chairman, David Herbert, was succeeded by Ken Purslow, who also served as Chairman of the annual Hucknall Byron Festival, first held in 1998. Taking place in Hucknall and at Newstead Abbey, the Byron Festival offers a variety of activities for all ages. Many events are free to attend and, over the years, many local authors and publishers have taken part. One regular speaker is the Nottinghamshire librarian and Byron scholar Ralph Lloyd-Jones.

When Lord Byron died, his long-time companion and valet, William Fletcher (1777–1837), the stout yeoman of *Childe Harold's Pilgrimage*, accompanied his body back from Greece. Byron's body lay overnight at the Blackamoor's Head Inn behind the Exchange in Nottingham, where thousands paid their respects. Among them was the writer Mary Howitt (1799–1888), who wrote, 'We laid our hands upon the coffin. It was a moment of enthusiastic feeling to me...' Her husband William Howitt followed the funeral procession before writing his poem "A Poet's Thoughts".

During Byron's final illness at Missolonghi, in Greece, he requested, 'Let not my body be hacked or be sent to England. Here let my bones moulder. Lay me in the first corner without pomp or nonsense.' But Byron's remains were taken to England, not to Newstead Abbey, nor to Westminster Abbey due to his "questionable morality"; his final destination was to be the Byron family vault in Hucknall, a vault in St Mary Magdalene Church that had been built in the seventeenth century by Newstead Abbey's Sir John Byron, whose wife Cecile was the first to be laid to rest there.

Mourners attending Byron's funeral included his friends Colonel Wildman, owner of Newstead Abbey, John Cam Hobhouse, a constant friend since his Cambridge days, John Hanson, family lawyer and father figure, and William Fletcher, who was inconsolable.

An album was presented to the church in 1825 to be used to register the names of visitors and record their comments. In 1834 the contents of this album were published in a book entitled *Byroniana*, edited by JM Langford. The Nottingham poet Philip James Bailey, later to write *Festus*, was one of many notable names listed in the book.

In 1852, Lord Byron's only legitimate daughter, Ada, Lady Lovelace (1815–52), was buried in the vault. This extract,[1] from *Gossip of the Century* (1852), explains why:

> Sixteen months before her death she paid a visit to the home of her ancestors, and in the great Library at the Abbey, Colonel Wildman quoted a passage from Byron's works to Byron's daughter, and she, touched by the beauty of the words, enquired the name of the author. For reply, Colonel Wildman pointed to the painting of her father which hung on the Library wall. It came as a revelation to her. Instantly she confessed that she was brought up in complete ignorance of all regarding her father. From that time Lady Lovelace devoted herself to a close study of her father's life and works. The loss of the affection of that noble heart, which had so long been kept from her, preyed upon her mind. She fell ill – so ill that she knew she could never hope to recover. In this last illness she wrote to Colonel Wildman a letter, begging to be buried beside her father: 'Yes, I will be buried there; not where my mother can join me, but by the side of him who so loved me, and whom I was not taught to love; and this reunion of our bodies in the grave shall be an emblem of union of our spirits in the bosom of the Eternal'.

A gambler who most likely had extra-marital affairs, Ada Lovelace was a true Byron. Like her father, she died aged thirty-six and was touched by genius. It was her mother, Anne Isabella ("Annabella") Milbanke, who steered her away from poetic pursuits and towards science. Ada Lovelace is credited with having written the first computer programme, her famous "notes on the translation", which followed her collaboration with Charles Babbage, being arguably the most important paper in the history of digital computing before modern times.

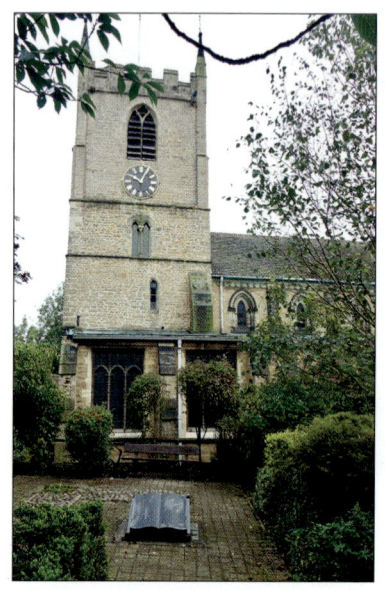

There are many memorials to Lord Byron and Ada Lovelace in St Mary Magdalene Church, such as the marble floor-slab donated by the King of Greece in 1881 in recognition of Byron's heroics in their War of Independence. Among the interesting artefacts is a memorial to Ann Jackson, placed high on a wall. Jackson was a girlfriend of Byron's when he was in Southwell. He almost hit her in a shooting accident, an incident he immortalised in an early poem.

St. Mary Magdalene Church and Byron's memorial, Hucknall.

Born in Sherwood Rise, Thomas Gerrard Barber arrived in Hucknall in 1904. Twenty years later, as vicar of St Mary Magdalene Church, he founded a Byron memorial committee on the centenary of the poet's death. Frustrated by rumours that Byron's body was not in the vault, and intrigued by the idea that there may be an ancient crypt, Canon Barber sought to investigate. Obtaining the approval of the Home Office and Rev Lord Byron of Thrumpton Hall, Canon Barber got permission to open the vault, and, in June 1938, with those involved sworn to secrecy, his meticulously-planned undercover operation took place.

A lorry dropped off the required tools and, at staggered times, those involved arrived largely unseen. Present in the church were Canon Barber and his wife, Seymour Cocks (the local MP), NM Lane (the surveyor of the Diocese), Holland Walker, Captain

McCraith and his wife, Dr Llewellyn, GL Willis (the vicar's warden) and his wife, CG Campbell and his wife, Geoffrey Johnstone, James "Jim" Bettridge (the caretaker/church fireman) and Claude Bullock (a photographer). The Press was excluded.

It took an hour to ease open the first of the six-inch-thick flagstones, beneath which were eleven stone steps descending from the nave of the church towards the vault. Barber went first, followed by the surveyor. On examination, there were signs that the vault had been disturbed. Souvenir-hunters had taken items and the poet's coffin had previously been opened. Had Byron's body been snatched?

Within the vault's rectangular chamber were three stacks of coffins in varying states. The right stack – the children's coffins – had perished. The middle pile belonged to the women, the uppermost of these containing the remains of Ada Lovelace, the last of the Byrons to be buried there. Her coffin was in good condition, her coronet intact. Underneath Lady Lovelace was Lord Byron's mother, resting upon the debris of other Byron women and their coffins.

The mostly crushed left stack held the peers. At the top, placed above the coffin of the "wicked" Fifth Lord Byron, was the poet Lord Byron's oak coffin. There was no name plate on the lid and some handles were missing. Nearby was an upright chest within which was an urn encased in lead containing the poet's heart and brain.

The party disbanded at midnight and operations were delayed until the morning, but Canon Barber, the caretaker and the photographer, later returned for closer inspection. Barber noticed that the lid of Lord Byron's coffin was loose and the leaden case within it had been cut open. This was Barber's chance to prove that the poet's remains were there. A year later, in his book *Byron and Where he is Buried* (1939), published by Henry Morley & Sons of Hucknall, Canon Barber described what he saw when sneaking a look at the poet:

> Reverently, very reverently, I raised the lid, and before my eyes there lay the embalmed body of Byron in as perfect a condition as when it was placed in the coffin one hundred and fourteen years ago. His features and hair easily recognisable from the portraits with which I was so familiar. The serene, almost happy expression on his face made a profound impression upon me. The feet and ankles were uncovered, and I was able to establish the fact that his

lameness had been that of his right foot. But enough – I gently lowered the lid of the coffin – and as I did so, breathed a prayer for the peace of his soul.

Canon Barber's midnight visit has been well documented. What's less well known is his secret third descent into the vault, taken with the novelist Cecil Roberts. Barber had previously promised Roberts that if he ever got permission to open the vault to check for an ancient crypt, he'd invite him along, knowing he was an admirer of the poet. Barber had written to Roberts informing him that the vault would be opened, but the novelist arrived a day late. Fortunately for Roberts, the vault had not yet been sealed.

Cecil Roberts was taken by Barber to the church where he entered the vault. Under his feet were several inches of debris, decayed wood and innumerable bones. At Byron's coffin, Roberts felt uneasy as he watched Canon Barber slowly lifting the lid, allowing him to look upon the face of the poet. In the fourth volume of his autobiography, *Sunshine and Shadow* (1972), he described what he saw.

In 1971, Roberts returned to the church and met up with James Bettridge, the former caretaker, and they shared their memories of visiting the opened vault. They were probably the last two survivors of the vault's opening.

Meanwhile, in 1938, the last year the vault had been opened, the Hucknall-born actor Robin Bailey (1919–99) made his professional stage debut with the Court Players, as George in *The Barretts of Wimpole Street,* at Nottingham's Theatre Royal, having first been on stage in Hucknall at the Church Hall. The son of a local china and glass merchant, Bailey had been educated at the Henry Mellish Grammar School. His stage career was surpassed by a long TV career that included an appearance in *The Adventures of Robin Hood* (1955), a series featuring scripts by Hollywood writers blacklisted during the McCarthy era (a subject of Nottingham writer Michael Eaton's screenplay *Fellow Traveller*). For a while, Bailey presented the quiz show, *The 64,000 Question* (based on the US show *The $64,000 Question*), but his favourite roles were in comedies. He is best-remembered for playing Uncle Mort in the TV show *I Didn't Know You Cared* (1975–79).

Later in life, Robin Bailey voiced audio books, including Nevil Shute's *A Town Like Alice,* and many crime novels such as Ruth

Rendell's *The Veiled One*, Catherine Aird's *A Religious Body*, and Agatha Christie's masterpiece, *The Murder of Roger Ackroyd*.

Hucknall boasts many literary plaques, most of which are on the ground in front of the church and public library. Several of these are associated with Byron and Ada Lovelace, while the poet and his daughter are also two of the portraits featured on the railing in front of the library.

Outside the church and in the Market Place are other fine tributes, including Nottinghamshire's only full-size statue of Byron, erected by Elias Lacey in 1903. The statue looks over the Market Place from its position high on the side of the Co-op Building.

Opposite the statue on the other side of the market is Hucknall Library. The library was built in 1887 and gifted to the town by John Edward Ellis and Herbert Byng Paget, two partners of the Hucknall Colliery Company. By the turn of the twentieth century, 13,500 books were being borrowed, with around 500 readers visiting each day. Extended in the 1960s, the large library is now run by Inspire for Nottinghamshire County Council. It hosts a crime café.

Byron's statue, Market Place, Hucknall.

Hucknall's oldest pub, the Red Lion, has a plaque outside its entrance letting us know that back in the eighteenth century it was at one time the rent house of Lord Byron. To the rear of the

The Red Lion, Hucknall.

pub was a row of terraced cottages rented at seven pounds a year. In 2011 Christy Fearn performed a speech here titled "Lord Byron – The First Rockstar?" in which she compared Byron to David Bowie.

Hucknall is associated with a number of writers, past and present. The most famous of these is Eric Coates (1886–1957), one of Britain's most familiar names in light music. Coates' autobiography, *Suite in Four Movements* (1953), came out a year before he wrote what became his most famous score. Within days of his writing this piece of music, some film producers happened to need a march for their soundtrack and Coates' music fitted perfectly. That film was *The Dambusters*.

Maureen Newton is chair of the Hucknall Heritage Society, having started as an officer for the society in 1985. It was a local history course at the University of Nottingham in 1990 that prompted Newton's writing, which often explores and expands upon details from two significant books about Hucknall, Beardsmore's *History of Hucknall Torkard* (1909) and Horriben's *Hucknall: Of Lowly Birth and Iron Fortune* (1974).

David Edwards grew up on Carlingford Road and now lives in Montreux, Switzerland, from where he told me, 'Byron used to live here. It's where he wrote the poem, *The Prisoner of Chillon*. I was inspired by Lord Byron [back in Hucknall], and he is still stalking me!'

Edwards, who also writes as Jack George Edmunson, made the news in 2010 when he left his high-flying career and luxury home to devote his time to writing, something he did from a caravan in

Wales. He still visits Hucknall where he has many strong memories.

NTU Creative Writing MA graduate, Kristina Adams, lives in Hucknall. Her debut, *What Happens in New York* (2016), is the first in a successful series from an author whose books about friendship and supporting each other aim to inspire people. Nottingham plays a role in two of her *What Happens in...* novels, and the city centre provides the setting for *Behind the Spotlight* (2019). Adams' blog, The Writer's Cookbook, attracts more than 30,000 aspiring authors each month, seeking advice on all aspects of writing.

The transgender rights activist and *Vogue* columnist Paris Lees was born in Hucknall. The former Holgate School pupil (now The Holgate Academy), is the author of *What It Feels Like for a Girl* (2021), part-memoir, part-fiction. It's a story about growing up poor in 2000's Hucknall. The novel is written in Nottingham dialect and its thirteen-year-old protagonist is called Byron.

A new Hucknall Book Festival hoped to launch in 2021 as the town continues its relationship with literature.

---

[1]Beardsmore, 1909.

Chapter 75
St Mary's Church, Edwinstowe –
Of Phrase and Fable

'The labour of all this writing out and indexing has been very great, though a labour of love for me.'

Ebenezer Cobham Brewer

St. Mary's Church, Edwinstowe.

Clergyman and cricketer Henry Hayman and his family moved from Nottingham's St Andrew's Church to Ruddington after he became vicar there in 1877. A year later they were joined by Hayman's father-in-law, the writer Dr Ebenezer Cobham Brewer (1810–97), who had moved up to Nottinghamshire after his wife died.

Hayman remained Vicar of Ruddington for seven years before he and his wife, their children, and her father, all moved to the vicarage at Edwinstowe. Ordained forty years earlier, Ebenezer Cobham Brewer assisted with the preaching and with the children, regaling them with his stories and experiences and paying regular visits to the village school. Brewer was a mine of information and stories, as his millions of readers could attest.

The Hayman family outside the vicarage (E. Cobham Brewer seated).

His forty or so books included *A Reader's Handbook to Literature* and the famous *Brewer's Dictionary of Phrase and Fable*, a book that had been under consideration for twenty years before its publication. The publisher, Mr Cassell, thought it a 'doubtful speculation, quite beyond the wildest reach of the imagination,' but his demands that it was 'not too learned' were heeded and the book became a huge seller. First published in the 1870s, it has received many updates and Brewer spent much of his time in Nottinghamshire revising the book.

On the walls of his room at the Edwinstowe vicarage, Brewer attached paper which he used to write on.[1] He had a lifelong habit of making notes which he typically kept in bundles of slips arranged alphabetically. It was a love he retained well into his eighties, and he'd often refer to them when working into the early hours of the morning. His advice for a long life: 'Little to eat, less to drink, little sleep and plenty to do,' served him well. Gardening, he once said, was his only vice.

Brewer graduated in law in 1836 from Trinity Hall, Cambridge, returning to his home of Norwich to work at his father's school, succeeding him as headmaster. During this time Brewer had been compiling his *Guide to the Scientific Knowledge of Things Familiar* (c1840). Money from this bestseller allowed him to travel through Europe, and make his notes. It was in the 1850s that he joined the publisher Cassell.

John Cassell's first publication was *The Standard of Freedom*, a weekly newspaper that advocated religious, political and commercial freedom. Cassell began publishing serialised work with affordable sections (a penny a week), making them accessible to the masses. With other volumes aimed at children, Brewer wrote his twelve-book series *My First Book of....* in which a different subject was explored in each edition.

Many educational books came from Brewer's pen. He told a reporter from *The Westminster Budget* that 'The *Phrase and Fable Dictionary* and the other books of that class may be said to be merely different sections of one gigantic commonplace book.' After his death, the "Brewer's" name continued to be attached to new works and, incredibly, more than 200 years after his birth, new versions of his most famous dictionary are still being published. In 2018, the twentieth edition of *Brewer's Dictionary of Phrase and Fable* was released, edited by the Dame of Dictionary Corner, Susie Dent.

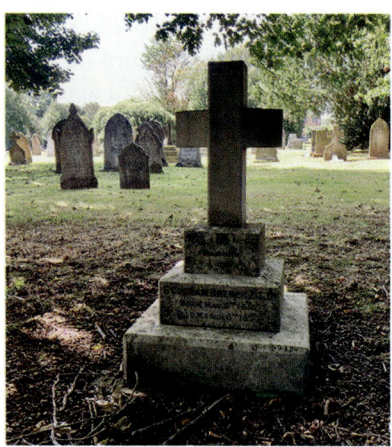

Ebenezer Cobham Brewer's headstone, St. Mary's Church, Edwinstowe.

It was in the Edwinstowe vicarage that Brewer took his last breath. He had ended his days writing and enjoying his family's company, as well as taking a close interest in St Mary's Church. The church's restoration work, which he had keenly followed, was completed just after his death in 1897. Brewer is buried in the churchyard a short distance from the west side of the tower.

The parish church dates from the twelfth century. The first stone building in Edwinstowe, it was built on the site of a church from 633AD. Local legend will tell you that it was here at St Mary's Church that Robin Hood and Maid Marian were married – folklore Brewer would have noted down.

Taking over from Henry Hayman as the vicar of St Mary's was Edward Bond. He was followed by Frank Day-Lewis in 1918, father of the future Poet Laureate Cecil Day Lewis (1904–1972), who was fourteen years old when the family moved to Edwinstowe. In his autobiography, *The Buried Day* (1960), Day Lewis ('As a writer I do not use the hyphen in my surname – a piece of inverted snobbery which has produced rather mixed results,' he wrote) recalled his father being in debt after furnishing the vicarage and purchasing a second-hand car. On Edwinstowe, he wrote:

> When we first went there, the black-faced miners cycling home from work with their snap-tins bumping at their sides were outnumbered by the farm labourers whom they passed in the village street, exchanging a curt Midland 'How-do?' Twenty years later, almost every man would be working in the pits.

'Remote though the miners' lives were from me,' wrote Day Lewis, 'it is at Edwinstowe that my social conscience was born.'

Cecil Day Lewis' father remained as vicar of St Mary's until his death in 1937. As a teenager Cecil sang in the choir. Poet Laureate from 1967 to his death in 1972, Day Lewis has also been a successful mystery writer as, to boost his income from poetry, he wrote twenty detective novels under the pseudonym Nicholas Blake. Most of the books featured the protagonist Nigel Strangeways (named after the prison), a character modelled on WH Auden. A stand-alone, *A Penknife in My Heart* (1958), featured a character named Ned/Edwin Stowe.

Edwinstowe Book Group produced *A Creative Dictionary of Edwinstowe* (2005), a book that was loosely based on the idea of *Brewer's Dictionary of Phrase and Fable*. The book was edited by Stephan Collishaw and Liz Stewart-Smith with a preface by Alan Sillitoe. The group, based at Edwinstowe Library, also held a big event on the life of Cecil Day Lewis, which included a lecture by his biographer Peter Stanford.

---

[1]Collishaw/ Stewart-Smith, 2005.

Chapter 76
Stapleford – It's All About Mee

> 'Oh for a book that will answer all the questions!'
> Arthur Mee, *The Children's Encyclopaedia*

The Arthur Mee Centre, Stapleford.

Arthur Mee wrote around a million words a year for fifty years, helping to teach and inspire generations of young people.

Close to Stapleford Library is the Arthur Mee Centre on Church Street. Now part of Nottingham College and no longer officially titled the Arthur Mee Centre, it was Stapleford Board School when its most famous former pupil learned the importance of self-discipline and hard work, along with a devotion to God and England. His teacher was George Byford, a conservative man from Essex who instilled in Mee a view that the British Empire was always a force for good. Mee's formal education left him well-schooled in English but with no aptitude for chemistry, mechanics or geometry, subjects he'd later make more attractive to his young readers by avoiding the technical terms he had struggled with in class. 'Never would he use such words, for example, as "diameter" or "circumference," but always width, and so many feet or yards round. If a technical term was not familiar to him, he argued, then it might be unfamiliar to thousands of others, both adult and juvenile,' said Bryant (1946).

In 2011 a blue plaque was placed on the wall of Mee's old school announcing:

Arthur Henry Mee – 1875–1943 –
Journalist and prolific author –
Originator and editor of The Children's Encyclopedia,
The Children's Newspaper and The King's England – Born in
Stapleford and attended school here

Arthur Mee was born in Stapleford's Church Street to a working-class Baptist family. He was the second child of ten, his father Henry a liberal man with a social conscience, his mother Mary a former cotton lace-winder. The Mees moved to Orchard Street, then to 7 Pinfold Lane, a two-bedroomed terraced house. Arthur left school aged fourteen just as his family left Stapleford, moving to the north of the city. He joined the local newspaper, the conservative *Nottingham Daily Guardian*, as a proofreader's copy-holder and he taught himself shorthand.

By 1891, with the Mee family living at 126 Manning Street in St Ann's/Mapperley Park, Arthur became an apprentice reporter for the *Nottingham Daily Express*, a radical Liberal newspaper with offices on Upper Parliament Street. He was working for the editor John Derry, and it suited him. *The Nottingham Guardian* was a Tory paper, Mee was a Liberal.

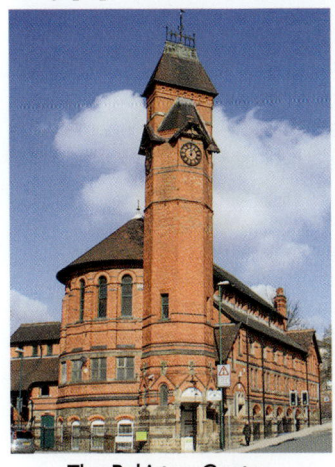

The Mees moved to 213 Woodborough Road, moving again to 237 (now 311) where Arthur's parents lived out their days. The house was close to the Woodborough Road Baptist Chapel (now the Pakistan Centre at 163 Woodborough Road) where the Mee family all worshipped. Arthur Mee was also a member of the Nottingham Mechanics' Institute.

Aged twenty, Mee was made editor of the *Express*' evening news edition. It was the paper's new editor, a Scot called John "Sandy" Hammerton, that appointed Mee, and the two men became lifelong friends and collaborators, Mee becoming "journalist in chief to British youth", and Hammerton "the most successful creator of large-scale works of reference in Britain".

The Pakistan Centre,
Woodborough Road,
Nottingham.

Sir John Hammerton was also a reputed biographer (of Dickens and Barrie), and he wrote a biography of Arthur Mee entitled *Child of Wonder* (1946), in which he examined his friend's ability to explain complex science, writing:

> [Mee] had the power to make plain to the average man, woman, and child the aspects and imports of the problems which the very men who had wrested them from nature could not make so plain.

Hammerton greatly encouraged Mee's career, including his contributions to the popular working-class penny weekly *Tit-Bits*, owned by George Newnes. Impressed by Mee's articles, Newnes invited him to join the London staff of *Tit-Bits*, and Mee made his move to the capital in 1896. He met Amelia "Amy" Fratson whilst holidaying in Skegness and they married in 1897. A year later Mee joined the staff of the *Daily Mail,* becoming their literary editor in 1903. He was now writing for Sir Alfred Harmsworth's *Amalgamated Press* and, together with Hammerton, Mee moved away from journalism, taking an editorial role for Harmsworth earning a thousand pounds a year. Wealthy and no longer needed in London, Mee ditched Lambeth for Hextable in Kent.

Mee and Hammerton produced *The History of the World* (1907–09) and *Natural History* (1909–11), but it was the fortnightly magazine *The Children's Encyclopaedia* that would make the biggest impact. It was Mee's six-year-old daughter Marjorie's constant questions, and her mother's response, that got Mee thinking. Of this he wrote:

> ...there came into [Marjorie's] mind the great wonder of the Earth. What does the world mean? And why am I here? Where are all the people who have been and gone? Where does the rose come from? Who holds the stars up there? ... And as the questions came, when the mother had thought and thought, and answered this and answered that until she could answer no more, she cried out ... for a book that will answer all the questions!

Mee began *The Children's Encyclopaedia* with a message for his readers:

> It is a Big Book for Little People, and it has come into the world to make your life happy and wise and good. That is what we are meant to be. That is what we will help each other to be, Your affectionate friend, Arthur Mee.

The encyclopaedia was an immediate hit and went on to educate millions of readers. The US edition, known as *The Book of Knowledge*, sold three-and-a-half million sets. A special bound copy of the encyclopaedia was presented to President Roosevelt at his inauguration in 1941. The Google of his day, Mee had revolutionised home-school learning. Together with his researchers, he popularised general knowledge in ways they thought patriotic and optimistic, using writing that was influenced by both the Bible's teachings and Mee's distorted version of Darwinism. This first edition contained an illustration depicting a controversial "racial hierarchy" that was removed in later editions. The encyclopaedia was known to favour the fascinating over the factual, such as the idea that lemmings throw themselves off cliffs, a myth that originated in *The Children's Encyclopaedia*. Other writing proved prophetic. Mee told his readers that they would one day carry telephones in their pockets.

In 1914 Arthur Mee moved to Eynsford, near Sevenoaks, to a house he'd commissioned and would live in for the rest of his life. The family's garden featured a children's "garden of knowledge".

Mee founded *The Children's Newspaper* in 1919, which he continued to edit along with his encyclopaedia. His other children's publications included *Arthur Mee's Gift for Boys and Girls who Love the Flag* (1917), *The Children's Bible* (1924), *The Children's Shakespeare* (1933), and *Arthur Mee's 1000 Heroes* (1933). The British Library has over 400 works attributed to Mee. In addition to writing for children he produced biographies and travel books, as well as *1940: Our finest hour* (1940) and *Immortal Dawn* (1941), published while his only child Margorie was serving as a member of a voluntary aid detachment.

Mee's final project was a guide to *The King's England*, a series of guidebooks he'd started in 1936. Aiming to become 'a new Domesday Book of 10,000 towns and villages,' the series romanticised the English countryside. Nottinghamshire gets an edition (copies are in the libraries). The King's England Press, founded in

1989, reprinted this historical series. Mee wrote that '[Stapleford] was a quiet village' but has now 'given away its rural charm and accepted its place in industry.' And on Nottingham: 'She is the Queen of the Midlands, and is making herself more beautiful than ever.'

Having twice refused the offer of a knighthood, Arthur Mee died unexpectedly in 1943, aged sixty-eight, following an operation at King's College Hospital in London. In his office safe was a copy of his obituary, written several years earlier by his former editor in Nottingham, John Derry, who described Mee as 'one of the most successful journalists in the world.'

So popular were Mee's *Children's Encyclopaedia* and *Newspaper* that they continued to be revised and published decades after his death. Though his work may be romanticised, sentimental, and occasionally unpalatable, his young readers saw him as a friend and his influence was wide-ranging. Enid Blyton read and reread *The Children's Encyclopaedia* and, aged eleven, she entered a poem into a competition in Mee's monthly *My Magazine,* which resulted in her poem being published.

In the 1970s, Arthur Mee was played by Terry Jones in a 1972 episode of *Monty Python's Flying Circus.* Not bad for a lad from Stabbo.

Chapter 77
Thrumpton Hall – An Obsession

> 'May your Paths be safe, your Floors unbroken and may the House fill your eyes with Beauty.'
>
> Susanna Clarke, *Piranesi*

Thrumpton Hall.

The small village of Thrumpton, originally called Turmodeston, is known for its grand English country house on the south bank of the Trent. A turreted gatehouse and long driveway lead to the mansion, constructed with rosy bricks and crowned with curved stone gables. It's the place that Miranda Seymour calls home. The author was two years old when her parents moved into Thrumpton Hall, her father, George FitzRoy Seymour, the tenth Lord Byron's nephew, had embarked on a lifelong obsession with the house some twenty-five years earlier, growing up at Thrumpton and spending the war years there with his aunt and uncle.

Miranda Seymour first wrote novels in her twenties, often featuring grand residences. After her father's death she realised that he too had written stories of beautiful homes after she found them unpublished and assembled in a file. Discovering her father's diaries and many letters, Seymour decided to write a family memoir, *In My Father's House*, charting her eccentric father's life which, in his later years, saw him take up the riding of motorbikes around the countryside, clad in black leather and in the company of a young male friend. The book was published in America as *Thrumpton Hall*, winning the 2008 Pen Ackerley Prize for Memoir of the Year.

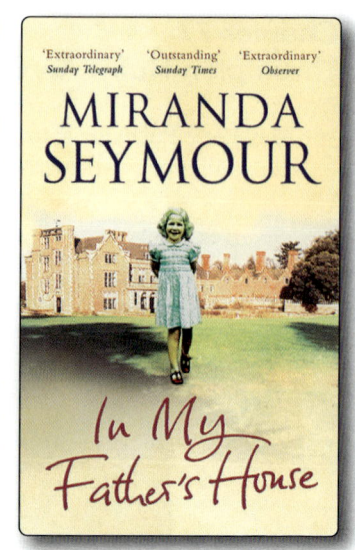

'I can never hope to banish my father's presence from the house that possessed his heart. I can make my peace by trying to understand what made him the man he was,' wrote Miranda Seymour. *In My Father's House* is dedicated to her husband, Ted Lynch, who lives with her at Thrumpton Hall.

Seymour has written many successful biographies – of Lady Ottoline Morrell, Mary Shelley, Robert Graves and, in 2022, Jean Rhys – as well as children's books and several historical novels, including *Count Manfred*, which weaves together Byron's life with the story of the Nottinghamshire riots. The ubiquitous Lord Byron has had a presence in the life of Thrumpton, too.

The actor Dennis Price, when playing Lord Byron in the film *The Bad Lord Byron*, visited Thrumpton Hall in 1948. Between shoots at Newstead Abbey, Price was sent to appease Thrumpton's owner, the seventy-eight-year-old Rev Lord Byron, who was unhappy with the film's title. It was arranged that the vicar would watch a rough copy of the film, and discuss the title with its director Sydney Box, only Rev Lord Byron was too ill. 'It was in this year that I was born,' Seymour told me, 'and apparently I had the honour of spending a few minutes lying in Mr Price's arms.'

Dennis Price may be the first esteemed guest whose company Miranda Seymour shared, but he's not the last. Many writers became familiar with Thrumpton as the author built up a large circle of literary friends. When she was Visiting Professor at Nottingham Trent University, she arranged for many of them to speak at events there. Writers received at Thrumpton Hall include several associated with the Booker Prize: Pat Barker (*The Ghost Road*, Booker Prize winner 1995), Alan Hollinghurst (*The Line of Beauty*, Booker Prize winner 2004), Michael Frayn (*Headlong*, shortlisted 1999), Alan Judd (*A Breed of Heroes*, shortlisted 1981), and Michèle Roberts (*Daughters of the House*, shortlisted 1992).

Seymour also welcomed fellow biographers Michael Holroyd (*Bernard Shaw*), Kathryn Hughes (*George Eliot: The Last Victorian*), Claire Tomalin (*Charles Dickens: A Life*) and Fiona MacCarthy (*Byron: Life and Legend*), as well as the novelist Paul Mendez, poet Alan Jenkins, critic and satirist Craig Brown, novelist and screenwriter Deborah Moggach, and a certain Alan Sillitoe, who was another to give talks at NTU.

Sillitoe often visited Thrumpton Hall with his wife, the poet Ruth Fainlight, both being long-term friends of Seymour's, who told me:

> Alan was adoring of Thrumpton. He often talked to me about his cycle rides along the roads over Barton Moor, soon to become a new town, and what a huge inspiration it was to him. That was back in the days when he worked at the Raleigh factory. He gave me a map from Russia that showed Nottinghamshire when they planned to bomb the county's industrial sites during the cold war.

Over a century before Sillitoe set eyes on Thrumpton, another of Nottinghamshire's most celebrated writers was here – Ada, Countess Lovelace. The mathematician and pioneering computer programmer, and Lord Byron's daughter, visited her relations at Thrumpton Hall from her mother's home at Kirkby Mallory.

Miranda Seymour wrote about Ada and Lady Byron (Anne Isabella Milbanke) in her 2018 award-winning double biography, *In Byron's Wake*. The book reveals the ways in which Byron, long after his death, continued to shape the turbulent lives and reputations both of his wife and his daughter. In researching the book, Seymour uncovered some personal connections. 'I was fascinated to discover that Ada visited Thrumpton in 1850, while paying her first ever visit to Newstead,' said Seymour. 'Ada's favourite cousin George (later the eighth Lord Byron) had married a family friend, Lucy Wescomb, with whose family he and his brother had travelled out to Geneva, to see where *Frankenstein* had been conceived and where Byron had lived in 1816. Ada's visit resulted in the bringing of a sprig of the famous Byron oak to Thrumpton.'

The sprig has fared much better than Byron's oak, the classic oak tree a duplicate of the one from which it came. 'I'm about to send a cutting out to Euboea,' said Seymour, 'where Ada's relatives still live on land bought by Lady Byron in the 1830s for her young cousin Edward Noel, in a tribute to her husband's Greek connection.'

A tree from the Newstead acorn is impressive enough, but there are many more Byron-related gems inside the property. As the author explains, 'We have a box of Byron treasures which were given by Ada to her cousin. These include a fragment of the hanging from Byron's bed at Newstead, and a bit of the hangings from his honeymoon bed at Halnaby (a house belonging to his wife's family). We also have a strand of Byron's hair and a pair of Ada's court gloves in white kid.'

There's also an inscribed first copy of Byron's poem, *Childe Harold's Pilgrimage*; a fragment of the flag which he famously carried on his journey to fight in Greece; and Byron's signet ring. 'The ring is by far my favourite,' said Seymour. 'It's the first ring ever made for Byron that carries the Byron crest and motto (*Crede Byron*). He had many rings, but this was for his hand as a boy, so it's tiny. I often wear it.'

Thrumpton Hall's library contains original reviews of Byron's poetry among its 5,000 volumes, including the *Quarterly Review*, the *Edinburgh Review* and *Blackwood's*, in bound copies dating back to the 1780s. The library and Baronial Hall are two of the most impressive rooms at Thrumpton, but it is its famous staircase that attracts the most interest. Carved in wood from the estate, and supervised by John Webb, a pupil of Inigo

The Gatehouse, Thrumpton Hall.

Jones, the sweeping cantilever Jacobean staircase is a standout structure.

More of Thrumpton's glory is found in its spectacular landscaped gardens, part of which date to the seventeenth century. The house itself goes back a century earlier, when it belonged to the Powdrills, a Roman Catholic family. The Powdrills forfeited the house and the land after being involved in the Babington Plot to kill Queen Elizabeth and put her cousin, Mary, Queen of Scots, on the English throne. The plot is named after the young man that hatched it, Anthony Babington, the Powdrills' neighbour.

Following the fall of the Powdrills, the socially ambitious and politically amoral Pigotts took over. The second Gervase Pigott used his wife's fortune to transform the house, removing much of the interior and creating the magnificent staircase and a reception room overlooking a formal garden. Ambition ruined the Pigotts. Unable to maintain the mortgage payments to their lawyer, Mr Emerton, they sold the estate to him in 1685.

By 1820, Thrumpton was held by the last of the Emertons, John, a bachelor, said to be the most handsome man in Nottinghamshire. His lavish improvements included the creation of the library, the lake in front of the house, and the landscaped park. It was his seventeen-year-old niece, Lucy Wescomb, that became heir to the estate in 1840, inheriting it three years later. She married George, the eighth Lord Byron and, whilst they had no children, the estate was to remain in the hands of the Byron family for over a hundred years. Lucy may have refused to allow the village to have a pub, still missing to this day, but she did oversee the period in its history that brought most of the fascinating Byron relics to the house, and she welcomed Ada Lovelace on her visits to Nottinghamshire.

As George, the ninth Lord Byron, had no children, the estate passed sideways to his brother Frederick, a vicar, and the tenth Lord Byron, in 1917. The novelist Cecil Roberts visited that Lord Byron at Thrumpton Hall when the reverend was sixty. Roberts (1970) wrote that, 'He was the only man I ever knew who could approach a peacock, stroke its head and cause it to expand its gorgeous tail feathers.' Thrumpton's peacocks were later known to scratch at their reflections in the polished side panels of cars, with guests' black Rolls Royces being a prime target.

Nearly thirty years after his visit, Roberts returned to open a church garden fete. He met a young couple now living there, striving to keep the place going by opening it up to visitors. That couple were Miranda Seymour's parents. The tenth Lord Byron had married Anna, who became Lady Anna FitzRoy. Their nephew was the Thrumpton-obsessed George FitzRoy Seymour, but the house was due to be sold, leaving George heartbroken. Thrumpton Hall was taken off the market for a year in 1945, as a solution was sought. Might the house even be left to a Byron cousin? George was frantic. 'I'd do anything to save Thrumpton,' he wrote. 'I realise now that it means more to me than anything else in the world.'

At this point, the tenth Lord Byron died, and George's devout aunt Anna offered the gift of life tenancy, if George could find £50,000 for the decrepit mansion. Bachelor George's luck was in when he met Rosemary Scott-Ellis, unmarried daughter of the wealthy Lord Howard de Walden. You might think he pursued her for the money, but his letters show otherwise. This was a love story. And what luck, his new wife shared his love of Thrumpton Hall.

George and Rosemary secured the house in 1949, a year after their first child, Miranda, was born. In 1950 they moved in, spending half a century restoring and preserving the near-derelict property. It was George's vision. His house.

George reached for a grander life than they could afford. With no household staff, parties had George offering his guests a drink then disappearing upstairs to arrange the rooms, with Rosemary doing the cooking and washing up. It was a real team effort. Rosemary lived at Thrumpton for seventy years and for many of those she looked after a four-acre garden singlehandedly. She was just Rosemary to everyone. Very kind, very beloved. She died in 2018 and is buried in Thrumpton's churchyard.

Miranda Seymour became the owner of Thrumpton Hall after her father's death in 1994. Back in 1950 George Seymour had begun opening the house and gardens to raise money through the National Garden Scheme for Macmillan and Marie Curie, and Seymour maintains these fundraising efforts to this day. Over the years she has had help from a range of sources, including Alan Sillitoe.

Seymour has increasingly taken on her father's causes, and weddings have provided a welcome income for the house. The wedding business has now closed and other changes are afoot, with Miranda Seymour's son taking over the administration and Thrumpton Hall now being run as a family collective.

The estate owns thirteen beautiful old properties in the village, all lovingly curated. The old village schoolroom and separate schoolhouse were designed and paid for by Ada Lovelace's cousin and his wife. Seymour and her father both attended the village school, and she told me, 'My dad's last wish was that we would return these lovely Victorian buildings to their old form, with the schoolroom entrance back in place, and bury the disgraceful past.'

That "disgraceful past" refers back to the 1970s when a local photographer lived in the old schoolhouse and opened up the deserted schoolroom as a photographic studio for "naughty pix" as Seymour calls them. 'Everybody knew,' she said, 'including my dad, who was rather excited by it all.'

In a last contribution as owner before her son took over, Miranda Seymour honoured her father's dying wish and oversaw the restoration of the schoolhouse, returning the two buildings to their former separate state.

Thrumpton continues to offer tours of the estate and hold charitable events, in addition to hosting yoga, painting and writing retreats. But it's not all rosy. 'Currently, our greatest fear is that the lack of flood protection will make the house unsustainable,' said Seymour. 'The levels are rising due to the lack of protection on the riverbanks and to the erosion of the old banks in the area near to the railway.'

As one of Nottinghamshire's finest historic homes, let's hope Thrumpton Hall can remain a thriving location for centuries to come.

Chapter 78
University of Nottingham –
A Special Collection

"...that Nottingham lights would rise and say by Boots: I am M.A. ..."

DH Lawrence, *Nottingham's New University*

Highfield House, University of Nottingham.

Highfield House was built in 1797 for Joseph Lowe, thrice Mayor of Nottingham. Over the following decade Lowe and his son Alfred carried out the landscaping that has formed much of the existing Highfields Park. The Highfield estate remained with the Lowes for several generations.

Joseph Lowe's great-grandson, Edward Joseph Lowe (1825–1900), was born at Highfield House. At the age of fifteen he began making meteorological observations and later gained a prominent reputation as an astronomer, botanist and scientist.[1] A Fellow of the Royal Society, Lowe wrote papers on a wide variety of subjects, including luminous meteors, sunspots and his meteorological observations, publishing *A Treatise on Atmospheric Phenomena* (1846), helping to shape human understanding of the Earth's atmosphere. His interest in ferns, grasses and other plants led to his most noted work, *Ferns: British and Exotic* (1856), which consisted of eight illustrated volumes. Known as "Big Snowflake" because of his beard, Lowe was one of Nottinghamshire's most eminent scientists. There is a blue plaque commemorating Lowe's life and work at Broadgate House, Beeston, the home and observatory he had built in the early 1850s.

Highfield House was sold by the Lowes in 1881. It passed through various hands until it was bought by Sir Jesse Boot in 1919. He then purchased the surrounding buildings and their land. A few years later, whilst living in Jersey, Boot learned of plans for the development of Nottingham's University College. He said, 'From all I hear, the university extension movement seems to be making but little progress. I do not like to think that my native city should fall in any way short of other large towns.'

Broadgate House, Beeston.

Sir Jesse decided to split his Highfields site, and he gifted land above the lake for the establishment of a new East Midlands University, largely funding the project himself. The new University College building (today known as the Trent Building) was designed and built between 1922 and 1928, with the addition of a new road system and an improved park to the south. The original Highfields House became part of the campus.

Morley Horder, a designer of Boots' outlets – including Nottingham's first "wonderstore" branch – planned University College's palace of education, the Trent Building, with its iconic tower, which was opened by King George V. Over the course of ten years, Sir Jesse Boot gave donations totalling over £440,000 (over £9,000,000 in today's money). It was a further twenty years before independent university status was bestowed upon what is now the University of Nottingham.

In 1929, perhaps having read Rolf Gardiner's report of the new building, DH Lawrence wrote a disparaging poem in *Pansies* (1929), entitled "Nottingham's New University". It began:

> In Nottingham, that dismal town
> where I went to school and college,
> they've built a new university
> for a new dispensation of knowledge.
> Built it most grand and cakeily
> out of the noble loot
> derived from shrewd cash-chemistry
> by good Sir Jesse Boot.

Gardiner described Lawrence's poem as '...an excellent bit of Lawrencian buffoonery, to be recited with gusto!'

Pansies, its title derived from the French "pensées" meaning thoughts, attracted the attention of the Home Office on grounds of indecency, and typescripts of the poems were intercepted by postal workers.

Following his donated "noble loot", Sir Jesse Boot was elevated to the peerage and named the first Lord Trent. South of the lake, at Highfield Park's entrance, is Charles Doman's bust of the benefactor, erected in 1934.

Near the University's Hallward Library is a full-size statue of DH Lawrence. Created by the sculptor Diana Thomson, the statue depicts Lawrence holding a blue gentian flower, referencing his poem "Bavarian Gentians". The statue is often to be found decorated by students! Lawrence trained as a teacher at University College, and it was at that time that he experimented with poetry and short stories, and wrote a version of his first novel.

Jesse Boot's bust, University of Nottingham.

The University's Manuscripts and Special Collections (from now on abbreviated to M&SC) owns a study notebook of Lawrence's from 1910, containing draft versions of his poems. This is one of many items in the University's Lawrence collections, covering all aspects of his life and work including published and archival writings, photographs, biographies and critical literature.

DH Lawrence's statue, University of Nottingham.

It took decades for the University to acknowledge and celebrate Lawrence due to a loyalty to Professor Ernest Weekley, whose wife had left him for the young writer. It wasn't until Weekley died in 1954 that the University finally recognised Lawrence. An exhibition was held in 1960, which one newspaper covered with the headline, "With Apologies to a Genius". That exhibition, DH Lawrence After Thirty Years 1930–1960, held accompanying lectures, including one by the University's own Department of English professor, Vivian de Sola Pinto, a champion of Lawrence's work. Pinto appeared for the defence in the famous trial of *Lady Chatterley's Lover* in 1960. Penguin had wanted to publish a set of works by Lawrence to commemorate the thirtieth anniversary of his death, and they took advantage of the Obscene Publications Act, which stated that any book considered obscene by some, but that could be shown to have redeeming social merit, might still be published. Penguin sent twelve copies of the banned book to the Director of Public Prosecutions, challenging him to prosecute. He did, leading to a trial at the Old Bailey that gripped the nation. Professor Pinto was one of the defence's thirty-five witnesses, including leading literary figures. An eyewitness described the trial as a 'circus so hilarious, fascinating, tense and satisfying that none who sat through all its six days will ever forget them.' Penguin won, allowing publication of the unexpunged version of *Lady Chatterley's Lover*.

Supporting Pinto in the promoting of Lawrence's work at the University and collecting Lawrence-related material for the archives was Lawrence's boyhood friend Jonathan "David" Chambers, who was a Professor of History at the University.

Another of the University's DH Lawrence exhibitions, A Phoenix in Flight, was opened by Philip Larkin in 1980. He purchased a Lawrence T-shirt which he'd wear whenever he mowed his lawn.[2] Larkin was a firm admirer of Lawrence, and his poem "The Explosion" was partly inspired by the author's description of mining communities. In 1985, Larkin was back for a Lawrence centenary festival, A Life in Literature.

Over three and a half million documents are housed in the M&SC in a converted television studio on the University's King's Meadow Campus. They include donations from writers, such as the Stephen Lowe collection: around sixty box files of his scripts, publicity material, tapes, photos and letters. The Sneinton-born playwright was awarded an honorary doctorate by the University in 2011.

The M&SC has a large number of rare publications, including first or early editions of works by notable local writers including Lord Byron, whose life and work has been commemorated with a series of high-quality memorial lectures, Muriel Hine, Hilda Lewis, James Prior, Cecil Roberts, JC Snaith, Geoffrey Trease and Dorothy Whipple.

There is a letter from Mary Howitt to her sister, plus a copy of the short-lived *Howitt's Journal*. There is also one of Henry Kirke White's legal notebooks c1800, which has a summary of his studies alongside verses of his poetry.

Another notebook in storage belonged to Stanley Middleton, containing a handwritten draft of *Beginning to End*. Middleton contributed stories and poetry to the student magazine *The Gong*, for which he later became an editor. *The Gong* ran intermittently from 1895 to 1995, publishing poetry, prose and art.

M&SC has research notes c1940 on the lace trade, compiled by Hilda Lewis for her historical novel *Penny Lace* (1946). Lewis' husband was Professor M Michael Lewis, a specialist in the education of the deaf. A lecturer in education at University College, Dr Lewis was later appointed Director of the Institute of Education. His work inspired his wife's novel, *The Day is Ours* (1946), about a young deaf girl, a book which formed the basis of the film *Mandy*.

M&SC also hold a copy of *The Trent: a record of friendship*, the long poem for which a young Cecil Roberts won the Kirke White Memorial Prize. Here's an extract:

> Yes, poet though you would be, or you are,
> You answer to a chord which stirs us all,
> And, could I speak in song, I would express
> The joyous beauty of this river Trent.

Some of these items were displayed as part of the University's Collected Words Exhibition, held in 2017 at the Lakeside Arts Centre's Weston Gallery. Taking part in the event was the author Alison Moore, who had previously worked as an assistant to the director of Lakeside before becoming a full-time writer and honorary lecturer at the University. Moore's debut novel, *The Lighthouse* (2012), was shortlisted for the Booker Prize.

BS Johnson's *The Unfortunates* (1969) takes the form of memories of his friendship with Anthony ("Tony") Tillinghast, a University of Nottingham student and academic, whose early death from cancer had a profound effect on Johnson and inspired his "Nottingham" novel. Johnson met Tillinghast in the late 1950s when he came here to assist him with the editing of a new inter-university magazine, *Universities' Poetry*. Tillinghast also edited *The Gong*.

The Gong isn't the only University publication its students have written for. There's *Scribble*, edited by Andrew Bailey, winner of the 1996 Kirke White Prize for poetry, *Pulp*, and current outputs: *Impact*, *Her Campus* and *The Letters Page*.

The Letters Page is edited by Professor Jon McGregor and produced by the Creative Writing section of the School of English. Students gain editing and publishing experience through this literary journal which publishes essays, stories, poetry, memoir, travelogue, and criticism; all in the form of letters. Each new edition puts out a call for submissions, and letters have been received from Naomi Alderman, George Saunders, Joanna Walsh and Colum McCann. These have been added to the M&SC's Letters Page Archive, placed alongside other collections of letters by leading literary figures such as Percy Shelley and Philip Larkin.

Jon McGregor was the youngest contender for the Booker Prize when his first novel, *If Nobody Speaks of Remarkable Things* (2002), was long-listed. He won the IMPAC Dublin Literary Award for *Even the Dogs* (2010), and his fourth novel, *Reservoir 13* (2017), won the Costa Novel Award. His latest book, published in 2021, is the novel *Lean Fall Stand*.

The Creative Writing MA explores contemporary writing and its hybrid forms. Other lecturers on the course include the poet Matthew Welton, the novelist and playwright Thomas Legendre, poet and editor Lila Matsumoto and the author Spencer Jordan.

The university celebrated ten years of its Creative Writing MA and BA in 2021. One of their success stories is the novelist Clare Harvey, an alumna of the MA course, who has fond memories of the 'hours spent discussing books with her tutor and a handful of other writing-nerds in a tiny room beneath the University clock tower.' She told me:

> My debut novel, *The Gunner Girl*, which began as MA coursework, not only bagged me an agent and a deal with a major publisher, but also went on to win both the Exeter Novel Prize and the Joan Hessayon Award for new fiction. Moreover, the discipline I learnt as

an MA student (wordcounts and deadlines, responding to criticism) stood me in good stead for the rigours of a career as a published author.

In addition to Clare Harvey, DH Lawrence, Stanley Middleton and others mentioned above, the University of Nottingham has many literary figures among its alumni. There's the poet and crime writer John Harvey, who took an MA in American Studies here and briefly taught Film and American Literature. In 2009, Harvey was awarded an Honorary Degree, making him a Doctor of Letters.

Jonathan Emmett developed his writing and illustration skills when studying Architecture at the University in the mid-1980s. A decade later he pursued a career in children's literature and now has over sixty children's books to his name.

The multi-award-winning poet, novelist and scholar Meena Alexander (1951–2018) achieved a PhD in Romantic Literature with a dissertation that was later developed and published as *The Poetic Self: Towards a Phenomenology of Romanticism* (1980).

Christopher Bigsby came here for his PhD (1964–6) and has since published over fifty books including a two-volume biography of Arthur Miller and books on Joe Orton and David Mamet.

Trent Building and boating lake, University of Nottingham.

The novelist and non-fiction writer Michael Bracewell graduated in English and American Studies. The screenwriter and producer Michael Hirst received a first-class degree in English and American Literature. Blake Morrison, whose best-known works are the memoirs *And When Did You Last See Your Father?* (2007) and *Things My Mother Never Told Me* (2002), studied English Literature. Emma Barnett, presenter of BBC *Women's Hour* and *Newsnight*, graduated with a degree in History and Politics, and is the author of *Period* (2019), in which she draws on female experiences and attitudes to menstruation. And Nottingham UNESCO City of Literature's first Young Poet Laureate, Georgina Wilding, graduated in 2015 with a first-class degree in Creative and Professional Writing.

The first (and so far, only!) Poet Laureate for Nottinghamshire was Adrian Buckner in 1999, who used to write a weekly article on poetry for the *Evening Post*. Buckner edited *Poetry Nottingham*, renamed *Assent*, from 2004–2013, and he worked in the University's Creative Writing department, on the Creative and Professional Writing course that arose out of Adult Education and the WEA.

Many of the University's lecturers have been published writers, including the Northern Irish poet Tom Paulin who worked at the University from 1972 to 1994, first as a lecturer in English and then as a Reader of Poetry, and, more recently, Chris Leavers, a lecturer in the School of Geography, who explores the animal kingdom in *Why Elephants Have Big Ears* (2001).

Since 2009, the University's Off the Page events have welcomed notable speakers, not least their inaugural guest, Roddy Doyle. Organised by the Creative Writing lecturers, these talks, readings and conversations are often open to members of the public.

Professor John Beckett has written a book about the University of Nottingham, from its early days as University College in 1881 to 2016. It's called *Nottingham: a history of Britain's global university*.

---

[1]Mellors, 1916.
[2]Thwaite, 1992.

Chapter 79
Welbeck Abbey – Going Underground

'Without our histories we are vacated.'
Mick Jackson, *The Underground Man*

Welbeck Abbey.

Welbeck Abbey has been the home to some fascinating characters that have inspired classic fiction. Originally a twelfth-century monastery, Welbeck Abbey in north Nottinghamshire has been a Cavalier residence and an army training college – visited by Bill Bryson, see *Notes from a Small Island* (1995) – but it's best known for being home to the Dukes of Portland and their families.

In 1854 William John Cavendish-Scott-Bentinck (1800–79), the Marquis of Titchfield, became the Fifth Duke of Portland. The title gave him a seat in the House of Lords, and he was later made Deputy Lord Lieutenant of Nottinghamshire. The eccentric aristocrat commissioned a vast building programme that included the construction of a labyrinth of tunnels. A lonely, self-isolated man, the fifth duke employed 1,500 people to fulfil his designs for a mysterious underground system that enabled him to move around in privacy and access the local railway without being seen. Ranging from a pigsty to a grand ballroom, the many subterranean spaces were ingeniously ventilated and lighted by either gas or natural skylight. The duke also built the world's second largest riding school with tunnels specifically designed for his hundred horses to exercise.

The duke would usually access his underground living areas via a trap-door, denying staff knowledge of his whereabouts. He could then pop up unannounced to check on his workforce. Archard (1907) wrote that:

> It was no uncommon thing for the Duke to rise up out of a tunnel and appear in the midst of a gang of workmen when they were little expecting him, and when, perhaps, they were idling their time, or making uncomplimentary remarks about him.

The duke wore a tall silk hat with a broad brim and a long brown cape, and walked around with an umbrella, all making him stand out, and yet he remained virtually withdrawn from observation. This inadvertently encouraged visiting onlookers, who would try to catch sight of him as if he was a rare bird. Opposed to company, he would write down his orders, then ring a bell for a servant to come and read his demands. Food arrived warm on a miniature railway track that came direct from the underground kitchens.

His Grace was a committed reader, taking all the national and provincial daily issues and weekly journals. These were hoarded, making up the largest private collection outside the British Museum. 'Though His Grace took no active part in politics, he exhibited, amid the magnificent solitude of Welbeck, a very keen interest in matters of national importance, and current literature found its way into his hands,' wrote Jacks (1881). Among the interesting artefacts in the library/gallery at Welbeck Abbey is an autographed letter from Mary Queen of Scots, signed 'Your very good friend,' and the large pearl drop earrings worn by Charles I throughout his life, including on the morning of his execution.

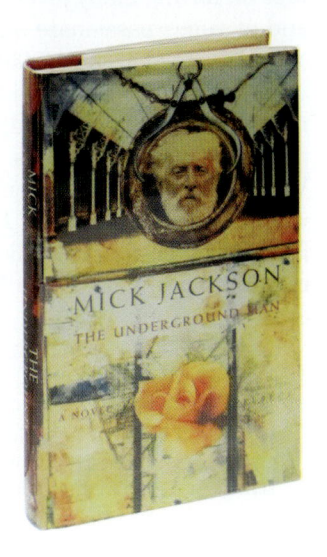

The Duke of Portland died in 1879, but the enigmatic aristocrat continues to intrigue. Mick Jackson's 1997 debut novel, *The Underground Man,* is a fictionalised diary based on the life of the fifth duke. In the book His Grace has finished his network of tunnels and is in reflective mood. It's a darkly comic character study and was shortlisted for the Booker Prize.

Nottingham playwright Nick Wood adapted Jackson's novel for the stage. *The Underground Man* was performed at Nottingham Playhouse in 2016. Together with the director Andrew Breakwell and cast (Mick Jasper and Iain Armstrong, one playing the Duke, the other playing his valet-cum-butler and all the other characters), Wood spent five days at Welbeck Abbey developing the play. He has described the Duke as, 'a man of great intelligence; he was confronting great changes, both in terms of science and with the certainties of religion being overthrown.'

Another inspirational literary figure is Lady Ottoline Morrell (1873–1938). If six-year-old Ottoline Cavendish-Bentinck's father had expected to succeed his cousin, the Fifth Duke of Portland, he was to be disappointed. Instead, it was to be Ottoline's half-brother William that took over the dukedom, with Ottoline still given the title "Lady". Her family immediately moved into Welbeck Abbey, where she grew up and later wrote of riding through Welbeck's 'great oaks and grass rides.'

Lady Ottoline grew to be six feet tall and with her flamboyant style and long red hair she cut a striking figure. She initially left Welbeck Abbey as a teenager and, in 1902, married the Liberal MP Philip Morrell, an open marriage that Lady Ottoline took advantage of, having many lovers, both male and female, including a long and at times passionate affair with Bertrand Russell, with whom she exchanged around 3,000 letters.

Most of her lovers were from her circle of friends that included many authors, artists, sculptors and poets. Lady Ottoline regularly played host to members of the Bloomsbury Group, including Virginia Woolf, and she entertained WB Yeats and TS Eliot. She was also a good friend of DH Lawrence, who depicted her as the fearsome Hermione Roddice in *Women in Love* (1920), 'the most remarkable woman in the Midlands.' Morrell was mortified by the characterisation.

This is how Lawrence introduces her:

> One of them she knew, a tall, slow, reluctant woman with a weight of fair hair and a pale, long face. This was Hermione Roddice, a friend of the Criches. Now she came along, with her head held up, balancing an enormous flat hat of pale yellow velvet, on which were

streaks of ostrich feathers, natural and grey. She drifted forward as if scarcely conscious, her long blanched face lifted up, not to see the world. She was rich. She wore a dress of silky, frail velvet, of pale yellow colour, and she carried a lot of small rose-coloured cyclamens. Her shoes and stockings were of brownish grey, like the feathers on her hat, her hair was heavy, she drifted along with a peculiar fixity of the hips, a strange unwilling motion. She was impressive, in her lovely pale-yellow and brownish-rose, yet macabre, something repulsive. People were silent when she passed, impressed, roused, wanting to jeer, yet for some reason silenced. Her long, pale face, that she carried lifted up, somewhat in the Rossetti fashion, seemed almost drugged, as if a strange mass of thoughts coiled in the darkness within her, and she was never allowed to escape.

We know from Lady Ottoline's two volumes of memoirs and her journals that at the end of 1914 and in early 1915 she read some 'very remarkable books': Lawrence's *The Prussian Officer* (1914), *Sons and Lovers* (1913) and *The White Peacock* (1911) among others. She described their 'scenes of which were laid in Nottinghamshire, and they had stirred up my early memories, which had lain dry and curled up'.[1]

After being 'excited and moved' by Lawrence's books, Ottoline wanted to get to know him, and did so through their mutual friend, the writer Gilbert Cannan. On a visit to Sussex to see Lawrence and his wife Frieda, Ottoline was 'extraordinarily happy and at ease,' adding, 'We at once went back to our memories of Nottinghamshire. We talked of the lovely wild commons, of Sherwood Forest, of the dark pit villages, of the lives of the colliers and their wives.' She appreciated the fact that Lawrence spoke to her in the Nottinghamshire dialect.

For three decades Lady Ottoline was London's leading literary hostess and, despite some snide comments from members of the Bloomsbury Group, she leaves an impressive literary legacy. Her influence came in many forms, as she was a lover, confidante, advisor, critic and mother figure to the writers she inspired.

A young Aldous Huxley described Lady Ottoline as having given him 'a complete mental re-orientation,' and he based his character Mrs Bidlake – from *Point Counter Point* (1928) – on her. She is said to have been the inspiration for Lady Caroline Bury in Graham Greene's *It's a Battlefield* (1934), and for Lady Sybilline Quarrell in Alan Bennett's 1968 play *Forty Years On*.

After her mother died, Lady Ottoline returned to Welbeck Abbey. Taking her ponies out on the 'dark dreary roads with their black hedges,' she described how she would 'feel excited and even a little nervous' when meeting groups of colliers returning from the pit, adding:

> These men, tall, black and mysterious, appeared rather fierce yet full of laughter and fun, joking together as they hurried pell-mell along the dark roads to tea, the grey winter light, a gleam of setting yellow sun behind them.

Ottoline Morrell: Life on the Grand Scale is a 1992 biography by Nottinghamshire author Miranda Seymour. The book benefits from Seymour's access to family papers, which include Lady Ottoline's "lost" correspondence with Lytton Strachey and the revealing private records she kept from her marriage until her death.

Lady Ottoline Morrell is buried in Nottinghamshire near Welbeck Abbey at St Winifred Churchyard in Holbeck. There is a memorial to her on the north aisle wall of St Winifred's Church by Eric Gill (1939).

---

[1]Gathorne-Hardy, 1974.

Chapter 80
Wilford Grove – Write by the River

'Who ever saw Wilford without wishing to become an inmate of one of its peaceful woodbined homes.'

Spencer T Hall

Kirke White's gazebo, St. Wilfrid's Church, Wilford Village.

An attrative Trentside aspect with idyllic woodland, Wilford Grove and its neighbour, Clifton Grove, attracted many a visitor from Nottingham and beyond. The area was a magnet for poets seeking inspiration and a place to write. In the words of Robert Mellors (1914), 'The spirit of poetry actively glided between Nottingham and Wilford for fifty years.'

It was in the churchyard of St Wilfrid's that teenage poet Henry Kirke White wrote his verse, inside a brick octagonal gazebo overlooking the Trent. The gazebo is still standing, and within it is a tired plaque that reads:

Wilford Gazebo
c1757
Listed historic building.
Built as a 'summerhouse'.
Associated with poet Henry Kirke White.
The basement was used as a mortuary
for river drownings.
Burnt out 1976.
Restored as a preserved structure
by community industry 1980.

Afflicted with tuberculosis, the young poet came to Wilford Grove for a month's leave of absence from the Bridlesmith Gate attorneys Coldham and Enfield. His repose was taken in the room of a little cottage opposite Wilford House, within the extended grounds of the church. To aid his recovery and provide uninterrupted study, he had chosen Wilford, as opposed to a sojourn on the coast, because it was close to his home in Nottingham and it was a peaceful place he loved, where he loved to write poetry. He was in poor health but 'determined not to leave the world without making myself known in literature,' he wrote.[1]

Wilford House.

In the midst of his painful, tiresome illness, when he couldn't walk ten yards before his knees buckled, Kirke White wrote to his mother, requesting that when he dies, he should be buried in the Wilford churchyard:

Here would I wish to sleep. This is the spot
Which I have long mark'd out to lay my bones in...

Inside the Grade II listed church of St Wilfrid's are two memorials to Kirke White, taking the form of a stained-glass window and a marble plaque of the poet in portrait. Based on his poem, *The Star of Bethlehem*, O'Connor's memorial window depicts a Nativity scene. Religion was important to the young poet, who attended Cambridge to pursue a career in the church, "Oft in danger, oft in woe", is his best-known hymn.

Clifton Grove was the subject of the longest poem in Kirke White's first short volume, *Clifton Grove, a sketch in verse with other poems* (1803), which contains the line: 'Bespeak, best Clifton! thy sublime domain.'

He adored Clifton Grove, writing:

These are thy charms;
the joys which these impart
Bind thee Best Clifton
close around my heart.

Clifton Grove.

Kirke White's principal poem incorporated the legend of the Fair Maid of Clifton, which told of a Clifton milkmaid, 'the beauteous Margaret,' as he called her. He also used the story in his ballad "O, The Fair Maid of Clifton". The story goes that Margaret, who lived here during the War of the Roses, had promised to wait for her sweetheart, a Wilford ferryman called Bateman, who had spent three years abroad. On his return, Bateman was distraught to discover that she'd been married for six months, having sold herself for wealth. He promptly drowned himself in the Trent. After giving birth, Margaret was dragged by vengeful spirits into the river, 'to the yawning wave, her own and murdered lover's mutual grave.'

The joys of the Groves aided Kirke White's health, and he recovered enough to follow his religious calling, attending St John's College, Cambridge. Family and friends provided money for his studies. Amongst those benefactors was the politician William Wilberforce (1759–1833), who contributed twenty pounds to Kirke White's education. Wilberforce had been a regular guest at Wilford House – the seat of his uncle, Abel Smith, of the Smith family of bankers – and he was here for several months between 1786 and 1789, when he would have been drawing up his first bill to abolish the transatlantic slave trade. Wilford House was later home to the Forman-Hardy family, who owned and ran the *Nottingham Evening Post* until 1994.

Once in Cambridge, Kirke White's health deteriorated and, in 1806, he died in his digs. His desire to be buried in Wilford was not met as, alas, his final destination was to be Cambridge.

The Homes and Haunts of Henry Kirke White (1908) by John T Godfrey and James Ward devotes twenty-seven pages to Wilford and thirty-five to Clifton. In his short life the poet immortalised both places and the walk between them, a tranquil avenue of beauty with the silvery river on one side and elm trees offering shade on the other.

In *The Broken Chariot* (1998) Alan Sillitoe wrote that:

> True country began when he navigated into Clifton Grove only if they ignored the new housing estate through trees to their left. He felt something magical and Grecian in the long avenue of beeches, oaks and elms, though he couldn't let Bert make such a comparison to Cecilia.

That picturesque route, from Wilford up through Clifton Grove (or vice versa), remained a place of much inspiration for over a century, its fine Nottingham vista attracting painters and poets alike.

Clifton Grove was formerly in the grounds of Clifton Manor, and it's likely that its elm trees were planted by Sir Gervase Clifton in the 1690s. In the nineteenth century, Nottingham possessed a greater literary circle than any comparable town in the world, and many of those writers came here. The Nottinghamshire poet Spencer T Hall (1812–85), writing of the decades after Kirke White's death, was not wrong when he wrote that 'Nottingham was remarkable for having turned out many excellent authors.'

In 1846 Hall said, 'Who ever saw Wilford without wishing to become an inmate of one of its peaceful woodbined homes.' Two decades later, he was living in Wilford when he published *The Upland Hamlet, and other Poems* (1867), in which he gives a description of its charms. On the subject of Wilford's notorious flooding, Hall wrote:

> Wilford! When first I gazed on thee.
> Whilst leaning o'er upland stile.
> Thy flooded meads were one vast lake.
> And thou a little bowery isle.

It was in a cottage in Wilford that William Howitt wrote part of his popular, *The Book of the Seasons, or the Calendar of Nature* (1831), written from his observations of nature's monthly changes. The book, inspired by Wilford, was dedicated to his wife and collaborator:

> To Mary Howitt, at home and abroad, in the fields of Nature and of Literature, the one true companion and Fellow Labourer.

The Howitts frequently lodged in Wilford between 1832 and 1936. William's younger brother, the poet and author Richard Howitt (1799–1869), known as "The Wordsworth of Sherwood Forest", emigrated to Australia with another brother, Godfrey, to a place near Melbourne that they named "Wilford".

In the spring of 1833, Mary Howitt wrote of the nearby Meadows, the gateway from Nottingham to Wilford. The Meadows was another local attraction; its acres of rare purple crocus flowers inspired her poem "Wild Crocus in Nottingham Meadows" (1833). It was a sight that led Daniel Defoe to describe Nottingham as 'one of the most pleasant and beautiful towns in England.'

The Howitts were friends with the journalist Henry S Sutton (1825–1901) whose first poetry was the mystical *Clifton Grove Garland* (1848). This work was the religious poet's tribute to his literary contemporaries from Nottinghamshire: People like Philip James Bailey, author of *Festus*, Edmund Larken, the county rector who was a patron of radical causes and an author on social matters, noted as possibly the first parish priest of his time to wear a beard, and Frederick Enoch, author of *Songs of Universal Brotherhood*. All of them spent time in Spencer T Hall's rustic study in Wilford.

Like Sutton, Edward Hind (1817–72) wrote here and produced lots of prose and verse informed by his rambles around the area. One of his poems, *Prometheus Bound: a Life-Drama*, was commented on by William Wylie, 'coming generations... will regard it as one of the most remarkable works ever produced in that town which first saw *Festus* given to a wondering world.'

Other writers frequenting the Groves in the mid-nineteenth century included the Radford-born poet Jane Jerram (1815–72) and the poet and novelist Thomas Miller (1807–74).

A keen explorer of rural subjects, Miller enjoyed Wilford's beauty and quietude. He was also around to see its deterioration. 'Where are the famous cherry eatings of Wilford now?' he wrote. 'The poetry around the neighbourhood is fast fading. The flower-sellers who used to stand under the sunny rocks of Sneinton have vanished. The green footpath that led along the river bank to Colwick is closed; even the pathway that leads to the old ballad-haunted grove is altered, and all old things seem to be passing away.'

By this time the Meadows had lost much of its charm. Ann Gilbert's *The Last Dying Speech of the Crocuses* (1852) was written as the famous crocuses were about to be lost to new housing. In fairness, the Meadows has maintained a wide embankment of lawns and playing fields, but to see the crocuses we must turn to paintings, such as the one that resides in Nottingham Castle's museum, by local artist SW Oscroft. Inspired by the painting, Cathy Grindrod wrote "The Crocus Gatherers, Nottingham Meadows", which appears in *Ten Poems About Nottingham* (2015).

In the year of Miller's death, *Shaw's Guide to Nottingham* was still hailing Clifton Grove as a big draw:

> At Easter and Whitsuntide, if the weather permits, thousands of the Nottingham artizans with their wives and families, young men and maidens, either with sweethearts or to gain sweethearts flock to...the Grove.

Nottinghamshire writers were also still flocking there, and to Wilford.

John Deane (1679–1761) took service with the Czar of Muscovy, and commanded a war ship before retiring to Wilford in 1738, where he wrote his life story. Deane was once cast upon a desert island, where the crew drew lots for their lives, one having to die to save (feed) the rest. The writer for boys, WHG Kingston used Deane's incredible story for one of his Boys' Own books, entitled *John Deane; Historic Adventures by Land and Sea* (c1888). The adventurer is buried in Wilford churchyard.

Nottingham folk were known to spend summer days out in Wilford Village, with its tea rooms and gardens. One popular location was the Ferry Inn. Briefly a coffee house during the eighteenth century, part of the pub dates back to a fourteenth-century farmhouse. Once a Charter was issued granting permission for the operation of a ferry boat across the river, the venue was converted into a place of refreshment. The Ferry Inn sits facing the river at the point where people were taken across the Trent to the Meadows, prior to the construction of Wilford Bridge.

It was on this spot that James Prior set the opening of his first published work. 'Good-day to you, madam; and good-day to you, sir. Welcome to Nottingham,' begins James Prior's *Three Shots from a Popgun* (1880), the "three shots" being three stories. Prior wrote:

> So we are now at the end of the Walk, and by the banks of the Trent. This thing that fronts us is not an iron bridge, but a rustic ferry – Wilford Ferry, worked by one man's arm. We enter the boat, and cross in company with a milk-cart, a Nottingham stockinger, with fishing-rod and mat basket in hand, and a pair of sweethearts bound for Clifton Grove.

The poet Edward Hind wrote a farewell sonnet to a real ferryman in charge of the crossing and barge at Wilford: Samuel Wilkinson.

In Sillitoe's *The Broken Chariot* (1998), Bert and Eileen 'went hand in hand over the Ha'penny Toll Bridge (the best tuppence ever spent) and so many packets of rubbers were called for that there were few hedge bottoms around Wilford and Clifton he and Eileen hadn't snuggled into.'

In "A Scream of Toys", from Sillitoe's *The Second Chance* (1981), Mario and Edie cross the bridge which 'seemed the only real way to get out of Nottingham.' The toll costing 'ha'penny' because 'somebody private owns it.' It seemed worth the price. 'The air seemed fresher beyond Wilford Village, where the smell of water lingered from the river which rounded it on three sides.'

The Trent itself has often been a source of literary inspiration. Sillitoe's Arthur Seaton may have called it 'turgid' but Sillitoe, like many of our writers, also wrote glowingly of the river. The Trent's admirers include Henry S Sutton, EC Roberts, Edward Hind, Rev Luke Booker, Cecil Roberts, Eliza S Oldham and Philip James Bailey, whose *To The Trent* includes the lines:

> Of all the rivers in the land
> Thee most I love fair Trent,
> For in thy streams, and by thy banks,
> My happiest hours I've spent.

Eliza S Oldham's novel *By the Trent* is set in Wilford Village or, as the author calls it, St Wilfrid's. Oldham's book won £250 in 1864, after been given first prize by the Scottish Temperance League in Glasgow. From *By the Trent*: 'Upon the river the wind rode, and with playful hands turned back the ripples, and curved them curiously, and whipped their edges softly into foam.'

DH Lawrence, who shared a publisher with James Prior, wrote of Clifton Grove in Chapter Twelve of *Sons and Lovers* (1913). In the novel, Paul and Clara visit the Grove, noting that, unlike Wilford and the Meadows, it had barely changed in a century:

> They were at the entrance to the Grove. The wet, red track, already sticky with fallen leaves, went up the steep bank between the grass. On either side stood the elm-trees like pillars along a great aisle, arching over and making high up a roof from which the dead leaves fell (...) All was silent and deserted. On the left the red wet ploughland showed through the doorways between the elm-boles and their branches. On the right, looking down, they could see the tree-tops

of elms growing far beneath them, hear occasionally the gurgle of the river. Sometimes there below they caught glimpses of the full, soft-sliding Trent, and of water-meadows dotted with small cattle.

'It has scarcely altered since little Kirke White used to come,' he said.

Reverend Rosslyn Bruce (1871–1956), rector of Clifton, published *The Clifton Book* in 1906, a historical account of Clifton through the ages. He wrote that, 'A book about Clifton to be characteristic should smell of the fresh-ploughed soil and resound with the song of thrushes.'

Much of Clifton is unrecognisable since Bruce's days. It was a small village until 1943, when Nottingham City Council acquired the land for new housing. The council had been in lengthy negotiation with the Clifton family before they secured the deal that would turn the land into one of the largest housing estates in Europe, incorporating it into the City of Nottingham in 1952.

In 1906, the year that Rev Bruce's *Clifton Book* was published, Cecil Roberts and his family lived at Wilford Grove, on the edge of a colliery district, 'in the days when miners were regarded as subhuman, brawling drunkards living in hovels,' said Roberts, who visited Clifton Colliery in that year.

When Roberts was ten, his brother nicknamed him "inky" because he was always writing. By the age of fourteen his writing was in print, with a piece entitled *Down a Coal Mine*, inspired by his journey into his local mine. After experiencing Clifton Colliery first-hand, and being shocked to learn that boys even younger than him had been sent down to the coal-face, Roberts wrote about the 'toilers who are working in the bowels of the earth.' The article appeared in his school magazine.

Although a follower of Asquith and Lloyd George, the author's sympathies were always 'with the underdog' and for Roberts, the underdog meant the coal miners living around Clifton Colliery. Decades later, when conducting research for a semi-autobiographical novel, Roberts revisited the colliery to check his memories. He was pleasantly struck by the improved working conditions. That planned novel became *A Terrace in the Sun* (1951), about a small boy, a miner's son, who became a famous artist. The book was a success, with 300,000 copies shifting within a month. Roberts regretted not calling it *A Nottingham Lad* as there was so much of his early life in its pages. He always referred to the book as his Nottingham novel.

Wilford makes an appearance in Stephen Booth's Cooper & Fry series, as it was Wilford that Booth's DS Diane Fry moved to from the Peak District.

Clifton Grove has one final literary legend, as it's said that it was here that JM Barrie had the idea for Peter Pan after being inspired by the sight of a ragged urchin wandering around. 'See that lad,' Barrie is said to have told fellow writer George Basil Barham, 'his name's Peter and he has lost his shadow. His sister's pinned that rag on him for a shadow.'

Maybe you should take the literary pilgrimage from Wilford to Clifton Grove. Who knows, the one-point-seven-mile walk might become an awfully big adventure.

---

[1] Godfrey and Ward William, 1908.

The Journey Continues...

In focusing on a limited number of locations, it has not been possible to cover all the places or local authors deserving of recognition, and that number continues to grow. An exhaustive list would certainly include many more academic writers, such as Andreas Bieler (international development), Stephen Roberts (Lorca), Thomas Waters (witchcraft), Emma Mardlin (psychology) and Richard King (Hannah Arendt). Other important writers outside of "place", yet Nottingham-based, must include the journalist Frances Ryan, a regular writer for the *Guardian* on disability issues — her book being *Crippled: austerity and the demonization of disabled people*, and there's Manjit S Sahota co-founder of Poets Against Racism, who is often seen supporting demonstrations.

As ever, our literature never sleeps. New writers to break through recently include the children's authors Darren Simpson (middle school, speculative fiction), Jasbinder Bilan (adventure stories with Asian characters), and Leicester-based Mahsuda Snaith whose novel *How to Find Home* follows a group of homeless people living in Nottingham, while MA Kuzniar's first adult novel *Midnight in Everwood* is set in early 20th century Nottingham.

If more parts of the county could have been featured, we'd have headed to Gotham, home to the many stories of "wise" men, and Jacksdale, the setting for Tony Hill's novel of the Margaret Thatcher era, *If the Kids are United*. Hill is also the author of *The Palace and the Punks*, a book about the famous/infamous Grey Topper music venue in north Nottinghamshire where everybody, but everybody, played on their way up or way down.

Maybe next time...

Acknowledgements

This book began as a literary locations series for the Nottingham UNESCO City of Literature blog. In writing the posts, and subsequently this book, I have called on many people for help. I would particularly like to thank Catharine Arnold, Barry Baker, Panya Banjoko, David Belbin, Ross Bradshaw, Heather Brown, Chris Cook Cann, Tony Challis, John Stuart Clark, Sarah Colborne, Michael Eaton, David Edgley, Ruth Fainlight, Adrian Gray, Norma Gregory, Andrew Harrison, Clare Harvey, John Harvey, Pippa Hennessy, Mars Hill, Sam Hope, Kevin Jackson, Siobhan Keenan, Mike Kirton, Patrick Limb, Karin Lindley, Ralph Lloyd-Jones, Sandeep Mahal, Angela Meads, Leanne Moden, Maureen Newton, Andy Nicholson, Henry Normal, Philipp at The Sparrows' Nest, Ken Purslow, Robert Rathbone, Miranda Seymour, Tony Simpson, Jenny Swann, Bridget Swinden, Matt Turpin, Victoria Villasenor, Felicity Whittle, Gregory Woods, Jon Wright and all those writers and historians on whose shoulders I squat, particularly Rowena Edlin-White for her pioneering work on Nottinghamshire authors. Finally, thanks to my wife Mel, for picking up the slack.

Photographs were taken by the author and John Baird Smith Senior, except for:
Black Boy Hotel, from Turner and Co. (advert).
Broxtowe Hall, from a collection belonging to Henry Belcher, courtesy nottshistory.co.uk
Caledon Road, taken by Dave Whittle.
Edwinstowe vicarage (Cobham Brewer and family), from the Edwinstowe Historical Society.
Five Leaves Bookshop, linocut by Gemma Curtis and photography by Pippa Hennessy.
Haggs Farm, from the collection of the Haggs Farm Preservation Society.
Lowdham Book Festival, taken by Clare Dudman.
Mechanics' Hall, from nottingham-mechanics.org.uk
Mushroom Bookshop – photographer unknown.
NRT Hyson Green, from postcard (unknown).
Philip James Bailey at his desk (unknown).
Sherwood Lodge (unknown).
Welbeck Abbey (unknown).

Printed Primary Sources

Michael Bache, "A Church Guide", in *Nottingham Evening Post*. CCN, March 2007.

Stephen Bailey & Chris Nottingham, *Heartlands: A Guide to DH Lawrence's Midlands Roots*. Leicestershire: Matador, 2013.

Valerie Baker, "Robin Hood Theatre Averham: The first 21 years, an account of the formation and early history of the Robin Hood Theatre". 1981.

Thomas Gerrard Canon Barber, *Byron and Where he is Buried*. Hucknall: Henry Morley & Sons, 1939.

John Beckett and Cathy Smith, "Dr Charles Deering: Nottingham's First Historian", *The Nottinghamshire Historian* 63:Autumn/Winter, 1999.

Various, *Bouchercon 26 Souvenir Programme*. London: Ringpull, 1995.

Richard Bradford, *The Life of a Long-Distance Writer: The Biography of Alan Sillitoe*. Pennsylvania: Peter Owen Books, 2008.

Cornelius Brown, *Lives of Nottinghamshire Worthies*. London: H Sotheran and Co, 1882.

Emrys Bryson, *Portrait of Nottingham*. London: Robert Hale and Co, 1974.

Roger Dobson, "Southwell's 'Old Theatre'", Southwell Local History Group, *Folio*, pp 4–5.

John Doherty, "A Memoir of Robert Blincoe", first published 1828 by Richard Carlile in *The Lion*. Reprinted by Carlile in *The Poor Man's Advocate*, 1832.

Rowena Edlin-White, *Exploring Nottinghamshire Writers*. Nottingham: Five Leaves Publications, 2017.

Ray Gosling, *Personal Copy*. London: Faber and Faber, 1980.

Ray Gosling, *Sum Total*. London: Faber and Faber, 1962.

Adrian Gray, *From Here We Changed the World*. Nottinghamshire: Bookworm of Retford, 2016.

Duncan Gray, *The Life and Work of Lord Byron*. Newstead Abbey Publications no 4, Corporation of Nottingham, 1950.

Graham Greene, *A Sort of Life*. London: The Bodley Head, 1971.

Richard Gurnam, *A History of Nottingham*. Hampshire: Phillimore, 2010.

Clare Hartwell, Nikolaus Pevsner, Elizabeth Williamson, *Nottinghamshire (Pevsner Architectural Guides: Buildings of England)*. Yale University Press, 2020.

Margaret Howitt (ed), *Mary Howitt, an autobiography*, two volumes. London: Wm. Ibister Ltd, 1889.

BS Johnson, *The Unfortunates*. London: Panther Books Ltd, 1969.

Henry Kirke White, *The poetical works and remains of Henry Kirke White, with life by Robert Southey*. London: G Routledge, 1853.

DH Lawrence, *New Poems*. London: Martin Seeker, 1918.

DH Lawrence, "Nottingham & the Mining Country", written in 1929, in *The New Adelphi*, 1930, and *Phoenix*, 1936.

DH Lawrence, *The Rainbow*. London: Methuen Publishing, 1915.

DH Lawrence, *The Selected Letters of DH Lawrence*, Compiled and edited by James T. Boulton. Cambridge University Press, 1997.

DH Lawrence, *Sons and Lovers*. New York: The Viking Press, 1913.

DH Lawrence, *The White Peacock*. London: Heinemann, 1911.

DH Lawrence, *Women in Love*. New York: Thomas Seltzer, 1920.

Hilda Lewis, *Penny Lace*. London: Jarrolds, 1946.

Leslie A Marchand, *Byron's Letters and Journals*. Massachusetts: Belknap Press of Harvard University Press, Cambridge, 1975.

Arthur Mee, *The King's England: Nottinghamshire*. London: Hodder & Stoughton, 1938.

Robert Mellors, *Men of Nottingham and Nottinghamshire*. London: J & H Bell, 1924.

Robert Mellors, *Old Nottingham Suburbs: then and now*. London: J & H Bell, 1914.

Stanley Middleton, "My Childhood in Bulwell", in *Contemporary Authors Autobiography Series*, 23. Detroit: Thomson Gale, 1996.

Andrew H Morton and John Hayes, *Tolkien's Gedling*. Warwickshire: Brewin Books, 2008.

Hannah Neate, "Because the Trent Book Shop is in Nottingham", in Geraldine Monk (ed), *Cusp: Recollections of Poetry in Transition*. Bristol: Shearsman Books, 2012.

Rev James Orange, *Narrative of the Late George Vason of Nottingham 1840*. London: Henry Mozley and Sons, 1840.

Michael Payne, "Dickens in Nottingham", *The Nottingham Historian* 73:Autumn/Winter, 2004.

Mike Phillips, "Len Garrison" (obituary), *The Guardian*. Fri 28 Feb, 2003.

Christopher Richardson, *A City of Light: Socialism, Chartism and Co-operation – Nottingham 1844*. Nottingham: Loaf on a Stick Press, 2013.

Cecil Roberts, *Autobiography vol 1: The Growing Boy*. London: Hodder and Stoughton, 1967.

Cecil Roberts, *Autobiography vol 3: The Bright Twenties*. London: Hodder and Stoughton, 1970.

Celia Robertson, *Who was Sophie? The lives of my grandmother, poet and stranger*. London: Virago Press, 2008.

Alan Sillitoe, *Life without Armour – an autobiography*. London: HarperCollins, 1995.

Alan Sillitoe, *Saturday Night and Sunday Morning*. London: WH Allen, 1958.

Alan Sillitoe, *Alan Sillitoe's Nottinghamshire*. London: Grafton Books, 1987.

Christopher Thompson, *The Autobiography of an Artisan*. Nottingham: J Shaw and Sons, 1847.

Geoffrey Trease, *Nottingham: A Biography*. London: Macmillan, 1970.

George Walker, account included in John F Sutton, *Date–Book of Remarkable and Memorable Events Connected with Nottingham and its Neighbourhood, 1750–1850*. Nottingham: R Sutton, 1852.

James Walker, "The Nottingham Essay: Geoffrey Trease", *LeftLion*, 23 March 2015. Also in *Dawn of the Unread*, online.

References

Book One – Nottingham City Centre

Chapter 1: The Arboretum
Arthur Mee, *The King's England: Nottinghamshire*. London: Hodder & Stoughton, 1938.

Robert Mellors, *Men of Nottingham and Nottinghamshire*. London: J & H Bell, 1924.

Helen Kirkpatrick Watts, *Papers of Helen Kirkpatrick Watts*. 1909. Held at Nottinghamshire Archives.

Stanley Middleton, *Harris's Requiem*. London: Hutchinson, 1960.

DH Lawrence, *The Rainbow*. London: Methuen Publishing, 1915.

Chapter 2: Arkwright Building
DH Lawrence, *The Rainbow*. London: Methuen Publishing, 1915.

DH Lawrence, *New Poems*. London: Martin Seeker, 1918.

Slavomir Rawicz, *The Long Walk*. The Companion Book Club, 1957.

Chapter 3: Broadway Cinema
Robert Mellors, *Men of Nottingham and Nottinghamshire*. London: J & H Bell, 1924.

Bouchercon 26 Souvenir Programme. London: Ringpull, 1995.

Chapter 4: Bromley House Library
Abigail Gawthern, *The Diary of Abigail Gawthern of Nottingham 1751–1810*. The Thoroton Society of Nottinghamshire Record Series, 1980.

Cecil Roberts, *Autobiography vol 1: The Growing Boy*. London: Hodder and Stoughton, 1967.

Chapter 5: The Council House
Alan Sillitoe, *The Broken Chariot*. London: Flamingo, 1998.

Cecil Roberts, *Autobiography vol 4, The Pleasant Years*. London: Hodder and Stoughton, 1974.

Chapter 7: Exchange Arcade
John Thomas Godfrey; Robert Southey; James Ward, *The homes and haunts of Henry Kirke White; with some account of the family of White, of Nottingham and Norfolk*. London: Simpkin, Marshall, Hamilton, Kent & Co.; Nottingham, HB Saxton, 1908.

Harry Gill, *A Guide to Old Nottingham*. Compiled for The Patriotic Fair of 1917, 1904.

Henry Kirke White, *The poetical works and remains of Henry Kirke White, with life by Robert Southey*. London: G Routledge, 1853.

Roger Beckwith, warden of Latimer House, Oxford. "The Maddock Brothers of Nottingham: A Family of Evangelical Clergy", www.biblicalstudies.org.uk.

Cecil Roberts, *Autobiography vol 2: The Years of Promise*. London: Hodder and Stoughton, 1968.

Cecil Roberts, *Autobiography vol 3: The Bright Twenties*. London: Hodder and Stoughton, 1970.

Chapter 8: Express Building

Graham Greene, *A Sort of Life*, London: The Bodley Head, 1971.

Lytton Strachey, *Eminent Victorians*. (first published 1918), London: Penguin, 1948.

Richard Greene, *Graham Greene: A Life In Letters*. London: Little Brown, 2007.

Norman Sherry, *The life of Graham Greene: vol 1, 1904–1939*. London: Jonathan Cape, 1989.

Graham Greene, *A Gun for Sale*. London: Heinemann, 1936.

Graham Greene, *Brighton Rock*. London: Heinemann, 1938.

Michael Shelden, *Graham Greene, The Enemy Within*, New York: Random House, 1994.

Cecil Roberts, *Autobiography vol 3, The Bright Twenties*. London: Hodder and Stoughton, 1970.

Chapter 9: Five Leaves Bookshop

Robert Mellors, *Old Nottingham Suburbs: then and now*. London: J and H Bell, 1914.

Thomas Miller, *Gideon Giles, The Roper*. London: James Hayward and Co, 1841.

Christopher Richardson, *A City of Light: Socialism, Chartism and Co-operation – Nottingham 1844*. Nottingham: Loaf on a Stick Press, 2013.

Chapter 10: The Loggerheads (former)

J Holland Walker, "An Itinerary of Nottingham: Narrow Marsh", *Transactions of the Thoroton Society*, 30, 1926.

Nicola Monaghan, *Dead Flowers*. Essex: Verve Books, 2019.

Chapter 11: Mechanics Hall (former)

Michael Payne, "Dickens in Nottingham", *The Nottingham Historian* 73:Autumn/Winter, 2004.

"Victorian Nottingham: A story in Pictures 1837–1901", article on Nottingham Mechanics Institute, vol 14.

Chapter 12: Mushroom Bookshop (former)

Richard Bradford, *The Life of a Long-Distance Writer: The Biography of Alan Sillitoe*. Pennsylvania: Peter Owen Books, 2008.

Alan Sillitoe, *The Open Door*. London: Grafton Books, 1989.

Hannah Neate article "Because the Trent Book Shop is in Nottingham", in Geraldine Monk (ed), *Cusp: Recollections of Poetry in Transition*. Bristol: Shearsman, 2012.

Chris Cook Cann, *Face Blind in Berlin, Suffolk and Gedling*. Nottingham: Loaf on a Stick Press, 2019.

"Mushroom Christmas/New Year Catalogues" via The Sparrows' Nest Library and Archive – www.thesparrowsnest.org.uk

Sylvia Riley, *Winter at the Bookshop*. Nottingham: Five Leaves Publications, 2019.

Chapter 13: New Foresters

Tony Scupham-Bilton, *Robin Hood: Out of the Greenwood: His Gay Origins*. Kindle edition, 2019.

Jo Willett, *The Pioneering Life of Mary Wortley Montagu*. Barnsley: Pen & Sword History, 2021.

Fiona MacCarthy, *Byron: Life and Legend*. London: John Murray, 2002.

Peter Cochran, *Byron and Orientalism*. Cambridge Scholars Publishing, unabridged edition, 2006.

Xavier Mayne, *The Intersexes*. Privately printed, 1909.

DH Lawrence, *Letters of DH Lawrence, vol 2: 1913–16*, 1981. Cambridge University Press; Revised Edition, 2002.

DH Lawrence, *The Rainbow*. London: Methuen Publishing, 1915.

Mark Kinkead-Weekes, *DH Lawrence, vol 2: Triumph to Exile 1912–1922*. Cambridge University Press, 1996.

Paul Baker, *Fabulosa!: The Story of Polari, Britain's Secret Gay Language*. Reaktion Books, 2019.

Francis King, *Yesterday Came Suddenly*. London: Constable, 1993.

"Nottingham's LGBT newspapers", from The Lesbian, Gay, Bisexual and Transgender history project for Nottingham & Nottinghamshire, www.nottsrainbowheritage.org.uk.

Chapter 14: Newstead House

Robert Chambers, *Memoir of Robert Chambers*. London: W and R Chambers, 1872.

Notes and Queries 4th series, vol. 3, 1870.

Chapter 15: Nottingham Arts Theatre

George Vason, *An Authentic Narrative of Four Years' Residence at Tongataboo, one of the Friendly Islands, in the South-Sea*. London: Longman, Hurst, Rees, and Orme: L B Seeley, and Hatchard, 1810.

Rev James Orange, *Narrative of the Late George Vason of Nottingham 1840*. London: Henry Mozley and Sons, 1840.

John Potter Briscoe, "The Weekday Cross at Nottingham, and its Associations", *Transactions of the Thoroton Society*, 21, 1917

Chapter 16: Nottingham Castle

Robert Thoroton, *Antiquities of Nottinghamshire*. London, 1677.

Georgina Lock, "Lucy Hutchinson: a truly revolutionary writer", www.nottinghamcityofliterature.com/blog/lucy-hutchinson, 2017.

Margaret Howitt (ed), *Mary Howitt, an autobiography,* two volumes. London: Wm. Ibister Ltd. 1889.

Lucy Hutchinson, *Memoirs of the Life of Colonel Hutchinson*. London: Henry G Bohn, 1863.

Alan Sillitoe, *A Man of His Time*. Flamingo, 2004.

Hilda Lewis, *Penny Lace*. London: Jarrolds, 1946.

DH Lawrence, *The White Peacock*. London: Heinemann, 1911.

DH Lawrence, *Sons and Lovers*. New York: The Viking Press, 1913

Alan Sillitoe, *Saturday Night and Sunday Morning*. London: WH Allen, 1958

Ian Fleming, *Thunderball*. London: Jonathan Cape, 1961.

Bob Egan, "Bob Dylan at the Nottingham Castle Gates", www.popspotsnyc.com/nottingham, 2017.

Chapter 17: Nottingham Mechanics

Francis Vivian, *The Death of Mr. Lomas*. London: Jenkins, 1941.

Alan Sillitoe, *Life Without Armour – an Autobiography*. London: HarperCollins, 1995.

Nottingham Writers' Club, "A History of the Nottingham Writers' Club", *Nottingham Post, Bygones.*

Richard Bradford, *The Life of a Long-Distance Writer: The Biography of Alan Sillitoe*. Pennsylvania: Peter Owen Books, 2008.

Chapter 18: Nottingham Playhouse

Dennis McCarthy, *Local Boy Makes Good*. Nottingham: Wm. J Butler & Co, 1971.

Emrys Bryson, *Portrait of Nottingham*, London: Robert Hale and Co, 1974.

Mel Gussow, *Conversations with Tom Stoppard*, London: Nick Hern, 1995, p132

Hermione Lee, *Tom Stoppard: A Life*. London: Faber & Faber, 2020.

Chapter 18: Nottingham Playhouse

Joan Wallace, *Ragtime Joe*. Nottingham: Colinprint, 1998.

John Bailey, *A Theatre For All Seasons*. Gloustershire: Alan Sutton Publications Ltd, 1994.

Chapter 19: Pitcher and Piano

Geoffrey Oldfield, *The Lace Market, Nottingham*. Nottingham Civic Society, 2002.

Gilbert Wakefield, *Memoirs of the life of Gilbert Wakefield*. vol 1:i.227, 1804.

Alexander Gordon, "Walker, George. 1885–1900", *Dictionary of National Biography*, 59.

Malcolm I Thomis, *Old Nottingham*. Newton Abbot: David & Charles, 1968.

Paul Magnuson *Subscribers to Coleridge's Poems (1796), or Duckings and Drubbings in Nottingham*. Online at New York University, www.friendsofcoleridge.com, 2003.

George Walker, *Substance of the speech of the Rev. Mr. Walker, at the general meeting of the county of Nottingham, held at Mansfield, on Monday the 28th of Febuary 1780*. Gale ECCO, Print Editions, 2010.

George Walker, *Essays, vol 2: A Life Of The Author*. 1809.

John Blackner, *The History of Nottingham*. Nottingham: Sutton and Son, 1815.

Richard Gurnham, *A History of Nottingham*. Hampshire: Phillimore, 2010, p85.

Malcolm I Thomis, *Politics and Society in Nottingham, 1785–1835*. New York: Augustus Kelley, l969.

George Walker, account included in John F Sutton, *Date-Book of Remarkable and Memorable Events Connected with Nottingham and its Neighbourhood, 1750–1850*. London: Simpkin & Marshall; Nottingham: R Sutton, 1852.

Rowena Edlin-White, *Exploring Nottinghamshire Writers*. Nottingham: Five Leaves Publications, 2017.

Chapter 20: The Playwright

Ray Gosling, *Sum Total*. London: Faber and Faber, 1962.

Siobhan Keenan, "The King's Men perform in Nottingham", online at www.bbc.co.uk/programmes/articles/53WtR0YKry39RY4M5mnZR1z/the-king-s-men-perform-in-nottingham, 2016.

Zoë Wilcox, "Shakespeare on Tour 2016". online at www.bbc.co.uk/programmes/articles/1hjZNMx67HLK2HcLkrCcZXM/ira-aldridge-the-first-black-shakespearean-actor, 2016.

DH Lawrence, "When I Read Shakespeare", *Pansies*. London: Alfred A. Knopf, 1929.

Emrys Bryson, *'Owd yer tight*. Ray Palmer Limited, 1967.

William Frederick Wallett, *The Public Life of WF Wallett, the Queen's Jester: An Autobiography*. London: Remrose and Sons, 1870.

Chapter 21: Raleigh Street

Ken Brand, *Thomas Chambers Hine; Architect of Victorian Nottingham*. Nottingham Civic Society, 2003.

Muriel Hine, *A Great Adventure*. London: Hodder & Stoughton, 1939.

Muriel Hine, *The Man With the Double Heart*. London: The Bodley Head, 1914.

Clare Hartwell, Nikolaus Pevsner, Elizabeth Williamson, *Nottinghamshire (Pevsner Architectural Guides: Buildings of England)*. Yale University Press, 2020.

Chapter 22: Regent Street

Constance Penswick Smith, *The Revival of Mothering Sunday*. Macmillan, 1921.

Michael Bache, "A Church Guide", *Nottingham Evening Post*. CCN, March 2007.

Chapter 23: School of Art

Mary Cadogan, *The William Companion*. London: Macmillan Publishers, 1990.

Alan Clark, *Dictionary of British Comic Artists, Writers and Editors*. The British Library, 1998, pp30–31.

Alan Clark, *The Best of British Comic Art*. London: Boxtree Ltd., 1989, pp95–120.

Denis Gifford, *The International Book of Comics*. London: Hamlyn; Reprint edition, 1988.

Timothy Wilcox, *Laura Knight at the Theatre*. London: Unicorn Press, 2008.

Dennis McCarthy, *Local Boy Makes Good*. Nottingham: Wm. J Butler and Co, 1971, p60.

Chapter 24: St Mary's Church and the Lace Market

Jane Jerram, *The Child's Own Story Book; Or, Tales and Dialogues for the Nursery*. Philadelphia: George S Appleton, 1850.

Nicholas Carlisle, *A Concise Description of the Endowed Grammar Schools in England and Wales*. London: Baldwin, Craddock and Joy, 1818.

Charles Deering, *History of Nottingham* (County Historical Reprints). SR Publishers, 1970.

John Beckett and Cathy Smith, "Dr Charles Deering: Nottingham's First Historian", *The Nottinghamshire Historian*, 63:Autumn/Winter, 1999.

Syndney Evelyn, "Evelyn Papers" (letters), at British Library, 1738.

Robert Mellors, *Men of Nottingham and Nottinghamshire*. Nottingham: J & H Bell, 1924.

CA Creffield, *Helen Zimmern, ODNB*. Oxford University Press, 2004.

Derrick Buttress, *Music While You Work*. Nottingham: Shoestring Press, 2007.

Geoffrey Oldfield, *The Lace Market, Nottingham*. Nottingham Civic Society, 2002.

Chapter 25: Tanners

Andrew Birkin, *JM Barrie and the Lost Boys: the real story behind Peter Pan*, (first published 1979). Yale University Press, illustrated edition, 2003.

Cecil Roberts, *Autobiography vol 3: The Bright Twenties*. London: Hodder and Stoughton, 1970, p68 & p71.

Pretty Boys, "Barrie", *Nottingham Journal*, 28 Jan, 1884.

Robert Mellors, *Men of Nottingham and Nottinghamshire*. London: J & H Bell, 1924.

Chapter 26: Theatre Royal

Geoffrey Oldfield, *The Lace Market, Nottingham*. Nottingham Civic Society, 2002.

Nottingham Theatre Royal's excellent archive: www.ourtheatreroyal.org.

J. Holland Walker, Percy Whatnall (eds), *Links With Old Nottingham*. 1928.

DH Lawrence, *Sons and Lovers*. The Viking Press, 1913.

Cecil Roberts, *Autobiography vol 1: The Growing Boy*. London: Hodder & Stoughton, 1967.

Chapter 27: Weavers

Ann Thwaite, "Obituary: Geoffrey Trease", *Independent*, Friday 30 January, 1998.

James Walker, "The Nottingham Essay: Geoffrey Trease, Dawn of the Unread". *LeftLion*, 23 March 2015.

Geoffrey Trease, *Nottingham: A Biography*. London: Macmillan, 1970.

DH Lawrence, *Sons and Lovers*. The Viking Press, 1913.

Chapter 28: The White Lion

Thomas Berdmore, *A treatise on the disorders and deformities of the teeth and gums: explaining the most rational methods of treating their diseases: illustrated with cases and experiments*. London: Printed for the author; Sold by Benjamin White, James Dodsley and Becket and De Hondt, 1770.

J Holland Walker, "An Itinerary of Nottingham: Clumber Street", *Transactions of the Thoroton Society* 39, 1935.

Chapter 29: Yates's (former)

BS Johnson, *The Unfortunates*. London: Panther Books Ltd, 1969.

Celia Robertson, *Who was Sophie? The lives of my grandmother, poet and stranger*. London: Virago Press, 2008.

Chapter 30: Zara Building

Richard Gurnam, *A History of Nottingham*. Hampshire; Phillimore, 2010, p133.

Ruth Sears, "Boots Booklovers Library 1898–1966", *The Nottinghamshire Historian*, 81:Autumn/Winter, 2008.

Jackie Winter, *Lipsticks and Library Books*. CreateSpace Independent Publishing Platform, 2016.

Book Two – Nottingham

Chapter 31: Basford House
Philip James Bailey, *Festus*. Arkose Press, 2015.

Cornelius Brown, *Lives of Nottinghamshire Worthies*. London: H Sotheran and Co, 1882.

Robert Mellors, *Old Nottingham Suburbs: then and now [Basford]*. London: J & H Bell Ltd, 1914.

Chapter 32: Beaconsfield Street
Mike Phillips, "Len Garrison" (obituary), *The Guardian*. Fri 28 Feb, 2003.

Norma Gregory, *Jamaicans in Nottingham: Narratives and Reflections*. Hertford, Hansib Publications, 2015.

Chapter 33: Bertrand Russell House
Tony Simpson, "Violence of the 'lambs'", *The Spokesman: Another Europe is Possible*, 132, 2016, p67.

Lady Ottoline Morrell, *Ottoline at Garsington, Memoirs of Lady Ottoline Morrell 1915–1918*. US: Random House, 1974.

Bertrand Russell, *Portraits from Memory*. G. Allen & Unwin, 1958.

Gail Chester and Andrew Rigby (eds), *Articles of Peace: Celebrating fifty years of Peace News*. UK: Prism Press, 1986.

Chapter 34: Broxtowe
WT Whitley, "Thomas Helwys of Gray's Inn and of Broxtowe Hall, Nottingham", *Baptist Quarterly*, New Series 7, 1935, pp241–255.

Adrian Gray, *From Here We Changed the World*. Nottinghamshire: Bookworm of Retford, 2016.

Derrick Buttress, *Broxtowe Boy*. Nottingham: Shoestring Press, 2004.

Chapter 35: Caledon Road
Philip Davies, "Stanley Middleton" (obituary), *The Guardian*, 29 July 2009.

Stanley Middleton, "My Childhood in Bulwell", *Contemporary Authors Autobiography Series*, 23. Detroit: Thomson Gale, 1996.

David Belbin (ed), *Stanley Middleton at Eighty*. Nottingham: Five Leaves Publications, 2009.

Stanley Middleton, *Poetry and Old Age*. Nottingham: Shoestring Press, 2019.

Chapter 36: Danethorpe Vale

Peter Mortimer, *Made in Nottingham*. Nottingham: Five Leaves Publications, 2012.

Alan Sillitoe, *Birthday*. Flamingo, 2010.

Chapter 37: Ebers Road

Dorothy Whipple, *Greenbanks*. London: John Murray, 1932.

Dorothy Whipple, *They Were Sisters*. London: John Murray, 1943.

Dorothy Whipple, *Random Commentary*. London: John Murray, 1966.

Chapter 38: First Avenue

Andrew M Colman, *Argyle, (John) Michael (1925–2002), social psychologist*. Oxford University Press, 2004–6.

R Lamb and M Sissons Joshi, "Michael Argyle", *The Psychologist*, 15, 2002, pp624–5.

Peter Robinson, "Michael Argyle" (obituary), *The Guardian Higher Education Supplement*, 3 October 2002.

Michael Argyle, *Bodily Communication*. International Universities Press Inc, 1975.

Michael Argyle, *The Psychology of Happiness*. London: Methuen, 1987.

Chapter 39: The Forest Recreation Ground

Richard Gurnham, *A History of Nottingham*. Hampshire: Phillimore, 2010, p92.

George Eliot, *The George Eliot Letters, Vol 2*, (letter 30, November 1858). London: Oxford University Press, 1954.

Alan Sillitoe, *Alan Sillitoe's Nottinghamshire*. London: Grafton Books, 1987.

Alan Sillitoe, *The Loneliness of the Long-distance Runner*. London: W H Allen, 1959.

Alan Sillitoe, *Saturday Night and Sunday Morning*. London: WH Allen, 1958.

JB Priestley, *English Journey*. London: Heinemann, 1934.

Jacques Morrell, *The Showman*. Nottingham: Porchester Press, 2017.

Aly Stoneman, "Kathy Pimlott interviewed by Aly Stoneman", *LeftLion*, online at www.leftlion.co.uk/read/2016/october/you-bring-out-the-nottingham-in-me-a-poem-by-kathy-pimlott-8617, 6 October 2016.

Cecil Roberts, *Autobiography vol 1: The Growing Boy*. London: Hodder and Stoughton, 1967.

Cecil Roberts, *Goose Fair*. London: Frederick A Stokes Company, 1928.

Chapter 40: Maggie's Cancer Centre

Ivory Longley, "Maggie's Magic Moments", Poem courtesy of Ivory Longley, 2019.

Chapter 41: Nottingham Girls' High School

Maggie Brown, "Helen Cresswell" (obituary), *The Guardian*, 29 September 2005.

Chapter 42: The Old General (former)

John Potter Briscoe, *Nottinghamshire Facts and Fictions*. 1877. Republished by RareBooksClub.com, 2012.

J. Holland Walker, "An Itinerary of Nottingham: Broad Marsh", *Transactions of the Thoroton Society*, 30, 1926.

Ztan Zmith, "The "Green" – A Journey through time", in the publication by Basford and District Local History Society.

Geoffrey Searle, writing for Australian Dictionary of Biography, online at adb.anu.edu.au/biography/hatfield-william-6598.

Chapter 43: The Park Estate

Rose Fyleman, *A Princess Comes to Our Town*. London: Methuen, 1927.

Cecil Roberts, *Autobiography vol 1: The Growing Boy*. London: Hodder and Stoughton, 1967.

WT Pike (ed), *Nottinghamshire and Derbyshire at the Opening of the Twentieth Century; [and] Contemporary Biographies*, (1901)

Chapter 44: Sneinton Market

William Booth, *In Darkest England and the Way Out*. London: Salvation Army, 1890.

WH Wylie, *Old and New Nottingham*. London: Longman, Brown, Green & Longmans, 1853.

Robert Mellors, *Old Nottingham Suburbs: then and now* [Sneinton]. London: J and H Bell, 1914.

DH Lawrence, *Women in Love*. Thomas Seltzer, 1920.

Colin Haynes, *Stories of Sneinton Market*. Sneinton Market Heritage project, 2016.

Chapter 45: St Ann's

Ray Gosling, *St Ann's*. The Civic Society Nottingham, 1967.

George Powe, *Don't Blame the Blacks*. Printed Dane Street, (copy via Sparrows' Nest Library and Archive archive.org/details/sparrowsnest-8466/page/n1/mode/2up), 1956.

Ray Gosling, *Personal Copy*. London: Faber and Faber, 1980.

Sylvia Riley, *Winter at the Bookshop*. Nottingham: Five Leaves Publications, 2019.

Ken Coates and Richard Silburn, *St Ann's*, Nottingham University, 1967.

Bea Udeh, "Mufaro Makubika interviewed by Bea Udeh", *LeftLion*, 9 June 2018.

Chapter 46: Victoria Crescent

Annabel Abbs, *Frieda: the original Lady Chatterley*. Two Roads, 2018.

DH Lawrence, *The Selected Letters of DH Lawrence*, Compiled and edited by James T Boulton. Cambridge University Press, 1997.

Chapter 47: The White Horse

Alan Sillitoe, *Saturday Night and Sunday Morning*. London: WH Allen, 1958

Richard Bradford, *The Life of a Long-Distance Writer: The Biography of Alan Sillitoe*. Pennsylvania: Peter Owen Books, 2008.

Alan Sillitoe, *Life Without Armour – an autobiography*. London: HarperCollins, 1995.

Herbert Spencer, *An Autobiography*, illustrated in two volumes, vol 1. New York: D. Appleton and Company, 1904.

Book Three – Nottinghamshire

Chapter 48: All Hallows Church
Wayne G Hammond and Christina Scull, *JRR Tolkien: Artist & Illustrator*. London: HarperCollins, 2001.

Andrew H Morton and John Hayes, *Tolkien's Gedling*. Warwickshire: Brewin Books, 2008.

Chapter 49: Annesley Hall
John Granby, "Notts Villages: Annesley", *The Nottinghamshire Guardian*, 1942.

Margaret Howitt (ed), *Mary Howitt, An Autobiography*, two volumes. London: Wm. Ibister Ltd., 1889.

Leonard Jacks, *The Great Houses of Nottinghamshire and the County Families*. Nottingham: W & AS Bradshaw Collection, 1881.

DH Lawrence, *The White Peacock*. London: Heinemann, 1911.

Chapter 50: Aslockton
Claire Ridgway & Beth Von Staats, "Thomas Cranmer's Everlasting Gift: The Book of Common Prayer", interview with Claire Ridgway about the book *Thomas Cranmer: In a Nutshell* by Von Staats. MadeGlobal Publishing, 2015.

Chapter 51: Bingham
Cornelius Brown, *A History of Nottinghamshire*, E Stock, 1896.

Arthur Mee, *The King's England: Nottinghamshire*, London: Hodder & Stoughton, 1938.

Various contributors, *Bingham Parish Church: A History and Guide*, Nottingham.

Chapter 52: Bridgford Road
Mark Valentine, "The Genius of JC Snaith", *Wormwoodiana*. 22 June 2009.

Kevin Telfer, *Peter Pan's First XI: The Extraordinary Story of JM Barrie's Cricket Team*. London; Hodder and Stoughton, Sceptre, 2010.

JC Snaith, *The Sailor*. New York: D Appleton and Co, 1916.

Chapter 53: Car Colston
TM Blagg, "Autumn Excursion, 1908: Car Colston Church/Dr Robert Thoroton", *Transactions of the Thoroton Society*, 12, 1908.

Southwell and Nottingham Church History Project, *Car Colston, St Mary*.

Chapter 54: Devonshire Avenue

John Lucas, *Remembered Acts*. Nottingham: Shoestring Press, 2020.

John Lucas (ed), *Ten Poems About Nottingham*. Nottingham: Candlestick Press, 2015.

Chapter 55: Eastwood

DH Lawrence, Harry T Moore (ed), *The Collected Letters of DH Lawrence*, two volumes. New York: The Viking Press, 1962.

DH Lawrence, *Sea and Sardinia*. New York: Thomas Seltzer, 1921.

DH Lawrence, "Nottingham & the Mining Country", written in 1929, published in *The New Adelphi*, 1930, and *Phoenix*, 1936.

DH Lawrence, *Sons and Lovers*. The Viking Press, 1913.

Enid Hilton, *A Nottingham Childhood with DH Lawrence*. Alan Sutton Publishing, 1993.

DH Lawrence, *Love Poems and Others*. First published in 1913. London: Edward Hulton, 1958.

Richard Bradford, *The Life of a Long-Distance Writer: The Biography of Alan Sillitoe*. Pennsylvania: Peter Owen Books, 2008.

Chapter 56: Elston

Ed Smith, Christopher Simon, "How Charles Darwin's grandfather prophesied the theory of evolution in his poetry". alternet.org, 30 May 2019, originally published on aeon.co.

Martin Priestman, *The Poetry of Erasmus Darwin: Enlightened Spaces, Romantic Times*. Routledge, 2013.

CJ Duffin, RTJ Moody, C Gardner-Thorpe, *A History of Geology and Medicine*. Geological Society. London: Geological Society special publication. 2013, p336.

Charles Darwin, *The Life of Erasmus Darwin*. 1879, unabridged edition, ed by Desmond King-Hele, Cambridge University Press, 2002.

Samuel Butler, *Evolution, Old & New Or, the Theories of Buffon, Dr. Erasmus Darwin and Lamarck, as compared with that of Charles Darwin*, 1879. Reprinted by HardPress Publishing, 2013.

Erasmus Darwin, *Zoonomia*. 1794. Republished by Cambridge University Press, 2010.

Erasmus Darwin, *The Temple of Nature*. London: J Johnson, 1803.

Chapter 57: Gonalston Mill

John Doherty, "A Memoir of Robert Blincoe", first published 1828 by Richard Carlile in *The Lion*. Reprinted by Carlile in *The Poor Man's Advocate*, 1832.

John Waller, *The Real Oliver Twist*. London: Icon Books, 2005.

Chapter 58: Haggs Farm

Paul Fussell, *Abroad: British Literary Traveling between the Wars*. New York: Oxford University Press, 1980.

DH Lawrence, *John Thomas and Lady Jane* (1927), London: Heinemann, 1972.

Jessie Chambers, *A Personal Record* (1965), Cambridge University Press, 1980.

Chapter 60: The Hemlock Stone

John Potter Briscoe, *Bypaths of Nottinghamshire History*. Privately printed, 1905.

DH Lawrence, *Sons and Lovers*. New York: The Viking Press, 1913

Chapter 61: Keyworth

"A fond farewell to "Baggy" Palmer", *Hold the Front Page*, 25 June 2007.

Chapter 62: Langar

Ian Brown, *Samuel Butler at Langar*. Nottinghamshire County Council Leisure Services, 1990.

Clara G Stillman, *Samuel Butler: a Mid-Victorian Modern*. New York: The Viking Press, 1932.

AH McLintock (ed.), An Encyclopaedia of New Zealand. 1966. online at www.teara.gov.nz.

Roger Robinson, *Dictionary of New Zealand Biography*. 1990.

Samuel Butler, *The Way of All Flesh*. R Streatfeild, 1903.

Chapter 63: Lowdham

James Walker, "Jane Streeter interview with James Walker". *Leftlion*, 25 July 2010. online at www.leftlion.co.uk/read/2010/july/jane-streeter-interview-the-bookcase-lowdham-book-festival-alan-sillitoe-pen-pal/.

Chapter 64: Newark

Duncan Gray, *The Life and Work of Lord Byron*. Newstead Abbey Publications no 4, Corporation of Nottingham, 1950.

TM Blagg, *Newark as a Publishing Town*. S Whiles, 1898.

Thomas Gerrard Canon Barber, *Byron and Where he is Buried*. Hucknall: Henry Morley & Sons, 1939.

Peter Cochran, "The Correspondence between Byron and Walter Scott, 1812–22". March 2010. online at petercochran.files.wordpress.com.

Samuel Smiles, *A Publisher and his Friends: Memoir and Correspondence of John Murray, with an Account of the Origin and Progress of the House, 1768–1843*. London: John Murray, 1891.

Roderick S Speer, *Byron and Scott: The Waverley Novels and Historical Engagement Hardcover*, unabridged edition. Cambridge Scholars Publishing, 2009.

Clement Eaton, "Winifred and Joseph Gales, Liberals in the Old South", in *Journal of Southern History 10*, 1944.

Tim Warner, article on newarkcivictrust.org.uk, *Newark Civic Trust*, 68:Feb 2013.

Michael R Booth, "Robertson, Thomas William (1829–1871), playwright", *Oxford Dictionary of National Biography*, Oxford University Press, 2004.

Matt Haig, "Made in Newark-on-Trent", *The Guardian*, 14 July 2018.

Chapter 65: Newstead Abbey

Emily Brand, *The Fall of the House of Byron*. London: John Murray, 2020, p74.

Rosalys Coope, *Lord Byron's Newstead*. City of Nottingham booklet.

Lord Byron, *Fugitive Pieces*. Newark: S and J Ridge, 1806.

Duncan Gray, *The Life and Work of Lord Byron*. Newstead Abbey Publications no 4, Corporation of Nottingham. 1950, p21.

LA Marchland, (ed), *Byron's Letters and Journals, Vols 1–4,* 1973–75.

Cornelius Brown, *A History of Nottinghamshire*. E Stock, 1896.

Washington Irving, *Abbotsford and Newstead Abbey*. London: John Murray, 1835.

Miranda Rijks, *The Eccentric Entrepreneur, a biography of Sir Julien Cahn*. Cheltenham: The History Press Ltd, 2008.

BS Johnson, *The Unfortunates*. London: Panther Books Ltd, 1969.

Chapter 66: Old Church Farm, Eakring

Maggie Brown, "Helen Cresswell" (obituary), *The Guardian*. 29 September 2005.

BBC, "Author Helen Cresswell dies at 71" (obituary), *BBC News website*, 27 September 2005.

Chapter 67: The Old Library
Christopher Thompson, *The Autobiography of an Artisan*. Nottingham: J Shaw and Sons, 1847.

Chapter 68: Rancliffe Arms
Arthur Mee, *The King's England: Nottinghamshire*. London: Hodder & Stoughton, 1938.

"The Spring Excursion: Bradmore and Bunny", *Transactions of the Thoroton Society*, 6, 1902.

Chapter 69: Retford
Tamara S Wagner, "Catherine Gore: Brief Biography", online, National University of Singapore/University of Cambridge.

Chapter 70: The Robin Hood Theatre
Valerie Baker, "Robin Hood Theatre Averham: The first 21 years, an account of the formation and early history of the Robin Hood Theatre". 1981

Chapter 71: Rufford Abbey
Helen Cresswell, *The Secret World of Polly Flint*. Republished Nottingham: Five Leaves Publications, 2008.

Anna Groundwater, "Rufford Abbey: a House's Changing Character". online at www.blogs.hss.ed.ac.uk/ben-jonsons-walk/rufford/, 28 July 2013.

Emily White, "Ghost hunters capture 'chilling' images of England's 'lost queen'", online at www.lincolnshirelive.co.uk/news/local-news/retford-ghost-white-lady-rufford-4542744, 26 September 2020.

Chapter 72: Sherwood Lodge
Leonard Jacks, *The Great Houses of Nottinghamshire and the County Families*. Nottingham: W & AS Bradshaw Collection, 1881.

Lord Mottistone, *My Horse Warrior*. London: Hodder & Stoughton, 1934.

General Jack Seely, Brough Scott, *Warrior: The Amazing Story of a Real War Horse*. Racing Post Books, 2011.

Chapter 73: Southwell
BS Johnson, *The Unfortunates*. London: Panther Books Ltd, 1969.

Alan Sillitoe, "A Trip to Southwell", from *Men, Women and Children*. Charles Scribner's Sons, 1973.

M Boussahba-Bravard, *Suffrage Outside Suffragism: Britain 1880–1914*. Palgrave Macmillan UK, 2007, pp108–110.

DH Lawrence, *Women in Love*. Thomas Seltzer, 1920.

Leslie A Marchand, *Byron's Letters and Journals*. Cambridge, Massachusetts: Belknap Press of Harvard University Press, 1975.

David Herbert, "Byron's Southwell Dramatics", Newstead Abbey Byron Society, April 2007.

Roger Dobson, "Southwell's 'Old Theatre'", *Folio*, pp4–5.

Richard Smedley, *The Life and Times of Joseph E Smedley*. London: Clink Street Publishing, 2018.

Alexander Gordon, "Hutton, William (1723–1815)", *Dictionary of National Biography, 1885–1900*, 28. 1900, p361.

Chapter 74: St Mary Magdalene Church, Hucknall

Margaret Howitt (ED), *Mary Howitt, an autobiography*, two volumes. London: Wm. Ibister Ltd. 1889.

JH Beardsmore, *The History of Hucknall Torkard*, Mansfield: Linney, 1909.

Thomas Gerrard Canon Barber, *Byron and Where he is Buried*. Hucknall: Henry Morley & Sons, 1939.

Cecil Roberts, *Autobiography vol 4: Sunshine and Shadow*. London: Hodder and Stoughton, 1972.

Chapter 75: St Mary's Church

Collishaw & Stewart-Smith (eds), *A Creative Dictionary of Edwinstowe*. Edwinstowe Reading Group, 2005.

Edwinstowe Historical Society, "Cobham Brewer's Labour of Love". Online at edwinstowehistory.org.uk/local-history/people/author/cobham-brewer/.

Edwinstowe Historical Society, "Cecil Day Lewis", based on research by Dennis Wood. Online at edwinstowehistory.org.uk/local-history/people/author/cecil-day-lewis-cbe/.

Cecil Day Lewis, *The Buried Day*. London: Chatto & Windus, 1960.

Chapter 76: Stapleford

Ernest Bryant, quoted in Sir John Hammerton, *Child of Wonder: An Intimate Biography of Arthur Mee*, London: Hodder & Stoughton, 1946, pp27–28.

Chapter 77; Thrumpton Hall

Miranda Seymour, *In My Father's House*. London: Simon & Schuster UK, 2008.

Cecil Roberts, *Autobiography vol 3: The Bright Twenties*. London: Hodder and Stoughton, 1970, pp 80–81.

Arthur Mee, *The King's England: Nottinghamshire*. London: Hodder & Stoughton, 1938.

Chapter 78: University of Nottingham

Robert Mellors, *Beeston: then and now*, booklet. 1916.

DH Lawrence, *Pansies*. Alfred A Knopf, 1929.

Anthony Thwaite, *Philip Larkin, Selected Letters of Philip Larkin 1940–1985*. London: Faber and Faber, 1992.

Cecil Roberts, "The Trent", from University of Nottingham, Manuscripts and Special Collections.

Chapter 79: Welbeck Abbey

Charles J Archard, "The Eccentric Duke and his Underground Tunnels", *The Portland Peerage Romance*, ch.7. London: Greening & Co Ltd, 1907.

Leonard Jacks, *The Great Houses of Nottinghamshire and the County Families*. Nottingham: W & AS Bradshaw Collection, 1881.

Lady Ottoline Morrell, Robert Gathorne-Hardy (ed), *Ottoline at Garsington, Memoirs of Lady Ottoline Morrell 1915–1918*. London: Faber and Faber, 1974.

DH Lawrence, *Women in Love*. Thomas Seltzer, 1920.

Chapter 80: Wilford and Clifton Grove

John T Godfrey and James Ward William, *The Homes and Haunts of Henry Kirke White: with some account of the family of White, of Nottingham and Norfolk*. London, Simpkin, Marshall, Hamilton, Kent & Co. Nottingham, HB Saxton, 1908.

Alan Sillitoe, *The Broken Chariot*. Flamingo, 1998.

Robert Mellors, *Old Nottingham Suburbs: then and now [Wilford]*. London: Bell, 1914.

Henry Kirke White, Robert Southey (ed), *The Poetical Works and Remains of Henry Kirke White*. London, G Routledge, 1835.

James Prior, *Three Shots from a Popgun*. 1880. Reproduced by Wentworth Press, 2019.

Alan Sillitoe, "A Scream of Toys", from *The Second Chance and other stories*. London: J Cape, 1981.

DH Lawrence, *Sons and Lovers*. The Viking Press, 1913.

Reverend Rosslyn Bruce, *The Clifton Book*. Nottingham: Henry B Saxton, 1906.

Cecil Roberts, *Autobiography vol 1: The Growing Boy*. London: Hodder and Stoughton, 1967.

Index

A

Dave **Ablitt**, 232
Derek **Acorah**, 259
Kristina **Adams**, 89, 375
Thomas **Adams**, 145
Catherine **Aird**, 373
Naomi **Alderman**, 397
Ira **Aldridge** (the African Roscius), 125
Meena **Alexander**, 398
Zayneb **Allak**, 25
Maria **Allen**, 25
Kirsty **Allsop**, 164
David **Almond**, 25
Katharine **Amberley**, 185–186
Viscount **Amberley**, 184–186
Hans Christian **Andersen**, 53
Joe **Andrews**, 89
Norman **Angell**, 51
Maya **Angelou**, 216
Jane **Anger**, 56
Narvel **Annable**, 85
Amanda **Arbouin**, 182
Lee **Arbouin**, 182
George **Argyle**, 208
(John) Michael **Argyle**, 208–210
Phyllis **Argyle** (née Hawkins-Ambler), 208
Simon **Armitage**, 31, 361
Iain **Armstrong**, 401
Jane **Armstrong**, 217
Catharine **Arnold**, 37, 141, 309
Chris **Arnot**, 303
Joan **Ashmore**, 195
Arthur **Askey**, 152
Herbert **Asquith PM**, 412
Richard **Attenborough**, 153
WH **Auden**, 379
Jane **Austen**, 206, 345
George **Ayscough**, 143
William and Anne **Ayscough**, 340

B

Charles **Babbage**, 370
Anthony **Babington**, 389
Francis **Bacon**, 111
Elizabeth **Baguley**, 309
Philip James **Bailey**, 52, 97, 101 175–178, 212, 225, 248, 328, 369, 409, 411
Robin **Bailey**, 372
Thomas **Bailey**, 97, 175–178, 248
Roy **Bainton**, 109–110
John **Baird**, 11, 12, Panya **Banjoko**, 181–183, 239–240
Alan **Baker**, 276
Paul **Baker**, 79
Roger **Baker**, 81
Valerie **Baker**, 348
F **Bakewell**, 134
Dr Hongwei **Bao**, 89
Alfred **Barber**, 33
Canon Gerrard **Barber**, 370–372
George Basil **Barham**, 413–414
Pat **Barker**, 387
Linda **Barnes**, 30
Emma **Barnett**, 399
Andy **Barrett**, 163
Jane **Barrie**, 147
JM **Barrie**, 15, 18, 52, 112, 147–149, 153–154, 266, 269, 301, 382, 413
Henry **Barrow**, 193
Mark **Barry**, 217
Lydia **Beardsall**, 229
Rev. JT **Becher**, 312, 364
Thomas **Becket**, 320
John **Beckett**, 241, 399
David **Belbin**, 24, 28, 29, 37, 61, 85, 200, 226
Gary **Bell**, 61, 238
Jo **Bell**, 366
Kathleen **Bell**, 276
Bouncing **Bella**, 58
Marco **Bellocchio**, 31
Alan **Bennett**, 117, 403

Arnold **Bennett**, 51, 274
Richard **Bentley**, 283
Samuel **Berdmore**, 161
Scrope **Berdmore**, 161
Thomas **Berdmore**, 159–161
Thomas **Berdmore** (the elder), 160
Richard **Bernard**, 191
Sarah **Bernhardt**, 152
Vicki **Bertram**, 24
John **Betjeman**, 167
James **Bettridge** (Jim), 371–372
AH **Betts**, 98
Bad **Betty**, 89
Christopher **Bigsby**, 398
Jasbinder **Bilan**, 414
Max Dalman **Binns**, 61
Ottwell **Binns**, 61
Richard **Birkin**, 144
Max **Blagg**, 345
Isla **Blair**, 349
William **Blake**, 286
Sebastian **Blanchard**, 345
Edith **Bland**, 144
Brian **Blessed**, 113
Lady **Blessington**, 53–54
Robert **Blincoe**, 287–290
Lawrence **Block**, 30
Geoff and Richard **Blore**, 74–75
Enid **Blyton**, 220, 332, 384
Gilbert **Bohun**, 271
Henry **Bolingbroke** (Duke of Lancaster), 263–264
Jessie **Bond**, 348–349
Rev. Luke **Booker**, 411
Florence **Boot**, 169, 171
Jesse **Boot**, 51, 112, 169, 393–394
John **Boot**, 167–168
Sarah **Boot**, 167
Jason **Booth**, 247
Stephen **Booth**, 61, 100, 301, 343, 345, 357, 413
William **Booth**, 26, 227

Anthony **Boucher**, 29
Nina **Boucicault**, 154
Matthew **Boulton**, 283
David **Bowie**, 238, 260, 374
Sydney **Box**, 386
Megan **Boyes**, 363
Michael **Bracewell**, 399
Malcolm **Bradbury**, 24
Richard **Bradford**, 246
Rebecca **Bradley**, 61
Don **Bradman**, 269
Ross **Bradshaw**, 55, 71, 310
William **Bradshaw**, 226
Emily **Brand**, 343
Ken **Brand**, 128, 130
Martin **Brandon-Bravo** MP, 180
Andrew **Breakwell**, 402
David **Brett**, 116
Kev and Kel **Brett**, 137
Simon **Brett**, 110
Dr Ebenezer Cobham **Brewer**, 376–379
John **Bridgeford**, 338
John Potter **Briscoe**, 16, 149–150, 221, 299, 338
Mary **Brittan** 305
Ellen **Brookes-Smith**, 254
Tim **Brooke-Taylor**, 348
Henry **Brougham**, 63
Arthur **Brown**, 230
Cornelius **Brown**, 318
Craig **Brown**, 387
Ephraim **Brown**, 338
Jane **Brown** (née Bailey), 178
John **Brown**, 287
John Henry **Brown**, 178
Pete **Brown**, 69
Tom **Browne**, 135–137
Pitman **Browne**, 240
Alan **Brownjohn**, 69
Rev. Rosslyn **Bruce**, 412
Ruth **Bryan**, 122, 328
Emrys **Bryson**, 113–4, 126, 153
Rebecca S **Buck**, 61, 86, 88
Adrian **Buckner**, 399
Sara **Bullimore**, 319

Claude **Bullock**, 371
Edward **Bulwer-Lytton**, 53, 64, 175
Gladys **Bungay**, 110
Mrs **Burden**, 282
Louie **Burrows**, 294
Wayne **Burrows**, 276
Matt **Busby**, 301
Samuel **Butler**, 78, 304–308
Rev. Thomas **Butler**, 304
Derrick **Buttress**, 146, 191, 196, 276
AS **Byatt**, 200
George **Byford**, 380
Douglas **Byng**, 81
Sue **Byrne**, 217
Augusta **Byron**, 361
Catherine **Byron**, 24
Cecile **Byron**, 369
Captain John **Byron** (Mad Jack), 91
Frederick **Byron**, 389
George **Byron**, 91, 387, 389
George Anson **Byron** (Eighth Lord Byron), 387
George Frederick William **Byron** (Ninth Lord Byron) 389
Lord Byron (George Gordon), 37, 41, 53, 77, 91–93, 111, 118, 122, 149, 157, 176, 256–258, 284, 312–329, 336, 361, 368–374, 385–390
Fifth **Lord Byron** (wicked), 256
Sir John **Byron**, 321, 369
Bill **Bryson**, 343, 400

C

Sir Julien **Cahn**, 326–327
Michael **Caine**, 153
Philip **Callow**, 17, 200
Alastair **Campbell**, 301
CG **Campbell**, 371
Phyllis **Calvert**, 206
Chris **Cann**, 68, 70
Gilbert **Cannan**, 403
George **Carey**, 176
Richard **Carlile**, 288

WD **Caröe**, 359
Liz **Carney-Marsh**, 343
Barbara **Cartland**, 235
Major John **Cartwright**, 120
Mr **Cassell**, 378
Fidel **Castro**, 235
William **Cavendish** (Duke of Newcastle), 100
William Henry **Cavendish-Bentinck** (Third Duke of Portland), 119
William John **Cavendish-Scott-Bentinck** (Fifth Duke of Portland), 400–402
Graham **Caveney**, 56
Lady **Cayley**, 119
Lukas **Chalandritsanos**, 78, 84, 285
Tony **Challis**, 84, 88
Jessie **Chambers**, 292–294
Prof. John **Chambers** (David), 293–294, 395
May **Chambers**, 292
Chambers family, 291–295
Ada **Chance**, 246
Raymond **Chandler**, 231, 302
Charlie **Chaplin**, 47, 136, 152,
King **Charles I**, 99, 361, 401
Leslie **Charteris**, 107
Pauline **Chase**, 153–154
Thomas **Chatterton**, 42
George **Chaworth**, 256
Mary Anne **Chaworth-Musters** (née Chaworth), 257–259
William **Chaworth**, 256, 321
GK **Chesterton**, 48, 63
Noam **Chomsky**, 189
Agatha **Christie**, 107, 113, 153, 373
Russell **Christie**, 87
Winston **Churchill**, 355
Marcus Tullius **Cicero**, 119

Sir John **Clanvowe**, 76, 90
John **Clare**, 274
John Stuart **Clark** (Brick), 69, 137, 311
Lynda **Clark**, 25
John Cooper **Clarke**, 73
Lilleth **Clarke**, 182
Susanna **Clarke**, 385
John **Clarkson**, 80
Hercules **Clay**, 318
John **Cleese**, 348
Colin **Clews**, 82
Sir Gervase **Clifton**, 408
Henry **Pelham-Clinton** (Fourth Duke of Newcastle), 100
Jeremy **Clyde**, 349
Eric **Coates**, 374
Ken **Coates**, 71, 188–189, 235, 237
Thomas FG **Coates**, 227
Peter **Cochran**, 78
Constable **Cock**, 58
Seymour **Cocks** MP, 370
Jonathan **Coe**, 30
Henry **Colburn**, 53
S **Coleman**, 123
Samuel Taylor **Coleridge**, 41, 119, 285–286
Dallas **Collins**, 286
Wilkie **Collins**, 63–64
Stephan **Collishaw**, 25, 379
John **Collyer**, 340
Edward **Compton**, 112
Ellen **Compton**, 112
Fay **Compton**, 112
Viola **Compton**, 112
Virginia Bateman **Compton**, 112
Sir Arthur **Conan Doyle**, 63, 107, 227, 269
Alfred **Coney**, 58
Henry **Constable**, 315–316
Paul **Cookson**, 343
Helen **Cooper**, 220
Wendy **Cope**, 275, 366
Marie **Corelli**, 63
Billy **Cotton**, 152
Julie **Covington**, 349
Noel **Coward**, 167

Ike **Cowen**, 81
Sidney William **Coxon**, 130
Emma **Craddock**, 56
Baron Gottfried von **Cramm**, 81
Thomas **Cranmer**, 260–261
Thomas **Cranmer** (the elder), 261
Anne **Crawford**, 206
Michael **Crawford**, 114
Helen **Cresswell**, 106, 219–220, 330–333, 350, 352
Andy **Croft**, 366
Giles **Croft**, 115
Louis **Crompton**, 78
Richmal **Crompton**, 135
Anthony **Cropper**, 24
Gillian **Cross**, 333
Helen **Cross**, 217
Lucy **Cullen**, 145
Rebecca **Cullen**, 25
Graeme **Cumming**, 345
Sophie **Curly** (born Joan Easdale), 162–166
Mary Ann **Cursham**, 259
Simon **Cutts**, 69
Czar of Muscovy, 410

D

Florence **Dale**, 155
Sarah **Dale**, 218
Charles **Darwin**, 249, 258, 285–286, 305–306
Erasmus **Darwin**, 119, 282–286, 306
Henrietta **Darwin**, 285
Robert & Elisabeth **Darwin**, 282, 286
Sonia **Davies**, 234
Pete **Davis**, 290
Prof. Philip **Davis**, 201
Alan **Dawson** (Jacques Morrell), 61, 214
Cecil **Day Lewis** (Nicholas Blake), 347, 379
Frank **Day-Lewis**, 379
Vivien **Dayrell-Browning**, 47
Christopher **Dean**, 354
John **Deane**, 410

William **Dearden**, 229
Charles **Deering** (born Georg Karl Dering), 142–144
Daniel **Defoe**, 211, 409
Judi **Dench**, 347
Robert **Denison**, 121
Susie **Dent**, 378
John **Derry**, 381, 384
Colin **Dexter**, 28, 31, Lord Howard de **Walden**, 390
Pemberton de **Wanderer**, 337
Catherine **Dickins**, 64
Charles **Dickens**, 53–67, 116, 184, 212, 274, 287–290, 301, 364, 382, 387
Katey **Dickens**, 66
Noel **Dilke**, 69
Benjamin **Disraeli**, 53
Jo **Dixon**, 25
Lanky **Dobbs**, 58
Ken **Dodd**, 35
Robert **Dodsley**, 337
John **Doherty**, 288
Maura **Dooley**, 366
Charles **Doman**, 394
Sir Alec **Douglas-Home**, 303
Joan **Downer**, 239
Roddy **Doyle**, 399
Sonia **Dresdel**, 331
John **Drinkwater**, 149
Melanie **Duffill-Jeffs**, 84
Carol Ann **Duffy**, 275, 311, 366
Maureen **Duffy**, 83
Peter **Duncan**, 116
Frank **Dunlop**, 114, 116
Anthony Van **Dyck**, 321
Bob **Dylan**, 104–105
Sue **Dymoke**, 25

E

Brian **Easdale**, 164
Michael **Eaton**, 25, 27–30, 59, 67, 116, 372,
David **Edgley**, 82, 88
John **Edleston**, 78
Rowena **Edlin-White**, 34, 122

King **Edward I**, 144, 263
King **Edward III**, 314
King **Edward VI**, 261
David **Edwards** (Jack George Edmunson), 374
Dwight D **Eisenhower**, 35
George **Eliot** (Mary Ann Evans), 107, 212, 215, 387
TS **Eliot**, 402
Janice **Elliott**, 219–220
WE **Elliott**, 249
John Edward **Ellis**, 373
Joseph **Else**, 15
Bob **Emerton**, 82
John **Emerton**, 389
Rowland **Emett**, 39–40
Jonathan **Emmett**, 398
Friedrich **Engels**, 235
Frederick **Enoch**, 409
Richard **Eyre**, 114, 231

F

Ruth **Fainlight**, 34, 68–69, 280, 387
Michael **Faraday**, 32
Paul **Farley**, 366
Sarah **Farmer**, 126
Christy **Fearn**, 374
Barry **Feinstein**, 104
Elaine **Feinstein**, 366
Marty **Feldman**, 80
John **Fellows**, 119
C **Ferraby**, 154
Jasper **Fforde**, 311
Shirley Anne **Field**, 73, 213
Yvette **Fielding**, 259
Gracie **Fields**, 107
Paul **Fillingham**, 138
Albert **Finney**, 245, 348
Catherine **Fisher**, 275
Thomas Henry **Fisher**, 134–137
Robert **Fisk**, 189
Lady Anna **FitzRoy**, 390
George **FitzRoy Seymour**, 390
James Elroy **Flecker**, 269
Ian **Fleming**, 40, 103
Gustav Albert **Flersheim**, 140

Alan **Fletcher**, 317
William **Fletcher**, 368–369
Raymond **Flynn**, 31, 61
Ken **Follett**, 301
Jean **Forbes-Robertson**, 154
Forman-Hardy family, 407
George **Formby**, 107
Barry **Forshaw**, 297
EM **Forster**, 79, 308
Barry **Foster**, 60
Caroline Bell **Foster**, 182
Watson **Fothergill**, 45, 46, 107, 128
Charles James **Fox**, 119
George **Fox**, 142
Kate **Fox**, 366
Samuel **Fox**, 108
Katherine **Frank**, 24
Benjamin **Franklin**, 160
Charles Ian **Fraser**, 326–327
Amelia **Fratson** (Amy), 382
John Foster **Frazer**, 52
Michael **Frayn**, 387
Stephen **Frears**, 31, 237,
Alderman HJ **Freckingham**, 230
Lee **Froch**, 247
Sam **Fuller**, 27
Neil **Fulwood**, 276
Frances **Fyfield**, 30
Rose **Fyleman**, 32, 224
Freddy **Fynn**, 182

G

Faith **Gakanje**, 182
Joseph **Gales**, 316
Winifred Marshall **Gales**, 316
Sheelagh **Gallagher**, 216
Graeme **Garden**, 349
Rolf **Gardiner**, 393–394
General Giuseppe **Garibaldi**, 353
Rosie **Garner**, 213–214, 366
Robert **Garioch**, 69

Lenford Alphonso **Garrison** (Len), 179–181
Marie **Garrison**, 180
Mark **Gatiss**, 117
John of **Gaunt**, 263–264
Abigail **Gawthern**, 32, 142
Robert **Gent**, 275
Boy **George**, 81
King **George III**, 12, 159, 160, 283
King **George V**, 393
Eustathios **Georgiou**, 78
Harry **German**, 326
Evelyn **Gibbs**, 195
Denis **Gifford**, 136
Ann **Gilbert**, 158, 409
Jane **Gilbert**, 158
Sidney **Giles**, 229, 338
Eric **Gill**, 404
Rev. John **Girardot**, 272
Malcolm **Gladwell**, 157
Mr and Mrs **Gladwin**,141
Canon **Glaister**, 359
Elizabeth **Glaister**, 359
John T **Godfrey**, 407
Johann Wolfgang von **Goethe**, 175
Lise **Gold**, 89
Denis **Goldberg**, 180
John **Goodridge**, 232
Rich **Goodson**, 25, 89,
Anne **Goodwin**, 88, 217
Mark **Goodwin**, 25
Nadine **Gordimer**, 199
Catherine **Gordon**, 91–92
Hannah **Gordon**, 331
Catherine Grace Frances **Gore**, 344–345
Ray **Gosling**, 17, 69, 80–81, 124, 184, 232–237, 248,
Piers **Gough**, 216
Tala **Gouveia**, 60
Sue **Grafton**, 30
Herol **Graham** (Bomber), 247
James **Graham**, 117
Prof. F **Granger**, 42
Bernie **Grant** MP, 180
Gwen **Grant**, 36
Andrew **Graves**, 366

Robert **Graves**, 386
Adrian **Gray**, 344
Dulcie **Gray**, 206
Mrs **Gray**, 92
Zane **Gray**, 235
Doreen **Greatorex**, 73
King of **Greece**, 370
George **Green**, 32
William **Green**, 160
Graham **Greene**, 18, 45–52, 62, 231, 301, 403, 413
Germaine **Greer**, 349
Norma **Gregory**, 181
Lord **Grey**, 91
Frank **Griffin**, 19
Elly **Griffiths**, 311
Cathy **Grindrod**, 55, 410
Alan **Guest**, 85
Everard **Guilford**, 340
André van **Gyseghem**, 113

H

Stephen **Haddelsey**, 296
Matt **Haig**, 312, 316–317
Flight Lieutenant **Hales**, 108
Madge **Hales**, 108
Henry Thomas **Hall**, 125
John **Hall**, 107
Dr Spencer Timothy **Hall**, 300, 337, 338, 405, 408
Duncan **Hamilton**, 309
John (Sandy) **Hammerton**, 381–382
Sophie **Hannah**, 311
John **Hanson**, 256, 369
Thomas **Hardy**, 120, 266
Jane **Harley** (Countess of Oxford), 324
Sir Alfred **Harmsworth**, 382
GW **Harris**, 151
Joanne **Harris**, 311
Robert **Harris**, 303
Noel **Harrower**, 100
Dorothy **Hartley**, 138
Clare **Hartwell**, 359

John **Harvey**, 19, 29–31, 36, 58–61, 110,115, 214, 226, 311, 366, 398, 415
Barney **Harwood**, 154
Nicki **Hastie**, 86, 88
William **Hatfield** (born Ernest Chapman), 223
Spike **Hawkins**, 69
Lucinda **Hawksley Dickens**, 66
John **Hayes**, 254–255
Henry **Hayman**, 376, 379
Colin **Haynes**, 232
Jaq **Hazell**, 61
W Carew **Hazlitt**, 315
Joan **Heal**, 116
Seamus **Heaney**, 73
Tina **Heath**, 331
John **Hegley**, 366
Edmund **Helwys**, 191–194, 197
Joan **Helwys** (née Ashore), 192
Margaret **Helwys**, 191
Thomas **Helwys**, 191–194
Felicia Dorothea **Hemans**, 254
Ernest **Hemingway**, 301
Paul **Henderson**, 68–69
Darren **Henley** OBE, 38
Pippa **Hennessy**, 55, 89
Caroline **Hennigan**, 31
Adrian **Henri**, 69
King **Henry I**, 99
King **Henry II**, 99, 320
King **Henry IV**, 264
King **Henry VII**, 99
King **Henry VIII**, 142, 321
George **Henty**, 129
John **Heppell**, 55
David **Herbert**, 368
Robert **Herrick** 131
Rev. John **Herring**, 192
Paul **Herring**, 16
Joan **Hessayon**, 397
Charlton **Heston**, 107
George **Hickling** (Rusticus), 145, 215
David **Higgins** (Stickman), 182

Patricia **Highsmith**, 30
Thomas **Hill**, 42
Tony **Hill**, 414
Tony **Hillerman**, 30
Sara **Hillier**, 154
Enid **Hilton**, 279
Edward **Hind**, 409, 411
George Thomas **Hine**, 128–129, 246
Muriel Florence **Hine**, 128–130, 396
Thomas Chambers **Hine**, 101, 128–132, 144, 224
Michael **Hirst**, 399
Victoria **Hislop**, 311
John Cam **Hobhouse**, 369
William Henry **Hocking**, 79
Rev. George Francis **Holcombe**, 354
Merlin **Holland**, 78
Stephen L **Holland**, 138
Alan **Hollinghurst**, 387
Buddy **Holly**, 152
Miss **Hogarth**, 64
John **Holmes** (builder), 221
John **Holmes** (author/radio presenter), 303
John **Holmes** (author), 344
Joseph **Holmes**, 221
Michael **Holroyd**, 387
Sam **Hope**, 86
Anthony **Hopkins**, 347
Percy Richard Morley **Horder**, 169, 393
WA **Hottinger**, 269
Harry **Houdini**, 152
Caroline **Howitt**, 108
Margaret **Howitt**, 100
Mary **Howitt**, 32, 100, 141, 175, 258–259, 328, 369, 396, 408–409
Richard **Howitt**, 175, 229, 296, 338, 409
TC **Howitt**, 36
Godfrey **Howitt**, 338
William **Howitt**, 32, 100–101, 175, 256, 259, 328, 369, 408–409
Michelle **Hubbard** (Mother), 182, 231, 240

Mr **Hudson**, 222–223
Madox **Hueffer** (later Ford Madox Ford), 293
Kathryn **Hughes**, 24, 387
Evan **Hunter** (Ed McBain), 28
Colonel John **Hutchinson**, 99, 195
Lucy **Hutchinson**, 99–100
Catherine **Hutton**, 367
William **Hutton**, 366–367
Aldous **Huxley**, 306, 403

I

Eric **Idle**, 349
Washington **Irving**, 320, 325
Isabella of France, 101
William **Ivory**, 25, 360

J

Leonard **Jacks**, 354
Ann **Jackson**, 370
Kevin **Jackson**, 88
Lisa **Jackson**, 182
Mick **Jackson**, 400–402
Philip **Jackson**, 60
Sarah **Jackson**, 24
Maxim **Jakubowski**, 30
Clive **James**, 349
King **James**, 191, 192
Peter **James**, 311
Anna **Jarvis**, 131–133
Mick **Jasper**, 401
Alan **Jenkins**, 387
Troy **Jenkinson**, 90
Pete **Jermy** & Roger **Westerman**, 74
Jerome K **Jerome**, 51, 63, 269
Jane **Jerram** (Jane Elizabeth Holmes), 143, 248, 409
King **John**, 320
Mervyn **Johns**, 206
Ruth L **Johns**, 239
Boris **Johnson**, 85
BS **Johnson**, 162–163, 274, 328, 358, 396–397
Joseph **Johnson**, 283
Geoffrey **Johnstone**, 371

Inigo **Jones**, 389
Philip **Jones**, 33
Terry **Jones**, 384
Ben **Jonson**, 316, 337, 352
Pat **Jordan**, 71, 235
Spencer **Jordan**, 397
Graham **Joyce**, 24
Rachel **Joyce**, 311
Lucy **Joynes**, 141
Alan **Judd**, 387
Joshua **Judson**, 89

K

Ken **Kamoche**, 182
Kadiatu **Kanneh-Mason**, 310
Siddharth **Katragadda**, 309
Patrick **Kavanagh**, 11
Campbell **Kay**, 115
Jackie **Kay**, 275, 311, 366
Joyce Lesley **Keating**, 345
Buster **Keaton**, 47
Fanny **Kemble**, 63
Marshall Dennis **Kemp**, 208
Sonia **Kemp**, 208
Duke of **Kent**, 81
Gordon **Kermode**, 348
John Maynard **Keynes**, 79
Rev. Mr **Killer**, 132
Herbert **Kilpin**, 211
Francis **King**, 80, 85
Richard **King**, 414
Desmond **King-Hele**, 285
Charles **Kingsley**, 290
Rory **Kinnear**, 360
Mark **Kinkead-Weekes**, 79
Carolyn **Kirby**, 297
Joseph **Kirby**, 154
Christopher Pious Mary **Kirk** (Kris), 81
Lily **Kirk**, 266–267
Pat **Kirkwood**, 154
Naomi **Klein**, 189
Harold **Knight**, 138
Jill **Knight**, 84–85
Laura **Knight** (née Laura Johnson), 138–139

Sarah **Kolawole** (Rain), 182

L

Elias **Lacey**, 373
Allan **Ladd**, 50
Veronica **Lake**, 50
Caroline **Lamb**, 324
Mr **Lamb**, 255
William and John **Lambert**, 151, 288–289
David **Lane**, 72
NM **Lane**, 370
Bonnie **Langford**, 154
JM **Langford**, 369
Lillie **Langtry**, 265
LD **Lapinski**, 343
Edmund **Larken**, 408
Philip **Larkin**, 395, 397
Birger **Larsen**, 60
Laurel & Hardy, 152
John **Lavender**, 92
Debbie **Law**, 87
Arthur **Lawrence**, 278–279
DH **Lawrence**, 11, 19–23, 37, 47,68, 76–79, 102, 107, 112–118, 122–125, 128, 141, 152, 157–158, 184–187, 201, 214–215, 219, 226, 229–233, 242–243, 259, 266, 269, 276–281, 289–295, 300, 328, 358–359, 392–398, 402–403, 411
Ernest **Lawrence**, 157
Frieda **Lawrence**, 277, 295
Lydia **Lawrence**, 277, 279, 291
Nigel **Leach**, 82
Captain John **Leacroft**, 362
John and Julia **Leacroft**, 362–364
Hannah **Leaf**, 334
David **Lean**, 167
Arthur **Leatherland**, 236
Chris **Leavers**, 399
Miss **Leavers**, 97
John **le Carré**, 189, 302
Robert **Lee**, 347
Giselle **Leeb**, 87

Paris **Lees**, 90, 375
Thomas **Legendre**, 397
Clive **Leivers**, 295
Dennis **Lemon**, 82
Mark **Lemon**, 64
Vladimir **Lenin**, 235
Keith **Leonard**, 70
Cathy **Lesurf**, 217
Alice **Levine**, 211
Hilda **Lewis**, 99, 101, 145, 152,195, 246, 396
Prof. M Michael **Lewis**, 396
Patrick **Limb**, 12
Karin **Lindley**, 297
Maxine **Linnell**, 25
Clare **Littleford**, 25, 61
Dr David **Livingstone**, 326
Dr **Llewellyn**, 371
Harold **Lloyd**, 47
Noel **Lloyd**, 80
David **Lloyd George**, 412
Ralph **Lloyd-Jones**, 78, 368
Lockwood and **Mawson**, 20
Hugh **Lofting**, 44
TM **Logan**, 301
Christopher **Logue**, 69
Herbert **Lom**, 28
Mrs **Loney**, 49, 50
Ivory **Longley**, 216, 218
Alfred **Loughton**, 365
Sharmaine **Lovegrow**, 181
Lady Ada **Lovelace**, 64–65, 370–373, 389, 39
Peter **Lovesey**, 28
RD **Low**, 136
Edward Joseph **Lowe**, 392
Joseph **Lowe**, 392
Stephen **Lowe**, 97, 114, 230–231, 395
John **Lucas**, 200, 274–276
Pauline **Lucas**, 195
Ted **Lynch**, 386
Vera **Lynn**, 152

M

Gilbert **Mabbot**, 141
George **MacBeth**, 69
Fiona **MacCarthy**, 77, 387
Margaret **MacDermott**, 275
Robert **Macfarlane**, 38, 296–298
Mhairi **Macfarlane**, 301
Robert **Machray**, 136
Compton **Mackenzie**, 112
Frederick **Macquisten**, 79
William **Macready**, 111
Henry **Maddock**, 42
Rod **Madocks**, 61
Maurice **Magnus**, 79
Sarah **Maguire**, 275
Sandeep **Mahal**, 38, 233
Eve **Makis**, 24, 309
Mufaro **Makubika**, 240–241
Dr Thomas **Mallett**, 132
Eric **Malpass**, 108–109
David **Mamet**, 398
Steve **Mapp**, 31
Emma **Mardlin**, 414
Princess **Margaret**, 114
Ngaio **Marsh**, 107
Adam **Mars-Jones**, 85
GJ **Martin**, 297
Eleanor **Marx**, 144
Karl **Marx**, 156, 235
Andy **Maslen**, 204
James **Mason**, 206
F **Matcham**, 152
David **Mathers**, 181
Lila **Matsumoto**, 397
Judge Keith **Matthewman** QC, 86
Charles Skinner **Matthews**, 77
Somerset **Maugham**, 81
Armistead **Maupin**, 83
Robert **Maxwell**, 281, 302
Val **May**, 114
Xavier **Mayne**, 78
Benjamin **Mayo** (The Old General), 221–223
Captain **McCraith**, 370
Val **McDermid**, 28, 30, 302
Gavin and Oskar **McIntosh**, 351

Ian **McMillan**, 275, 311, 366
Richard **McCance**, 83
Colum **McCann**, 397
Joseph **McCarthy**, 47
Vicky **McClure**, 60, 114
Nigel **McCrery**, 60, 311
Geraldine **McEwan**, 347
Roger **McGough**, 69, 275, 311
Jimmy **McGovern**, 73
Pat **McGrath**, 114, 248
Jon **McGregor**, 25, 309
Ian **McKellen**, 114, 116
Lisa **Mckenzie**, 237–238
"Leo" **McKern**, 114
Joyce **McKinney**, 302
Jenny **McLeod**, 183, 240
Jack **McNeill**, 154
Hollie **McNish**, 366
Jonathan **Meades**, 311
Angela **Meads**, 343
Arthur **Mee**, 271, 342, 380–384
Henry **Mee**, 381
Marjorie **Mee**, 382
Mary **Mee**, 381
David **Mellen**, 38
Dame Agnes **Mellers**, 142
Richard **Mellers**, 142
Robert **Mellors**, 195, 405
Paul **Mendez**, 387
Margaret **Middleton** (née Welch), 198, 200
Stanley **Middleton**, 19, 198–203, 309, 396, 398
Annabella (Anne Isabella) **Milbanke**, 324, 328, 370, 387
George Francis (Frank) **Miles**, 264–265
Mary **Miles**, 266
Arthur **Miller**, 398
Claude **Miller**, 27
Kei **Miller**, 366
Thomas **Miller**, 53–54, 338, 409
Marian **Millhouse**, 228
Robert **Millhouse**, 225–228, 337
Stuart **Mills**, 69–70

AA **Milne**, 269
John **Milton**, 227, 335
Adrian **Mitchell**, 69
Naomi **Mitchison**, 164
Leanne **Moden**, 233
Deborah **Moggach**, 387
Nicola **Monaghan**, 25, 36, 59, 196, 309,
Walter **Montgomery**, 151
Bill **Moody**, 30
Alison **Moore**, 25, 311, 396
Beth **Moran**, 217, 366
Caitlin **Moran**, 311
Eric **Morecambe**, 152
Samuel **Morley** 15–16,
Michael **Morpurgo**, 353
Lady Ottoline **Morrell** (née Cavendish-Bentinck), 184, 187, 386, 401–404
Philip **Morrell**, 402
Jackie **Morris**, 298
Blake **Morrison**, 399
Helen **Mort**, 366
Peter **Mortimer**, 202–204
Roger **Mortimer**, 101
Andrew H **Morton**, 254–255
Walter **Mosley**, 30, 53
Kate **Mosse**, 25
Andrew **Motion**, 366
Sir Alfred **Munnings**, 355
John **Murray**, 207, 314–315
John **Murton**, 193–194
Charles **Musters**, 258
John **Musters**, 257
Julie **Myerson**, 219

N

Daljit **Nagra**, 366
Suniti **Namjoshi**, 83
Christopher **Neame**, 349
Edwin **Neave**, 253–255
Trevor **Negus**, 61
AS **Neil** (Aaliyah), 354
E **Nesbit**, 332
John **Neville**, 114–115
Sir William **Neville**, 76
Duke of **Newcastle**, 100
George **Newnes**, 382

Chloe **Newsome**, 154
Sir Isaac **Newton**, 283, 341
Maureen **Newton**, 374
Trish **Nicholson**, 311
Leslie **Nielsen**, 107
Robert **Nieri**, 211
Edward **Noel**, 388
Henry **Normal**, 72, 275, 366
Ben **Norris**, 366
Ivor **Novello**, 81

O

Deirdre **O'Byrne**, 55
Feargus **O'Connor**, 17
Bill **Oddie**, 349
Bo **Olawoye**, 239
Geoffrey **Oldfield**, 146
Eliza S **Oldham**, 411
Laurence **Olivier**, 81, 107
Julie **O'Neill**, 364
Betty-Maxine **Onwuteaka**, 182
Rev. James **Orange**, 97
Baroness **Orczy**, 151, 152
Joe **Orton**, 81, 398
George **Orwell**, 156, 301
Sir Peter **O'Sullevan**, 353, 356
Amelia **Osborne**, 91
SW **Oscroft**, 410
Philip **Osment**, 85
Peter **O'Toole**, 153
Sally **Outram**, 343

P

Norman **Pace**, 116
Hugh **Paddick**, 80
Herbert Byng **Paget**, 373
Thomas **Paine**, 120–21
Frank **Palmer** (Baggy), 30, 61, 301–303
Geoffrey **Palmer**, 80
Nick **Palmer**, 302
Adela **Pankhurst**, 17
Emmeline **Pankhurst**, 17
Sara **Paretsky**, 28, 30
Chris **Parker**, 61
Richard **Parkes Bonington**, 43

Sir Thomas **Parkyns**, 340–342
Martin **Parnell**, 69–70
Joe **Pasquale**, 154
Brian **Patten**, 69, 213
William **Patterson**, 128
Charles **Pauli**, 78, 305–306
Tom **Paulin**, 275, 399
Charlie **Peace**, 58
Gregory **Peck**, 107
Henry **Pelham-Clinton** (Fifth Duke of Newcastle), 128
Henry **Pelham-Clinton** (Fourth Duke of Newcastle), 100
Adam **Penford**, 117
Nicholas **Penny**, 246
Charles **Penswick**, 133
Constance **Penswick Smith**, 131–133
Gareth **Peter**, 89
William **Peveril**, 99
Nikolaus **Pevsner**, 359
Sir Richard **Phillips**, 228
Charles J **Phipps**, 151
Nigel **Pickard**, 310
Tom **Pickard**, 70
EG **Pickering**, 338
Paul A **Pickering**, 17, 57
William **Pickering**, 175
Helena **Pielichaty**, 318
John Shadrach **Piercy**, 345
Elizabeth **Pigot**, 362–363
John **Pigot**, 362
Gervase **Pigott**, 389
Rosamund **Pike**, 360
Kathy **Pimlott**, 214
Prof. Vivian de Sola **Pinto**, 395
Dave **Pitt**, 82
Nigel **Planer**, 275
Samuel **Plumb**, 338, 364
Charles **Plumbe**, 338, 364
John **Plumptre**, 144
Alexander **Pope**, 283
Peter **Porter**, 25

Third Duke of **Portland** (William Henry Cavendish-Bentinck), 119
Fifth Duke of **Portland** (William John Cavendish-Scott-Bentinct), 400–402
Dukes of **Portland**, 400
Christopher **Pressler**, 89
Martin **Priestman**, 284
Dennis **Price**, 386
Peter **Price**, 71, 235
VS **Pritchett**, 307
FW **Pomeroy**, 359
Alexander **Pope**, 227
Ellen **Porter**, 132
Beatrix **Potter**, 144
The **Powdrill** family, 389
George **Powe**, 183, 234–235
JB **Priestley**, 206, 215, 354
Prince of Wales, 35, 160, 222, 282, 326, 355
Dorothy **Prior**, 265
James **Prior** (Kirk), 263, 265–267, 396, 410-411
Pritt, 97
Sheenagh **Pugh**, 275
Ken **Purslow**, 368

Q

Bernard **Quaritch**, 149
Queen **Elizabeth**, 261, 341, 389
Queen Mary, 261
Mary Queen of Scots, 389, 401

R

George **Ragg**, 228
Thomas **Ragg**, 228–229
Ian **Rankin**
William Dickinson **Rastall**, 360
Robert **Rathbone**, 302
Arnold **Rattenbury**, 101
Onjali **Raúf**, 343
Slavomir **Rawicz**, 23
Paula **Rawsthorne**, 217, 311

Nicola Davison **Reed**, 346
Sir John **Rees**, 51
Saskia **Reeves**, 360
Antonia Marie Therese **Regina**, 144
Miss **Reinhardt**, 151
Karel **Reisz**, 213
Thomas **Rempstone**, 263–264
Jim **Rendel**, 165
Ruth **Rendell**, 31, 61, 372
Kate **Reynolds**, 351
Jean **Rhys**, 386
King **Richard II**, 263
King **Richard III**, 99
Christopher **Richardson**, 83
FR **Richardson**, 169
Peter **Richardson**, 238
Séan **Richardson**, 88
George **Ridding**, 359
Lady Laura **Ridding**, 359–360
Sylvia **Riley** (Carol Lake), 71, 235
Stella **Rimington**, 219
Jean **Ritchie**, 104
Doug **Ritchie**, 146
Charles **Roach**, 116
Rosemary **Robb**, 110
Cecil **Roberts**, 32, 36, 43, 44, 47, 51–52, 80, 134, 153,176, 215, 225, 301, 326, 372, 389,396, 411–412
Michèle **Roberts**, 387
Rachel **Roberts**, 213
Celia **Robertson**, 165
Thomas William **Robertson**, 316
JB **Robinson**, 17,
Nicci **Robinson** (pen. Robyn **Nyx**), 88
Dummer **Rogers**, 92
President **Roosevelt**, 383
Michael **Rosen**, 275, 311
Patricia **Routledge**, 331
Brian **Rowe**, 332
Carrol **Rowe**, 182
Peter Paul **Rubens**, 321
Jane **Rule**, 83
AE **Russell**, 269

Bertrand **Russell**, 51, 72, 184–189, 402
Earl **Russell**, 184–185
Lord Grey de **Ruthyn**, 321
Samuel **Rutter**, 160
Frances **Ryan**, 414

S

Manjit S **Sahota**, 414
Thomas **Sanders**, 327
George **Saunders**, 397
Sir George **Savile** (8th Baronet of Thornhill), 351
Alice **Scanlon**, 108
Earl of **Scarborough**, 338
Michael (a.k.a. Mitzi) **Scholes**, 82
John Brough **Scott**, 356
Sir Walter **Scott**, 313, 315, 336
Rosemary **Scott-Ellis**, 390
Tony **Scupham-Bilton**, 76
Thom **Seddon**, 88
The **Seely** family, 353–356
Charles **Seely** MP, 353
Sir Charles **Seely**, 354
Sir Charles Hilton **Seely** MP, 354
Colonel Frank Evelyn **Seely**, 354
Hugh Michael **Seely**, 354
Jack **Seely** (Lord Mottistone, General John Edward Bernard Seely, JEB Seely) 355–356
Will **Self**, 301
Shreya **Sen-Handley**, 217, 311
Dr **Seuss**, 159
Dolly **Sewell**, 110
Miranda **Seymour**, 25, 385–387, 390–391, 404
William **Shakespeare**, 111–113, 116, 124–125, 220, 226–227, 263–264, 334, 336, 348
Sir Dodds **Shaw**, 52

George Bernard **Shaw**, 112–113, 149, 309, 365
Gilbert **Shelden**, 48
Mary **Shelley**, 283–284, 286, 386
Percy B **Shelley**, 186, 284, 286, 397
Arthur **Shelton**, 246
Norman **Sherry**, 49
Countess of **Shrewsbury** (Jane), 351
Nevil **Shute**, 372
Richard **Silburn**, 237–238
Alan **Sillitoe**, 12, 17, 25, 34, 35, 36, 68, 69, 72, 73, 87, 101–108, 116, 117, 145, 162, 184, 188, 203,213, 233, 244-248, 280, 309–311, 358, 379, 387, 390, 408, 411
Brian **Sillitoe**, 245, 246
Christopher **Sillitoe**, 245
David **Sillitoe**, 36
Michael **Sillitoe**, 245
Sabina **Sillitoe**, 245
Ron **Silver**, 27
Sheila **Sim**, 153
Alan **Simpson**, 27
Darren **Simpson**, 414
Mark **Simpson**, 137
Tony **Simpson**, 189
GF **Sinclair**, 151
William **Singleton**, 108
Lemn **Sissay**, 366
Jackie **Skinner**, 310
Di **Slaney**, 25
Kim **Slater**, 25, 61
Ioney **Smallhorne**, 182
Joseph **Smedley**, 364–365
Richard **Smedley**, 365
Abel **Smith**, 407
Alan and Roy **Smith**, 247
Dr Courtney Alexander **Smith**, 182
Delia **Smith**, 138
Freda Love **Smith**, 25
George **Smith**, 32
Mary C. **Smith**, 133
Michael RD **Smith**, 61
Paul **Smith**, 27, 216
Thomas **Smith**, 32

Ursula **Smith**, 116
John **Smyth**, 191, 194
JC **Snaith**, 212, 268–270, 396, 414
Mahsunda **Snaith**, 414
Lord **Snowdon**, 114
Mahendra **Solanki**, 24, 366,
Annie **Sophia**, 178
Robert **Southey**, 41, 42, 229
Roderick **Speer**, 315
Herbert **Spencer**, 248–249
Mark **Spencer** MP, 354
WJH **Sprott**, 186
Bridie **Squires**, 232
Michael **Standen**, 18
Peter **Stanford**, 379
Colin **Stanley**, 231
HM **Stanley**, 326
Sir Charles **Starmer**, 51
Edward **Staveley**, 97
Beth **Steel**, 117
Stan **Stennett**, 231
Debra **Stephenson**, 154
Clare **Stevens**, 25, 217–218,
Sharon RM **Stevens**, 182
Nick **Stevenson**, 238
William **Stevenson**, 33
David **Stirling**, 190
Rachael **Stirling**, 360
Dorothy **Stirrup**, 205
Paul **Stone**, 333
Bram **Stoker**, 149
Mary **Stokes**, 330
Michael **Stokes**, 61
Major Kenneth **Stoppard**, 115
Tom **Stoppard** (born Tom Straussler), 111, 115–116
Richard **Stott**, 302
Lytton **Strachey**, 46, 404
Jane **Streeter**, 309–311
Mercer **Stretch**, 169
Lady Arbella **Stuart**, 352
William **Stukeley**, 300
David **Such**, 236
(Emily) Jane **Suffield** (later Neave), 254–255

Lord Ronald Charles **Sutherland-Leveson-Gower**, 265
Charles **Sutton**, 249
Henry S **Sutton**, 299–300, 411
John **Sutton**, 119
Richard **Sutton**, 249, 300
Jenny **Swann**, 274–276
Bridget **Swinden**, 217
Rev. John Elliotson **Symes**, 225–226
Julian **Symons**, 28
Sylvia **Syms**, 154

T

Helen **Tamblyn-Saville**, 344
Dr Robert **Tansey**, 345
Quentin **Tarantino**, 28–29
Peter **Tatchell**, 180
Bertrand **Tavernier**, 31
Andrew **Taylor**, 24
Megan **Taylor**, 89, 311
Paul **Taylor**, 30
John **Tenniel**, 64
Alfred **Tennyson**, 175
William Makepeace **Thackeray**, 175
Margaret **Thatcher**, 85, 414
Frances **Thimann**, 25
Jeremy **Thomas**, 31
Sue **Thomas**, 24
Marie **Thompson**, 56
N **Thompson**, 154
Sue **Thompson**, 58
Christopher **Thomson**, 334–339
Diana **Thomson**, 394
Anne **Thoroton**, 272
Robert **Thoroton**, 99, 143, 271–273
Tony **Tillinghast**, 162, 396–397
Christopher **Timothy**, 349
Tinley family, 366
Titian, 321
Miriam **Toews**, 155
Albert **Toft**, 178
Hilary **Tolkien**, 254
Mabel **Tolkien**, 254
JRR **Tolkien**, 253–255
Claire **Tomalin**, 387

Elizabeth **Tomlinson**, 212
Rebecca **Tope**, 311
Barry **Took**, 80
Geoffrey **Trease**, 18, 112, 140, 155–157, 226, 396
Mary **Trease**, 157
Philip **Trease**, 157
Tommy **Trinder**, 152
Anthony **Trollope**, 63
Father **Trollope**, 48
Frances **Trollope**, 287, 289
Joanna **Trollope**, 311
Leon **Trotsky**, 235
Reuben **Trueman**, 335–336
CJ **Tudor**, 31, 61
Gael **Turnbull**, 69
Bob **Turner**, 302
Dick **Turpin**, 58
Mark **Twain**, 301
John **Tyson**, 232

U

Barry **Upton**, 345
Peter **Ustinov**, 114

V

George **Vason**, 94, 97
Eleftherios **Venizelos** (Prime Minister of Greece), 327
Queen **Victoria**, 126, 169, 175, 326, 353
Victoria **Villasenor** (pen. Victoria **Oldham** & Brey **Willows**), 87–88
Francis **Vivian** (Arthur "Ernest" Ashley), 61, 106–110
Mary **Voce** (née Mary Hallam), 212
Kurt **Vonnegut**, 189

W

Katherine Monica **Wade-Dalton**, 140
Gilbert **Wakefield**, 43, 118
Miranda **Walden**, 390
Rev. George **Walker**, 118–122
Holland **Walker**, 370
James **Walker**, 138, 233
Joseph Cyril **Walker**, 347–348
Peter **Walker** (pen. Nicholas **Rhea**), 109
Joan **Wallace**, 111
John **Waller**, 289
William **Wallett** (The Queen's Jester), 125–127
Hugh **Walpole**, 164
Joanna **Walsh**, 397
Minette **Walters**, 30
Edward **Ward**, 12
James **Ward**, 407
Simon **Ward**, 349
Heriot **Ware**, 152
Jackie **Washington**, 105
Rory **Waterman**, 24
Thomas **Waters**, 414
Dudley D **Watkins**, 136–137
Fothergill **Watson**, 107
James **Watt**, 283
Helen Kirkpatrick **Watts**, 17
Bishop Mark **Way**, 348
Gail **Webb**, 232
John **Webb**, 388
William Frederick **Webb**, 326
Josiah **Wedgwood**, 283
Prof. Ernest **Weekley**, 242–243, 269, 395
Frieda **Weekley** (née von Richthofen, finally Mrs Frieda Lawrence), 242, 243, 269, 294
Matthew **Welton**, 366, 397
Angus **Wells**, 60
Lucy **Wescomb**, 387, 389
Donald E **Westlake**, 28, 30
Jo **Weston**, 217
Alfred **Whipple** (Henry), 205
Dorothy **Whipple**, 205–207, 327, 396
Phil **Whitaker**, 61
Cathy **White**, 82
Henry Kirke **White**, 41, 43, 276, 328, 405, 407
John **White**, 41
AN **Whitehead**, 186

Amanda **Whittington**, 25, 116
Dave and Felicity **Whittle**, 201
Ann **Widdecombe**, 86
"Sam Weller" **Widdowson**, 212
William **Wilberforce**, 407
Oscar **Wilde**, 63, 78–79, 149, 264–265
Georgina **Wilding**, 366, 399
Colonel Thomas **Wildman**, 325–326, 369
Leah **Wilkins**, 56
Samuel **Wilkinson**, 411
Tom **Wilkinson**, 60
Hugh **Willatt**, 113–114, 195
Jo **Willett**, 77
William the Conqueror, 99
Alan **Williams**, 61
Joanna **Williams**, 338
Jonathan **Williams**, 70
Kenneth **Williams**, 80
Tennessee **Williams**, 116
Leslie **Williamson**, 281
GL **Willis**, 371
Colin **Wilson**, 231
Glenis **Wilson**, 61, 110
Harold **Wiltshire**, 237
Godfrey **Winn**, 106, 109
Jackie **Winter**, 171
Jeanette **Winterson**, 83
Ernie **Wise**, 152
PG **Wodehouse**, 156, 269, 301
Sir Donald **Wolfit**, 125, 347–349
Jack **Wood**, 295
Nick **Wood**, 116, 402
President **Woodrow Wilson**, 131
Gregory **Woods**, 24, 83, 84, 86, 89,
Virginia **Woolf**, 164, 402
Adrian **Wootton**, 27–31
William **Wordsworth**, 286
Frank **Wore**, 68
Lady Mary Wortley **Montagu**, 77

449

Keith **Wright**, 30, 61, 214
Susannah **Wright**, 57, 288
William **Wylie**, 409

Y

WB **Yeats**, 402
Jackie **Yelland**, 351
Ena **Young**, 110
Kerry **Young**, 25

Z

Benjamin **Zephaniah**, 275
Alice **Zimmern**, 144
Hermann Theodore **Zimmern**, 144
Ztan **Zmith**, 221